CORRECTION SYMBOLS

Ab	17	Improper abbreviation
Ad	4	Improper use of adjective or adverb
Agr	8	Error in agreement
Appr	42	Inappropriate level of diction
Awk	14	Awkward construction
Ca	2	Faulty pronoun case
CF	7	Comma fault
Comp	13	Faulty or incomplete comparison
CS	7	Comma splice
Dgl	12	Dangling modifiers
Dir	41	Indirectness, redundancy, weakening repetition
Emp	36	Lack of needed emphasis
End P	19	Faulty end punctuation
Ex	40	Inexact word
Frag	6	Unacceptable sentence fragment
FS	7	Fused (run-together) sentence
Glos	43	Check glossary
Gr	1-5	Faulty grammar
Int P	20-25	Faulty internal punctuation
K	14	Awkward construction
Log	37	Faulty logic
Mis Pt	11	Misplaced part

MS	15	Improper manuscript form
Nos	16	Error in use of numbers
Om	13	Careless omission, incomplete construction
P	19-30	Error in punctuation
¶ Coh	32c-d	Paragraph lacks coherence
¶ Con	32h	Paragraph lacks consistent tone
¶ Dev	32e-g	Paragraph is poorly or inadequately developed
¶ Un	32a-b	Paragraph lacks unity
‖	35	Faulty parallelism
Plan	31	Paper is poorly planned
PV	10	Shift in point of view
Q	26	Faulty punctuation of quoted material
Ref	9	Faulty pronoun reference
S	6-14	Poor sentence structure
Sp	44	Error in spelling
Sub	33	Poor subordination
Syl	18	Improper division of word
T	3	Wrong tense of verb
Var	34	Sentence structure lacks variety
Word P	27-30	Faulty word punctuation
X		Obvious error
?		Is this right? Do you mean this?

PROOFREADERS' MARKS

℮	Delete.	
℮	Delete and close up	
⌒	Close up	
#	Insert space	
stet	Let it stand (i.e., the crossed out material above the dots)	
¶	Begin a new paragraph	
no ¶	Run two paragraphs together	
(sp)	Spell out (e.g., 20 ft.)	
tr	Transpose	
lc	Lowercase a capital letter	
cap	capitalize a lowercase letter	
o/	Correct an error	
⌄	Superior number	
⌃	Inferior number	

∧	Caret (placed within the text to indicate the point at which a marginal addition to be inserted)	
⊙	Period	
⌃	Comma	
:/	Colon	
;/	Semicolon	
ᵛ/	Apostrophe or single quotation mark	
ᵛ/ᵛ	Quotation marks	
?/	Question mark	
!/	Exclamation point	
=	Hyphen	
⊥	Dash	
(/)	Parentheses	
[/]	Brackets	

PRENTICE-HALL
HANDBOOK
FOR WRITERS

7th edition

PRENTICE-HALL
HANDBOOK
FOR WRITERS

GLENN LEGGETT

Former President, Grinnell College

C. DAVID MEAD

Michigan State University

WILLIAM CHARVAT

Late of Ohio State University

PRENTICE-HALL, INC.
Englewood Cliffs, New Jersey
07632

Library of Congress Cataloging in Publication Data

LEGGETT, GLENN H. (date).
  Prentice-Hall handbook for writers.

  Includes indexes.
    1. English language—Rhetoric. 2. English
language—Grammar—1950-   I. Mead, Carl David,
(date), joint author. II. Charvat, William, (date),
joint author. III. Title. IV. Title: Handbook
for writers.
PE1408.L39 1978   808′.042   77-13084
ISBN 0-13-695767-6

PRENTICE-HALL HANDBOOK FOR WRITERS, 7 th edition

LEGGETT, MEAD, and CHARVAT

10 9 8 7 6 5

PRENTICE-HALL INTERNATIONAL, INC., *London*
PRENTICE-HALL OF AUSTRALIA PTY. LIMITED, *Sydney*
PRENTICE-HALL OF CANADA, LTD., *Toronto*
PRENTICE-HALL OF INDIA PRIVATE LIMITED, *New Delhi*
PRENTICE-HALL OF JAPAN, INC., *Tokyo*
PRENTICE-HALL OF SOUTHEAST ASIA PTE. LTD., *Singapore*
WHITEHALL BOOKS LIMITED, WELLINGTON, *New Zealand*

CONTENTS

CONTENTS

CONTENTS

PREFACE

The *Prentice-Hall Handbook* is both a reference work for the individual writer and a text for class use. As a summary of grammar, usage, and elementary rhetoric, it provides the essentials of clear writing. Its format provides the student with a convenient reference tool for both the preparation and the review of written work. It provides the instructor assistance in reading papers, allowing him or her to direct attention readily to specific essentials. Ample illustrations and exercises provide ready help in study, review, or class discussion.

The seventh edition has been extensively revised. Although slightly shorter than the sixth edition, it continues to cover fully the issues of grammar, usage, and rhetoric expected in writing courses. The basic structure and divisions of the text remain the same.

Sections 1–30 of the text address the basic materials of composition. The Introduction sketches the growth of English and describes briefly the variety of present-day English. "Grammar" (Sections 1–5) outlines the basic grammar of English—the structure of sentences, the parts of speech, the problems of case, tense, and mood, and the distinctions between adjectives and adverbs. "Basic Sentence Faults" (Sections 6–14) reviews the recurrent problems in sentence construction which most seriously interfere with clarity and effectiveness—fragments, comma splices, agreement, reference, misplaced and dangling modifiers, and shifted constructions.

"Manuscript Mechanics" (Sections 15–18) and "Punctuation" (Sections 19–30) describe the conventions of manuscript form and of punctuation, and the principles upon which those conventions rest. "Manuscript Mechanics" outlines the conventions of manuscript form, of writing numbers, of using abbreviations, and of word division (syllabication). "Punctuation" clarifies basic principles by dividing the problems into those of end punctuation (Section 19), internal punctuation (Sections 20–25), and word punctuation (Sections 27–30). Throughout, the emphasis is upon the understanding and solution of persistent problems.

Sections 31–44 turn from the more elementary problems of grammar, punctuation, and mechanics to the basic rhetorical questions of writing, the questions of skill and effectiveness in building and using well the writer's resources as opposed to the questions of correctness and clarity. "Larger Elements" (Sections 31–32) discusses the planning and organization of the complete paper and the structure of paragraphs. "Effective Sentences" (Sections 33–36) describes the principles of rhetorically sound sentences, from the elementary one of subordination to the more subtle one of emphasis. "Logic" (Section 37) discusses briefly how illogical thinking interferes with clear and honest communication. Information on dictionaries and on ways of improving vocabulary appears in the first two sections (38–39) under "Words." The last sections under "Words" (40–44) discuss the three principles of word choice (exactness, directness, appropriateness), include a glossary of troublesome words, and provide both exhortation and practical help for poor spellers.

The remaining sections of the *Handbook* deal with special matters. "The Library" (Section 45) describes the organization of a library and its facilities for research. "The Research Paper" (Section 46) gives instruction on research technique and provides a facsimile paper, with comment and analysis. Sections 47, 48, and 49 discuss the principles of summarizing, of writing examinations, and of writing the most common kinds of business letters. Section 50, the last, is a glossary of grammatical terms.

The *Handbook* is designed particularly to be a useful and easy reference guide in the preparation, correction, and revision of papers. It classifies the standards and conventions of writing and provides reference to them in three ways: (1) through a full index, (2) through a detailed table of contents, and (3) through the charts on the endpapers of the book. Each major rule is given a number and a symbol, and each subrule is designated by the number of the major rule plus a letter (5a, 16b, 22c, etc.). Thus in writing a paper the student may readily check any specific convention about which he or she is doubtful. The instructor, in reading papers, may conveniently call attention to a specific convention or to general principles by using either numbers or symbols, so that the student may refer quickly to the proper section of the *Handbook*. For an illustration of these possibilities, see the specimen paragraphs on pp. 93–94.

Acknowledgments

We are grateful to many colleagues who have suggested ways to improve both this and previous editions of the *Prentice Hall Handbook*. In preparing this edition, we are especially indebted to Patricia Graves, Georgia State University; Virginia C. Hinton, Kennesaw College; Richard Larson, Herbert H. Lehman College, City University of New York; Thomas H. Ohlgren, Purdue University; and Patrick B. Shaw, Texas Tech University for extensive comments on the sixth edition. Others who read all or part of the manuscript for the seventh edition and made valuable suggestions for its improvement include Dee Brock, Dallas County Community College District; Sandra Dooley, Richland College; Robert L. Kindrick, Central Missouri State University; and Nora B. Leitch, Lamar University.

Special thanks go to Melinda G. Kramer, Indiana University–Purdue University at Indianapolis who both offered extensive suggestions for the revision of the sixth edition and later read the manuscript of the seventh edition; to Holly Zaitchik, Boston University, and Joseph Zaitchik, University of Lowell, who assisted in the revision of the chapters on the library and research paper; and to Caren Mattice, who was endlessly patient and accurate in typing and retyping manuscript and attending to permissions correspondence.

We owe particular credit to Richard S. Beal, Boston University, who has been responsible for both the planning and most of the actual writing for this and the previous three editions.

Finally, we owe a continuing debt to William H. Oliver, our Prentice-Hall editor, who has offered his patient encouragement and advice throughout this and earlier editions; and to Barbara Kanski, our production editor, whose daily efforts ensured that a manuscript became a book.

For allowing us to reprint papers that were part of their course work, we are grateful to Claire McDermott, Stephen Kelley, and Thomas Bonenfant, all students at the University of Lowell. Throughout the *Handbook* we have quoted from copyrighted material and are grateful to the copyright holders acknowledged below for their permission.

ACKNOWLEDGMENTS

Jacques Barzun, *Teacher in America.* By permission of Little, Brown and Company, in association with the Atlantic Monthly Press.

Monroe Beardsley, *Practical Logic.* Copyright © 1950 by Prentice-Hall Inc.

Isaiah Berlin, *Mr. Churchill in 1940.* By permission of the author and John Murray (Publishers) Ltd.

Pierre Berton, *The Klondike Fever* (Alfred A. Knopf, Inc., 1958).

Newman and Genevieve Birk, *Understanding and Using English.* By permission of the Odyssey Press, Inc.

Daniel J. Boorstin, *The Image.* Atheneum. Copyright © 1971 by Daniel J. Boorstin.

D. W. Brogan, *The American Character.* By permission of Alfred A. Knopf, Inc.

Claude Brown, *Manchild in the Promised Land* (The Macmillan Company, 1965).

Stokely Carmichael, "What We Want," *New York Review of Books,* Sept. 22, 1966.

Rachel Carson, *Silent Spring* (Houghton Mifflin Company, 1962).

C. W. Ceram, *Gods, Graves, and Scholars.* By permission of Alfred A. Knopf, Inc.

Winston Churchill, *Blood, Sweat and Tears.* By permission of G. P. Putnam's Sons and Cassel and Company Ltd.

John Ciardi, "Confessions of a Crackpot," *Saturday Review,* Feb. 24, 1962.

Walter Van Tilburg Clark, *Track of the Cat.* By permission of Random House, Inc.

R. P. T. Coffin and Alexander Witherspoon, *Seventeenth Century Prose.* By permission of Harcourt, Brace and Company, Inc.

Malcolm Cowley, "Artist, Conscience, and Censors," *Saturday Review,* July 7, 1962, by permission of the publisher.

E. E. Cummings, "a man who had fallen among thieves." Copyright 1926 by Horace Liveright; published by Harcourt, Brace and Company, Inc.; used by permission of Brandt and Brandt.

Annie Dillard, *Pilgrim at Tinker Creek.* Copyright © 1974 by Annie Dillard. By permission of Harper & Row, Publishers, and Blanche C. Gregory, Inc.

John Dewey, *How We Think* (D. C. Heath and Company, 1933).

Peter Drucker, "How to Be an Employee," *Fortune,* May 1952. Copyright © 1952 by Time, Inc.

Kent Durden, *Flight to Freedom.* Reprinted by permission of Simon & Schuster, Inc.

Loren Eiseley, "Little Men and Flying Saucers," copyright © 1953 by Loren C. Eiseley. Reprinted from *The Immense Journey* by permission of Random House, Inc.

T. S. Eliot, *Collected Poems.* By permission of Harcourt, Brace and Company, Inc.

William Faulkner, *Delta Autumn* and *Sanctuary.* By permission of Random House, Inc.

William H. Gass, *In the Heart of the Heart of the Country.* Copyright © 1967 by William H. Gass. Reprinted by permission of International Creative Management.

Walker Gibson, *Tough, Sweet, and Stuffy.* Copyright © 1970. Indiana University Press.

Alice Glasgow, *Sheridan of Drury Lane.* By permission of J. B. Lippincott Company.

Paul Goodman, "Confusion and Disorder," *Earth,* August 1971.

Edith Hamilton, *The Greek Way.* Copyright 1930, 1943 by W. W. Norton and Company, Inc.; renewed 1958 by Edith Hamilton. By permission of the publisher.

From *Language in Thought and Action,* Third Edition, by S. I. Hayakawa, copyright © 1972 by Harcourt Brace Jovanovich, Inc. and reprinted with their permission and the permission of George Allen & Unwin Ltd.

Eric Hoffer, *The Ordeal of Change.* Copyright © 1956 by Eric Hoffer. Reprinted by permission of Harper & Row, Publishers, Inc. and Sidgwick & Jackson Ltd.

From the book, *How Children Fail* by John Holt. Copyright © 1964 by Pitman Publishing Corporation. Reprinted by permission of Fearon-Pitman Publishers, Inc.

W. H. Ittelson and F. P. Kilpatrick, "Experiments in Perception," *Scientific American,* August 1951.

Jane Jacobs, "How City Planners Hurt Cities," *Saturday Evening Post,* Oct. 14, 1961.

Wendell Johnson, "You Can't Write Writing." Reprinted from *Language, Meaning, and Maturity,* ed. S. I. Hayakawa, by permission of Mr. Hayakawa.

Okakura Kakuzo, *The Book of Tea.* By permission of Charles E. Tuttle Company.

Donald Keene, *Japanese Literature.* By permission of Grove Press, Inc.

Elaine Kendall, "An Open Letter to the Corner Grocer," *Harper's* Magazine, December 1960. Reprinted by permission.

George F. Kennan, "Training for Statesmanship," *The Atlantic,* May 1953.

Jerzy Kosinski, NBC's *Comment.* By permission of Jerzy Kosinski.

Joseph Wood Krutch, *The Desert Year,* copyright © 1952, used by permission of William Sloane Associates, Inc.; *Human Nature and the Human Condition,* copyright © 1959 by Joseph Wood Krutch, used by permission of Random House, Inc.; "Should We Bring Literature to Children, or Children to Literature?" *New York Herald Tribune Book Review,* July 22, 1951, copyright © 1951 by New York Herald Tribune, Inc., used by permission of the author and the publisher.

Susanne K. Langer, "The Lord of Creation," *Fortune,* January 1944. Copyright © 1944 by Time, Inc.

Henry S. Leonard, *Principles of Right Reason.* Published by Holt, Rinehart and Winston, Inc.

Max Lerner, *America as a Civilization.* Copyright © 1957. Reprinted by permission of Simon & Schuster, Inc.

Sinclair Lewis, *Main Street.* By permission of Harcourt, Brace and Company, Inc.

Staughton Lynd, "The New Radical and 'Participatory Democracy,'" *Dissent,* Summer 1965.

From p. 16 in *Guests: or How to Survive Hospitality* by Russell Lynes. Copyright, 1951 by Harper & Row, Publishers, Inc. By permission of Harper & Row, Publishers, Inc.

Archibald MacLeish, "The Conquest of America," *The Atlantic,* August 1949.

Bill Mauldin, *Back Home.* Copyright 1947. By permission of William Sloane Associates, Inc.

G. H. McKnight, *English Words and Their Background.* Copyright 1923 by Appleton-Century, Inc. By permission of Appleton-Century-Crofts, Inc.

Margaret Mead, "What Women Want," *Fortune* Magazine, December 1964. Reprinted by permission of the publisher.

H. L. Mencken, "Bryan," from *Selected Prejudices;* "The Human Mind," from *Prejudices 6th Series;* and *in Defense of Women.* By permission of Alfred A. Knopf, Inc.

Michael Vincent Miller, "The Student State of Mind," *Dissent,* Spring 1965.

Edmund S. Morgan, "What Every Yale Freshman Should Know," *Saturday Review,* Jan. 23, 1960.

Jack Newfield, *The Prophetic Minority* (New American Library).

Bernard Pares, *Russia: Its Past and Present.* Copyright 1943, 1949 by The New American Library of World Literature, Inc.

ACKNOWLEDGMENTS

Roy H. Pearce, *Colonial American Writing.* By permission of Rinehart & Company, Inc.

S. J. Perelman, *Keep It Crisp.* By permission of Random House, Inc.

John Radar Platt, *Style in Science.* Reprinted from *Harper's* Magazine, October 1956.

Herbert Read, *The Eye of Memory.* Copyright 1947 by Herbert Read. By permission of Harold Ober Associates, Inc.

Edwin O. Reischauer, *Japan Past and Present.* By permission of Alfred A. Knopf, Inc.

James Harvey Robinson, *The Mind in the Making.* By permission of Harper & Brothers.

Lionel Ruby, *The Art of Making Sense.* Copyright © 1968. Reprinted by permission of the publisher, J. B. Lippincott Company.

Herbert H. Sanders, *How To Make Pottery.* Copyright © 1974 by Watson Guptill Publications. Reprinted by permission.

Ben Shahn, *The Shape of Content.* By permission of Harvard University Press.

Susan Sontag, "The Double Standard of Aging," *Saturday Review,* Sept. 23, 1972. Copyright © 1972. SR Publishing Assets Industries, Inc.

George Summey, Jr., *American Punctuation.* Copyright 1949 The Ronald Press Company, New York.

Deems Taylor, *Of Men and Music.* By permission of Simon and Schuster, Inc.

James Thurber, *The Years with Ross.* Copyright © 1959 by James Thurber. Published by Atlantic-Little Brown. Originally printed in *The New Yorker.*

John Updike, from "The Dogwood Tree," in *Five Boyhoods,* edited by Martin Levin (Doubleday). Copyright © 1962 Martin Levin. Reprinted by permission of Martin Levin.

Hendrik Willem Van Loon, *Van Loon's Geography.* By permission of Simon and Schuster, Inc.

Paul Velde, "Psychedelics: You Can't Bring the Universe Home," *The Village Voice,* October 6, 1966.

Gerald Weales, "The Bogart Vogue," *Commonweal,* Mar. 11, 1966.

E. B. White, *One Man's Meat.* By permission of Harper & Brothers.

Leslie A. White, *The Science of Culture.* By permission of Farrar, Straus and Giroux, Inc.

A. N. Whitehead, *Science and the Modern World,* copyright 1925. By permission of The Macmillan Company.

Harold Whitehall, *Structural Essentials of English.* Reprinted by permission of Harcourt Brace Jovanovich, Inc. and Longman Group.

William Zinsser, *On Writing Well.* Copyright © 1976 by William K. Zinsser. Reprinted by permission of William K. Zinsser.

Blot out, correct, insert, refine,
Enlarge, diminish, interline;
Be mindful, when invention fails,
To scratch your head, and bite your nails.

INTRODUCTION

All life therefore comes back to the question of our speech, the medium through which we communicate with each other; for all life comes back to the question of our relations with one another.

HENRY JAMES, *The Question of Our Speech*

The Growth of English

Like all languages, English changes constantly. Changes in vocabulary are the most rapid and obvious. A *butcher* was once a man who slew goats; *neutron* and *proton,* key terms in physics today, were unrecorded fifty years ago; *biofeedback* appears in dictionaries only in the 1970's. But language changes in more complex ways also. Today educated speakers avoid the multiple negatives of *She won't never do nothing*. But Shakespeare's *nor this is not my nose neither* was good Elizabethan English. Even the sounds of language change. For Shakespeare, four hundred years ago, *deserts* rhymed with *parts,* and *reason* sounded much like our *raisin;* for Pope, two hundred years ago, *join* rhymed with *line,* and *seas* with *surveys.*

The changes we see if we look back at the history of our language are far more dramatic. English is a Germanic language, descended from the language of the Germanic tribes (Angles, Saxons, and Jutes) who invaded the British Isles in the fifth and sixth centuries. In the centuries following, their language was subjected to a variety of influences. Its structure was loosened by the effects of the Danish invasions in the ninth and tenth centuries and by the Norman Conquest in 1066. To its vocabulary were added thousands of Latin, Scandinavian, and particularly French words. Spelling and pronunciation changed. Word meanings were modified or extended.

Perhaps most important of all the changes was a gradual change in the syntax of English, the ways of showing relationships among words in a sentence. The English of the sixth, seventh, and eighth centuries—Old English—was a highly inflected language depending largely upon changes in the forms and particularly the endings of words to show their relation to one another. Gradually, the order of words for the most part replaced such endings as the main way of showing relation among words. At the same time, function words—words like *the,* and connecting words, our prepositions and conjunctions—grew in number and importance. Thus, one of the great differences between Old English and English as we know it is that our ancestors depended heavily upon inflection to show relation among words, whereas we depend mainly on word order. When we discuss grammar later, we shall see that it is important to understand this difference if we are to manage our own use of language well.

If we look at the following brief passages, we can see something of the great changes that occurred between the time of King Alfred in the late ninth century and that of Shakespeare in the late sixteenth century.

Ða gemette hie   Æpelwulf aldorman on Englafelda, ond
Then met   them Aethelwulf alderman in Englefield, and

him þær   wiþ gefeaht ond sige nam.
them there against fought and victory won.

KING ALFRED, Anglo-Saxon Chronicle, C. 880

But now, if so be that dignytees and poweris be yyven to gode men, the whiche thyng is full selde, what aggreable thygnes is there in tho dignytees or power but oonly the goodnesse of folk that usen them?   CHAUCER, from the translation of <i>Boethius,</i> C. 1380

Hit befel in the dayes of Uther Pendragon, when he was kynge of all Englond, and so regned, that there was a myghty duke in Cornewaill that helde warre ageynst hym long tyme, and the duke was called the duke of Tyntagil.

SIR THOMAS MALORY, Morte d'Arthur, C. 1470

A Proude Man contemneth the companye of hys olde friendes, and disdayneth the sight of hys former famyliars, and turneth hys face from his wonted acquayntaunce.

HENRY KERTON, The Mirror of Man's Lyfe, 1576

To us, these passages illustrate a steady growth toward the English we know. But to men living then, the changes often seemed not growth but chaos. English, it appeared, would not hold still long enough to have any value as a means of communication. Some, like Sir Thomas More and Francis Bacon, preferred to write their greatest works in Latin. But others, like Chaucer and Malory, chose their native language, staking their reputations on the survival of this language. In so doing, they gave English part of the prestige it needed. This support, coupled with the development of English printing and the growth of a national spirit, helped dignify and standardize the language. By the end of the sixteenth century, English had become a national language, as indicated by the great English translation of the Bible in 1611. Printing, together with the great increase in the number of people who could read and write, tended to slow change in the language, particularly in its written form. But though less rapid, change remains continuous as the language adapts itself to the changing needs of those who speak and write it.

As always, change is most easily seen in vocabulary. In its very early history, the coming of Christianity brought into the language such Latin words as *angel, candle, priest,* and *school.* The Danes gave us such basic words as our pronouns *they, their,* and *them,* and *skull, skin, anger, root,* and *ill.* After the Norman Conquest in 1066, an endless variety of French words poured into the language for nearly three hundred years, touching nearly every corner of life with words which are part of our everyday vocabulary: *dance, tax, mayor, justice, faith, battle, paper, poet, surgeon, gentle, flower, sun*—the list extends to thousands. In the seventeenth century, when Latin became greatly respected and avidly studied, thousands upon thousands of Latin words flooded into English. They included not only the words we think of as learned, but also many that are common such as *industry, educate, insane, exist, illustrate, multiply, benefit, paragraph, dedicate,* and the like. And as English reached into other parts of the world, it continued its habit of borrowing. It has played no favorites, drawing on Arabic (*alcohol, assassin*), Hebrew (*cherub, kosher*), East Indian (*jungle, yoga*), Japanese (*jujitsu, tycoon*), Spanish (*adobe, canyon*), and many others.

The borrowing process continues into our own day. But in the past hundred years two other developments have had major consequences for English. The first is the rapid development of mass education and the resulting rise in literacy. The second is the advancement in science and technology. Both of these developments have had complex effects upon our language and will doubtless continue to exert great influence in the future. Though the effect of the first is difficult to measure, it is clear that a language that can reach many of its users in print, and an even greater number through radio and television, will develop differently than a language in which writing is addressed to a special minority, or in which speech occurs largely in face-to-face exchange. The effect of the technological revolution and rapid specialization is clearer. It has given us a burgeoning vocabulary of technical terms ranging from the names of the drugs our doctors prescribe to the specialized words in everything from do-it-yourself kits to space engineering.

Changes in grammar since the sixteenth century, though very minor compared with the loss of inflections and the accompanying fixing of word order that came earlier, have continued in Modern English. Since the sixteenth century, reliance upon word order and what we call function words has become even greater. Questions in the form of *Consents he?* and negations in the form of *I say not, I run not* have disappeared, to be replaced by the use of the auxiliary verb *do,* as in *Does he consent? I do not say, I do not run.* Verb forms with *be* in the pattern of *He was speaking, We are going, It is being built* have multiplied greatly. Today we can observe such changes as the increase in the number of verbs made from verbs combined with adverbs or with prepositions, as in *He <u>looked up</u> the word, He <u>looked over</u> Bill's new house, The fireplace <u>was smoking up</u> the room.* Similarly, at least in some kinds of writing, nouns used as modifiers of other nouns, as in *college student, radio station, mathematics course, ice-cream stand,* have become more common. Though these are but a few of the developments of Modern English, such changes make it clear that the evolution of our language is unending.

The following passages, though less strikingly dissimilar than those we saw earlier, demonstrate that language was hardly static between 1600 and 1900. Many of the differences among these selections are those of idiom or style rather than of grammar. The distinctions are important, but are less important for us than the basic fact that the differences represent aspects of language change that are continuous.

> I had often before this said, that if the Indians should come, I should chuse rather to be killed by them than taken alive but when it came to the tryal my mind changed; their glittering weapons so daunted my spirit, that I chose rather to go along with those (as I may say) ravenous Bears, then that moment to end my dayes; and that I may better declare what happened to me during that grievous Captivity, I shall particularly speak of the severall Removes we had up and down the Wilderness.
>
> MARY ROWLANDSON, *The Narrative of the Captivity,* c 1682

> About the twelfth year of my age, my Father being abroad, my Mother reproved me for some misconduct, to which I made an Undutifull reply & the next first-day, as I was with my Father returning from Meeting, He told me he understood I had behaved amis to my Mother, and Advised me to be more careful in future.
>
> JOHN WOOLMAN, *The Journal,* 1756

> I had stopped in Boston at the Tremont House, which was still one of the first hostelries of the country, and I must have inquired my way to Cambridge there; but I was sceptical of the direction the Cambridge horsecar took when I found it, and I hinted to the driver my anxieties as to why he should be starting east when I had been told that Cambridge was west of Boston.
>
> WILLIAM DEAN HOWELLS,
> *Literary Friends and Acquaintances,* 1894

Variety and standards

Language not only changes with time, as we have seen in our brief glance at the history of English, it also varies widely at any given time. It varies from one geographical area to another, and from one occupational and social group to another. Further, the language each of us uses varies from situation to situation. The language of our conversation differs from that in a public address, and that in turn differs from written language. And even carefully written English—what we call EDITED ENGLISH—varies according to its audience and purpose.

One of the most important kinds of variation is that between STANDARD and NONSTANDARD English. This distinction rests largely on the educational, economic, and social status of the people using the language. STANDARD ENGLISH describes the spoken and written language of educated people. It is the written language of business, journalism, education, law, public documents, and literature. But it is also the speech of our professional men and women, of the courtroom, and of our legislators. For all these and many other occupations, competence in its use is nearly always necessary.

NONSTANDARD ENGLISH describes the language of a great many people who have had relatively little formal education, who read and write but little in their daily lives, and who are normally limited to a kind of work that requires little or no writing. It differs most obviously from standard English in its use of verb and pronoun forms and the double negatives which are widely avoided in standard, such as *he give, growed, have saw; him and me is, hern, youse; can't never.* Although these are its most noticeable marks, nonstandard is also characterized by a relatively narrow range of vocabulary and a heavy dependence upon a small variety of sentence structures.

Distinctions between standard and nonstandard English are not distinctions between good and bad, or right and wrong. The function of language is to communicate, and any language that makes for clear and accurate communication is good language. Nonstandard English works perfectly well in the lives and work of millions. In fact, many varieties of nonstandard often have an easy directness, color, and force sometimes lacking in standard varieties. The reasons many of its forms are not used in business and the professions and do not ordinarily appear in print are social and historical, rather than because they do not communicate. Nonetheless, the standard spoken and written variety of language is a major part of the mainstream of our culture, and of our business and professions. It is the widely used and understood public language, and competence in its use is almost indispensable to taking part in the public functions in which it is used.

The following passages illustrate standard and nonstandard English. Note that since nonstandard is primarily spoken, the illustration can only approximately represent it.

Standard

Today, as never before, the sky is menacing. Things seen indifferently last century by the wandering lamplighter now trouble a generation that has grown up to the wail of air-raid sirens and the ominous expectation that the roof may fall at any moment. Even in daytime, reflected light on a floating dandelion seed, or a spider riding a wisp of gossamer in the sun's eye, can bring excited questions from the novice unused to estimating the distance or nature of aerial objects.

LOREN EISELEY, "Little Men and Flying Saucers"

The voice we hear in an ad is not the official voice of the corporation that pays the bill. The voice in the ad is a highly fictitious created person, speaking as an individual in a particular situation. In a bathtub, for instance. No corporation official could ever say, officially, "I never, never bathe without Sardo." The official voice of the corporation appears, I suppose, in its periodic reports to its stockholders, or in its communications with government agencies.

WALKER GIBSON, *Tough, Sweet, & Stuffy*

Nonstandard

So I said to him, I said, "You was dead wrong thinking you'd get away with that dough. We had you spotted from the beginning, smart boy. And we was sure when we seen you put that roll in your pocket." So I starts to move in on him, easy-like, and all at oncet he grabs in his pocket and comes out with a gun. "Don't nobody move," he yells, and starts for the door. But he trips over his own big feet and goes down, hard. Right then I lets him have it with five quick shots. He was the deadest double-crosser you ever seen.

Standard English itself varies according to its use or function, such varieties sometimes being called FUNCTIONAL VARIETIES. The most general variation may be described as that between INFORMAL and FORMAL. In broadest terms, INFORMAL describes the English of everyday speaking and writing, casual conversation between friends and business associates, personal letters, and writing close to general speech. FORMAL describes the language of books and articles, particularly those dealing with special subjects, the reports of business, industry, and science, most legal writing, and literary prose.

The line between informal and formal cannot be sharply drawn, for there are wide ranges of degree in each. In general, as we move toward casual speech, we become more informal. At the extreme of informality is the casual speech of educated people in familiar situations and the writing that tries to catch the flavor of such speech. Such speech and writing are marked by a relatively free use of contractions, loose sentence structures, and the use of many words and expressions such as *deal, flunk, wise up, fall for, make off with, shape up, get going,* and the like.

At the extreme of formality is careful scientific, scholarly, and legal writing, in which the need for exactness is most important. In the examples below, note the elaborate sentence structure of the more formal selections, their Latinate vocabulary, and their serious tone. As the examples move toward the informal, note the increasingly relaxed sentences, the everyday vocabulary, and the conversational tone. But if you catch yourself thinking that one is better than the other, remember that the purpose, subject matter, audience, temperament, and hence style of each author are quite different.

Formal

An antibiotic is a chemical substance, produced by microorganisms, which has the capacity to inhibit the growth of and even destroy bacteria and other microorganisms. The action of an antibiotic against microorganisms is selective in nature, some organisms being affected and others not at all or only to a limited degree; each antibiotic is thus characterized by a specific antimicrobial spectrum. The selective action of an antibiotic is also manifested against microbial vs. host cells. Antibiotics vary greatly in their physical and chemical properties and in their toxicity to animals. Because of these characteristics, some antibiotics have remarkable chemotherapeutic potentialities and can be used for the control of various microbial infections in man and in animals.

Quoted in SELMAN A. WAKSMAN,
The Actinomycetes and Their Antibiotics

Dean Donne in the pulpit of old Paul's, holding his audience spellbound still as he reversed his glass of sands after an hour of exposition and application of texts by the light of the church fathers, of mortification for edification, of exhortation that brought tears to the eyes of himself and his hearers, and of analogies born of the study, but sounding of wings—there was a man who should have had wisdom, surely. For if experience can bring it, this was the man.

R. P. T. COFFIN and A. M. WITHERSPOON,
"John Donne," in *Seventeenth Century Prose*

Informal

All scientists are not alike. Look at any laboratory or university science department. Professor Able is the kind of man who seizes an idea as a dog seizes a stick, all at once. As he talks you can see him stop short, with the chalk in his fingers, and then almost jump with excitement as the insight grips him. His colleague, Baker, on the other hand, is a man who comes to understand an idea as a worm might understand the same stick, digesting it a little at a time, drawing his conclusions cautiously, and tunneling slowly through it from end to end and back again.

JOHN RADAR PLATT, "Style in Science"

Of all the common farm operations none is more ticklish than tending a brooder stove. All brooder stoves are whimsical, and some of them are holy terrors. Mine burns coal, and has only a fair record. With its check draft that opens and closes, this stove occupies my dreams from midnight, when I go to bed, until five o'clock, when I get up, pull a shirt and a pair of pants on over my pajamas, and stagger out into the dawn to read the thermometer under the hover and see that my 254 little innocents are properly disposed in a neat circle round their big iron mama.

E. B. WHITE, *One Man's Meat*

The colossal success of the supermarkets is based upon the fact that nobody, but nobody, can sell you something as well as you can by yourself. As a result, supermarkets now stock clothing, appliances, plastic swimming pools, and small trees. The theory is that if you succumb to an avocado today, tomorrow you may fall for an electronic range or a young poplar.

ELAINE KENDALL, "An Open Letter to the Corner Grocer"

The terms COLLOQUIAL and EDITED ENGLISH are often used in discussing varieties of English. COLLOQUIAL means simply *spoken,* and is used to describe the everyday speech of educated people, and the kind of writing that uses the easy vocabulary, the redundancy, the loose constructions, the contractions, and other characteristics of that speech. In this sense, COLLOQUIAL may be applied to the informal style of E. B. White and Elaine Kendall illustrated above. EDITED ENGLISH is the written language of books, good magazines, and many newspapers. It may be more or less formal or informal, but it is always marked by close adherence to the established conventions of spelling, punctuation, standard grammar, and sentence structure.

The very fact that English has such variety means that there can be no unvarying and absolute standard of correctness. But it does not mean that we can do without standards at all, or that what is good enough for familiar conversation is appropriate for all kinds of communication. It is true that if people were to write as naturally as they talk, they might rid their writing of a great deal of affectation. But it is also true that for much of its force conversational English depends upon the physical presence of the speaker. Personality, gesture, and intonation all contribute to the success of spoken communication. Written English, on the other hand, whether formal or informal, requires a structure that makes for clarity without the physical presence of the writer. It must communicate through the clarity of its diction, the orderliness of its sentence and paragraph structure, and the relative fullness of its detail. And if it is to be taken seriously by a general audience, it must observe the conventions of spelling, punctuation, and grammar to which an audience is accustomed and which it expects. In short, the writer must meet certain standards if he is to get his meaning across.

A handbook somewhat arbitrarily classifies standards of "good English" into rules or conventions that cannot always be defended on logical grounds. Rather, they reflect the practices—some old, some new—of English and American writers. Most of these conventions are quite flexible. The rules for punctuation, for instance, permit many variations, and so do the standards for diction, sentence structure, and paragraphing. The truth is that the rules of writing represent "typical" or "normal" practices. Skillful writers interpret them very loosely and occasionally ignore those that seem too restrictive for their purposes. For most writers, however, the rules are a discipline and a security. Observing them will not make a writer great, but it will help make his writing clear and orderly. And clarity and order are the marks of all good writing.

BASIC GRAMMAR
GR

Good grammar is not merely grammar which is free from unconventionalities, or even from the immoralities. It is the triumph of the communication process, the use of words which create in the reader's mind the thing as the writer conceived it; it is a creative act. . . .

JANET AIKEN, *Commonsense Grammar*

To begin, it is useful to separate two different ways we use the term "grammar." In one sense, grammar is the system by which a language works. In this sense, learning to speak a language *is* learning its grammar. If we grew up speaking English, as soon as we learned the difference between such pairs as *toy* and *toys, home run* and *run home,* or *tiger tails* and *tiger's tail,* we had learned a good deal of English grammar. And by the time we could put together sentences such as *Howard's father gave him some new toys,* or *See the monkeys jumping around in the cages,* we had learned very complicated things about English grammar.

In another sense, grammar is a description of language. In this sense, grammar is in the same class as physics. Physics describes how light, sound, and electricity and other kinds of energy and matter work. Grammar describes the way a language works. It describes the kinds of words in a language (nouns, verbs, prepositions, etc.) and how speakers and writers put single words together into larger groups that have meaning.

The following pages describe some of the details about English grammar which have proved useful to less experienced writers. One basic concept about language may be helpful in keeping these details in perspective. Any language is composed of individual words and of GRAMMATICAL DEVICES for putting them together into larger meaningful combinations. A series of words such as *age, buggy, the, and, horse* is pretty much just a series of isolated words in English. Each word makes sense, but they aren't related to one another in any particular way. But *the horse-and-buggy age* makes a quite different kind of sense; the words have been put together into a meaningful combination. English has several devices for putting words into such combinations, and it is useful to keep these in mind. The three most important are WORD ORDER, FUNCTION WORDS, and INFLECTIONS.

In English, grammatical meaning is largely determined by WORD ORDER. *Blue sky* and *sky blue* mean different things: in the first, *blue* describes *sky;* in the second, *sky* describes *blue.* We can see the principle in action in the following:

The thief called the lawyer a liar.
The lawyer called the thief a liar.
The liar called the lawyer a thief.
Our new neighbors bought an old house.
Our old neighbors bought a new house.

We see how important word order can be in such a sentence as *The man in the black shoes with the sandy hair knocked on the door*. The sentence confuses us because word order tells us that *with the sandy hair* describes *shoes,* but common sense tells us that shoes do not have sandy hair.

FUNCTION WORDS, sometimes called GRAMMATICAL WORDS, are words such as *the, and, but, in, to, at, because,* and *while,* whose main use is to express relationships among other words. Compare the following:

I am lonely *at* dark.   The cook prepared *a* rich feast.
I am lonely *in the* dark.   The cook prepared *the* rich *a* feast.

INFLECTIONS, less important in Modern English than they were in earlier stages of the language, are changes in the form of words which indicate differences in grammatical relationship. Inflections account for the differences in the following:

The boy*s* walk slowly.   Stop bother*ing* me.
The boy walk*s* slowly.   Stop*s* bother me.

These three grammatical devices—word order, function words, and inflections—are the principal ones we must learn to control if we are to write clearly and effectively.

A distinction is sometimes made between grammar and usage. GRAMMAR is concerned with generally applicable principles about a language. USAGE, in contrast, is concerned with choices, particularly with differences between standard and nonstandard English, and between formal and informal English. The differences between *tile floor* and *floor tile, he walks* and *he walked, he was biting the dog* and *the dog was biting him* are grammatical differences. The differences between *I saw* and *I seen, he doesn't* and *he don't, he ought to do it* and *he had ought to do it,* and *let me do it* and *leave me do it* are differences in usage. They identify those persons who use them as educated or uneducated. But they do not mean different things. Since this book is concerned with providing guidelines for writing standard English, it is concerned with both grammar and usage. And since many questions of grammar and usage overlap, the two are not set apart sharply.

We can make useful generalizations about some usage differences. It is true, for instance, that, in standard English, verbs almost always agree in number with their subjects, and that the objective case is almost always used for pronouns that are the objects of verbs and prepositions. But a good many matters of usage are not readily reducible to neat "rules." For one thing, writing is slower to change and more orderly than speech. For another, the language an educated person uses in writing differs

1

1a

in a good many rather slight but important ways from the language he uses in casual and hasty conversation. Finally, the habits of language are simply not as regular and logical as we might like them to be.

Speakers of standard English in most sections of the country regularly use *It's me/him/them/us,* for example, but in writing they tend strongly to prefer *It's I/he/they/we.* Standard English allows the double negatives *not infrequently* and *not uncommon,* but rejects *can't scarcely* and *can't hardly. Anywheres* is sometimes used by educated speakers in some parts of the country, but *anywhere* appears in written English.

However minor such differences of our language may seem, they are real and important. A college student who wants to write like other educated people must be willing to learn and to observe these differences and to turn to some reference such as this book when in doubt about the forms or words of standard English. He must also be willing to learn enough of the basic grammar of English to be able to judge where difficulties may arise in his writing, acquire enough understanding of English sentences to work toward greater flexibility in his writing, and learn enough grammatical terminology to discuss his writing.

Properly understood and applied, such a knowledge of basic grammar and its relation to problems of usage can be a very useful tool rather than a collection of useless, confusing detail.

1 Sentence Sense* SS

1a Recognizing sentences

A sentence is grammatically independent and complete. It may contain words that we cannot fully understand unless we read the sentences before and after, but it is grammatically self-sufficient even when lifted out of context and made to stand alone.

> People said old Dinger's ghost lived in the surrounding hills.
> They had seen it several times from the tavern window.

Both sentences are grammatically complete. True, the full meaning of the second sentence depends on our identifying *they*

---

*The grammatical terms used in these sections are defined in the Glossary of Grammatical Terms, pp. 437–50.

with *people* and *it* with *Old Dinger's ghost* in the first sentence. But the second sentence is structurally independent because the pronouns *they* and *it* are acceptable substitutes for *people* and *Dinger's ghost.*

1a

The main parts of an English sentence are a SUBJECT and a PREDICATE. Usually the SUBJECT names something or someone; the PREDICATE tells something about the subject. In the simplest sentence the subject is a noun or a pronoun, and the predicate is a verb, which may be either a single word or a group of words such as *was eating, has been finishing,* or *will have gone.*

Basic sentence patterns. All English sentences are built on a limited number of basic patterns, to which all sentences, however long and complex, can be reduced. The five most basic patterns are listed below. Note that in all basic patterns the subject remains a simple noun or pronoun. Differences among the patterns lie in the kind of verb and in what follows the verb.

PATTERN 1

Subject	*Verb*	*(Optional Adverb)*
Red	fades	(easily).
The woman	arrived	(late).
The snow	fell	(everywhere).

Though sentences as simple as these are relatively rare in mature writing, they show the core of all English sentences. When we think, we think about something; and we think something about that something. When we write, we follow this same pattern.

PATTERN 2

Subject	*Transitive Verb*	*Direct Object*
Dogs	eat	bones.
The carpenter	repaired	the roof.
John	prefers	movies.
Someone	insulted	her.

The verbs in this pattern are always action words. Such verbs are called TRANSITIVE verbs, meaning that they can pass their action along to OBJECTS. The object is always a noun, a pronoun, or a group of words serving as a noun, which answers the question "what" or "whom" after the verb.

1a

Subject	Transitive Verb	Direct Object	Objective Complement
Henry	called	him	a traitor.
They	appointed	Shirley	chairwoman.
We	made	the clerk	angry.
People	judged	her	innocent.

This pattern occurs only with a special, quite limited group of verbs. The OBJECTIVE COMPLEMENT provides another name for the object, or an adjective which modifies the object.

Subject	Transitive Verb	Indirect Object	Direct Object
His father	gave	Sam	a car.
The college	found	me	work.
Wellington	brought	England	victory.
John	sold	her	a book.

The INDIRECT OBJECT occurs with verbs of asking, giving, telling, receiving, and the like. It names the receiver of the message, gift, or whatever, and always comes before the DIRECT OBJECT. The same meaning can usually be expressed by a prepositional phrase placed after the direct object, as in *Wellington brought victory to England.*

Subject	Linking Verb	Complement	
		Predicate Noun	Predicate Adjective
Napoleon	was	a Frenchman.	
My brother	remains	an artist.	
Natalie	may become	president.	
The book	seemed		obscene.
Work	was		scarce.
The fruit	tasted		bitter.

This pattern occurs only with a special kind of verb, called a LINKING VERB. The most common linking verb is *be* in its various forms: *is, are, was, were, has been, might be,* etc. Other common linking verbs include *appear, become, seem,* and in some contexts such verbs as *feel, grow, act, look, taste, smell,* and *sound.* Linking verbs are followed by a COMPLEMENT, which may be either a PREDICATE NOUN or a PREDICATE ADJECTIVE. A complement following a linking verb, in contrast to an object after a transitive verb, is related to the subject of the sentence. Predicate nouns rename the subject; predicate adjectives modify the subject.

Other sentence patterns. These patterns are the basis of English sentence structure. Other kinds of English sentences may be thought of as additional patterns, or as changes—called transformations by some grammarians—in these basic patterns. Thus we can create questions by inverting the subject and verb, as in *Will he run?* or by using a function word before the basic pattern, *Does he run?* We create commands by omitting the subject, as in *Open the can, Know thyself, Keep calm.*

1a

Two kinds of sentences which involve changes in the usual word order of the basic patterns are important because they change the usual order of subject and predicate.

The first of these is the PASSIVE SENTENCE. The passive sentence is made from one of the basic patterns which use a transitive verb and a direct object. The verb in passive sentences consists of some form of the AUXILIARY, or helping, verb *be* and the PAST PARTICIPLE.

Active

The carpenter *repaired* the roof.
Someone *insulted* her.
Henry *called* him a traitor.
Wellington *brought* England victory.

Passive

Subject	Passive Verb	(Original subject)
The roof	was repaired	(by the carpenter).
She	was insulted	(by someone).
He	was called a traitor	(by Henry).
Victory	was brought to England	(by Wellington).

Notice that in all passive sentences the original subject can be expressed by a prepositional phrase, but the sentence will be complete without that prepositional phrase.*

The second important kind of sentence that involves change in the word order allows us to postpone the subject of the sentence until after the verb by beginning with the EXPLETIVE *there* or *it*.

Expletive	Verb	Complement	Subject
It	is	doubtful	that they will arrive.
There	is		no reply.
There	are		seven students.
There	will be		an opportunity.

*It is this characteristic of the passive construction which makes it especially useful when we do not <u>know</u> the doer (subject) of an action. Thus we normally say <u>*He was killed*</u> in action rather than <u>*Someone killed*</u> him in action. See pp. 257–58 on the use of the passive.

The great variety of English sentences is created, not by variety in the basic sentence patterns, but by the addition of modifying words and word groups in the position of subjects and objects. Learning to recognize the subjects and predicates of sentences, and to distinguish verbs, objects, and complements within the predicate, is the first step in analyzing sentences.

1b

EXERCISE 1a Label verbs, direct and indirect objects, and predicate nouns and predicate adjectives in the following sentences. Be prepared to indicate which of the basic patterns each sentence follows.

1 War is a disease.
2 The geese circled slowly.
3 Recent studies prove the dangers of cigarettes.
4 To be useful, a dictionary must be used.
5 His friends gave Sam a reception when he returned.
6 Local citizens sent the police many complaints about burglaries in the neighborhood.
7 Poverty deprives many children of an education.
8 The blue Buick raced down the narrow road.
9 Television and radio bring us the news daily.
10 People who live in glass houses shouldn't throw stones.

1b Recognizing parts of speech

Grammarians classify words as particular PARTS OF SPEECH in three ways: (1) by their grammatical function, such as subject or modifier; (2) by their grammatical form, such as the distinctive -s of most nouns in the plural, or the -ed of most verbs in the past tense; (3) by their type of meaning, such as the name of a thing, or the statement of an action.

The class we assign a particular word to may differ according to which kind of classification we use. In *the army cannon,* for example, *army* is an adjective if we ask what function it performs (that of modifying *cannon*), but a noun if we ask what form it can take (a plural, *armies*). In *She seemed tired, seemed* is a verb clearly enough if we have defined verbs as words that can form a past tense with -ed or the equivalent; but one might question whether *seemed* states an action.

Many words in English can function in more than one way, and a good many can have more than one set of forms:

Noun	The *place* to be is New York. The *places* to be are New York and San Francisco.
Verb	*Place* the book on the desk. He *placed* the book on the desk.
Modifier	She bought *place* mats for the table.

In English it is most useful to classify words according to their most common function (keeping in mind that some words will belong to more than one part of speech), and to note their other characteristics as convenient ways of identifying them when we have any doubt. The basic functions in English and the kinds of words that usually perform them are as follows:

1b

Function	Kinds of Words
Naming	Nouns and pronouns
Predicating (stating or asserting)	Verbs
Modifying	Adjectives and adverbs
Connecting	Prepositions and conjunctions

Nouns and verbs are the basic elements. They are the bones of the sentence patterns we have described. We use modifying and connecting words to expand and refine these basic patterns. One other part of speech, the interjection (*ouch, wow*), is used to express emotion and is grammatically independent of other elements.

1. Nouns. Words that function as the basic part of sentence subjects are most commonly NOUNS (*Carl, Detroit, studio, committee, courage, wealth*). Nouns also function as objects of verbs and prepositions (*Send <u>John</u> to the <u>store</u>*). Most nouns name or classify things, people, places, activities, and concepts. They usually add -*s* to make a plural (*boy, boys; song, songs*), although a few irregular (*sheep, sheep; man, men; child, children*), and others (like *courage,* which names a quality, and *Detroit,* which names a particular place) do not usually have plurals. The great majority of nouns show a possessive in writing by adding an -*s* preceded by an apostrophe in the singular, or in some cases merely by adding an apostrophe (*cow's horns, the committee's decision, Archimedes' law*).

2. Pronouns. The most common PRONOUNS substitute for nouns. We can usually discover the full meaning of a pronoun only by referring to the noun that serves as its antecedent. In the sentence *Clara Barton is the woman who founded the American Red Cross,* the pronoun *who* refers to its antecedent, *woman.* In the sentence *Whichever he chooses will be acceptable,* we can tell what *whichever* means only if we know from a larger context what is referred to. In such sentences as *He who hesitates is lost,* the meaning is implied by the context itself; that is, *he* refers to any person who hesitates to take action. Words called INDEFINITE PRONOUNS (*anybody, everybody, somebody*) act as nouns and require no antecedent.

The PERSONAL PRONOUNS *I, we, he, she,* and *they,* and the pronoun *who,* which is used either to relate one group of words to another or to ask a question, have distinctive case forms for the nominative, possessive, and objective cases; *you* and *it* have distinctive forms for the possessive only. (See Section 2.)

1b

3. Verbs and verbals. VERBS serve as the heart of sentence predicates. They are the minimum of the second part of the typical subject-predicate word group. Typical verbs are *ask, eat, give, describe, criticize, exist, seem, appear, become.* Most verbs make some sort of assertion about their subjects. They indicate some kind of action, the occurrence of something, or the presence of some condition.

In form, verbs can usually be recognized by the fact that they add *-s* to the plain form to make the third person singular of the present tense (*I run, he run<u>s</u>; we ask, she ask<u>s</u>*). Most verbs also form a past tense by adding *-ed* (*we walk, we walk<u>ed</u>*), although some form the past in irregular ways (*we eat, we ate; we go, we went*). Verbs can almost always be placed immediately after such words as *please* and *let's,* and after simple noun subjects: *Please <u>go</u>, Let's <u>eat</u>, John <u>hit</u> Henry.* Verbs can combine with AUXILIARIES, which precede the main verb form, to make a variety of verb phrases such as *is eating, should have been eating, should have been eaten,* and *will be eating,* which convey special shades of meaning.

VERBALS are special verb forms which have some of the characteristics and abilities of verbs but <u>cannot function as predicates by themselves</u>. Verbs make an assertion. Verbals do not; they function as nouns and modifiers. There are three kinds of verbals: INFINITIVES, PARTICIPLES, and GERUNDS.

INFINITIVES are usually marked by a *to* before the actual verb (*to eat, to describe*). They are used as nouns, adjectives, or adverbs.

> *To see* is *to believe.* (both used as nouns)
> It was time *to leave.* (used as adjective)
> I was ready *to go.* (used as adverb)

PARTICIPLES may be either present or past. The present form ends in *-ing* (*eating, running, describing*). The past form usually ends in *-ed* (*described*). But note that some end in *-en* (*eaten*), and a few make an internal change (*begun, flown*). Participles are always used as adjectives.

> *Screaming,* I jumped out of bed. (present participle)
> *Delighted,* we accepted his invitation. (past participle)

GERUNDS have the same *-ing* form as the present participle. The distinctive name GERUND is given to *-ing* forms only when they function as nouns.

Writing requires effort. (subject of *requires*)
You should try *swimming*. (object of *try*)

Although verbals can never function by themselves as predicates, they can, like verbs, take objects and complements, and like verbs, they are characteristically modified by adverbs. Note the following:

1b

I prefer *to believe him*. (*him* is the object of *to believe*)
It was time *to leave the house*. (*house* is the object of *to leave*)
Screaming loudly, I jumped out of bed. (the adverb *loudly* modifies the participle *screaming*)
Swimming *in the Atlantic* is refreshing. (the adverb phrase *in the Atlantic* modifies the gerund *swimming*)

4. Adjectives and adverbs. Adjectives and adverbs are the principal modifiers in English. MODIFIERS are words or word groups which limit, or make more exact, or otherwise qualify other words or word groups to which they are attached.

ADJECTIVES modify nouns or pronouns. Typical adjectives are the underlined words in the following: <u>brown</u> dog, <u>Victorian</u> dignity, <u>yellow</u> hair, <u>one</u> football, <u>reasonable</u> price, <u>sleek</u> boat. Adjectives have distinctive forms in the COMPARATIVE and SUPERLATIVE: *happy, happier, happiest; beautiful, more beautiful, most beautiful; good, better, best.*

ADVERBS modify verbs, adjectives, or other adverbs, although they may modify whole sentences. Typical adverbs are the underlined words in the following: *stayed <u>outside</u>, walked <u>slowly</u>, <u>horribly</u> angry, <u>fortunately</u> the accident was not fatal.*

For a discussion of the special forms by which adjectives and adverbs show comparison, and of certain distinctions between the two, see Section 4.

5. Prepositions and conjunctions. Prepositions and conjunctions are the connecting words in English. A PREPOSITION links a noun or pronoun (called its OBJECT) with some other word in the sentence and shows the relation between the object and the other word. The preposition, together with its object, almost always modifies the other word to which it is linked.

The dog walks *on* water. (*on* links water to the verb *walks; on water* modifies *walks*)
The distance *between* us is short. (*between* links *us* to the noun *distance; between us* modifies *distance*)

Typical prepositions in English are *above, among, at, before, beside, down, during, from, in, of, over, through, to, toward, until, up,* and *with.*

Although a preposition usually comes before its object, in a few constructions it can follow its object.

1b

> *In what town* do you live?
> *What town* do you live *in?*

Note: Some words, such as *below, down, in, out,* and *up,* occur both as prepositions and as adverbs. Used as adverbs, they never have objects. Compare *He went below* with *He went below the deck.*

A CONJUNCTION joins words, phrases, or clauses. Conjunctions show the relation between the sentence elements that they connect.

COORDINATING conjunctions (*and, but, or, nor, for*) join words, phrases, or clauses of equal grammatical rank. (See **1d,** "Recognizing Clauses."*)

Words Joined	We ate ham *and* eggs.
Phrases Joined	Look in the closet *or* under the bed.
Clauses Joined	We wanted to go, *but* we were too busy.

SUBORDINATING conjunctions (*because, if, since, when, where,* etc.) introduce subordinate clauses and join them to main clauses. (See **1d,** "Recognizing Clauses.")

> We left the party early *because* we were tired.
> *If* the roads are icy, we shall have to drive carefully.

6. Interjections. An INTERJECTION is an exclamatory word that expresses emotion. It has no grammatical relation to other words in the sentence. Mild interjections are usually followed by a comma: *Oh, is that you? Well, well, how are you?* Stronger interjections are usually followed by an exclamation point: *Ouch! You are hurting me. Oh! I hate you!*

EXERCISE 1b Indicate the part of speech of each word in the following sentences.

1 The blizzard raged from the northeast.
2 Stop! I've heard that excuse before.
3 Pollution increases though scientists warn that it threatens our survival.

---

*For a discussion of the punctuation of clauses separated by a coordinating conjunction, see Section 20.

4 Newspapers, magazines, and books are the most powerful weapons against ignorance.
5 The streets of seaside resorts are strangely desolate in winter.
6 Misreading directions is a common student mistake in taking examinations.
7 That cave is unsafe; even the bats have left it.
8 Sally soon recovered from her severe injuries.
9 Einstein said that a man has at the most only two or three ideas in his lifetime.
10 A man should never wear his best suit when he goes out to fight for freedom and truth.

1c

1c Recognizing phrases

A PHRASE is a group of related words that has no subject or predicate and is used as a single part of speech. Typical phrases are a preposition and its object (*I fell on the sidewalk*), or a verbal and its object (*I wanted to see the parade*).

Phrases are usually classified as PREPOSITIONAL, INFINITIVE, PARTICIPIAL, or GERUND phrases.

PREPOSITIONAL PHRASES consist of a preposition, its object, and any modifiers of the object (*under the ground, without thinking, in the blue Ford*). Prepositional phrases function as adjectives or adverbs and occasionally as nouns.

> He is a man *of action.* (adjective modifying *man*)
> The plane arrived *on time.* (adverb modifying *arrived*)
> We were ready *at the airport.* (adverb modifying *ready*)
> She came early *in the morning.* (adverb modifying *early*)
> *Before breakfast* is too early. (noun, subject of *is*)

INFINITIVE PHRASES consist of an infinitive, its modifiers, and/or its object (*to see the world, to answer briefly, to earn money quickly*). Infinitive phrases function as nouns, adjectives, or adverbs.

> I wanted *to buy the house.* (noun, object of verb)
> It is time *to go to bed.* (adjective modifying *time*)
> We were impatient *to start the game.* (adverb modifying *impatient*)

PARTICIPIAL PHRASES consist of a present or past participle, its modifiers, and/or its object (*lying on the beach, found in the street, eating a large dinner*). Participial phrases always function as adjectives.

> The dog *running in the yard* belongs to my mother.
> The man *walking his dog* is my father.

Covered with ice, the road was dangerous.

Beaten twice by Susan, Jim fought to win the last game.

GERUND PHRASES consist of a gerund, its modifiers, and/or its object (*telling the truth, knowing the rules, acting bravely*). Gerund phrases always function as nouns.

Collecting stamps is my hobby. (subject)

She earned more by *working overtime.* (object of preposition)

He hated *living alone.* (object of verb)

Making a profit is his only purpose. (subject)

1d Note that since both the gerund and the present participle end in *-ing,* they can be distinguished only by their separate functions as nouns or adjectives.

VERB PHRASES consist of a main verb and its auxiliaries. A verb phrase always functions as a verb.

She *will have arrived* by noon.

We *had been working* for three hours.

EXERCISE 1c In the following sentences identify the prepositional phrases by underlining them once and the verbal phrases by underlining them twice.

1 Both little girls and little boys dream of becoming astronauts.
2 Watching football on TV is the favorite sport of millions.
3 Language is the most amazing invention of man.
4 After working late into the night, Mary went to bed.
5 The tornado struck the town, ripping roofs from houses, wrenching trees from the ground.
6 Smith wanted to hold the foreman to his promise.
7 For many years the gap between the rich and the poor in South America has been widening.
8 Being loyal to her principles was more important to Jane than gaining approval from her friends.
9 Rising in a graceful arc, the space ship swung into orbit.
10 Reports of flying saucers grew frequent in the summer.

1d Recognizing clauses

A CLAUSE is a group of words containing a subject and a predicate. The relation of a clause to the rest of the sentence is shown by the position of the clause or by a conjunction. There are two kinds of clauses: (1) main or independent clauses, and (2) subordinate or dependent clauses.

1. Main clauses. A main clause has both subject and verb but it is not introduced by a subordinating word. A main clause makes an independent statement. It is not used as a noun or as a modifier.

2. Subordinate clauses. Subordinate clauses are usually introduced by a subordinating conjunction (*as, since, because,* etc.) or by a relative pronoun (*who, which, that*). Subordinate clauses function as adjectives, adverbs, or nouns, and express ideas that are less important than the idea expressed in the main clause. The exact relationship between the two ideas is indicated by the subordinating conjunction or relative pronoun that joins the subordinate and the main clause.

A. An ADJECTIVE CLAUSE modifies a noun or pronoun.

1d

This is the jet *that broke the speed record.* (The subordinate clause modifies the noun *jet.*)

Anybody *who is tired* may leave. (The subordinate clause modifies the pronoun *anybody.*)

Canada is the nation *we made the treaty with.* (The subordinate clause modifies the noun *nation,* with the relative pronoun *that* understood.)

B. An ADVERB CLAUSE modifies a verb, adjective, or adverb.

The child cried *when the dentist appeared.* (The subordinate clause modifies the verb *cried.*)

I am sorry *he is sick.* (The subordinate clause modifies the adjective *sorry,* with the subordinating conjunction *that* understood.)

He thinks more quickly *than you do.* (The subordinate clause modifies the adverb *quickly.*)

C. A NOUN CLAUSE functions as a noun. It may serve as subject, predicate noun, object of a verb, or object of a preposition.

What John wants is a better job. (The subordinate clause is the subject of the verb *is.*)

This is *where we came in.* (The subordinate clause is a predicate noun.)

Please tell them *I will be late.* (The subordinate clause is the object of the verb *tell.*)

He has no interest in *what he is reading.* (The subordinate clause is the object of the preposition *in.*)

EXERCISE 1d(1) Underline the subordinate clauses in the following sentences and identify each as an adjective, adverb, or noun clause.

1 We tried our new speedboat when the sea was calm.

2 The apples that make the best pies are the sour ones.
3 She enrolled in college because she wanted to be a lawyer.
4 What annoyed him was the clerk's indifference.
5 While he was telephoning, the doorbell rang.
6 Many parents think that education is to be gotten only in school.
7 What one thinks at twenty often seems silly at thirty.
8 Many would be rich if success depended only on work.
9 She had the quality of innocence that the director needed.
10 We left before the movie was over.

EXERCISE 1d(2) In the following sentences point out the main and subordinate clauses. Indicate the function of each subordinate clause as an adjective, an adverb, or a noun.

1d

1 As the class ended, the teacher sighed with relief.
2 Many of the unemployed lack skills that they need for jobs.
3 One objection to capital punishment is that it is inconsistently administered.
4 The ideal summer job is one that involves little work and much money.
5 A clause is subordinate if it serves as a single part of speech.
6 The price that John wanted for his car was too high.
7 If marijuana is not addictive, why shouldn't it be legal?
8 An educated person is one who knows not only the extent of his knowledge but also its limits.
9 Some parents let their children do whatever they please.
10 The most valuable of all talents is that of never using two words when one will do.

The number of main or subordinate clauses in a sentence determines its classification: SIMPLE, COMPOUND, COMPLEX, or COMPOUND-COMPLEX.

A SIMPLE SENTENCE has a single main clause.

The wind blew.

Note that a sentence remains a simple sentence when either the subject or the verb or both are compounded.

The cat and the dog fought.
The dog barked and growled.
The cat and the dog snarled and fought.

A COMPOUND SENTENCE has two or more main clauses.

The wind blew and the leaves fell.

A COMPLEX SENTENCE has one main clause and one or more subordinate clauses.

When the wind blew, the leaves fell.

A COMPOUND-COMPLEX SENTENCE contains two or more main clauses and one or more subordinate clauses.

When the sky darkened, the wind blew and the leaves fell.

EXERCISE 1d(3) Indicate whether each of the following sentences is simple, compound, complex, or compound-complex.

1 Thinking requires practice.
2 An addict needs more and more heroin, and he needs it all the time.
3 Anyone who likes rock music can listen to it all day long.
4 He tries to be a man of the world, but he doesn't succeed.
5 Though I enjoy the country, bugs scare me and flowers make me sneeze.
6 The professor told his class he was retiring, and they applauded.
7 Teachers frown on cramming for an exam, but it's better than flunking.
8 Before elections, all politicians promise to cut taxes.
9 The judge wondered why the jury had deliberated so long.
10 If you give me your address, I will write you next week.

2   Case CA

CASE shows the function of nouns and pronouns in a sentence. In the sentence *He gave me a week's vacation,* the NOMINATIVE CASE form *he* indicates that the pronoun is being used as subject; the OBJECTIVE CASE form *me* shows that the pronoun is an object; the POSSESSIVE CASE form *week's* indicates that the noun is a possessive.

Case endings were important in early English, but modern English retains only a few remnants of this complicated system. Nouns have only two case forms, the possessive (*student's*) and a common form (*student*) that serves all other functions. The personal pronouns *I, we, he, she,* and *they,* and the relative or interrogative pronoun *who,* are inflected in three cases—nominative, possessive, and objective; the personal pronouns *you* and *it* have distinctive forms in the possessive (see table, p. 28).

In contrast, adjectives, which were once declined in five cases, now have no case endings at all. Consequently, English has had to rely increasingly on word order to show the relation of a particular word to other parts of the sentence. For example, the object of a verb or preposition normally follows the verb or preposition and thus is easily identified. In the following sentences, the nouns are identical; it is the position of each noun that determines its function.

2a

Jack threw Bill the ball.   Bill threw Jack the ball.

PERSONAL PRONOUNS

	Nominative	Possessive	Objective
Singular			
First Person	I	my, mine	me
Second Person	you	your, yours	you
Third Person	he, she, it	his, her, hers, its	him, her, it
Plural			
First Person	we	our, ours	us
Second Person	you	your, yours	you
Third Person	they	their, theirs	them

Relative or Interrogative Pronoun

Singular	who	whose	whom
Plural	who	whose	whom

2a   Nominative case

1. Use the nominative case for the subject of a verb. No English speaker is likely to say "Us are happy" or "Him is tired" instead of "We are happy" and "He is tired." But there are several types of sentence in which the subject is not easily recognized and can be confused with the object.

A. In formal English use the nominative case of the pronoun after the conjunctions *as* and *than* if the pronoun is the subject of an understood verb. In informal English there is a growing tendency to use *as* and *than* as prepositions.

Formal	She gets her work done faster than *I*. (*I* is the subject of *get mine done,* which is understood by the reader.)
Informal	She gets her work done faster than *me*.
Formal	She is as rich as *they* (are).
Informal	She is as rich as *them*.

B. Remember that the pronoun *who* used as subject of a verb will not be changed by such expressions as *I think, he says* intervening between it and its verb.

We invited only the people *who* he said were his friends. (*Who* is the subject of *were*.)

Barbara is a woman who I think deserves praise. (*Who* is the subject of *deserves*.)

Who do you think *will buy* Joe's car? (*Who* is the subject of *will buy*.)

If you are not sure which form to use in sentences such as these, try testing by temporarily crossing out the interrupting words.

Barbara is a woman (who, whom) deserves praise.
(Who, whom) will buy Joe's car?

The test will help you determine in each case whether the pronoun *who* is the subject of the verb in the subordinate clause.

C. Use the nominative case for any pronoun that is the subject of a clause, even though the <u>whole</u> clause may function as an object of a verb or preposition.

I shall welcome *whoever* wants to attend. (*Whoever* is the subject of *wants*. The object of *welcome* is the entire clause *whoever wants to attend*.)

A reward is offered to *whoever* catches the escaped lion. (The entire clause is the object of the preposition *to*.)

2. In formal English use the nominative case of the personal pronoun after forms of the verb *be*, such as *is, are, were, have been*. The forms *it's I, she, he*, and *they* continue to be preferred in formal speech and carefully edited writing. But *it's me* is very widely used by educated speakers, and *it's her, him*, and *them* are increasingly heard among such speakers.

Formal   It was *I*. I thought it was *he*. It was not *we*.
Informal   It's *me*. I thought it was *him*. It wasn't *us*.

3. In formal English use the nominative case for a pronoun following the infinitive *to be* when the infinitive has no expressed subject. Informal English commonly uses the objective case of the pronoun in this construction. (See **2c(3)** for the case of the pronoun after the infinitive when the subject is expressed.)

Formal   I would not want to be *he*. (The infinitive *to be* has no expressed subject.)
Informal   I would not want to be *him*.

2b Possessive case

2b

1. Generally, use the *s*-possessive (*boy's, Jane's*) with nouns naming living things. With nouns naming inanimate things, the *of*-phrase is sometimes preferred, but the *s*-form occurs very often.

Animate	Jane's hair; an outsider's view; inspector's approval
Inanimate	the point of the joke; the wheel of the aircraft; the name of the paper; the city's newsstands; the magazine's tone

The *s*-possessive is commonly used in expressions that indicate time (*moment's notice, year's labor*) and in many familiar phrases (*life's blood, heart's content*). Which possessive form to use may also depend on sound or rhythm: The *s*-possessive is more terse than the longer, more sonorous *of*-phrase (the President's signature, the signature of the President).

2. In formal English use the possessive case for a noun or pronoun preceding a gerund. In informal English, however, the objective case rather than the possessive case is often found before a gerund.

Formal	What was the excuse for *his* being late?
Informal	What was the excuse for *him* being late?
Formal	He complained of *Roy's* keeping the money.
Informal	He complained of *Roy* keeping the money.

Even in formal English the objective case is frequently used with plural nouns.

The police prohibited *children* playing in the street.

The choice of case sometimes depends on the meaning the writer intends to convey.

Fancy *his* playing the violin. (The act of playing the violin is emphasized.)
Fancy *him* playing the violin. (The emphasis is on *him. Playing* is here used as a participle modifying *him.*)

And note the difference in the meaning of the following sentences:

I hate that *woman* riding a bicycle.
I hate that *woman's* riding a bicycle.

We must confess, however, that the illustrations above are a little artificial. A person wishing to state dislike for a *woman's riding a bicycle* would say *I hate the way that woman rides a bicycle* or *I hate the fact that that woman rides a bicycle.*

3. Use *which* to refer to impersonal antecedents. However, substitute *whose* where the phrase *of which* would be awkward.

We saw a house *whose* roof was falling in. (*Compare:* We saw a house the roof of which was falling in.)

This is the car *whose* steering wheel broke off when the driver was going seventy miles an hour. (*Compare:* This is the car the steering wheel of which broke off when the driver was going seventy miles an hour.)

2c

2c Objective case

1. Use the objective case for the object of a verb, verbal, or preposition.

Object of a verb
I saw *him. Whom* did you see?

Object of a Verbal
Visiting *them* was enjoyable. (*Them* is the object of the gerund *visiting.*)
Whom does he want to marry? (*Whom* is the object of the infinitive *to marry.*)

Object of a Preposition
Two of *us* policemen were wounded. With *whom* were you dancing?

Formal English usage requires *whom* in the objective case. Informal English uses *who* in similar situations.

Formal   *Whom* are you discussing? (*Whom* is the object of *are discussing.*)
Informal *Who* are you discussing?

Formal   *Whom* are you looking for? (*Whom* is the object of the preposition *for.*)
Informal *Who* are you looking for?

The following sentences illustrate the use of the pronoun in the objective case after the conjunction *and.*

He found Tom and *me* at home. (Not "Tom and *I*." *Me* is an object of the verb *found.*)
He must choose between you and *me*. (Not "between you and *I*." *Me* is an object of the preposition *between.*)

3

She had dinner with *him* and *me*. (*Him* and *me* are objects of the preposition *with*.)

2. After the conjunctions *than* and *as,* use a pronoun in the objective case if it is the object of an understood verb.

She needs him more than [she needs] *me*.
I called him as well as [I called] *her*.

3. When the infinitive *to be* has an expressed subject, both that subject and the object of the infinitive are in the objective case.

He took *him* to be *me*. (*Him* is the subject of the infinitive; *me* is its object.)

EXERCISE 2 In the following sentences correct the errors in case in accordance with formal usage. Be prepared to give reasons.

1 He has lived in Cleveland longer than me.
2 It was her who was elected to the student council.
3 When we heard the footsteps, we knew it was him.
4 I appreciate soul music without him telling me what to listen for.
5 They considered the logical candidate to be I.
6 We found Mark and she in the swimming pool.
7 The teacher reported Dick as well as I for cheating.
8 Burgess was the candidate who all educated people voted for.
9 We will consider whomever applies for it.
10 There was no reason for me staying any longer.

3   Tense and Mood T

TENSE indicates the time of the action expressed by a verb.
English verbs have three PRINCIPAL PARTS, or forms: a PLAIN FORM, or INFINITIVE (*talk*), a PAST TENSE FORM (*talked*), and a PAST PARTICIPLE (*talked*). In most English verbs the past tense and the past participle are identical, both being created by adding -*ed* to the plain form: *smoked, hammered, played, worked.* Such verbs are called REGULAR verbs. Other English verbs indicate their past tense and past participle forms by more individualistic changes, frequently a vowel change within the word: *grow, grew, grown; swim, swam, swum.* Such verbs are called IRREGULAR. A few verbs have only one form for all three principal parts (*burst, cost, split*). By themselves these verbs cannot indicate differences in time but depend entirely on auxiliary verbs (*I was splitting the wood*) or modifying words or phrases (*I split the wood yesterday*).

3

With few exceptions, the difference between present and past in English is shown by a difference in the form of the verb. All other time relationships that verbs indicate are shown by combining forms of the main verb with auxiliaries. Thus, future time is shown by *shall* and *will* before the plain form (*will go, shall win*). The PERFECT TENSES, which usually indicate that an action is completed before a given point in time, combine the various forms of *have* with the past participle (*have gone, had won*). For the future perfect, *shall* and *will* are added (*will have gone, will have won*).

English verbs can also make PROGRESSIVE FORMS which show that an action continues in the time indicated. These are made by using the forms of the auxiliary *be* with the *-ing* form of the main verb (*is going, was winning*).

The usual form of the verb is the *active* form (or *active voice*) in which the subject performs or initiates the action described by the verb. The PASSIVE FORMS indicate that the subject is the object or receiver rather than the doer of the action. They can be formed only with verbs that can take objects in the active voice. We can say *The elephant dragged him,* or *He was dragged by the elephant; The poison drove him mad,* or *He was driven mad by the poison;* but only *He talked,* not *He was talked.*

The most common uses of the tenses of the ACTIVE VERB FORMS are illustrated in the following:

Present Tense (expressing a present or habitual action)

He *is talking* to the students now. He *talks* to the students at least once every year.

Past Tense (expressing an action that was completed in the past)

He *talked* to the students yesterday.

Future Tense (expressing an action yet to come)

He *will talk* to the students tomorrow.

Present Perfect Tense (usually expressing an action carried out before the present and completed at the present; sometimes expressing an action begun in the past and continuing in the present)

He *has talked* to the students before.
(action carried out before the present and now completed)
He *has* always *talked* to the students.
(action begun in the past and continuing in the present)

3

Past Perfect Tense (expressing a past action completed before some other past action)

This morning I saw the speaker who *had talked* to the students last month.

Future Perfect Tense (expressing an action that will be completed before some future time)

He *will have talked* to the students before next Thursday.

PARADIGM OF REGULAR AND IRREGULAR VERBS

	Simple Form	Progressive Form
Active Voice		
Present	I ask/drive	I am asking/driving
Past	I asked/drove	I was asking/driving
Future	I shall/will ask/drive	I shall/will be asking/ driving
Present Perfect	I have asked/driven	I have been asking/ driving
Past Perfect	I had asked/driven	I had been asking/ driving
Future Perfect	I shall/will have asked/driven	I shall/will have been asking/driving
Passive Voice		
Present	I am asked/driven	I am being asked/ driven
Past	I was asked/driven	I was being asked/ driven
Future	I shall/will be asked/ driven	I shall/will be being asked/driven
Present Perfect	I have been asked/ driven	I have been being asked/driven
Past Perfect	I had been asked/ driven	I had been being asked/driven
Future Perfect	I shall/will have been asked/driven	I shall/will have been being asked/driven

3a **Make sure that the tense of the verb in a subordinate clause is logically related to the tense of the verb in the main clause.**

Faulty	As the day *ends,* a few stars *appeared* in the sky.
Revised	As the day *ends,* a few stars *appear* in the sky.
Revised	As the day *ended,* a few stars *appeared* in the sky.
Faulty	If he *tried,* he *could have avoided* the accident.
Revised	If he *had tried,* he *could have avoided* the accident.

3b **Use a present infinitive after a verb in a perfect tense; a perfect infinitive may sometimes be used after a verb not in a perfect tense.**

Faulty	I would have liked *to have gone.*
Revised	I would have liked *to go.* (At the time indicated by the verb, I desired *to go,* not *to have gone.*)
Revised	I would like *to have gone.*
Faulty	I hoped *to have visited you.*
Revised	I had hoped *to visit* you.

3c **Use the present tense in statements that are generally true or that have no reference to time.**

Brevity *is* the soul of wit.
Corn *grows* rapidly in warm, humid weather.

3d **Distinguish carefully between the principal parts of irregular verbs.**

If you are in doubt about the principal parts of a particular verb, go to your dictionary. There you will find the present infinitive (*begin*), the past tense (*began*), and the past participle (*begun*) of irregular verbs. For regular verbs, you will find only the present infinitive, since they always form the past tense and past participle simply by adding *-d* or *-ed* (*live, lived, lived*).

The principal parts of some irregular verbs are listed below. When two or more forms are listed, both are acceptable, although the first is that first given in most dictionaries. Add to the list any other verbs that you may have used incorrectly.

Present Infinitive	Past	Past Participle
beat	beat	beaten
become	became	become
begin	began	begun

3d

Present Infinitive	Past	Past Participle
blow	blew	blown
break	broke	broken
bring	brought	brought
burst	burst	burst
buy	bought	bought
choose	chose	chosen
come	came	come
cut	cut	cut
dive	dived, dove	dived
do	did	done
draw	drew	drawn
drink	drank	drunk
drive	drove	driven
eat	ate	eaten
fall	fell	fallen
feel	felt	felt
find	found	found
fly	flew	flown
forget	forgot	forgot, forgotten
freeze	froze	frozen
get	got	got, gotten
give	gave	given
go	went	gone
grow	grew	grown
hang (suspend)	hung	hung
hang (execute)	hanged	hung
hit	hit	hit
hurt	hurt	hurt
keep	kept	kept
know	knew	known
lead	led	led
leave	left	left
let	let	let
lose	lost	lost
read	read	read
ride	rode	ridden
ring	rang	rung
rise	rose	risen
run	ran	run
see	saw	seen
shake	shook	shaken
shine	shone	shone
sink	sank, sunk	sunk
speak	spoke	spoken
spring	sprang, sprung	sprung
stand	stood	stood
steal	stole	stolen
strike	struck	struck
swim	swam	swum

Present Infinitive	Past	Past Participle
swing	swung	swung
take	took	taken
teach	taught	taught
tell	told	told
think	thought	thought
throw	threw	thrown
wear	wore	worn
write	wrote	written

Two pairs of irregular verbs—*lie, lay,* and *sit, set*—are particularly troublesome. *Lie* and *sit* are INTRANSITIVE, which means they do not take objects or occur in the passive; *lay* and *set* are TRANSITIVE and either have objects or occur in the passive. The principal parts of *lie* (meaning *to recline*) are *lie, lay, lain.* The principal parts of *lay* (meaning *to place*) are *lay, laid, laid.* The distinction between the two verbs continues to be quite carefully observed in standard English.

3d

LIE

Present	*Lie* down for a while and you will feel better.
Past	The cat *lay* in the shade and watched the dog carefully.
Present Participle	His keys were *lying* on the table where he dropped them.
Past Participle	After he *had lain* down for a while, he felt better.

LAY

Present	*Lay* the book on the table and come here.
Past	He *laid* the book on the table and walked out the door.
Present Participle	*Laying* the book on the table, he walked out the door.
Past Participle	*Having laid* the book on the table, he walked out the door.

The principal parts of *sit* (meaning *to occupy a seat*) are *sit, sat, sat;* the principal parts of *set* (meaning *to put in place*) are *set, set, set.*

SIT

Present	*Sit* down and keep quiet.
Past	The little girl *sat* in the corner for half an hour.

| Present Participle | *Sitting* down quickly, he failed to see the tack in the chair. |
| Past Participle | *Having sat* in the corner for an hour, the child was subdued and reasonable. |

SET

Present	*Set* the basket on the table and get out.
Past	Yesterday he *set* the grocery cartons on the kitchen table; today he left them on the porch.
Present Participle	*Setting* his spectacles on the table, he challenged John to wrestle.
Past Participle	*Having set* the basket of turnips on the porch, Terry went to play the piano.

3e EXERCISE 3a–d Correct the verb forms in the following sentences. Consult your dictionary when necessary.

1 The trash laid on the office floor for days.
2 Plans for the space launch were began in the spring.
3 Soon after the fire started, rats come rushing out of the basement.
4 The spy denied that he had stole the blueprints.
5 My new bikini shrunk when I washed it.
6 He was prejudice against the city because he had always lived on a farm.
7 On its first trial, the new speedboat has broke the record.
8 I would have liked to have seen Garbo in the movies.
9 If he tried, he could have avoid skidding off the road.
10 When I got home, I found I had tore my new jacket.

The MOOD of a verb indicates whether an action is to be thought of as a fact, a command, or a condition contrary to fact. In modern English the INDICATIVE MOOD, which expresses ordinary statements (*He is happy*), and the IMPERATIVE MOOD, which expresses commands (*Be happy*), serve almost all purposes.

The SUBJUNCTIVE MOOD survives only in a few formal phrases and in the forms *if I were, if he/she/it/were.*

3e Use the subjunctive mood in formal idioms.

Far be it from me to advise you.
Come what may, I am going to buy a car.

Such idioms have survived from earlier times, when the subjunctive was more common in English.

3f In formal English use the subjunctive in stating conditions contrary to fact, and in expressing doubt, regrets, or wishes.

Formal	If I *were* tired, I would go home.
Informal	If I *was tired,* I would go home.
Formal	The elm tree looks as if it *were* dying.
Informal	The elm tree looks as if it *was* dying.
Formal	If this man *be* guilty, society will condemn him.
Informal	If this man *is* guilty, society will condemn him.
Formal	I wish that I *were* taller.
Informal	I wish that I *was* taller.

3g Use the subjunctive in *that* clauses which express formal demands, resolutions, or motions.

I demand that he *resign* his position.
Resolved, that Mr. Smith *investigate* our financial condition.
I move that the meeting *be* adjourned.

3f

3g

EXERCISE 3a–g In the following sentences make whatever changes are demanded by formal usage. Indicate those sentences that would be acceptable in informal English.

1 After the crash, the injured were laying all over the highway.
2 The *Titanic* was considered unsinkable, but it sunk in a few hours.
3 Roosevelt lead the nation through some difficult times.
4 The revolution might have succeeded, if people was ready to fight.
5 Anyone would be happier if he was a millionaire.
6 I won't invite them because they drunk too much at my last party.
7 World peace would be assured if all nations set down together and talked.
8 The president demands that Jane resigns her position.
9 Both Jake and I swum across the lake and back.
10 Had I knowed I could have rode, I would have went.

4 Adjectives and Adverbs AD

4

Both adjectives and adverbs are modifying words; that is, they are words that limit or qualify the meaning of other words. Adjectives modify nouns, and they are usually placed either immediately before or immediately after the word they modify.

Adverbs normally modify verbs, adjectives, and other adverbs, although they may sometimes modify whole sentences. When they modify adjectives or other adverbs, they are adjacent to the words they modify. When they modify verbs, they are frequently but not always adjacent to the verbs.

4a

Most adverbs are distinguished from their corresponding adjectives by the ending *-ly: strong–strongly, happy–happily, doubtful–doubtfully, hasty–hastily, mad–madly.* But the *-ly* ending is not a dependable indication of the adverb since some adjectives also end in *-ly* (*gentlemanly, friendly*);* some adverbs have two forms (*quick, quickly; slow, slowly*); and still others have the same form as adjectives (*fast, much, late, well*).

4b

Most uses of adjectives and adverbs are common to both standard and nonstandard English and to all levels. But formal English makes more frequent use of distinctive adverb forms than ordinary conversation does. Since certain distinctions in the use of adjectives and adverbs are especially clear markers of differences between standard and nonstandard, and between formal and informal English, they must be observed closely.

Where there is a choice between a form with *-ly* and a form without it, formal English prefers the *-ly* form—*runs quickly* rather than *runs quick, eats slowly* rather than *eats slow*—even though the shorter forms are widely used in informal English, particularly in such commands as *Drive slow.* Note particularly that *good* and *bad* as adverbs are nonstandard. The sentence *He talks <u>good</u> but writes <u>bad</u>* is nonstandard. Standard English requires *He talks well but writes badly.*

4a Do not use an adjective to modify a verb.

Incorrect	He writes *careless.*
Correct	He writes *carelessly.* (The adverb *carelessly* is needed to modify the verb *writes.*)
Incorrect	She talks *modest.*
Correct	She talks *modestly.* (The adverb is needed to modify the verb.)

4b Do not use an adjective to modify another adjective or an adverb.

Incorrect	He was *terrible* wounded.
Correct	He was *terribly* wounded. (The adverb *terribly* is needed to modify the adjective *wounded.*)

---

*The ways in which adjectives are formed from nouns are discussed in Section 39, "Vocabulary."

Incorrect	She works *considerable* harder than he does.
Correct	She works *considerably* harder than he does. (The adverb *considerably* is needed to modify the other adverb *harder*.)

The use of adjectives in place of adverbs is more common in conversation than in writing. Indeed, the use of the adjective *real* as an emphatic *very* to modify adjectives and adverbs is often heard in educated speech.

Formal	You will hear from me *very* soon.
Colloquial*	You will hear from me *real* soon.

4c Use an adjective to modify the subject after a linking verb.

The common LINKING VERBS are *be, become, appear, seem,* and the verbs pertaining to the senses: *look, smell, taste, sound, feel.* Predicate adjectives after such verbs refer back to the subject and should be in the adjectival form. In each of the following sentences, for example, the predicate adjective modifies the subject. The verb simply links the two.

Jane looks *tired* tonight. (*Tired* modifies *Jane.*)
The butter smells *sour.* (*Sour* modifies *butter.*)

One of the most frequent errors in this construction is *I feel badly* in place of the correct subject–linking verb–predicate adjective form *I feel bad.* Though *badly* is common even in educated speech, *bad* is strongly preferred by many speakers.

Formal	He feels *bad* (ill).
Colloquial	He feels *badly.*

Formal	He felt *bad* about it.
Colloquial	He felt *badly* about it.

4d Use an adverb after the verb if the modifier describes the manner of the action of the verb.

He looked *suspiciously* at me. (The adverb *suspiciously* modifies the verb *looked.* Contrast *He looked suspicious to me.*)
The thief felt *carefully* under the pillow. (The adverb *carefully* modifies the verb *felt.*)

In these examples the verbs *look* and *feel* express action, and

*We use the term *colloquial* to signify the qualities of familiar spoken English.

4c

4d

must be modified by adverbs. But in constructions like *She looks tired* or *He feels well,* the verbs serve, not as words of action, but as links between the subject and the predicate adjective. The choice of adjective or adverb thus depends on the function and meaning of the verb—in other words, on whether or not the verb is being used as a linking verb. Ask yourself whether you want a modifier for the subject or for the verb.

4e Distinguish between the comparative and superlative forms of adjectives and adverbs.

Adjectives and adverbs show degrees of quality or quantity by means of their positive, comparative, and superlative forms. The POSITIVE form (*slow, quickly*) expresses no comparison at all. The COMPARATIVE, formed by adding *-er* or by prefixing *more* to the positive form (*slower, more quickly*), expresses a greater degree or makes a comparison. The SUPERLATIVE, formed by adding *-est* or by putting *most* before the positive form (*slowest, most quickly*), indicates the greatest degree of a quality or quantity among three or more persons or things. Some common adjectives and adverbs retain old irregular forms (*good, better, best; badly, worse, worst*).

Whether to use *more* or *most* before the adjective or adverb or to add the *-er, -est* endings depends mostly on the number of syllables in the word. Most adjectives and a few adverbs of one syllable form the comparative and superlative with *-er* and *-est*. Adjectives of two syllables often have variant forms (*fancier, more fancy; laziest, most lazy*). Adjectives and adverbs of three or more syllables always take *more* and *most* (*more beautiful, most regretfully*). Where there is a choice, select the form that sounds better or that is better suited to the rhythm of the sentence.

Some adjectives and adverbs, such as *unique, empty, dead, perfect, round,* are sometimes thought of as absolute in their meaning and thus not able to be logically compared. Logically, a room is either *empty* or *not empty,* a person is either *dead* or *alive.* But phrases such as "emptier than," "more perfect than," and "more dead than alive" are common.

Formal	His diving form is *more nearly perfect* than mine.
Informal	His diving form is *more perfect* than mine.
Formal	The new stadium is *more clearly circular* than the old one.
Informal	The new stadium is *more circular* than the old one.

4f In formal usage, use the comparative to refer only to one of two objects; use the superlative to refer only to one of three or more objects.

Comparative   His horse is the *faster* of the two.

Superlative   His horse is the *fastest* in the county.

Comparative   Ruth is the *more* attractive but the *less* good-natured of the twins.

Superlative   Ruth is the *most* attractive but the *least* good-natured of his three daughters.

EXERCISE 4   In the following sentences correct any errors in the use of adjectives and adverbs in accordance with formal usage.

1 Student leaders must take their obligations more serious.
2 I felt very badly about not seeing him.
3 The South Pole is the coldest of the two poles.
4 John is the tallest of the two brothers.
5 Our society is based on the belief that all men are created equally.
6 Owls can see good at night.
7 Would a rose by any other name smell as sweetly?
8 At first even the critics didn't understand *Lolita* because it is a very unique book.
9 The accident was not near as bad as it would have been if he had not been driving slow.
10 The tall ships sailed majestic into the harbor.

4f

5 Diagraming Grammatical Relationships

5

Diagrams can be used in grammar for the same general purpose as in the sciences: to help us visualize the way the parts of something work or go together. The chemist represents the structure of molecules by diagrams. The grammarian may construct diagrams to represent his conception of how the parts of a sentence go together. The kind of diagram that either the chemist or the grammarian draws will depend, of course, on his ideas of how, in fact, the parts of what he is representing <u>do</u> go together. We must remember that neither of them uses diagrams as ends in themselves. A diagram can only add a graphic dimension to our understanding of how something works or is constructed, be it a molecule or a sentence. But by so doing, it someitimes enables us to grasp more readily an abstraction that would otherwise remain vague.*

5a

The conception of a sentence presented in this book is that it consists of a subject and a predicate, the latter consisting of a verb alone, or of a verb plus one or two objects or a complement. (See "Basic Grammar," pp. 15–17.) Such sentences as *Boys play, Boys ride bicycles, Boys give parents trouble, Boys consider teachers unnecessary,* and *Boys are trouble* are basic sentence types. These basic sentences can be expanded by three means. First, the parts may be <u>modified</u> by adding words that qualify or restrict one or more of the basic parts. Second, word groups—clauses, or verbal or prepositional phrases—may be <u>substituted</u> for one or more of the basic parts, or for a single-word modifier. Third, any one of the basic parts or modifiers can be <u>compounded</u>; that is, another similar part may be added to it.

A well-developed system which translates this conception of the sentence into diagrams has long been in use. Essentially, it consists of four devices. First, the <u>basic sentence parts</u>—subject, verb, and objects or complements—are represented <u>on a horizontal base line</u>. Second, <u>modifiers of the basic parts</u> are placed <u>below the line</u> and attached to one of the basic parts. Third, <u>word groups that function as subjects, objects, or complements</u> are placed above the base line. Fourth, <u>compound parts</u> of any kind are placed in <u>parallel arrangements</u>. The mechanics of the system can be seen in the following.

5a The basic sentence

The <u>subject-predicate division</u> is indicated by a vertical line cutting the base line to suggest the major division within the sentence. <u>Direct objects</u> are indicated by a vertical line extending upward from the base line.

Boys	eat	hotdogs

<u>Complements</u> after linking verbs and <u>objective complements</u>

---

*The great usefulness of some sort of diagram as a way of making grammatical conceptions clear can be seen from an examination of their use by linguists. The "Chinese box" diagrams of W. Nelson Francis (see p. 49) and the various diagrams of Eugene A. Nida and others are examples. One of the readiest ways to "see" some of the basic differences between different grammatical descriptions is to compare their various diagrammatic representations. The fact that diagrams have sometimes been misused as ends in themselves, or that unrealistic claims have been made for what they can accomplish, ought not to deter us from using them judiciously to clarify systems of grammatical analysis.

(see Section 50) after direct objects are indicated by a line slanted back toward the words they complete.

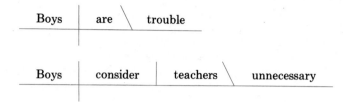

5b Modifiers

Modifiers are always placed below the base line, attached by slant lines to the words they limit or describe.

The white rooster crowed proudly.

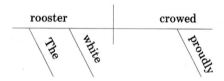

Continuing this principle, words that modify modifiers are attached to the words they modify.

The light blue airplane disappeared very quickly.

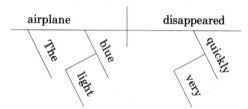

Since an indirect object is thought of as equivalent to a modifying phrase beginning with *to* or *for,* it is also placed below the line, as follows:

We gave him money.

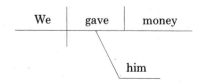

45

5c Word groups that function as basic sentence parts and as modifiers

<u>Word groups that function as subjects, objects, or complements</u> are placed <u>above the base line</u> on stilts. Note the special kinds of lines that are used to represent clauses, gerunds, and infinitives. Note also, especially, that the diagram for the internal parts of a clause or a verbal phrase merely repeats the system for diagraming basic parts and modifiers.

5c

NOUN CLAUSE AS COMPLEMENT

His weakness was *that he had no ambition.*

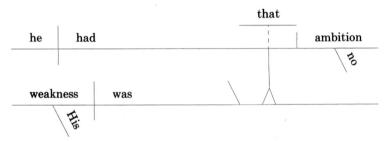

GERUND PHRASE AS SUBJECT

Breaking a forest trail is strenuous work.

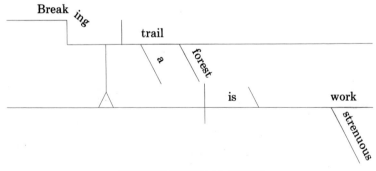

INFINITIVE PHRASE AS OBJECT

Kate is learning *to drive an automobile.*

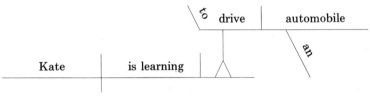

Word groups that function as modifiers are placed, in accordance with the principle for modifiers, below the base line. The connecting slant line carries the connecting word.

PREPOSITIONAL PHRASE USED AS AN ADJECTIVE

She is the owner *of the store.*

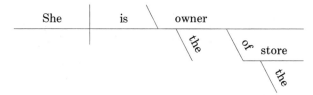

PREPOSITIONAL PHRASE USED AS AN ADVERB

The cow jumped *over the moon.*

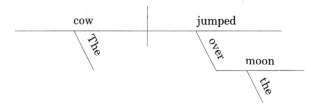

PARTICIPIAL PHRASE

Having made his fortune, he retired.

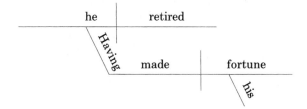

ADJECTIVE CLAUSE

The girl *who won the contest* is a college freshman.

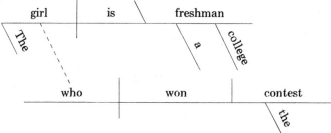

ADVERB CLAUSE

We will meet him *when the train arrives*.

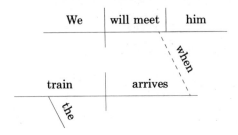

5d   Compound constructions

Compound constructions are always represented in parallel arrangements. If a connecting word is present, it is indicated on the line that joins the compound parts.

Susan and *Nancy* ran.

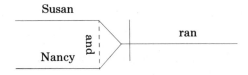

Fish *swim* and *splash*.

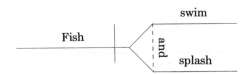

Hawkeye *was pursued* by Indians, but they *did* not *catch* him.

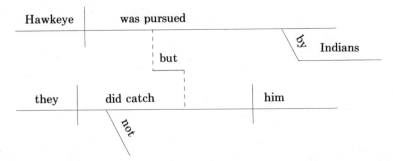

This system of diagraming offers devices for representing other elements also, such as absolutes, expletives, words of direct address, and the like. In its complete form it provides a means of representing almost all English sentences in graphic form.*

5e   Other types of diagrams

We can, of course, think of the grammatical structure of an English sentence differently from the representation in the diagrams we have been looking at. Many grammarians do think of it differently today, and have devised other kinds of diagrams to help make their ideas clear.

The idea of the sentence we have been diagraming is essentially that of a basic subject and predicate to which other less important parts are somehow attached. Suppose we think instead of the subject and predicate each as divisible into two parts, just as the sentence is divisible into a subject and a predicate. And then suppose we think of these parts in turn as again divisible, and so on until we reach individual words. The principle may be represented in this way:†

If we were to carry such a system of diagraming through so that it would permit us to make blueprints of all sentences, we should have to devise conventional ways for indicating all the different kinds of grammatical relations, just as the traditional system of diagraming has. We might, for instance, decide to show modification by an arrow connecting two boxes, and the subject-predicate relation by a *P* between boxes:

Obviously we should have to develop ways of indicating various kinds of objects and complements, compound constructions, and the like. And the finished system would have to let us always

---

*For a clear and thorough explanation of all the conventions of traditional diagraming, with very full illustrations, see R. W. Pence and D. W. Emery, *A Grammar of Present Day English,* 2nd ed. (New York: The Macmillan Company, 1963), pp. 369–426.

†This is based on diagrams used by W. Nelson Francis in *The Structure of American English* (New York: The Ronald Press, 1958).

represent our sentences in accordance with the basic idea that any sentence is successively divisible into two parts until we reach single words, just as traditional diagraming is consistent with its basic ideas about sentence construction.

Naturally, if we didn't like either of the kinds of diagrams above, we could try inventing others. If we wished, we could borrow a different kind of trick from the mathematicians and the logicians; instead of working with diagrams, we could work out formulas for our grammar. To do this, we would have to agree on symbols to represent each kind of word, word group, and grammatical relation. But once we had worked out our symbols, we could then reduce our statements about grammar to a set of formulas. Some recent grammarians have done something like this, trying to develop convenient shorthand ways of talking about some of the more complicated problems of language.

5e

Such devices as these are not grammar, of course; they are merely convenient ways of understanding our language better.

EXERCISE 5(1) Diagram the following sentences.

1 Life is short.
2 Russia invaded Czechoslovakia.
3 Marijuana offered them escape.
4 The rising floodwaters overflowed the riverbanks.
5 The outdated regulations irritated the students severely.

EXERCISE 5(2) Which word groups in the following sentences would go above the base line on stilts? Which would be attached by slant lines under the base line?

1 Balancing the national budget is a difficult task.
2 The excited reporters besieged him with questions.
3 His ambition was to marry well and retire soon.
4 His passion was hunting for antiques.
5 To ignore others' misery is to aggravate it.

EXERCISE 5(3) Which of the clauses in the following sentences would be placed above the base line? Which below it? For those below, indicate the words to which they would be attached.

1 A minority group's main problem is that it has little power.
2 This is the mixed economy toward which both communism and capitalism are moving.
3 The student militants insisted that their demands were non-negotiable.
4 The continent of Africa is now divided into nations, but tribal divisions are more faithfully observed.
5 Martin Luther King's basic principle was that violence is not a viable alternative.

"BASIC GRAMMAR" REVIEW EXERCISE Correct the grammatical errors in the following sentences according to formal usage:

1 If Judy was coming home tomorrow, I would not leave today.
2 Cleveland was the first major city that has a black mayor.
3 Many policemen feel badly over reports of police brutality.
4 After the play ended, the cast appears for curtain calls.
5 That snake looks as if he was getting ready to strike.
6 The boxer seen at once that his opponent was a harder puncher than him.
7 It was him and not I who forgot the date.
8 International relations may improve greatly if China and the United States established diplomatic relations.
9 She did not say it was me who she wanted to see.
10 After the war ended, everyone begins making plans for the next one.
11 His sister works considerable harder than he does.
12 NASA was sure delighted when the space shot proceeded on schedule.
13 It would be interesting to have watched a debate between Eisenhower and Stevenson.
14 All of we recent employees must attend orientation meetings.
15 All families were prepared when the blizzard strikes.

5e

BASIC SENTENCE FAULTS
SEN FLT

The purpose of writing is to communicate facts, feelings, attitudes, and ideas clearly and effectively. Having something to say, thinking about it clearly, developing general ideas with ample fresh, specific, and accurate details—these are all indispensable to effective writing. But so also are many details of basic sentence structure and punctuation. Unless our sentences observe the limits of English grammar and conform to the conventions of written English, we are not likely to have any readers to ask whether our ideas are interesting and our writing vivid. A reader confronted, for instance, with *In Yellowstone Park driving down the road some bears were seen having climbed down from the trees* doesn't worry much about effectiveness. He worries about the basic grammatical difficulties which make the statement such an incoherent mishmash. And the writer, if he wishes to be read, must worry about them, too.

6 Sentence Fragment FRAG

The usual sentence contains a subject and a verb, and at least one independent clause. In writing, we indicate sentences by capitalizing the first word and placing appropriate end punctuation, usually a period, after the last. Any group of words that is set off as a sentence but that lacks a subject, a verb, or an independent clause is a SENTENCE FRAGMENT.

Such fragments are common in speech, and they are sometimes used for certain special purposes in writing. But in most writing, incomplete sentences, or fragments, are very infrequent. The subject-verb sentence is what readers expect, and they will want some special effectiveness if that expectation is not met.

✗ 6a **Avoid punctuating phrases, dependent clauses, and other fragments as sentences.**

Most fragments in student writing are phrases, clauses, and occasionally other constructions which are dependent for their meaning on independent clauses that immediately precede them. The most common types of fragments, together with revisions, are illustrated on page 55. Because fragments are usually improperly punctuated parts of an adjacent sentence, they can almost always be revised by joining them to that sentence, although other revisions may be possible and sometimes desirable.

6a

1. Prepositional phrase.

Fragment	Lisa and Sally had just come home. From their trip to New Orleans, Miami, and Atlanta.
Revised	Lisa and Sally had just come home from their trip to New Orleans, Miami, and Atlanta.
Fragment	There must always be secrets. Even between you and me.
Revised	There must always be secrets, even between you and me.
Or	There must always be secrets—even between you and me.

(Here both revisions join the prepositional phrase introduced by *between* with the main statement, to which it clearly belongs. But the dash gives greater emphasis. See **24a.**)

2. Verbal phrase.

Fragment	The Dean finally agreed to see me. To talk about my financial problems.
Revised	The Dean finally agreed to see me to talk about my financial problems.
Fragment	The Egyptian pyramids are a remarkable accomplishment. Showing much knowledge of the laws of modern physics.
Revised	The Egyptian pyramids are a remarkable accomplishment, showing much knowledge of the laws of modern physics.
Fragment	The citizens voted against the proposed town budget. Being angry at the continued tax increases.
Revised	The citizens voted against the proposed town budget, being angry at the continued tax increases.
Or	The citizens voted against the proposed town budget; they were angry at the continued tax increases.

(Note that the second revision has changed the participle phrase beginning with *being* to an independent clause. The two sentences could thus be separated by a period, but the semicolon suggests the close relation between the two clauses. See **20b.**)

3. Subordinate clause.

Fragment	He took both English and mathematics. Because both were required.
Revised	He took both English and mathematics because both were required.
Or	He took both English and mathematics; both were required.
	(Here the fragment has been made independent by dropping the subordinating conjunction *because,* but the close relation of the second clause to the first is suggested by separating the two with a semicolon rather than a period.)
Fragment	The resentment which his attack on the children caused lasted for many years. Although it was seldom openly expressed.
Revised	The resentment which his attack on the children caused lasted for many years, although it was seldom openly expressed.
Fragment	Prospectors invaded the newly discovered gold field. Which was reported to be the richest yet found.
Revised	Prospectors invaded the newly discovered gold field, which was reported to be the richest yet found.

4. Appositive.

Fragment	The supervisor on my job was a kind person. A thorough man, but always sympathetic and thoughtful.
Revised	The supervisor on my job was a kind person, a thorough man, but always sympathetic and thoughtful.
Or	The supervisor on my job was a kind person. He was thorough, but always sympathetic and thoughtful.
	(Here the fragment has been made independent by adding a subject and verb. Note that this revision gives greater emphasis to the qualities of the supervisor.)
Fragment	McBride knew better than to mix ten beers with driving. Particularly driving in city traffic.
Revised	McBride knew better than to mix ten beers with driving, particularly driving in city traffic.
Or	McBride knew better than to mix ten beers with driving—particularly driving in city traffic.
	(Here the dash rather than the comma gives greater emphasis to what follows. See **24a.**)

6a

5. Other fragments.

Fragment	She was offered one position in a law office. And another in the Bureau of Indian Affairs.
Revised	She was offered one position in a law office and another in the Bureau of Indian Affairs.
	(Here the fragment is the second part of a compound object of the verb *offered*.)

6b

Fragment	After packing Saturday night, they left early Sunday morning. And reached Denver Monday evening.
Revised	After packing Saturday night, they left early Sunday morning and reached Denver Monday evening.
	(Here the fragment is the second part of a compound predicate: *They left . . . and reached . . . .*)

Fragment	No rain for three months. The reservoirs were low and the streams were drying up.
Revised	With no rain for three months, the reservoirs were low and the streams were drying up.
	(This is an uncommon form of fragment. Revision here requires either that the disconnected initial phrase be given a beginning preposition and be joined to the main clause, as illustrated; or made into an independent clause, as in *There had been no rain for three months.*)

6b Recognize acceptable incomplete sentences.

Incomplete sentences are common in the questions and answers of speech and in the written representation of speech. Exclamations and requests in English ordinarily are incomplete sentences. Also in certain situations incomplete sentences appear in more formal writing. The following will illustrate such uses.

1. Questions and answers in speech, or the rhetorical question and answer.

Why go? To see the game.
When? At 2:30.
How much does welfare do for the poor? Not enough.

2. Exclamations and commands or requests.

Look out!	Let the buyer beware!
Close the door.	Please pass me the spinach.

3. Transitional phrases and a few familiar expressions.

So much for this point. Now for my second.
The quicker, the better.

7

7a

4. Experienced writers sometimes use incomplete sentences for special purposes. In description, particularly when recording *sense* impressions, writers occasionally rely on verbless sentences, as in the first example below. In expository writing, writers sometimes use a sentence fragment to gain special emphasis, as in the second example.

> Howland & Gould's Grocery. In the display window, black, overripe bananas and lettuce on which a cat was sleeping. Shelves lined with red crepe paper which was now faded and torn and concentrically spotted. SINCLAIR LEWIS, *Main Street*

> The voice in the ad is a highly fictitious created person, speaking as an individual in a particular situation. In a bathtub, for instance. WALKER GIBSON, *Tough, Sweet & Stuffy*

EXERCISE 6 In the following sentences eliminate ineffective fragments by (1) combining them with the main clause or (2) making them into complete sentences.

1 The two candidates have the same plans. The only difference being their party.
2 Carter's first budget was one of the largest in history. Even though he had promised to cut it.
3 Many young people consider social work as a career. Not for the money, but for the satisfaction it provides.
4 The Beatles decided to stop giving concerts. Just as they were at the peak of their form.
5 Violence has become a tool of political dissent. Chiefly because nonviolence can be so easily ignored.
6 He visited on Tuesday afternoon. Immediately after he had arrived from Los Angeles.
7 I think that we should ignore their insults. Or leave quickly.
8 Linda has saved $700. Enough to make a down payment on a car.
9 Congress has investigated the Kennedy assassination several times. Trying to determine whether there was a conspiracy.
10 Many doctors refuse to prescribe birth control pills. Some women having serious side effects from them.

7 Comma Splice CS or CF
Run-together or Fused Sentence FS

7a Comma splice CS or CF

Do not connect two main clauses with only a comma. Placing a comma between two main clauses without a coordinating conjunction (*and, but, for, or, nor, yet*), results in the COMMA FAULT or COMMA SPLICE. If two main clauses are joined by a coordinating conjunction, a comma may precede the conjunction. If no conjunction is used, the two clauses must be separated by a semicolon or a period.

Comma splices may be corrected in one of the following ways:

1. Connect the main clauses with a coordinating conjunction.
2. Replace the comma with a semicolon.
3. Make a separate sentence of each main clause.
4. Change one of the main clauses to a subordinate clause.

Comma Splice	The witness was unwilling to testify, he was afraid of the accused man.
Revised (1)	The witness was unwilling to testify, *for* he was afraid of the accused man.
Revised (2)	The witness was unwilling to testify; he was afraid of the accused man.
Revised (3)	The witness was unwilling to testify. He was afraid of the accused man.
Revised (4)	*Because* he was afraid of the accused man, the witness was unwilling to testify.

Revision 4 would ordinarily be the most effective, for it not only corrects the comma splice but also indicates a specific relationship between the clauses. A good revision of a comma-splice error often entails reworking the sentence rather than merely inserting a punctuation mark. The kind of revision you choose will depend on the larger context in which the sentences occur.

A comma splice can sometimes be justified if it joins two clauses that are in balance or contrast:

As I have said elsewhere, a journalist's work is not important, it is indispensable.　　　　　BERNARD DE VOTO

But note that in this sentence a dash would serve the same purpose as a comma. The inexperienced writer will be wiser to follow the more common convention.

Note: Do not allow a conjunctive adverb (words such as *accordingly, also, consequently, furthermore, however, instead, likewise, moreover, nevertheless, otherwise, then, therefore, thus*) or a transitional phrase (such as *for example, in fact, on the other hand, that is*) to lead you into a comma splice. When such words and phrases connect main clauses, they are always preceded by a semicolon.

Everything seemed quiet; then the explosion came.
John must be sick; otherwise he would be here.

He disliked college; however, he studied every day.
He wanted a job; in fact, he needed a job very badly.

7b   Run-together or fused sentence FS

7b

<u>Do not omit punctuation between main clauses.</u> Such omission
<u>results in run-together or fused sentences</u>—that is, two gram-
matically complete thoughts with no separating punctuation.
Correct these errors in the same way as the comma splice.

Fused	Balboa gazed upon the broad Pacific his heart was filled with awe.
Revised	Balboa gazed upon the broad Pacific, *and* his heart was filled with awe.
Revised	Balboa gazed upon the broad Pacific; his heart was filled with awe.
Revised	Balboa gazed upon the broad Pacific. His heart was filled with awe.
Revised	*When* Balboa gazed upon the broad Pacific, his heart was filled with awe.

EXERCISE 7   Eliminate comma splices and fused sentences from the following items.

1 The automobile crashed headlong into the wall then all was quiet.
2 The best way to publicize a movie is to say it's "For Adults Only"
then everyone will flock to see it.
3 After the blood transfusion, the patient was comfortable, the doctor left for coffee.
4 My brother must be color-blind, he calls all colors blue.
5 Eisenhower wrote a book about World War II, he called it *Crusade
in Europe.*
6 Population continues to increase in most of the world we will soon
not have enough food for all.
7 Most of Hemingway's novels have similar subjects, love and war
are two of the most frequent.
8 Water is becoming scarce in many parts of the country, our children may have to ration it.
9 Russia and China were close allies for many years however they
are now very suspicious of each other.
10 We are never challenged by television, it's much easier to watch the
screen than to read a book.

8 Faulty Agreement AGR ✳

Agreement is the grammatical relationship between a subject
and a verb, or a pronoun and its antecedent, or a demonstrative
adjective and the word it modifies. Since modern English nouns
and verbs have few inflections, or special endings, agreement
usually presents few problems. However, there are some grammatical patterns, such as the agreement in number of a subject
and verb, or a pronoun and its antecedent, that you must watch
carefully.

number refers to singular & plural.

8a Make every verb agree in number with its subject. ←

Sometimes a lack of agreement between subject and verb results
from carelessness in composition or revision. But more often,
writers use a singular subject with a plural verb or a plural
subject with a singular verb, not because they misunderstand
the general rule, but because they are uncertain of the number
of the subject. This problem in agreement is most likely to arise
when other words intervene between the subject and verb.

**1. Do not be confused by words or phrases that inter-
vene between the subject and verb. Find the subject and
make the verb agree with it.** ①

> The first two *chapters* of the book *were* exciting. (The verb agrees
> with the subject, *chapters,* not with the nearest noun, *book.*)
> The *size* of the bears *startles* the spectators.

Singular subjects followed by such expressions as *with, together with, accompanied by,* and *as well as* take singular verbs.
The phrases introduced by such expressions are not part of the
subject, even though they do suggest a plural meaning.

Faulty	The *coach,* as well as the players, *were* happy over the victory.
Revised	The *coach,* as well as the players, *was* happy over the victory.
Faulty	*Sally,* together with her friends, *were* here.
Revised	*Sally,* together with her friends, *was* here.

**2. Remember that singular pronouns take singular
verbs.** All speakers observe this convention when pronouns
such as *everyone* and *nobody* immediately precede a verb. No

everyone, nobody

8a

English speaker is likely to say *Everyone are present,* or *Nobody win all the time.* But formal and informal English differ in their handling of pronouns that refer to antecedents such as *anyone, everyone, nobody.* Informal English frequently has sentences such as <u>*Everyone*</u> took off <u>*their*</u> coats, and <u>*Nobody*</u> ate <u>*their*</u> dinner. Formal English, however, clearly prefers <u>*Everyone*</u> took off <u>*his*</u> coat, and <u>*Nobody*</u> ate <u>*his*</u> dinner. [See **8b** (1).]

None, all, some, more, most, any <u>may</u> be followed by either <u>a singular or a plural</u> verb, dep<u>ending on whether you in</u>tend a singular or a plural meaning.

Singular   *None* but a fool *squanders* his time.
Plural   *None* but fools *squander* their time.

3. Use a plural verb with two or more subjects joined by *and.*

A do<u>g and a cat</u> <u>*are*</u> seldom friends.

However, use a <u>singular verb</u> when the tw<u>o parts of a</u> compound subject refer to the same person or thing.

My friend and benefactor *was* there to help me.

4. Use a singular verb with two or more singular sub-jects joined by *or* **(or** *nor***). If the subjects differ in number or person, make the verb agree with the subject nearer to it.**

Either the dean or his assistant *was* to have handled the matter.
Neither the farmer nor the chickens *were* aware of the swooping hawk.
Either you or he *has* to be here.

5. When the verb precedes the subject of the sentence, be particularly careful to find the subject and make the verb agree with it.

There *are* only a chair and a table left to auction.
In the balcony there *are* many seats.

In informal English a singular verb is often used when it is followed by a compound subject.

Formal   As a result, there *are* confusion, trouble, and uncertainty.
Informal   As a result, there *is* confusion, trouble, and uncertainty.

6. Use a singular verb with *collective nouns* to indicate that the group is considered as one unit. Use a plural verb to indicate that the individual members of the group are acting separately.

8a

The committee *is* meeting today.
The committee *are* unable to agree on a plan of action.

7. Make the verb agree with its subject, not with a predicate noun.

The best part of the program *is* the vocal duets.
Men *are* a necessity in her life.

8. With relative pronouns use a singular verb when the antecedent is singular, a plural verb when the antecedent is plural.

He is the only one of the councilmen who *is opposed* to the plan.
(The antecedent of *who* is *one*, not *councilmen*.)
He is one of the best baseball players that *have come* from Texas.
(The antecedent of the relative pronoun *that* is *players*, not *one*.)

Expressions like *one of the best baseball players that* commonly take a singular verb in informal usage. Although the antecedent of *that* is the plural noun *players*, the writer or speaker is influenced in his choice of a verb by the fact that *one* is singular.

Formal	He is one of those people who *are* afraid to act.
Informal	He is one of those people who *is* afraid to act.

9. When the subject is the title of a novel, a play, or the like, or a word used as a word, use a singular verb even though the form of the subject is plural.

Romeo and Juliet is a Shakespearean play.
Songs and Satires is a book by Edgar Lee Masters.
Women is the plural of *woman*.

10. Use a singular verb with nouns that are plural in form but singular in meaning, such as *economics, news, physics*.

Mathematics *has* always been Betty's downfall.
The financial news *was* favorable last month.

EXERCISE 8a In the following sentences correct any errors in agreement in accordance with formal usage. Place an *I* before the sentences that might be correct in informal English.

1 His only interest are his studies.
2 A fool and his money is soon parted.
3 Among my favorite books are *Nine Stories* by Salinger.
4 The burden of sales taxes fall on the poor.
5 Taste in movies differ greatly.
6 Neither of the leaders were certain of popular support.
7 The farmer and not the city dweller are hurt when food prices fall.
8 Twenty dollars are more than many can afford for a pair of shoes.
9 He is one of those candidates who does not take a stand on specific issues.
10 There is a good many reasons for tensions between Arabs and Israelis.

8b **Use a singular pronoun in referring to a singular antecedent. Use a plural pronoun in referring to a plural antecedent.**

Singular	The small *boy* put *his* penny in the collection box.
Plural	The *drivers* lost *their* way in the storm.

Ambiguity in the use of pronouns is an offense against clarity. The following general rules will help you select proper pronouns:

1. In formal writing use a singular pronoun to refer to antecedents such as *person, man, woman, one, any, anyone, anybody, someone, somebody, each, every, everyone, everybody, either, neither.* Informal English frequently uses a plural pronoun to refer to antecedents such as *any, every,* and their compounds, and *each, someone, somebody, either, neither,* especially when a plural meaning is suggested.

Formal	*Everybody* held *his* breath.
Informal	*Everybody* held *their* breath.
Formal	He asked *each* of us to bring *his* own lunch.
Informal	He asked *each* of us to bring *our* own lunch.

Historically *he* (*him, his*) has been used to refer to such antecedents as *one, none, everybody,* and similar indefinite pronouns that designate either male or female. This "common gender" use of the masculine pronouns has been widely criticized in recent years. Some critics have suggested coining new pronouns such as *himmer,* which would refer to both men and women. Others have urged the regular use of *he or she* (*him or her, his or hers*) when the reference is general. But language strongly resists such changes as the first, and many writers and speakers find the second too awkward for regular use. The growing practice of writers who wish to avoid the common gender use of *he* (*him, his*) is to cast their sentences in the plural, or to rework their sentences to avoid the problem. Note the following.

8b

A careful writer will recast his sentences.
A careful writer will recast his or her sentences.
Careful writers will recast their sentences.

2. With a collective noun as an antecedent, use a singular pronoun if you are considering the group as a unit, a plural pronoun if you are considering the individual members of the group separately.

The *militia* increased *its* watchfulness.
The *band* raised *their* instruments at the conductor's signal.

3. If two or more antecedents are joined by *and,* use a plural pronoun to refer to them. If two or more singular antecedents are joined by *or* or *nor,* use a singular pronoun to refer to them. If one of two antecedents joined by *or* or *nor* is singular and one plural, make the pronoun agree with the nearer.

Jack and Jim *have* finished *their* work.
Neither Jack nor Jim *has* finished *his* work.
Neither the instructor nor the students *have* finished *their* work.

EXERCISE 8b In the following sentences make every pronoun agree with its antecedent in accordance with formal usage. Then place an *I* before any sentence that would be acceptable in familiar speech or informal writing.

1 A person should be willing to defend their own principles.
2 Neither of the leaders was willing to compromise on their demands.
3 Every American should be free to live wherever they can afford.
4 The Kennedy family has carried on in spite of their tragedies.
5 Everybody has their own solution to the race problem.
6 None of the students in the psychology class could analyze their own dreams.
7 If either a black woman or a white woman were qualified, they would get the job.
8 No child appreciates their parents until later in life.
9 The school board disagreed in its opinions about closing the Adams School.
10 The citizens' group submitted their report to the mayor.

8c <u>Make sure that a demonstrative adjective (*this, that, these, those*) agrees in number with the noun it modi-</u>fies.

These adjective forms seldom cause difficulty. One frequent error, however, occurs when the demonstrative adjective is used with *kind of* or *sort of* followed by plural nouns. Here you must remember that the demonstrative adjective modifies the singular noun *kind* or *sort* and <u>not</u> the following plural noun. Thus a singular demonstrative is used.

8c

Nonstandard	*These kind* of strawberries taste sweet.
Standard	*This kind* of strawberry tastes sweet.
Nonstandard	*These sort* of watches are expensive.
Standard	*This sort* of watch is expensive.

EXERCISE 8a-c   In the following sentences correct every error of agreement in accordance with formal usage.

1 Poverty is one of the major forces that encourage crime.
2 If someone wants to "do their thing," they should be allowed to.
3 These sort of planes can exceed the speed of sound.
4 Congress should pass a law that everyone must vote or they will be fined.
5 The President with his cabinet members are touring South America.
6 Two solutions to national traffic problems have been offered but neither have been tried.
7 After thirty, one loses both the rebelliousness and the inventiveness of their earlier years.
8 Although everyone wants the right to vote, they don't all exercise that right at election time.
9 If world peace is to be assured, either the Eastern bloc or the Western bloc must alter their position.
10 The committee on admission of new members do not approve the nomination of Mr. Smith.

another pronoun for meaning

9

9   Faulty Reference of Pronouns REF

pronoun depends on noun or

A pronoun depends for meaning upon a noun or another pronoun. Insure clarity in your writing by making pronoun antecedents clear and obvious. Place pronouns as close to their antecedents as possible and make pronoun references exact.

9a Avoid sentences in which there are two possible antecedents for a pronoun. ✳

Ambiguous	Jack told Carl that he was ungrateful. (Is *he* Jack or Carl?)
Clear	Jack said to Carl, "You are ungrateful."
Clear	Jack said to Carl, "I am ungrateful."
Clear	Jack confessed to Carl that he was ungrateful.
Ambiguous	After Mrs. Henry scolded little Sylvia, she regretted her rudeness. (To whom do *she* and *her* refer?)
Clear	After Mrs. Henry scolded her, little Sylvia regretted her rudeness.
Clear	After scolding little Sylvia, Mrs. Henry regretted her own rudeness.

EXERCISE 9a Revise the following sentences by eliminating the ambiguous reference of pronouns.

1 When Kathy visited her mother, she was very angry.
2 George had a dog with fleas which he was always scratching.
3 Dad told Ross that he had stayed up watching television too late.
4 He took the shutters off the window frames and painted them.
5 Take the baby out of the bath water and throw it away.
6 He dropped the phonograph arm on the record and broke it.
7 Sidney gave his brother a copy of *Catcher in the Rye,* which was one of his favorite books.
8 The American people have elected several inadequate Presidents, but Congress has kept them from ruining the country.
9 If Hitler had behaved differently with Stalin, he might not have had to take the action he did.
10 Marilyn told Susan she should never have married Jim.

9b Avoid references to an antecedent which is remote from the pronoun, or so placed as to confuse the reader.

Remote	The birds sang in the forest where the undergrowth was thick, and a brook wound slowly in the valley. *They* were of many colors. (The pronoun *they* is too far removed from its antecedent, *birds.*)
Clear	. . . The *birds* were of many colors. (Confusion in meaning avoided by repetition of the noun.)
Clear	The *birds,* which were of many colors, sang in the forest. . . . (Elimination of the remote reference by changing the second sentence of the example into a subordinate clause.)

Vague	When the President's committee was established, he appointed student representatives. (Reference to an antecedent in the possessive case is confusing.)
Clear	When the President established his committee, he appointed student representatives.
Vague	He leaned over the bench for hours working on the blueprints. It was too low to be comfortable. (Confusing: The reference of *it* is not clear until the reader completes the sentence.)
Clear	He leaned over the bench for hours working on the blueprints. The bench was too low to be comfortable.

9c

EXERCISE 9b Revise all sentences in which pronouns are too remote from their antecedents.

1 The school belongs to the community. Students and their parents should work closely with faculty and administrators in developing programs of instruction and recreation. It could be the meeting place for all community activities.
2 The delegates arrived in twos and threes for the emergency session at the UN. Interested spectators were also streaming in. They stopped only to pose for the press photographers at the entrance.
3 The crowd watched as the computer projected the election returns all across the nation. It moaned. It groaned. It was an unexpected defeat.
4 He argued that marijuana is simply a means of achieving relaxation, and that artists, writers, and even office workers find it necessary.
5 He and his opponent made promises to the people of the nation to augment and revitalize the various poverty programs. But they were soon forgotten after the election.

9c Avoid the vague use of *this, that,* or *which* to refer to the general idea of a preceding clause or sentence.

Informal English frequently uses *this, that,* or *which* to refer to the general idea of a preceding clause or sentence. Even relatively formal written English accepts such general antecedents when the reference is unmistakably clear. In general, however, it is preferable that a pronoun refer to a particular word in the sentence.

Formal	His *joining* a fraternity, *which* was unexpected, pleased his family. (*Which* refers specifically to *joining*.)
Informal	He joined a fraternity, *which* was unexpected and pleased his family. (The reference is clear, although *which* refers to the entire preceding clause, not to any specific word.)

Eliminate a vague pronoun reference by (1) recasting the sentence to eliminate the pronoun, or (2) supplying a specific antecedent for the pronoun.

Vague	The profits from the investment would be large, *which* I realized almost immediately.
Clear	I realized almost immediately that the profits from the investment would be large. (The pronoun is eliminated.)
Clear	The profits from the investment would be large, a *fact that* I realized almost immediately. (A specific antecedent is supplied for the pronoun *that.*)

EXERCISE 9c Revise all sentences in which the reference of pronouns is vague.

9d

1 Aid to Third World countries was very limited, which angered many blacks in South Africa.
2 People should always vote in elections. This indicates their interest in good government.
3 There is a part of the museum on the south side, which is open to the public.
4 She was self-conscious about her money, which didn't bother her friends.
5 General Motors is one of the largest companies in the United States. This was not done overnight.
6 A student who does not know how to study properly will have difficulty, which this booklet is designed to prevent.
7 The migrant worker is being exploited, and that should be corrected immediately.
8 The conservative position often has great merit. Senator Taft was a good example of this.
9 The motor of the car is very noisy, which should be repaired as soon as possible.
10 Martin Luther King was dedicated to nonviolence, which influenced him to become a minister.

9d Do not use a pronoun to refer to a noun that is not expressed but is merely implied by the preceding construction.

Weak	Because we put the wire fence around the chicken yard, *they* cannot escape. (The sentence implies the antecedent *chickens,* but the word is not expressed.)
Clear	Because we put the wire fence around the chicken yard, the *chickens* cannot escape.
Weak	Tom's brother is an engineer, and *this* is the profession Tom wants to study. (*This* cannot logically refer to *engineer.*)

| Clear | Tom's brother is an engineer, and *engineering* is the profession Tom wants to study. |

EXERCISE 9d In the following sentences eliminate all references to unexpressed antecedents.

1 There is a fire station near the school, and we called them when we saw smoke.
2 He had a slight heart attack, but after a month's rest it was as good as ever.
3 When he was young he was a good poker player, but now he seldom has time to do it.
4 We plucked off the feathers before we roasted them.
5 She is a good housekeeper because she learned it as a child.
6 After hearing a lecture on population control, Mrs. Eldon had great respect for them.
7 When the witness asked for police protection, four of them were assigned to guard him.
8 Although Barbara likes to talk about politics, she does not want to be one.
9 If children are irresponsible, a great deal of it is the fault of their parents.
10 My father is a lawyer, but I know nothing about this.

9e Avoid the indefinite use of *they, you,* and *it*.

The indefinite use of *they, you,* and *it* is very common in spoken English, but is generally avoided in all but the most informal written English.

Formal	In less industrialized areas, the problems of the city are not understood.
Informal	In less industrialized areas, *they* do not understand the problems of the city.
Formal	In some states motorists are not permitted to drive faster than fifty miles an hour.
Informal	In some states *you* are not permitted to drive faster than fifty miles an hour.
Formal	The newspaper says that Monday will be warmer.
Informal	*It* says in the newspaper that Monday will be warmer.*

EXERCISE 9e Revise the following sentences to avoid the indefinite use of *they, you,* and *it*.

1 In Central America you hear of revolutions every few months.

*The indefinite use of *it* is appropriate in such idioms as *It is cloudy, It is too late to go.*

10

10a

2 Throughout the development of the West, they drove back the Indians and took their land.

3 When I called the CIA, they said they didn't have any openings for summer jobs.

4 The government pays large sums everywhere except where you need it.

5 In the first few verses of the Bible, it describes the creation of the world.

6 In every society you have to expect that some people will not be able to provide for themselves.

7 In the Vietnam agreement, it said that all American POW's would be released.

8 In the Victorian era, they never talked about sex in public.

9 It says almost nothing in the textbooks about our real treatment of Chicanos and other minorities.

10 In every generation, you find a "generation gap."

10 Shifts in Point of View PV

Point of view is <u>consistent</u> when we continue to use one subject, one person and number in pronouns, and one tense, mood, and voice in verbs, as far as grammar allows. Sudden shifts in any of these elements tend to obscure meaning and make reading difficult.

10a Do not shift the subject of a sentence or the voice of the verb.

Faulty   Frogs could be heard croaking as we neared the swamp. (The subject shifts from *frogs* to *we*. The verb shifts from passive to active voice.)

Revised   We heard frogs croaking as we neared the swamp.

Faulty   Ellen stayed at a mountain resort, and much of her time was spent in painting. (The subject shifts from *Ellen* to *much*. The verb shifts from active to passive voice.)

Revised   Ellen stayed at a mountain resort and spent much of her time in painting.

Note that when we shift the subject we often shift the voice of the verb. If you avoid the passive voice as much as possible, your sentences generally will be stronger and you will be less likely to write the kind of ineffective sentence illustrated here. For further discussion of the weak use of the passive, see **36e.**

10b   Do not shift person or number. ✳

Faulty	When *you* have good health, *one* should feel fortunate. (a shift from second to third person)
Revised	When *you* have good health, *you* should feel fortunate.
Revised	When *one* has good health, *one* should feel fortunate.
Faulty	I like *an* occasional cup of coffee, for *they* give me an added lift. (a shift from singular to plural)
Revised	I like *an* occasional cup of coffee, for *it* gives me an added lift.
Revised	I like occasional *cups* of coffee, for *they* give me an added lift.

10b

10c

10d

10c   Do not shift tense or mood. ✳

Faulty	He *sat* down at his desk and *begins* to write. (The verb shifts from past tense to present tense.)
Revised	He *sat* down at his desk and *began* to write.
Faulty	*Hold* the rifle firmly against your shoulder, and then you *should take* careful aim. (The verb shifts from imperative mood to indicative mood.)
Revised	*Hold* the rifle firmly against your shoulder and then *take* careful aim.

10d   Do not needlessly shift from indirect to direct discourse.

Faulty	The manager told me he would have my car for me as soon as he can get it serviced. (shift from indirect to direct discourse)
Revised	The manager told me he would have my car for me as soon as he could get it serviced. (indirect discourse)
Revised	The manager told me, "I will have your car for you as soon as I can get it serviced." (direct discourse)

EXERCISE 10a–d Revise the following sentences, correcting all needless shifts in tense, mood, voice, person, and number, and any shifts from indirect to direct discourse. Be prepared to explain your changes.

1 First the surface should be carefully cleaned; then put the glue on.
2 No matter what political party you belong to, one should listen to all the candidates.
3 The Sunday drivers were out in full force, and suddenly there is an accident.
4 He said he had a copy of *Esquire,* and would I like to borrow it.
5 I shall be delighted to come if my sister might come with me.

6 The great supplies of gold are found in South Africa while Mexico leads in silver mining.

7 A public opinion poll is based on a cross-section of the population, but sometimes they have been wrong.

8 Mr. Jones put putty around the window panes, and then the broken sashes were repaired.

9 Ruth wondered whether her mother had left and did she say when she would be back.

10 A person needs more than intelligence to be a good legislator; you also have to be a student of human nature.

11 The manager decided to offer free samples, and the next day the store is packed with customers.

12 When one feels tired, a candy bar will give you quick energy.

13 He marked the distance from the crosswalk to the curb, and then a heavy yellow line was painted across the area.

14 The college is revising its programs and students were asked to submit suggestions.

15 He asked me if I had done the mathematics problems and would I lend my paper to him.

11 Misplaced Parts MIS PT

Modern English, as we have seen in our discussion of grammar, relies heavily upon word order to show relations among words. The Latin sentences *Puella amat agricolam* and *Agricolam amat puella* have the same literal meaning: *The girl loves the farmer.* Even though the subject and object are reversed, the special endings (*-a* and *-am*) make the meaning of the sentence unmistakable. But if the English words are reversed, so is the English meaning: *The girl loves the farmer; The farmer loves the girl.* Word order, in short, is crucial to meaning in English.

Just as word order is the principal means by which we keep our subject-verb-object relations clear, so it is the principal means by which we keep many of our modifiers attached to the words they modify. We have to be especially watchful of phrases and clauses that modify nouns, since they normally attach to the nearest noun preceding them. Unless we are careful we can write sentences such as

He bought a horse from a stranger with a lame hind leg.

We returned to Atlanta after a week's vacation on Monday.

Context usually—though not always—allows readers to work out the intended meaning of such sentences. But at best a reader is distracted by the necessary effort.

11a Be sure that adverbs such as *almost, even, hardly, just, merely, only, nearly, scarcely* refer clearly and logically to the words they modify.

11a

11b

The misplacement of these modifiers—particularly *only*—does not always result in confusion. The misplaced *only,* in fact, is rather common in informal English. However, if you are to avoid ambiguity you must exercise care in placing these modifiers.

Formal	We caught *only* three fish.
Informal	We *only* caught three fish.
Illogical	She *nearly* blushed until she was purple.
Clear	She blushed until she was *nearly* purple.
Misplaced	I *almost* read half the book.
Clear	I read *almost* half the book.

EXERCISE 11a In the following sentences place the adverbs nearer the words they modify.

1 He almost seemed amused.
2 The *U.S. Constitution* just docked here last week.
3 The prisoner only confessed when the victim confronted him.
4 Everyone nearly suffers when unemployment rises.
5 Since she had never appeared on a stage before, she nearly was faint from fright.
6 She merely refused our offer of help because she wanted to be independent.
7 Football is a sometimes violent sport, and even some players are badly hurt.
8 The earthquake victims needed nurses to bandage their wounds badly.
9 Reports will only be mailed after all the final examinations are finished.
10 The administration scarcely provided any funds for poverty programs.

11b Be sure that modifying phrases *and clauses* refer clearly to the words they modify.

Illogical	Who is the woman who gave you the candy *in the pink dress?*
Clear	Who is the woman *in the pink dress* who gave you the candy?

Illogical	This poison attracts mice *with the smell of cheese.*
Clear	This poison *with the smell of cheese* attracts mice.

EXERCISE 11b In the following sentences place the modifying phrases nearer the words they modify.

1 Joan borrowed a bicycle from a friend with ten speeds.
2 I kept thinking how religious my parents were for the rest of the night.
3 A small boy was found lost in a cowboy suit on Central Street.
4 The furnace exploded after the patrons left the theater with a loud crash.
5 The astronauts looked forward to landing on the moon for several years.
6 He stopped the car before the house on the street with the green shutters.
7 Susan reported the accident in a quivering voice.
8 The President announced that he would confer with his cabinet at his press conference last week.
9 He dropped out of school after three years' attendance on Friday.
10 The boy was rescued after he was nearly drowned by a lifeguard.

11c **Be sure that modifying clauses refer clearly to the words they modify.**

Illogical	He had a ribbon around his neck that was tied in a bow.
Clear	Around his neck he had a ribbon that was tied in a bow.
Illogical	There was a canary in the cage *that never sang.*
Clear	In the cage there was a canary *that never sang.*
Illogical	A dog is good company *that is well trained.*
Clear	A dog *that is well trained* is good company.

EXERCISE 11c In the following sentences place the modifying clauses nearer the words they modify.

1 I took a bus at Times Square that was going uptown.
2 The new apartment was in a park with three bedrooms.
3 Marty bought a Great Dane from a neighbor that was already housebroken.
4 Jones became seriously ill shortly after he married and died.
5 She bought an alarm clock for her husband that was guaranteed for life.
6 He bought a sports car from a dealer that had been completely repainted.
7 She secured a job with the government after she had graduated from college which lasted twenty years.

8 We seldom drive this car even though it is the most comfortable because the cost is so high.
9 She was knitting a sweater for her son that was warm.
10 We watched the football game on TV that our team won.

11d   Avoid "Squinting" Modifiers

A "squinting" modifier is one that may modify either a preceding word or a following word. It squints at the words on its right and left, and leaves the reader confused.

Squinting	His physician told him *frequently* to exercise.
Clear	His physician *frequently* told him to exercise.
Clear	His physician told him to exercise *frequently*.
Squinting	The committee which was studying the matter *yesterday* turned in its report.
Clear	The committee which was studying the matter turned in its report *yesterday*.
Clear	The committee *which spent yesterday* studying the matter turned in its report.
Squinting	She promised *on her way home* to visit him.
Clear	*On her way home,* she promised to visit him.
Clear	She promised to visit him *on her way home*.

EXERCISE 11d Recast the following sentences to eliminate squinting modifiers.

1 The pilot was told constantly to be prepared for emergencies.
2 The President said after the election he would raise taxes.
3 The story he was reading slowly put his daughter to sleep.
4 The motorcycle he was riding happily skidded off the road.
5 The person who succeeds in nine cases out of ten is intelligent.
6 The instructor told his students when the class was over they could ask their questions.
7 The passengers were told when it was noon the plane would take off.
8 Religious faith without doubt is a comfort to many people.
9 The men who were beating on the wall wildly began shooting.
10 I promised when the movie was over I would tell her all about it.

11e   Do not split infinitives awkwardly.

An infinitive is split when an adverbial modifier separates the *to* from the verb. There is nothing ungrammatical about splitting an infinitive, and sometimes a split is useful to avoid awkwardness. But most split infinitives are unnecessary.

Awkward	She tried *to* not carelessly *hurt* the kitten.
Clear	She tried not *to hurt* the kitten carelessly.
Awkward	You should try *to,* if you can, *take* a walk every day.
Clear	If you can, you should try *to take* a walk every day.

On the other hand, note the following sentence:

The course is intended *to* better *equip* graduates to go into business.

In this case, if *better* is placed before *to equip* it will squint awkwardly between *intended* and the infinitive; after *to equip* it will modify graduates; at the end of the sentence it will be at best awkward and unnatural, if not entirely unclear.

EXERCISE 11e Revise the following sentences by eliminating awkward split infinitives.

1 We agreed to once and for all resolve our partnership.
2 Because the Stephensons quarreled so much, they decided to permanently separate.
3 The problem in South Africa is to successfully persuade the wealthy white rulers to give blacks a genuine voice in the government.
4 The team plans to, if the weather permits, play the game tomorrow.
5 The major nations of the world regularly decide to one day in the near future reduce their armaments.
6 It's helpful to immediately send in your tax return after the first of the year.
7 You have to willingly accept the idea that you are your brother's keeper, or the condition of man will never improve.
8 The owner of the discotheque asked the boys to immediately produce proof of their age.
9 The availability of birth control information helps to effectively reduce the number of unwanted children.
10 The student body voted to once and for all abolish fraternities from campus.

11f In general, avoid separations of subject and verb, verb and object, or parts of verb phrases unless such separations add greatly to the effectiveness of the sentence.

Effective Separation	The captain, *seeing the ominous storm clouds gathering overhead,* ordered the crew to take in the sail.
Effective Separation	And so Pilate, *willing to content the people,* released Barabbas unto them,

12

and delivered Jesus, *when he had scourged him,* to be crucified.

MARK 15:15

Effective Separation

Only when a man is safely ensconced under six feet of earth, *with several tons of enlauding granite upon his chest,* is he in a position to give advice with any certainty, and then he is silent.   EDWARD NEWTON

Awkward Separation

She *found,* after an hour's search, the *money* hidden under the rug.

Clear

After an hour's search, she *found* the *money* hidden under the rug.

Awkward Separation

At the convention I saw Mr. Ward, whom I *had* many years ago *met* in Chicago.

Clear

At the convention I saw Mr. Ward, whom I *had met* many years ago in Chicago.

EXERCISE 11f Revise the following sentences by eliminating the unnecessary separation of related sentence elements.

1 Abe, realizing that he was in danger, looked for a way to escape.
2 In a pleasant house in Concord, Emerson, who was a neighbor of Thoreau, lived.
3 You should, if you ever see a suspicious prowler, immediately call the police.
4 They discovered, after many years, the sunken treasure.
5 Peggy is, despite strong objections from her parents, going to study music and painting.
6 John wrote, after discussing it with his sister, a letter resigning his position.
7 The Senator's hope was, after his long illness, to return to Washington.
8 Swenson made, after years of smoking heavily, a great effort to stop.
9 In a primitive hospital in the jungles of Africa, Albert Schweitzer for many years lived and worked.
10 Pollution, as many have discovered, is very hard to control.

12   Dangling Modifiers DGL

A modifier must have something to modify. A DANGLING MODI-FIER is one that has nothing to modify because what it ought to modify has not been clearly stated in its sentence. For example:

Driving through the mountains, three bears were seen.

Driving through the mountains is a participle phrase which can modify anything that can drive. But there is nothing in the sentence that can do this. The sentence <u>says</u> that the bears were driving, but common sense tells us this can't be so. The writer doubtless <u>meant</u> that the bears were seen by some person who was driving.

12a

Dangling modifiers may be verbal or prepositional phrases, or elliptical clauses **(12d).** They most commonly come at the beginning of a sentence, but they can come at the end as well. To write *There were three bears, driving through the mountains* still leaves the bears apparently doing the driving. We still have nothing that *driving* can sensibly modify. Nor is *When a baby, my grandfather gave me a silver cup* improved by moving the clause to the end of the sentence.

We can eliminate dangling modifiers by (1) reworking the sentence so that the modifier is clearly attached to the right word, or (2) expanding the dangler into a full subordinate clause. Thus we can correct the sentence in our illustration by revising it as follows:

Driving through the mountains, we saw three bears.
When we drove through the mountains, we saw three bears.

12a Avoid dangling participles.

Dangling	Coming home late, the house was dark. (There is nothing in the sentence that can sensibly be *coming home.* Thus a revision must identify some person.)
Revised	Coming home late, we found the house dark.
Revised	When we came home late, the house was dark.
Dangling	Being made of glass, Horace handled the tabletop carefully. (The *tabletop* is *made of glass,* not Horace.)

EXERCISE 12a Revise the following sentences to eliminate the dangling participial phrases.

1 Cooked in a sweet and sour sauce, he bakes a delicious ham.
2 Sitting in his cabin, his keen eyes followed the birds' flight.
3 Spanning the Narrows, I realized the bridge was one of the longest in the world.
4 The airport delays were endless, waiting for the fog to lift.
5 Fearless and uncaged, the visitors to wild game preserves must be careful not to excite the animals.
6 Howling through the treetops, I could hear the wind.

7 Knowing little mathematics, the problem was difficult.
8 Seated at an outdoor cafe, Paris reveals an eternal variety.
9 The dog chased me, riding my bicycle.
10 Having waited for the coffee to heat, the eggs burned.

12b Avoid dangling gerunds.

Dangling	Before exploring the desert, our water supply was replenished. (Who replenished it?)
Revised	Before exploring the desert, we replenished our water supply.
Dangling	After putting a worm on my hook, the fish began to bite. (A very accomodating fish which will bait the hook for you.)
Revised	After I put a worm on my hook, the fish began to bite.

EXERCISE 12b Revise the following sentences to eliminate the dangling gerund phrases.

1 In inspecting the car, a large dent was found in the fender.
2 After releasing the suspect, new evidence was submitted to the police.
3 In deciding where to live, the distance to one's work should be considered.
4 In preparing the launch, the space ship was examined several times.
5 By checking the answer sheet, my errors became clear to me.
6 By riding in an airplane, the landscape acquires a new beauty.
7 Before transferring to the new school, his mother took him to meet his future classmates.
8 Upon opening the closet door, the boxes on the shelf tumbled down.
9 By reading constantly, the doctor was forced to prescribe glasses.
10 After getting up in the morning, the day began with a good breakfast.

12c Avoid dangling infinitives.

Dangling	To take good pictures, a good camera must be used. (Who will use the camera?)
Revised	To take good pictures, you must use a good camera.
Revised	If you wish to take good pictures, you must use a good camera.
Dangling	To write effectively, practice is necessary.
Revised	To write effectively, you (or *one*) must practice.

EXERCISE 12c Revise the following sentences to eliminate the dangling infinitive phrases.

1 To save fuel, the thermostat is turned down.
2 To be a good citizen, some knowledge of government procedure is necessary.
3 To find out why the wheel shakes, the car must be driven over fifty miles an hour.
4 To plan a college program, career goals must be kept in mind.
5 To be a financial success, a minimum of 100 performances of a play is necessary.
6 To be appreciated properly, the volume on the record player should be high.
7 To be completely immune to polio, several innoculations may be necessary.
8 To become a concert pianist, many years of study are required.
9 To eliminate malnutrition, food stamps were issued to the poor.
10 To be extra safe, the lock on the new apartment door was changed.

12d

12d Avoid dangling elliptical clauses.

An ELLIPTICAL CLAUSE is one in which the subject or verb is implied or understood rather than stated. The clause dangles if its implied subject is not the same as the subject of the main clause. Eliminate a dangling elliptical clause by (1) making the dangling clause agree with the subject of the main clause, or (2) supplying the omitted subject or verb.

Dangling	*When a baby,* my grandfather gave me a silver cup.
Revised	*When a baby, I* was given a silver cup by my grandfather. (The subject of the main clause agrees with the implied subject of the elliptical clause.)
Revised	*When I was a baby,* my grandfather gave me a silver cup. (The omitted subject and verb are supplied in the elliptical clause.)
Dangling	*While rowing on the lake,* the boat overturned.
Revised	*While rowing on the lake,* we overturned the boat. (The subject of the main clause agrees with the implied subject of the elliptical clause.)
Revised	*While we were rowing on the lake,* the boat overturned (*or* we overturned the boat). (The elliptical clause is expanded into a full subordinate clause.)

EXERCISE 12d Revise the following sentences to eliminate the dangling elliptical clauses.

1 When well stewed, you remove the bones from the chicken.
2 While watching television, someone knocked at the door.

3 If sighted, the astronauts would report that the man in the moon really did exist.

4 If lost, we shall pay a reward for the ring.

5 When making use of birth control information, the child can arrive exactly when planned.

6 If highly polished, you may slip on the floor.

7 My bicycle tire went flat while hurrying to the dentist.

8 The car proved hard to drive when drinking heavily.

9 If well oiled, I find my motorcycle easier to handle.

10 Although a minor, the judge suspended the sentence.

13 Omissions OM
Incomplete and Illogical Comparisons COMP

A sentence will be confusing if the writer omits words needed to insure clarity and accuracy. Sometimes, of course, we omit words through haste or carelessness. The only cure for this sort of omission is careful proofreading. Most omissions not caused by mere carelessness occur in three kinds of construction: (1) some constructions in which the omission of a preposition or conjunction is common in informal speech, (2) some kinds of compound constructions, and (3) comparisons.

13a Proofread your writing carefully to avoid careless omissions.

The sample sentences below are confusing simply because they carelessly omit necessary words.

The opportunities for men television repair are varied.

Many millions people were unemployed last depression.

Learning by imitation is one of the most common in early life.

In the first two examples, one suspects that the writer has simply failed to write the necessary words: *in* after *men* in the first, and *of* before *people* and *during the* before *last* in the second. The only cure for this sort of ill is more careful proofreading. The third sentence, although somewhat more complex, is probably of the same sort. The sentence clearly requires something like *methods of learning* after *common*. Very probably the writer *thought out* the sentence with such a phrase and, was merely careless in getting his idea down on paper.

13b   Spell out relationships left implied in speech.

Informal speech sometimes omits prepositions and the conjunction *that* in certain constructions. Careful writing prefers to spell out such constructions to avoid any possible ambiguity for the reader.

Confusing	The instructor noticed the students in the examination were anxious to start.
Revised	The instructor noticed *that* the students in the examination were anxious to start. (The omission of *that* may lead the reader to take *students* as the object of *noticed;* the inclusion of *that* makes it clear that the whole clause is the object.)
Confusing	Space travel the last few years has been exciting.
Revised	Space travel during the last few years has been exciting.

Note that some expressions such as *He left Monday* are idiomatic. Informal speech often extends the pattern to such expressions as *We became friends spring semester,* or *The next few years we'll worry about prices.* Such relationships need to be spelled out in writing.

Colloquial	I have never driven this make car before.
Formal	I have never driven this make of car before.

The use of *type, make, brand* and some other similar words immediately before a noun (*this type show*) is common in speech but avoided by most writers.

13c   Include all necessary words in compound constructions.

When we connect two items of the same kind with coordinating conjunctions such as *and* or *but,* we often omit words that unnecessarily duplicate each other: *She could [go] and did go; He was faithful [to] and devoted to his job.* But we can make such omissions only if the two items are in fact the same. If they are not, the resulting construction will be incomplete. Such incomplete constructions usually result from omitting necessary prepositions or parts of verb phrases.

Incomplete	Martha was interested and skillful at photography.

Revised	Martha was interested *in* and skillful *at* photography. (*Interested* idiomatically requires the preposition *in;* if it is not present, we tend to read *interested at.*)
Incomplete	My cat never has and never will eat fish.
Revised	My cat never has *eaten* and never will *eat* fish.
Incomplete	Tom's ideas were sound and adopted without discussion.
Revised	Tom's ideas were sound and *were* adopted without discussion. (*Were* needs to be repeated here since the two verbs are not parallel; the first *were* is used as the main verb; the second is used as an auxiliary with *adopted.*)

13d

13d   Make all comparisons complete and logical.

A comparison expresses a relation between two things: *A is larger than B*. To make a comparison complete and logical, we must include both items being compared, include all words necessary to make the relationship clear, and be sure that the two items are in fact comparable.

Incomplete	I admire her more than Jane. (More than Jane admires her? More than you admire Jane?)
Revised	I admire her more than I admire Jane.
Revised	I admire her more than Jane does.
Incomplete	Our new Ford uses less gasoline. (Less than what?)
Revised	Our new Ford uses less gasoline than our old one did.
Illogical	The buildings here are as impressive as any other city.
Revised	The buildings here are as impressive as those in any other city.
Illogical	She is the best singer of any in the chorus.
Revised	She is the best singer in the chorus.
Incomplete	He is as strong, if not stronger than, Bob.
Revised	He is as strong as, if not stronger than, Bob.
Revised	He is as strong as Bob, if not stronger.
Incomplete	She is a very kind, if not the kindest, woman I know.
Revised	She is one of the kindest women I know, if not the kindest.

14

14a

EXERCISE 13 The following sentences all contain incomplete constructions. Revise each by supplying words that have been omitted.

1 His face is like a movie actor.
2 Ghetto children deserve to and should be getting better schools.
3 He made it seem he wanted to be caught.
4 This quality mechanism would not be sold in a reputable store.
5 He was both afraid and fascinated by the idea of skin-diving.
6 Midwesterners are as friendly as any section in the country.
7 He made a supreme effort senior year and graduated June.
8 Humphrey was as well known, if not better known, than any Vice President in history.
9 Which brand toothpaste reduces cavities?
10 His opinion is in agreement with the average individual.
11 She taught in elementary school because she was interested and capable with young children.
12 I like James Baldwin better than any writer.
13 Adults sometimes understand themselves less well than children.
14 He finally decided to and eventually wound up giving up smoking.
15 Water colors are much easier.

14 Awkward or Confused Sentences AWK

Sometimes a sentence goes wrong because we construct a predicate that says something about our subject that cannot sensibly apply to that subject. Or a sentence can go wrong because we have started it with one kind of construction in mind, lost sight of where we were going, and ended with a different kind of construction. The first of these faults is called FAULTY PREDICATION; the second, a MIXED CONSTRUCTION.

14a Do not combine subjects and predicates that do not make sense together.

Not all subjects and verbs make sense together. For example, all living things can be subjects for the verb *eat—women, boys, ants, panthers*. Figuratively, we can speak of *water eating away rock*. But nouns like *bed, fence,* and *idea* are not likely subjects for *eat*. Sometimes, however, in haste or carelessness, writers construct sentences in which they combine inappropriate verbs with their subjects. Such combinations are called FAULTY PREDICATIONS.

In each of the following sentences, the writer has combined a subject and a verb that do not fit together.

The *selection* of the committee *was chosen* by the students.

Many *settlers,* moving into a new part of the country, *expanded* into towns.

Any *member* who failed to do his job on the ship *meant* danger for the whole crew.

14a

As soon as we identify the subjects and verbs of such sentences, the inappropriateness of the combinations becomes clear to us.

Such illogical combinations of subject and verb are particularly likely to occur when the verb is the linking verb *to be* in its various forms. Linking verbs equate what comes before the verb with what comes after it—the subject with the complement. They say that something equals something else. Thus they cannot be used to connect things that are not equal. *My dog is a beagle* will do, but not *My dog is a reason.*

Faulty	The first step in writing is spelling. (*Step* equals *spelling?*)
Revised	The first step in writing is learning to spell.
Faulty	His first trick was a pack of cards. (*Trick* equals *pack?*)
Revised	His first trick was one with a pack of cards.
Faulty	Schools are a serious quarrel today.

Here *schools* clearly do not equal *quarrel.* But revision is not really possible because the subject *schools* is itself so vague. Perhaps the writer meant something like *Increased taxes for schools cause serious quarrels today.*

A common kind of faulty equation occurs with predicates that begin *is when, is where, is because.*

Faulty	Chemistry is where I have my greatest difficulty.
Revised	Chemistry is the subject in which I have my greatest difficulty.
Revised	Chemistry gives me my greatest difficulty.
Faulty	A hasty generalization is when you jump to conclusions.
Revised	Hasty generalization involves jumping to conclusions.
Revised	To make a hasty generalization is to jump to conclusions.
Faulty	The reason he went to Chicago was because he wanted to visit his sister.
Revised	The reason he went to Chicago was that he wanted to visit his sister.
Revised	He went to Chicago because he wanted to visit his sister.

14b Do not mix constructions.

A MIXED CONSTRUCTION is one in which a writer begins a sentence in one construction and then shifts to another. The result is a derailed sentence which must be put back on its track to be clear.

Mixed	In every effort the student made to explain his problem got him more confused.

Here the writer began with a prepositional phrase, but by the time he arrived at his verb *got* he is thinking of *every effort* as his subject. We can untangle the sentence either by giving *got* the subject *he;* or by dropping the preposition *in* and making *every effort* the subject.

Revised	In every effort the student made to explain his problem he got more confused.
Revised	Every effort the student made got him more confused.
Mixed	The fact that Ben was a good student he had many offers for good jobs.

The fact that as a beginning requires something like *results* or *leads to* as a main verb in the sentence. But the writer has forgotten that as his sentence develops.

Revised	The fact that Ben was a good student resulted in his having many offers for good jobs.
Revised	Because Ben was a good student, he had many offers.

Note that beginnings such as *the fact that, there are,* and *it is* often cause needless complexity and lead to mixed or confusing sentences.

EXERCISE 14 Correct the following sentences to eliminate faulty predications and mixed constructions.

1 By harnessing nuclear energy, it will lessen the need for other kinds of energy.
2 The copper wheel process is one of the best types of ornamentation.
3 Being a traveling salesman is difficult, for by the time he gets home he is too tired to talk or play with his children.
4 Having spent large sums for defense has left the government with fewer resources to help the poor.
5 As a center for the performing arts, most young actors and actresses yearn to go to New York.
6 Because he forgot the date was why he missed the meeting.

7 Another kind of dishonesty is taxes.
8 My first reaction to being in a large class frightened me.
9 The price of the car cost me over $3,000.
10 The reason for her leaving is because she has been offered a higher salary.

"BASIC SENTENCE FAULTS" REVIEW EXERCISE (Sections 6–14) Indicate what strikes you as the principal error in each of the following sentences (faulty agreement, faulty reference, misplaced parts, etc.) and then revise the sentence.

1 Harvard generally accepts more students from the Northeast than others.
2 Having been pickled in formaldehyde for a week, the lab instructor distributed the frogs for dissection.
3 Because Manhattan is an island, you have to take a bridge from New Jersey.
4 Having been battered to a pulp, the referee told the boxers the bout was over.
5 When a teenager begins to lecture to his parents, it always makes them feel uncomfortable.
6 He had forgotten how tall the skyscrapers were after a year in Vietnam he had grown more used to thatched huts.
7 However much he wanted to get there on time, and with all possible modes of transportation at his disposal.
8 The letter was mailed an hour ago by the new clerk with the red miniskirt in the corner mailbox.
9 She likes her better than any of the other girls.
10 Millicent went to work in the theater after being graduated from college as a chorus girl.

MANUSCRIPT MECHANICS
MS

It was very pleasant to me to get a letter from you the other day. Perhaps I should have found it pleasanter if I had been able to decipher it.

THOMAS BAILEY ALDRICH

A good many of the practices of written English are merely conventions. Logic does not justify them; they represent instead standard ways of doing things. The "mechanics" of manuscript form, of writing numbers and abbreviations, of word division (syllabication) are such conventions. We observe them chiefly because generations of readers have come to expect writers to observe them. To be ignorant of these conventions, or to violate them, is by no means to commit a cardinal sin—it is only to make nuisances of ourselves to our readers, who expect that anyone seeking their attention with a piece of writing will have the graciousness at least to do the little things properly.

15   Manuscript Form MS

15a   Use suitable materials for your manuscripts.

1. Paper. Your instructor will probably require you to use standard theme paper ($8\frac{1}{2}$ by 11 inches) with lines about a half inch apart. Unless specifically told to, do not use narrow-lined notebook paper for themes. If you typewrite your manuscript, use either regular typewriter paper or the unruled side of theme paper. Do not use onionskin paper.

2. Typewriter. Use a black ribbon and keep the keys clean.

3. Pen and ink. Write only on one side of the paper. Use a good pen and black or blue-black ink. Do not write in pencil.

15b   Make sure your manuscripts are legible.

1. Typewritten manuscripts. Use double spacing. Leave one space between words and two spaces between sentences.

2. Handwritten manuscripts. Provide adequate spacing between words and between lines. Avoid unnecessary breaks between letters and syllables at the ends of lines. Form all letters distinctly, with clear and conspicuous capitals. Cross all *t*'s. Dot all *i*'s with real dots, not with decorative circles. Avoid artistic flourishes. If your handwriting tends to be excessively large and sprawling, or small and cramped, or precariously tipped to right or left, make a conscious effort to improve it.

15c Keep your manuscripts physically uniform and orderly.

1. Margins. Leave a uniform one-and-a-half-inch margin at the top and at the left side of each page and about one inch at the right side and bottom. Resist the temptation to crowd words in at the right or bottom of the page.

2. Title. Center the title about two inches from the top of the page, or on the first line. Leave a blank line between the title and the first paragraph. Capitalize the entire title, or if your instructor prefers, capitalize the first word and all other words in the title except the articles, *a, an, the,* and short prepositions or conjunctions. Do not underline the title or put it in quotation marks unless it is an actual quotation. Use no punctuation after titles except when a question mark or exclamation point is required. Do not repeat the title after the first page.

15c

15d

3. Indenting. Indent the first line of each paragraph about an inch, or five spaces on the typewriter. Indent lines of poetry one inch from the regular margin, or center them on the page. If you are typewriting, use single spacing for poetry you are quoting.

4. Paging. Number all pages, after the first, in the upper right-hand corner. Use Arabic numerals (2, 3, 4, etc.).

5. Endorsement. The endorsement usually appears on the outside sheet of the folded composition and includes your name, the course, and the date, plus any other information required by your instructor. Below is a specimen:

Fold $\longrightarrow$ Doe, John
here   English 101, Section A
                October 18, 1978
                Instructor: Mr. Brown
                Class Paper 2

15d Carefully proofread your manuscripts before submitting them.

Give every manuscript a close, hypercritical reading before turning it in. Allow a cooling-off period between composition and proofreading. If you know you are poor in spelling, punctuation, or some other skill, give your paper a separate reading for each kind of error. If your proofreading reveals a great many errors, rewrite your composition. When rewriting is not necessary, make specific changes as follows:

1. If you want to delete words, draw a horizontal line through them. Do not use a series of parentheses to cancel words.

2. If you want to begin a new paragraph within an existing paragraph, put the sign ¶ or *Par.* before the sentence that is to begin the new paragraph. When you want to remove a paragraph division, write *No* ¶ or *No Par.* in the margin.

3. If you want to make a brief insertion, write the new material above the line and indicate the point of insertion by placing a caret (∧) below the line.

15e   After your instructor has returned a manuscript, make the necessary corrections and submit it again.

Correcting or rewriting your papers is invaluable practice. If your instructor indicates errors in your writing by using numbers or correction symbols that refer to specific sections of this handbook, study these sections before making revisions. Note that your instructor may not indicate all errors. Be alert to eliminate all faults before returning your corrected paper. Your instructor may want you to make corrections directly on your paper, particularly when these corrections involve grammar, punctuation, and mechanics. Or he or she may suggest that you try reworking a single paragraph or an entire brief paper.

On pages 93–94 are examples of paragraphs marked by an instructor and the same paragraphs corrected by a student. The first, on p. 93, has been marked by using handbook section numbers and corrected directly on the paper. The second has been marked with symbols and rewritten by the student.

16   Numbers NOS

16a   In nonscientific writing spell out numbers or amounts less than one hundred; use numerals for other numbers or amounts.

He spent ninety-seven dollars for a camera.
Miriam is twenty-two years old.
The boy saved $4.53.
On their vacation they drove 2,468 miles.

A Paragraph Marked with Handbook Section Numbers

41a — (In my opinion, I feel that) Freshman (Comp.) should not be — 17c

16a — a required course. If you haven't learned to write after

28d — (4) years in (High School), you'll never learn. Actually, writing

44d — is a gift that (your) either born with or not, nobody can teach — 7a

13a — you how to write. Why should (studnets) be forced to take a — 44b

17a — course they don't believe need? Many students feel that they

write well enough, and they don't want to hear (the same old stuff) — 42a

about spelling, punctuation, (etc.) If students are forced to

9b — take (it), they become resentful.

16a

The Same Paragraph Corrected

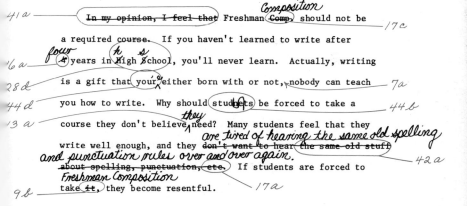

41a — ~~In my opinion, I feel that~~ Freshman (Comp.) should not be — 17c
Composition

16a — a required ~~course.~~ If you haven't learned to write after
four

28d — (~~4~~) years in ~~H~~igh ~~S~~chool, you'll never learn. Actually, writing

44d — is a gift that your 're either born with or not, nobody can teach — 7a

13a — you how to write. Why should (stud~~n~~ets) be forced to take a — 44b
they

course they don't believe need? Many students feel that they
are tired of hearing the same old spelling

write well enough, and they ~~don't want to hear~~ (the same old stuff)
and punctuation rules over and over again.

~~about spelling, punctuation, etc.~~ If students are forced to — 42a
Freshman Composition

9b — take ~~it,~~ they become resentful. — 17a

A Paragraph Marked with Correction Symbols

Try rewriting these as one sentence.

Freshman Composition should be required of (each and every) /Glos/
student. | Even after completing four years of intensive study /Dg /
in high school, mistakes in grammar are common. Even students, Int P
sp who (recieved) honor grades in high school, find that they make
mistakes in grammar. Writing, as my teacher used to say at
cs least once a week, <u>can</u> be taught, it sometimes takes a few
years to do it. I suppose this paragraph is the best evidence
sp in support of my (arguement). (Although I really (didn8t) make X
Frag any mistakes "on purpose." q

The Same Paragraph Rewritten

Freshman Composition should be required of all students.
Even after completing four years of intensive study in high
school, students--even those who received honor grades--make
mistakes in grammar. Writing, as my teacher used to say at
least once a week, <u>can</u> be taught, but it sometimes takes a
few years to do it. I suppose this paragraph is the best
evidence in support of my argument--although I really didn't
make any mistakes just to prove my point.

16b Ordinarily, use numerals for dates.

The ordinal numbers (*first, second, third, ninth*) or the forms *1st, 2nd, 3rd, 13th,* etc. should not be used after the days of the month if the year is given. If the year is not given, they may be used. Write out the year only in formal social correspondence.

16b

> May 4, 1914; July 2, 1847
> March 1, March first, March 1st

16c Use numerals for street numbers, decimals and percentages, page numbers, and hours followed by A.M. or P.M.

16c

> 13 Milford Avenue; 57 121st Street.
> The bolt is .46 inch in diameter.
> The price was reduced 15 percent.
> The quotation was in Chapter 4, page 119.
> A train arrived from Chicago at 11:20 A.M.

16d

16d Except in legal or commercial writing, do not repeat in parentheses a number that has been spelled out.

16e

> Commercial   The interest on the note was fifty (50) dollars.
> Standard   Carol has had four cars in four years.

16e Spell out numbers that occur at the beginning of a sentence.

> Inappropriate   217 bales of hay were lost in the fire.
> Revised   Two hundred seventeen bales of hay were lost in the fire.

If necessary, recast a sentence to eliminate numerals at the beginning.

> Inappropriate   2,655 entries were received in the puzzle contest.
> Revised   In the puzzle contest 2,655 entries were received.

EXERCISE 16 In the following sentences make any necessary corrections in the use of numbers.

1 John Kennedy was inaugurated on January 20th, 1961, at the age of 44.

2 The students' strike lasted ten (10) days.

3 The satellite model measured five and nineteen-hundredths inches in circumference.

4 Steven spent 2 years in the Peace Corps.

5 The seminar met at two-thirty P.M.

6 Some students spend as much as $.95 for bus fare daily.

7 85,000 people viewed the President's press conference.

8 Labor Day is the 1st Monday in September.

9 Retail prices were found to be nearly fifteen percent higher in the ghetto than in other areas of the city.

10 Of five hundred students in the senior class, only one hundred and fifty attended the prom.

17 Abbreviations AB

With a few standard exceptions, abbreviations are avoided in ordinary writing. The following sections describe standard exceptions, as well as some forms that should not be used.

17a The following abbreviations are appropriate in both formal and informal writing.

1. Titles before proper nouns. Use such abbreviations as *Mr., Mrs., Ms., Dr.* only when the surname is given: *Dr. Hart* or *Dr. F. D. Hart.*

Inappropriate	He has gone to consult the Dr.
Revised	He has gone to consult Dr. Hart (*or* the doctor).

Use *St.* (Saint) with a Christian name: *St. James, St. Theresa.*
Use abbreviations such as *Hon., Rev., Prof., Sen.* only when both the surname and given name or initials are given: *The Hon. O. P. Jones,* but not *Hon. Jones.* In more formal usage spell out these titles and use *The* before *Honorable* and *Reverend.*

Informal	Rev. W. C. Case delivered the sermon.
Formal	The Reverend W. C. Case delivered the sermon.

2. Titles after proper names. Use the following abbreviations only when a name is given: *Jr., Sr., Esq., M.D., D.D., LL.D., Ph.D.* You may, however, use academic titles by themselves.

John Nash, Jr., received an M.A.

F. D. Hart, M.D., is now studying for his J.D.

3. Abbreviations used with dates or numerals. Use the following abbreviations only when specific dates and numerals are given: B.C., A.D., A.M., P.M., *No.,* $.

Inappropriate	What was the No. of the play the coach discussed yesterday P.M.?
Revised	What was the number of the play the coach discussed yesterday afternoon?
Appropriate	He was No. 2 on the list posted at 6:30 P.M.

17b

17c

4. Latin abbreviations. Latin abbreviations such as *i.e.* (that is), *e.g.* (for example), *etc.* (and so forth) are common in most writing. In formal writing the English equivalent is increasingly used. Do not use *etc.* as a catch-all. It is meaningless unless the extension of ideas it implies is unmistakably clear. Do not write *and etc.;* the *and* becomes redundant.

Clear	The citrus fruits—oranges, lemons, etc.—are rich in Vitamin C. (The reader has no difficulty in mentally listing the other citrus fruits.)
Ineffective	We swam, fished, etc. (The reader has no clues to the implied ideas.)
Revised	We swam, fished, rode horses, and danced.

Use such abbreviations as *Bros., Inc.,* and the ampersand (&) only in names of firms where they are used in official titles.

Barnes & Noble, Inc.

17b In formal writing spell out personal names and the names of countries, states, months, and days of the week.

Inappropriate	Geo., a student from Eng., joined the class last Wed.
Revised	George, a student from England, joined the class last Wednesday.

17c In formal writing spell out the words *street, avenue, company,* and references to a subject, volume, chapter, or page, except in special contexts such as addresses and footnotes.

Inappropriate	The Perry Coal Co. has an office at Third Ave. and Mott St.
Revised	The Perry Coal Company has an office at Third Avenue and Mott Street.

18

18a

Inappropriate	The p.e. class is reading ch. 3 of the textbook.
Revised	The physical education class is reading the third chapter (*or* Chapter 3) of the textbook.

EXERCISE 17 In the following sentences correct all faulty abbreviations.

1 At two o'clock post meridian, the rocket was launched.
2 The Pres. and Amb. Smith discussed U.S. policy in the So. Pacific.
3 He enrolled in the U. of Me. because he liked the New Eng. climate.
4 Mister Turner spent his Aug. vacation working with a civil rights group in Ala.
5 Mister Downs noted the license No. of the motorcycle.
6 After yrs. of study in chem. he decided to become a Dr.
7 Many mt. passes are closed in the winter in Switz.
8 The Eng. prof. asked the students to draw on their personal experiences in writing comps.
9 The urban renewal project will cover the area from Main St. to Mich. Ave.
10 Next fall the university will offer courses in Black Lit. and Black Hist.
11 The dr. told his patient to take 3 tsp. of medicine every 2 hrs.
12 The shortest day of the year is in Dec.
13 Rev. Paul Crocker's sermons draw upon his training in phil.
14 The rds. are impassable because of a flood this A.M.
15 The capt. spent all his $$ on his Oct. furlough.

18 Syllabication SYL

When you find that you can write only part of a word at the end of a line and must complete the word on the next line, divide the word between syllables and use a hyphen to indicate the break. When you are in doubt about the syllabication of a word, consult a good dictionary.

Desk dictionaries normally use dots to divide words between syllables: *bank·rupt, col·lec·tive, ma·lig·nant, punc·ture*. Note that not every syllable marks an appropriate point at which to divide a word at the end of a line. (See **18b** and **18c**.)

18a   Never divide words of one syllable.

Wrong	thr-ee, cl-own, yearn-ed, plough-ed
Revised	three, clown, yearned, ploughed

18b   Never divide a word so that a single letter stands alone on a line.

Wrong   wear-y, e-rupt, a-way, o-val
Revised   weary, erupt, away, oval

18c   When dividing a compound word that already contains a hyphen, make the break where the hyphen occurs.

Awkward   pre-Shake-spearean, well-in-formed, Pan-Amer-ican
Revised   pre-Shakespearean, well-informed, Pan-American

EXERCISE 18   Which of the following words may be divided at the end of a line? Indicate permissible breaks with a hyphen. Refer to your dictionary if you are doubtful.

drowned	enough	walked
swimmer	twelve	automobile
learned	through	exercise
abrupt	acute	open
envelope	ex-President	preeminent

"MANUSCRIPT MECHANICS" REVIEW EXERCISE   (Sections 15–18) Correct the errors in the following sentences.

1 Some stores put a service charge on bills that are not paid within thirty (30) days.
2 I try not to enroll in classes that begin before ten forty-five A.M.
3 The vice-pres. of the Student Council is occasionally asked to act as chmn. of the mtgs.
4 The new Center for African Studies will be located at Maple and Main Sts.
5 3 boxtops must accompany every request for a "free" sample.
6 Paperback books, which once sold for a quarter, now cost as much as five dollars and ninety-five cents.
7 The local movie house will show a Bogart film on the 1st. Mon. of every mo.
8 Most tourists in N.Y. go to see the Empire St. Bldg. first.
9 Some people opposed extending suffrage to 18 yr. olds.
10 Students should have a voice in curriculum development, course selection, etc.
11 The Moore Mfg. Co. gave all old customers a five percent reduction on snow tires.
12 All heavyweight boxers must be over 175 lbs.
13 All perch measuring under 5 in. must be thrown back into Lk. Mendota.
14 Rev. Winters performed the marriage ceremony at the Lutheran Ch.
15 Mr. & Mrs. Hone entered their 3 yr. old filly in the race.

PUNCTUATION

P

Punctuation is far from being a mere mechanical device. It is mechanical as a matter of course, like word-spacing or the use of initial capitals; but punctuation is much more than that. It is an integral part of written composition.

GEORGE SUMMEY, JR.

When we speak, we use pauses and gestures to emphasize our meaning, and we vary the tempo, stress, and pitch of our voices to mark the beginning and end of units of thought. In other words, we "punctuate" our speech. We punctuate writing for the same purposes, drawing on a whole set of conventional devices we have developed to give the reader clues to what we are trying to communicate.

The first of these devices is SPACING: that is, closing up or enlarging the space between letters or words. For example, we do not runwordstogetherthisway. Instead, we identify a word <u>as a word</u> by setting if off from its neighbors. Spacing is the most basic of all punctuating devices. We use spacing also to set off paragraphs, to list items as in an outline, to mark lines of poetry, and the like.

But spacing, of course, is not the only punctuation we need. What, for example, can you understand from this string of words:

> yes madam jones was heard to say to the owl like old dowager without a doubt the taming of the shrew by shakespeare would be a most appropriate new years present for your husband

To make this passage intelligible, we need to add two other kinds of punctuation: (1) CHANGES IN THE SIZE AND DESIGN OF LETTERS (capitals and italics); and (2) MARKS OR "POINTS" (periods, commas, quotation marks, apostrophes, and other special signs).

> "Yes, Madam," Jones was heard to say to the owl-like old dowager, "without a doubt, *The Taming of the Shrew* by Shakespeare would be a most appropriate New Year's present for your husband."

This example shows us four functions of punctuation:

1. End punctuation. Capitals, periods, question marks, and exclamation points indicate sentence beginnings and endings.

2. Internal punctuation. Commas, semicolons, colons, dashes, and parentheses within sentences show the relationship of each word or group of words to the rest of the sentence.

3. Direct-quotation punctuation. Quotation marks and brackets indicate speakers and changes of speaker.

4. Word punctuation. Capitals, italics, quotation marks, apostrophes, and hyphens indicate words that have a special character or use.

In questions of punctuation there is often no absolute standard, no authoritative convention to which you can turn for a "correct" answer. But there are two general rules that serve as reliable guides:

19

1. Remember that punctuation is a part of meaning and <u>not a substitute for</u> clear and orderly sentence structure. Before you can punctuate a sentence properly, you must have constructed it properly. No number of commas, semicolons, and dashes will redeem a poorly written sentence.

19a

2. Observe conventional practice in punctuation. Though many of the rules are not hard and fast, still there is a community of agreement about punctuating sentences. Learning and applying the punctuation rules that follow will help you observe these conventions.

19b

19 End Punctuation END P

Periods, question marks, and exclamation points signal the end of a sentence. Use a period to terminate plain assertions or commands; use a question mark to terminate interrogative statements; use an exclamation point to terminate strongly emotional assertions or ejaculations. Ordinarily, the character of the sentence dictates the proper end punctuation. Occasionally, however, you must determine for yourself just what you <u>intend</u> the character of a sentence to be. Notice the different intentions behind these three sentences:

> He struck out with the bases loaded.
> He struck out with the bases loaded?
> He struck out with the bases loaded!

19a Use a period to signal the end of an assertion or a command.

| Assertion | He mowed the hay with easy strokes. |
| Command | Mow the hay with easy strokes. |

19b Use a period after an abbreviation.

> Dr.   Mr.   Mrs.   Ms.   R.N.   C.P.A.   Sen.   B.A.

Omit the period after abbreviations which serve as names of organizations or government agencies (NEA, AFL, UNESCO, AMA, TVA). If you are in doubt about whether or not to use periods in an abbreviation, consult a good dictionary for the standard practice.

19c Use a series of three spaced periods (. . .) to indicate an ellipsis within a sentence.

An ELLIPSIS is an intentional omission of words from quoted material. If you decide that it is unnecessary to reproduce all the words of the author you are quoting, use spaced periods to let your reader know that you have left something out.

For example, the first selection below is taken without any omission from Donald Keene's *Japanese Literature* (New York, 1955), p. 2. The second selection shows how a writer quoting from the original passage might use the ellipsis. Notice that when the ellipsis comes at the end of a sentence, four periods are used. The first is the usual sentence ending, and the last three indicate the ellipsis.

> The Korean Confucianists, on the other hand, tended towards extreme orthodoxy, and a chance remark attributed to Confucius, that the superior man did not talk while he ate, resulted in centuries of silent meals in Korea, though not in China, much less in Japan.
>
> The Korean Confucianists . . . tended towards extreme orthodoxy, and a chance remark attributed to Confucius, that the superior man did not talk while he ate, resulted in centuries of silent meals in Korea. . . .

19d Use a question mark after a direct question.

Direct questions often begin with an interrogative pronoun or adverb (*who, when, what,* etc.), and usually have an inverted word order, with the verb before the subject.

> When did you study science?
> Do you ever wonder what your future will be?
> You want to make a good impression, don't you?

19e Use a question mark inside parentheses (?) to indicate doubt or uncertainty about the correctness of a statement.

The device shows that, even after research, you could not establish the accuracy of the fact. It does not serve as a substitute for checking facts.

> John Pomfret, an English poet, was born in 1667 (?) and died in 1702.

Rather than using (?) you may simply say *about:*

> John Pomfret, an English poet, was born about 1667 and died in 1702.

Do not use this mark as a form of sarcasm.

> She was a very charming (?) girl.

19f Do not use a question mark after an indirect question.

An INDIRECT QUESTION is a statement implying a question but not actually asking one. Though the idea expressed is interrogative, the actual phrasing is not.

> They asked me whether I had studied science in high school.
> He asked me whether I wished to make a good impression.
> I wonder what my future will be.

A polite request phrased as a direct question is often followed by a period rather than a question mark.

> Will you please return this book as soon as possible.
> May we hear from you at your earliest convenience.

19f

19g

19g Use the exclamation point after an interjection or after a statement that is genuinely emphatic or exclamatory.

> Fire! Help! Absolutely not!
> What a vicious war!
> The examination has been stolen!

19h Do not overuse the exclamation point.

Used sparingly, the exclamation point gives real emphasis to individual statements. Overused, it either deadens the emphasis or introduces an almost hysterical tone in your writing.

> War is hell! Think of what it does to young men to have their futures interrupted and sometimes cut off completely! Think of what it does to their families! Think of what it does to the nation!

EXERCISE 19(1) Supply the appropriate punctuation marks in each of the following sentences. If you feel that a choice of marks is possible, state why you chose the one you did.

1 The reporter asked, "Mr. President, could you clarify that remark please"

2 "Yes," he replied, "let me make that absolutely clear"
3 Mr C P Johnson, who formerly worked with the law firm of Herrick, Noble, and Snow, is now with the U S Army
4 He has a Ph D from U C L A, but he earned his M A from M I T
5 I would live in N Y C if I could afford to live on Fifth Ave and E 68th St
6 Recently we have heard much about the F B I and the C I A
7 Is Mrs or Miss the abbreviation for Mistress
8 "May I quote you on that, Mr President" asked the reporter
9 "Oh, why do you insist on quoting everything" he cried
10 The guard yelled "Halt"

EXERCISE 19(2) Assume that in quoting the following passage you wish to omit the following elements: the phrase "when I was a boy"; the clause "kill the savages, kill 'em"; and the sentence beginning "But it takes time to become free." Show how you would indicate to a reader that you were omitting these elements.

I remember that when I was a boy, I used to go to see Tarzan movies on Saturday. White Tarzan used to beat up the black natives. I would sit there yelling, "Kill the beasts, kill the savages, kill 'em!" I was saying: Kill *me*. It was as if a Jewish boy watched Nazis taking Jews off to concentration camps and cheered them on. Today, I want the chief to beat hell out of Tarzan and send him back to Europe. But it takes time to become free of the lies and their shaming effect on black minds.

STOKELY CARMICHAEL, "What We Want"

20–25 Internal Punctuation INT P

End punctuation indicates whether a writer wants you to read a whole sentence as a question, an assertion, or an expression of emotion. Internal punctuation indicates the relations and relative importance of elements within the sentence. Five punctuation marks are used for this purpose: commas, semicolons, colons, dashes, and parentheses.

The most important uses of these marks, like those of end punctuation, are repeated over and over again. And like all uses of punctuation, they are a vital way of making the meaning of your sentences clear. In studying the following rules, notice not only how each mark is used but also how it contributes to the total meaning of the sentence.

20 Main Clauses

20a Use a comma to separate main clauses joined by a coordinating conjunction (*and, but, or, nor, for, yet,* and *so*). *

The patrol planes were delayed by a heavy rain, and they barely had enough fuel to get back to the carrier.

The patrol planes were delayed by a heavy rain, but they succeeded in making safe landings on the carrier deck.

The patrol planes could land near the enemy lines, or they could risk night landings on the carrier deck.

The return of the patrol planes must have been delayed, for they made night landings on the carrier deck.

Exceptions:

1. In compound sentences, when one or both main clauses are very short, you may omit the comma.

Ask no questions and you'll be told no lies.

The scene changes but the inspiration of men of good will persists.
VANNEVAR BUSH

2. You may use a semicolon to separate main clauses joined by a coordinating conjunction, especially when you have already used commas within the clauses themselves.

Babe Ruth, the greatest of home run hitters, was the most colorful figure in baseball; but many people think Ty Cobb was a better player.

The life of every man is a diary in which he means to write one story, and writes another; and his humblest hour is when he compares the volume as it is with what he vowed to make it.
SIR JAMES BARRIE

I first gave it a dose of castor-oil, and then I christened it; so now the poor child is ready for either world. **SIDNEY SMITH**

3. You may use a semicolon in place of a comma to separate long coordinated clauses or to indicate a stronger pause between clauses.

---

* In formal English *yet* is sometimes used to mean *but.* Spoken English often uses *so* as a coordinating conjunction, but written English tends to be very sparing of its use as a coordinator.

We haven't all had the good fortune to be ladies; we haven't all been generals, or poets, or statesmen; but when the toast works down to the babies, we stand on common ground.   MARK TWAIN

The cook was a good cook as cooks go; and as cooks go she went.
H. H. MUNRO

20b | **20b   Use a semicolon to separate main clauses not joined by a coordinating conjunction.**

20c | Children begin by loving their parents; as they grow older they judge them; sometimes they forgive them.   OSCAR WILDE

To educate a man is to educate an individual; to educate a woman is to educate a family.

Okinawa is sixty miles long and from two to ten miles wide; it is the largest of the Ryukyu Islands.

Exception: You may use a comma to separate very short main clauses not joined by coordinating conjunctions.

I stopped, I aimed, I fired.

20c   Use a semicolon to separate main clauses joined by a conjunctive adverb.

CONJUNCTIVE ADVERBS are words like *however, moreover, consequently, indeed,* and *then* which carry a thought from one main clause to the next. (See page 442 for a more complete list.) Unlike SUBORDINATING CONJUNCTIONS such as *although, because,* and *if* which nearly always stand at the beginning of the clause they introduce, CONJUNCTIVE ADVERBS can be moved from the beginning of a main clause to another position in the clause.

We could survive without running water; *indeed,* our ancestors survived without any modern conveniences.
We could survive without running water; our ancestors, *indeed,* survived without any modern conveniences.

Note that when the conjunctive adverb comes within the second main clause instead of at the beginning, the clauses still must be separated by a semicolon, and the conjunctive adverb set off by commas.

Americans spend millions of dollars for road-building; however, our roads are rapidly deteriorating.
Americans spend millions of dollars for road-building; our roads, however, are rapidly deteriorating.

20d Use a colon to separate two main clauses, the second of which amplifies or explains the first.*

His reasons are as two grains of wheat hid in a bushel of chaff: you shall search all day ere you find them, and when you do they are not worth the search. WILLIAM SHAKESPEARE

A gentleman of our day is one who has money enough to do what every fool would do if he could afford it: that is, consume without producing. G. B. SHAW

Over the piano was printed a notice: Please do not shoot the pianist. He is doing his best. OSCAR WILDE

20d

Note: The first word of a complete sentence following a colon may be capitalized or not. If the sentence is in quotation marks, the first word is always capitalized.

EXERCISE 20(1) Separate the main clauses in the following sentences, using a comma, a semicolon, or a colon as appropriate.

1 The telephone call brought them news they had been waiting for Doris had been offered a position with IBM.
2 One of Will Rogers' chief assets was his grin seldom is such a grin seen except on an Oklahoman.
3 The cat tried to catch the goldfish but in his excitement he fell into the bowl.
4 Very few of the workers had been able to get to the office the morning of the blizzard the manager decided to close the office.
5 Good intentions are not enough intelligence is needed also.
6 One record was lost and two were broken but the rest arrived safely.
7 Many students are ambitious to become lawyers however few realize the amount of work necessary.
8 Crime rates have been increasing rapidly therefore demands for stricter law enforcement increase rapidly.
9 Many scientists believe that marijuana is no more harmful than alcohol nevertheless alcohol is legal but marijuana is not.
10 Every winter the fear of energy shortages is renewed every summer the fear is forgotten.

EXERCISE 20(2) In each of the following sentences make the change requested. Then correct the punctuation accordingly.

1 Change *but* to *still*
   Public opinion polls indicated that Mrs. Kennedy's popularity had declined after her marriage to Onassis, but it was not clear whether this was the sole reason.

---

*Some writers prefer to use a dash instead of a colon, particularly when they wish to give an emotional emphasis to the amplifying statement. (See also **24a.**)

21

21a

2 Change *therefore* to *consequently*
European housewives shop daily; therefore they do not have left-over food to throw away.

3 Omit *because*
Because student demonstrations were becoming increasingly violent, school administrators adopted a "get tough" attitude.

4 Change *but* to *still*
There were some congested areas on the highway, but for the most part traffic flowed smoothly.

5 Change *who* to *they*
The witness was positive that these were the men who had rushed into the bank in broad daylight and held the employees at gunpoint.

6 Change *otherwise* to *or*
Strong efforts must be made to bridge the gap between the races; otherwise this nation will be split into two separate societies.

7 Change *and* to *therefore*
Common sense is not a very common quality and those who possess it are usually sought after.

8 Change *however* to *although*
At that time, the Smiths thought nothing of the occasional signs of oil on the floor of the garage; however, they recalled later that their oil tank needed constant refilling.

9 Omit the first *and*
The thundershower ended as quickly as it had begun and the spectators filed back into their seats and the baseball game was resumed.

10 Change *when* to *then*
The reporters waited patiently for the President until noon, when they began to batter the press secretary with questions.

21 Subordinate Phrases and Clauses

21a Use a comma to separate introductory clauses and phrases from a main clause.

When I saw the grizzly bear coming toward me, I raised the gun to my shoulder and took aim.

As soon as he finished studying, he left the library.

If you wish to avoid foreign collision, you had better abandon the ocean.   HENRY CLAY

After his long exile to France, Charles II returned to England in 1660.

Whenever I hear anyone arguing for slavery, I feel a strong impulse to see it tried on him personally.   ABRAHAM LINCOLN

The comma is frequently omitted after very short introductory clauses or phrases. Note, however, that even when the introductory clause or phrase is very short, a comma will be necessary if its omission can cause misreading.

Clear	When he arrived she was taking the cat out of the piano.
Clear	After his defeat he retired from public life.
Confusing	When he returned home was not what it used to be.
Confusing	After dark fireflies came in large numbers.

21b

21c

21b Use a comma to set off a beginning participial phrase modifying the subject or an absolute phrase* before the subject.

Having been an arbitrator between labor and management for a decade, he felt confident in tackling one more labor dispute.

Exhausted, the swimmer fell back into the pool.

To be quite honest about it, that dog has been known to climb trees.

Note: Do not confuse verbal modifiers with verbals used as subjects.

Having been an arbitrator between labor and management for a decade made him feel confident in tackling one more labor dispute.

21c Use a comma to set off phrases and clauses following the main clause and explaining, amplifying, or offering a contrast to it. Do not set off such clauses if they are closely related to the main clause.

Adverbial phrases and clauses, to which this rule applies (see Section 22 for adjectival modifiers), usually <u>restrict</u> the meaning of the main clauses to which they are joined. They are therefore essential to the meaning of the main clause and are not set off by a comma when they follow the main clause. When they merely introduce additional <u>nonrestrictive</u> information, however, a comma is used to indicate that they are not essential to the meaning. The writer must be guided by the logic of his sentence and the meaning he intends. Note the following.

You will not pass the examination unless you study carefully.

You did not pass the examination, although I am sure you studied carefully.

---

*For a definition of *absolute phrase,* see Section 50.

The first of these sets up *unless you study carefully* as an essential condition for passing the examination. In the second, the main clause makes an unqualified statement of fact; the *although* clause merely adds some sympathy not immediately related to the fact of the main clause.

> Jane loves John because he tolerates her petty moodiness.
> Jane knows that she loves John, because she can tolerate his petty moodiness.

21c

The first of these states that John's toleration is an essential condition of Jane's love for him. In the second, the *because* clause merely introduces explanatory information about how Jane knows that she loves John.

Note that in some constructions a comma or the lack of one will determine whether the reader will understand a phrase or a clause as a modifier of a final noun in the main clause or as an adverbial modifier.

> He has visited all the small towns in Pennsylvania.
> He has visited *all* the small towns, in Pennsylvania, in Ohio, in almost every state of the union.

In the first of these, *in Pennsylvania* restricts the location of the small towns and is an adjectival modifier of *towns*. In the second, however, the *in* phrase is additional information amplifying the assertion of the main clause but not essential to it.

EXERCISE 21(1) Supply commas in the following sentences to set off introductory phrases and clauses where necessary.

1 After visiting several hospitals she became interested in a career in physical therapy.
2 Because of the high risk of injury motorcycle riders in most states are required to wear helmets.
3 To one who is interested in farming land has beauty and character.
4 Having finished a course in photography she began taking pictures of all her friends.
5 As we expected prices continued to rise throughout the year.
6 After he had signed the contract was placed in the safe.
7 Sheila says she is interested in nursing although she really longs to become a doctor.
8 After he had finished his journalism courses he worked as a part-time reporter for the *Wakefield Times*.
9 In spite of their good intentions most parents don't understand their children.
10 Forced to make an emergency landing the pilot let the plane lose altitude rapidly.

EXERCISE 21(2) Some of the following sentences are punctuated correctly; some require commas to set off clauses or phrases which are introductory or which follow the main clause. Supply commas where necessary. If no comma is necessary in a sentence, be prepared to explain why.

1 During his final exile on the island of St. Helena Napoleon may have been poisoned.
2 Having turned state's evidence Crawford was given a lighter sentence.
3 When the exam was placed in front of him he realized how little he had studied.
4 With the shift to Daylight Time in spring everyone loses an hour's sleep.
5 If dry weather continues through the spring wheat crops will suffer greatly.
6 Shortly before the committee meeting ended.
7 Not long after Thanksgiving they met again.
8 Many psychiatrists argue that television has a bad effect on children because it makes them believe violence is acceptable.
9 Annoyed by the coughing in the audience John Barrymore once stalked off the stage during a performance.
10 From every direction came sounds of celebration.

22 Nonrestrictives
Other Parenthetical Elements

A NONRESTRICTIVE element in a sentence is a word or group of words that is an addition to, rather than an integral part of, the basic word or group of words it modifies. RESTRICTIVE elements identify or designate in some particular way that which they modify. Nonrestrictive elements introduce amplifying information beyond what is necessary for the purpose of identification. An illustration will help make our meaning clear.

Restrictive   A man *who is honest* will succeed.
Nonrestrictive   Jacob North, who is honest, will succeed.

In the first sentence the clause *who is honest* identifies the kind of man who will succeed; it restricts the subject of *will succeed* to men *who are honest* as opposed to *men who are not honest.* In other words, the clause is <u>restrictive</u>. It is thus <u>not</u> set off with commas. In the second sentence, however, the proper noun *Jacob North* identifies or designates the particular man who *will succeed;* the fact that Jacob North *is honest* is merely amplifying information about a person already sufficiently identified. The clause is <u>nonrestrictive</u>. It <u>is</u> set off with commas.

All the nonrestrictives in the following example have been italicized. The restrictives are not italicized. Notice that although the nonrestrictives contribute to the humor, they could be eliminated without destroying the basic meaning of the main clauses.

22a

One day not long ago, *idling through the pages of a sophisticated 35-cent monthly while waiting for the barber to give me my sophisticated 65-cent monthly haircut,* I was suddenly oppressed by the characteristic shortness of breath, *mingled with giddiness and general trepidation,* that results whenever one gets too near an advertisement for Tabu. This exotic scent, *in case you have been fortunate enough to forget it,* is widely publicized as "the 'Forbidden' Perfume," which means, *when all the meringue is sluiced away,* that it is forbidden to anyone who doesn't have $18.50 for an ounce of it.   s. j. perelman, *Keep It Crisp*

22a   Set off nonrestrictive elements with commas, dashes, or parentheses; do not set off restrictive elements.

Ordinarily you will use commas to set off nonrestrictives, though you may sometimes decide to use dashes or parentheses if you want to indicate a greater break in the sentence.

Nonrestrictive   Zachariah Wheeler, *the town marshal,* was once a professional wrestler.

Nonrestrictive   The town marshal, *Zachariah Wheeler,* was once a professional wrestler.

In each of these sentences the words to which the italicized phrases refer are sufficient by themselves to identify the person being talked about; the italicized phrases simply give additional or extra information about him. These phrases are nonrestrictive.

Now notice the differences among these sentences:

Restrictive   The ex-professional wrestler Zachariah Wheeler is the town marshal.

Nonrestrictive   An ex-professional wrestler, Zachariah Wheeler, is the town marshal.

The first sentence indicates by the use of the definite article *the* that one particular person is meant. We need to know that person's name to identify him and complete the meaning of the sentence. Thus, *Zachariah Wheeler* here is restrictive—it is essential to the meaning of the sentence.

In the second sentence, the indefinite article *an* indicates that the writer's purpose is to make a general statement about an ex-professional wrestler's being town marshal; the marshal's name is merely incidental. Here, then, *Zachariah Wheeler* is nonrestrictive—it is not essential to the meaning of the sentence.

Here is a rule of thumb to use in identifying restrictives and nonrestrictives: If the words in question may be omitted without seriously impairing the sense of the sentence, they are nonrestrictive and must be set off by punctuation marks. If they may not be omitted without impairing the sense of the sentence, they are restrictive and must not be set off by punctuation marks.

22b

Setting an element off with commas is a way of telling the reader your meaning. Sometimes a modifying element in a sentence may be either restrictive or nonrestrictive depending upon your meaning. And you must decide upon your meaning and purpose before you punctuate.

The house, built by my grandfather, faced the mountains.
   (*built by my grandfather* is nonessential information)
The house built by my grandfather faced the mountains.
The house built by my father stood only a hundred yards away.
   (In these sentences the two phrases beginning with *built* limit and define the particular houses.)

Texans, who have oil wells, can afford high prices.
   (All Texans have oil wells and can afford high prices.)
Texans who have oil wells can afford high prices.
   (Some Texans have oil wells; only they can afford high prices.)

Note: Always use <u>two</u> commas to set off a nonrestrictive unless it begins or ends the sentence:

Not   The old mare, half-blind and lame was hardly able to stand in the traces.

But   The old mare, half-blind and lame, was hardly able to stand in the traces.

Or   Half-blind and lame, the old mare was hardly able to stand in the traces.

22b   Set off nonrestrictive appositives with commas or dashes; do not set off restrictive appositives.

An APPOSITIVE is a noun (or group of words used as a noun) that renames another noun in the sentence. Appositives immediately follow the noun they rename. Often they are nonrestrictive because they merely give additional information not essential to the meaning of the sentence. The italicized appositives in the following sentences are nonrestrictive and are therefore set off by commas.

The professor, *an elderly and gentle man,* led the student from the class by the ear.

Daisy Mae, *our old Irish setter,* has never missed or won a fight.

"Hello, Mitty. We're having the devil's own time with McMillan, *the millionaire banker and close personal friend of Roosevelt.*"

JAMES THURBER, *The Secret Life of Walter Mitty*

Some appositives are restrictive because they give needed information. They are not set off by commas.

22c

The poet *Bryant* was a leader in New York literary circles.

Among the holiday visitors were Doris, Wilma, and my Aunt *Martha.*

But Notice   Among the holiday visitors were Ted Stevens, Gertrude Williams, and my aunt, Martha Johnson. (The speaker has only one aunt. Had he more than one he might have said "and Martha Johnson, my aunt.")

To prevent confusion, use dashes rather than commas to set off compound appositives. In the following sentence it is difficult to determine whether *Bill, Dave, and Blacky* are three additional men—or perhaps dogs or tame bears—or whether these are, in fact, the names of the men who were in the office.

Three men, Bill, Dave, and Blacky, were sitting in the office with their feet on the desk.

But when the commas are replaced by dashes, the meaning becomes clear:

Three men—Bill, Dave, and Blacky—were sitting in the office with their feet on the desk.

22c Use commas to set off words or expressions that slightly interrupt the structure of the sentence.

1. Words in direct address.

Yes, *Louise,* you should file your fingernails.

2. Mild interjections.

Oh, I never get *A*'s—always *C*'s and more *C*'s!

3. Parenthetical explanations, transitions, and afterthoughts.

Horses, *unlike tractors,* must be fed in winter.
You may, *if you wish,* leave your teeth in the bathroom.
Christians, *on the other hand,* are opposed to violence.
"The grave's a fine and private place,
But none, *I think,* do there embrace."

ANDREW MARVELL, "To His Coy Mistress"

Note: Always use two commas to set off a parenthetical element unless it begins or ends a sentence.

Not	She insisted, however that he bring her home before midnight.
But	She insisted, however, that he bring her home before midnight.
Or	She insisted that he bring her home before midnight, however.

22d

22d   Use dashes or parentheses to set off parenthetical expressions that abruptly interrupt the structure of the sentence.

The choice here is largely one of personal taste. Most writers use dashes to set off statements that they wish to emphasize, and parentheses to set off less emphatic statements.

Emphatic Parenthetical Statement	The power of the *Tribune*—one million people read it daily—is enormous.
Unemphatic Parenthetical Statement	The power of the *Tribune* (one million people read it daily) is enormous.

EXERCISE 22(1) Supply necessary punctuation in the following sentences. If a choice of punctuation is possible, be prepared to explain why you made the choice you did.

1 John L. Lewis an aggressive union leader was self-educated.
2 No one not even his wife knows what Tony paid for his collection of jazz records.
3 Commuters who know what they are talking about complain bitterly over the state of public transportation.
4 Students who do not wish medical insurance should turn in blank cards; the others who are evidently satisfied with the insurance should fill in all details.
5 Few Americans know very much about our nearest and best neighbor Canada.
6 Enrico Fermi who has been called the architect of the atomic age was born in Italy.

7 The siege of Troy which is the subject of the *Iliad* lasted for ten years.

8 He liked to attend movies which took his mind off his troubles.

9 His attempt to win her back was as you can guess unsuccessful.

10 Julian Bond although still a young man is being watched with interest by older politicians.

EXERCISE 22(2) Indicate which of the following sentences are correctly punctuated. Supply necessary punctuation in sentences that require it.

1 Mr. Wright who is the town's oldest citizen walks to work daily.

2 A man with a great deal of money should give generously to charity.

3 Binghampton, the largest city in the area was hard hit by floods.

4 Animals that hibernate in the winter are usually good fur-bearers.

5 The owner of the Green Dragon having been convicted of negligence was fined $1,000.

6 Heart transplants once confined to science fiction are now standard medical practice.

7 The Christmas shopping season, which all merchants look forward to, begins earlier and earlier each year.

8 The shopping area that my mother prefers is about three miles from our home.

9 Traveling in Asia if one is willing to experiment with new foods can be very exciting.

10 On Christmas which came on Friday last year there was a record-breaking storm.

23 Items in a Series

23a **Use commas to separate three or more words, phrases, or clauses that form a coordinate series.**

He talked fluently, wittily, penetratingly.

He is honest, he is courageous, and he is experienced.

There is not a more mean, stupid, dastardly, pitiful, selfish, spiteful, envious, ungrateful animal than the Public. It is the greatest of cowards, for it is afraid of itself.   WILLIAM HAZLITT

Some writers omit the comma before *and* in simple A, B and C series: violins, flutes and cellos; men, women and children. But since the comma is sometimes vital for clarity, it is preferable to establish the habit of always including it.

Note how necessary the final comma is in the following.

Our resort is equipped with comfortable cabins, a large lake with boating facilities, and a nine-hole golf course.

I am interested in a modern, furnished apartment with two bedrooms, kitchenette, living room, bathroom with shower, and garage.

If we omit the comma after *facilities* in the first sentence, the sentence seems to suggest that the resort has a lake with a golf course in it. If we omit it after the *shower* in the second sentence, the writer seems to be saying that he wishes an apartment with a garage in the bathroom.

23b

23b Use commas to separate coordinate adjectives in a series; do not use commas to separate adjectives that are not coordinate.

Adjectives in a series are coordinate if each adjective modifies the noun separately. They are not coordinate if each adjective in the series modifies the total concept that follows it.

Coordinate	You are a *greedy, thoughtless, insensitive* prig.
Not Coordinate	The boys are planning an *exciting holiday canoe* trip.

In the first sentence each adjective is more or less independent of the other two; the three adjectives might be rearranged without seriously affecting the sense of the sentence: *thoughtless, insensitive, greedy prig; insensitive, greedy, thoughtless prig.* Moreover, the conjunction *and* could be inserted in place of the commas and the basic meaning would remain—*greedy* and *thoughtless* and *insensitive* prig. But in the second sentence the adjectives are interdependent. Their order may not be changed, nor may *and* be substituted, without making hash of the original meaning—*canoe holiday exciting* trip; *holiday exciting canoe* trip; *exciting* and *holiday* and *canoe* trip. The adjectives in the second sentence constitute, in effect, a restrictive phrase, as distinct from the nonrestrictive quality of the adjectives in the first sentence, and therefore are not separated from one another by commas.

It must be said, however, that actual usage in punctuating coordinate adjectives varies a great deal. Though few writers would punctuate the sentences above other than we have, many of them would be unable to choose between the punctuation of the sentences below.

He presented the ambassador with a *dirty, yellowed, gnarled* hand to shake.
He presented the ambassador with a *dirty yellowed gnarled* hand to shake.

Some writers feel that the meaning of the two sentences is slightly different: that the latter sentence suggests a more unified image than the former. That is, they feel that in the latter case the three adjectives partake of one another's qualities—*dirty-yellowed-gnarled* rather than *dirty and yellowed and gnarled.*

23c **Use commas to set off items in dates, addresses, and geographical names.**

23c

23d

He left Detroit on July 19, 1967.
He left Detroit on July 19, 1967, and never returned.

But   He left Detroit in July 1967.
        He left Detroit in July 1967 and never returned.

When the day of the month is given, a comma is required between the day and the year. When the month-date-year date stands within a sentence, it is normally followed by a comma after the year. When only the month and year are given, a comma is used neither between them, nor after the year.

The military services and some other organizations now observe the practice of putting the day of the month before the name of the month, as 17 July 1931, 6 August 1950. If you follow this practice, remember not to put a comma after the day of the month.

Addresses	He gave 39 West 46th Street, Olean, New York, as his forwarding address.
Geographical Names	He pretended to make the grand tour in three months, but he spent a whole month at Bremen, Germany, and the rest of the time in Tunbridge Wells, Kent, a small village in England.

23d **Use semicolons to separate the items of a series if the items themselves contain commas.**

[See "Main Clauses," **20a**(2).]

The following people were present: John Smith, the doctor; Paul Brown, the dentist; and Elmer Wilson, the psychiatrist.

The bureaucracy consists of functionaries; the aristocracy, of idols; the democracy, of idolaters.   G. B. SHAW

EXERCISE 23 The following sentences all contain series which require punctuation. Supply commas or semicolons where they are necessary.

1 The warehouse had an aluminum roof a concrete floor and steel window sash.

2 His courses included algebra which he liked psychology which he at least found interesting and French which he hated.

3 Both candidates seemed to be promising peace prosperity and happiness.

4 He learned how necessary money is how hard it is to earn and how easy it is to spend.

5 He brought a pot of strong steaming hot coffee to the table.

6 Among the countries I visited last summer were Rumania Bulgaria and Poland all behind the Iron Curtain.

7 The telephone operator reported that there was no 33 Pine Drive in Austin that there is no Michael Stone listed at any other address and that there is no telephone exchange beginning with 254 in that area.

8 To pursue a career in the theater one must have talent a great deal of energy and a supreme confidence in himself.

9 If TV commercials are to be believed the American dream consists of a new car a color television set and a mate who uses an effective mouthwash.

10 Taking off his wrinkled old white cap lowering his tattered black umbrella and scraping his tennis shoes on the doormat he rang the bell.

24   Final Appositives and Summaries

24a   Use a dash to set off a short final appositive or summary.*

He had only one pleasure—eating.

These are the two culprits—Joe Green and Miller Berg.

Each person is born to one possession which overvalues all his others—his last breath.   MARK TWAIN

So I leave it with all of you: Which came out of the opened door—the lady or the tiger?   FRANK STOCKTON

24b   Use a colon to set off a long or formal appositive or summary, or a series or statement introduced by the words *the following* or *as follows*.

Out of these things, and many more, is woven the warp and woof of my childhood memory: the dappled sunlight on the great lawns of

---

*The comma is sometimes used as follows:

The human species, according to the best theory I can form of it, is composed of two distinct races, the men who borrow, and the men who lend.
                    CHARLES LAMB

The dash, however, makes the writer's intention more immediately clear.

Chowderhead, our summer estate at Newport, the bitter-sweet fragrance of stranded eels at low tide, the alcoholic breath of a clubman wafted on the breeze from Bailey's Beach.

S. J. PERELMAN, Keep It Crisp

I had three chairs in my house: one for solitude, two for friendship, three for society. HENRY DAVID THOREAU

24b

Humanity has but three great enemies: fever, famine and war; of these by far the greatest, by far the most terrible, is fever.

SIR WILLIAM OSLER

The great secret, Eliza, is not having bad manners or good manners or any other particular sort of manners, but having the same manner for all human souls: in short, behaving as if you were in Heaven, where there are no third-class carriages, and one soul is as good as another. G. B. SHAW

If you are interested in reading further on the subject, I would recommend the following books: Mencken, *The American Language;* Baugh, *A History of the English Language;* and Bryant, *Modern English and Its Heritage.*

To check out a book from our library, proceed as follows: (1) check the catalog number carefully, (2) enter the catalog number in the upper left-hand corner of the call slip, (3) fill out the remainder of the call slip information, and (4) hand in the call slip at the main desk.

EXERCISE 24 The following sentences all contain final appositives or summaries which require dashes or colons. Supply the appropriate mark in each sentence.

1 She was a good teacher good humored, clever, always clear.
2 He had absolutely no virtues at all he would lie, cheat, or steal at every opportunity.
3 These are the punctuation marks that give the most difficulty commas, semicolons, and colons.
4 He had only one pleasure eating.
5 His whole life seems devoted to one activity football.
6 Four complex civilizations existed in America many years before the white man arrived the Olmec, the Toltec, the Aztec, and the Mayan.
7 Everything for the trip will be ready the car checked, the baggage loaded, the money in hand.
8 He sometimes seems to care about only one thing his dog Ruffles.
9 To learn to play the piano well you need three things a good teacher, a great deal of patience, and several thousand hours of practice.
10 The short story was only a pot boiler estimated life one month.

25 Superfluous Internal Punctuation

Do not use a comma unless you have a definite reason for doing so. Occasionally you will need to use a comma for no other reason than to prevent misreading.

> Long before, she had left everything to her brother.
> Pilots who like to see sunbathers, fly low over apartment houses.
> Inside the house, cats are sometimes a nuisance.

The omission of a comma after *before* in the first sentence would be momentarily confusing; we get off to a false start by reading *Long-before-she-had-left* without interruption. If there were no comma in the second sentence, we might think we were reading about flying sunbathers. A similar difficulty arises in the third sentence if *house* is not separated from *cats*. Often it is best to rewrite such sentences to avoid confusion.

Too many punctuation marks, however, clutter sentences and confuse readers. The "comma-rash" is especially prevalent among untrained writers. The reader of the following sentence, for example, is constantly jarred by the unnecessary punctuation:

> The people of this company, have, always, been aware, of the need, for products of better quality, and lower price.

Not one of the commas is necessary.

25a Do not separate a single or final adjective from its noun.

> Not   He was a discourteous, greedy, deceitful, boy.
> But   He was a discourteous, greedy, deceitful boy.

25b Do not separate a subject from its verb unless there are intervening words that require punctuation.

> Not   The worth of real estate, is determined by the demand for it.
> But   The worth of real estate is determined by the demand for it.
> Or   The worth of real estate, tangible property, is determined by the demand for it. (The commas set off an appositive.)

25c   Do not separate a verb from its complement unless there are intervening words that require punctuation.

Not   Molly drove, her old car carefully down the road.

But   Molly drove her old car carefully down the road.

Not   The boys always made Peanut, the butt of their pranks.

But   The boys always made Peanut the butt of their pranks.

Or   The boys always made Peanut, an undersized and immature smart aleck, the butt of their pranks.

25d   Do not separate two words or phrases that are joined by a coordinating conjunction.

Not   He is very honest, and patient.

But   He is very honest and patient.

Not   I decided to work during the summer, and relax in the fall.

But   I decided to work during the summer and relax in the fall.

25e   Do not separate an introductory word, brief phrase, or short clause from the main body of the sentence unless clarity requires it.

Not   On Wednesday, the ice in the river began to break up.

But   On Wednesday the ice in the river began to break up.

Occasionally, however, a comma must be inserted to prevent misreading. (See introduction to Section 25.)

Not   Notwithstanding *Drums at Dusk* is a worthy successor to *Black Thunder.*

But   Notwithstanding, *Drums at Dusk* is a worthy successor to *Black Thunder.*

25f   Do not separate a restrictive modifier from the main body of the sentence.

(See "Nonrestrictives," **22a**.)

Not   The girl, who slapped my face, also kicked my shins.

But   The girl who slapped my face also kicked my shins.

Not   The band, in the park, played the same tired old marches we had heard, for fifteen years.

But   The band in the park played the same tired old marches we had heard for fifteen years.

25c

25d

25e

25f

Note that adverbial phrases and clauses usually <u>restrict</u> the meaning of the word or clause to which they are attached. They are therefore essential to the meaning and should <u>not</u> be separated by a comma from what they modify. (See also **21c.**)

Not   The product is available, in large and small sizes.

But   The product is available in large and small sizes.
        (The phrase *in large and small sizes* restricts the adjective available and is essential to the meaning.)

Not   Once darkness fell, over the trees, the dogs began to bark.

But   Once darkness fell over the trees the dogs began to bark.
        (The phrase *over the trees* restricts the meaning of the verb *fell.*)

25g   Do not separate indirect quotations, or single words or short phrases in quotation marks, from the rest of the sentence.

Correct   After drinking ten bottles of pop Henry said he could drink ten more.

Correct   Claude said he was "weary of it all" and that he had "absorbed" his "fill of monotony."

25g

25h   Do not separate a preposition from its object.

Not   Carol went to, New York, Washington, and Atlanta.

But   Carol went to New York, Washington, and Atlanta.

25h

25i

25i   Do not use a semicolon to separate a main clause from a subordinate clause, a phrase from a clause, or other parts of unequal grammatical rank.

Not   Mortimer rushed out of the house in his shirt sleeves; although it was raining.

But   Mortimer rushed out of the house in his shirt sleeves, although it was raining.

Not   The speaker rambled on and on; making everyone increasingly restless.

But   The speaker rambled on and on, making everyone increasingly restless.

EXERCISE 25   Eliminate any superfluous commas in the sentences below.

1 Across the river, was a protected cove, in which there were two rowboats, and one small sailboat.

2 The meeting began late, because Blackburn did not know where the Regency Hotel was, or when the meeting was scheduled.

3 The pilot, having received clearances, the plane circled the field, before landing.

4 Robbins decided he could not take the night job, and still take courses in chemistry, accounting, and history, in the mornings.

5 The ice, near the southern bank, was too thin, and soft, to support the child's weight.

6 Nobody knows what the men, who work under the Secretary of State, really think of him, or of his policies.

7 Nudity on the public stage, once undreamed of, but now commonly accepted, may eventually run out its course, and be received only with apathy.

8 The senator replied slowly, because he had not expected the question, and he really didn't know what to say.

9 The United States is slowly taking over the world, not with guns, but with Coca-Cola and television reruns.

10 The disenchantment with urban renewal, stems from the fact that, frequently, it is merely a matter of building new slums, to replace the old.

"INTERNAL PUNCTUATION" REVIEW EXERCISES (Sections 20–25)

EXERCISE A The following sentences contain various errors in internal punctuation. Correct all errors, and be prepared to explain the reasons for your corrections.

1 Outside the dog scratched on the door.

2 Judy went shopping Marty went to a movie and Lou stayed home to nurse her cold.

3 Answering the defense attorney Robbins said angrily he was sure of his evidence.

4 Uranium which is important in atomic processes is found in parts of Africa.

5 The Governor refused to everyone's surprise and bewilderment to sign the bill after the Senate passed it.

6 Mark our plumber who can bend iron pipe in his bare hands recited Shakespeare as he fixed our water pipes.

7 Words words words were all that came out of the meeting.

8 Common sense is not a common quality those who have it are often sought after.

9 The President critics say has gained too much power, in foreign affairs, at the expense of the Senate.

10 A quiet stretch of Sudbury farmland, set behind a row of tidy typical colonials is the setting of the story.

11 Mr. Goldberg, who was once U.S. Ambassador to the U.N. was also once an Associate Justice of the Supreme Court.

12 There's only one problem involved in "doing your own thing" that's that everyone else may want to do his own thing as well.

13 It's relatively easy to borrow money it's much harder to pay it back.

14 Jealousy, a debilitating emotion, can wreck a relationship for without genuine trust there can be no real love.

25i

15 There is some evidence to show that Christopher Columbus was not the first European to visit America recent discoveries reveal that there may have been Viking settlements on the northeastern tip of the continent.

26 Punctuation of Quoted Material Q

Direct speech and material quoted verbatim from other sources must always be set off distinctly from a writer's own words. Such distinctions are usually indicated by quotation marks, although longer quotations may be indicated merely by different spacing and indentation. The following sections describe conventional usage in punctuating quoted material.

26a Use double quotation marks to enclose a direct quotation, whether from a written or spoken source.

Direct   He said, "Don't dive from that rock."

Direct   Our handbook says, "Direct speech and material quoted verbatim from other sources must always be set off distinctly from a writer's own words."

Remember *not* to punctuate indirect quotations.

He said not to dive from that rock.

Our handbook says that direct speech and material quoted verbatim from other sources must always be set off distinctly from a writer's own words.

26b Use single quotation marks to enclose a quotation within a quotation.

She turned and said, "Remember Grandfather's advice, 'When other people run, you walk.'"

Notice that the end punctuation of the sentence within single quotation marks serves also as the end punctuation for the entire sentence unit of which it is a part.

26c If a quotation is relatively long—more than four lines—it is usually indented from both right and left margins, and not enclosed in quotation marks.*

Professor George Summey's comment on the writer's responsibility for accuracy in reporting the words of others is worth quoting.

> Anyone who quotes another person's words has the duty of keeping the words unchanged and continuous or of giving clear notice to the contrary. It is improper to alter wording or punctuation of quoted matter, to italicize words without due notice, or to make any other change. That would misrepresent the meaning of the quoted words in their context.†

No careful writer would question the need for such accuracy.

26d Use quotation marks to set off titles of poems and songs, and of articles, short stories, and other parts of a longer work.

(For the use of italics to set off titles of longer works, see "Italics," **27a** and **27b.**)

> "Preparing the Manuscript" is a chapter in *Report Writing,* a text for engineers.
> "The Easy Chair" is a section of informal literary review appearing in *Harper's.*
> "Wintergreen for President" is a song from the musical play *Of Thee I Sing.*

26e Words used in a special sense may be set off by quotation marks.

> When a new book comes into the library, it is first of all "accessioned."
> Is this what you call "functional" architecture?
> "Anarchy" means "without a leader," hence "without government."
> (*Or: Anarchy* means *without a leader,* hence *without government.* See **27c.**)

Do not use quotation marks around common nicknames. Do not use them for emphasis. And do not use them apologetically

---

* If quotation marks, rather than the usual indentation, are used for a passage of two or more paragraphs, they are placed at the beginning of each paragraph and at the end of the last; they are not placed at the end of intermediate paragraphs.
† George Summey, *American Punctuation* (New York: Ronald Press Co., 1949).

to enclose slang, colloquialisms, trite expressions, or for imprecise words or phrases when you cannot find the right word. If a word is appropriate, it will stand without apology. If it is not appropriate, it should be replaced.

26f Use brackets to set off editorial remarks in quoted material.

You will sometimes want to insert an explanatory comment in a statement you are quoting. By enclosing such comments in brackets, you let the reader know at once that <u>you</u> are speaking rather than the original author.

> John Dryden, a famous English poet, said, "Those who accuse him [Shakespeare] to have wanted knowledge, give him the greater commendation; he was naturally learned."
> The favorite phrase of their [English] law is "a custom whereof the memory of man runneth not back to the contrary."
>
> RALPH WALDO EMERSON

26f

In bibliographical notations, use brackets to enclose the name of a writer <u>reputed</u> to be the author of the work in question.

> [NED WARD], *A Trip to New England* (1699)

26g

26g Use the word *sic* (*"thus it is"*) in brackets to indicate that a mistake or peculiarity in the spelling or the grammar of a foregoing word appears in the original work.

26h

> The high school paper reported, "The students spoke most respectively [*sic*] of Mrs. Higginbottom."

26h Always place a comma or a period inside the quotation marks.

Commas are generally used to separate direct quotations from unquoted material.

> "There is no use in working," he complained, "when it only makes me more sleepy than usual."

Note that this rule <u>always</u> applies regardless of the reason for using quotation marks.

> According to Shakespeare, the poet writes in a "fine frenzy."
> While he insisted that he was a "beatnik," I certainly got tired of hearing him say that everything was "cool."

26i Always place a colon or a semicolon outside the quotation marks.

According to Shakespeare, the poet writes in a "fine frenzy"; by "fine frenzy" he meant a combination of energy, enthusiasm, imagination, and a certain madness.

26j Place a dash, question mark, or exclamation point inside the quotation marks when it applies only to the quotation; place it outside the quotation marks when it applies to the whole statement.

He said, "Will I see you tomorrow?"
Didn't he say, "I'll see you tomorrow"?
"You may have the car tonight"—then he caught himself abruptly and said, "No, you can't have it; I need it myself."

When a mark applies to both quotation and sentence, use it only once.

Has he ever asked, "May I come in?"

26k In punctuating explanatory words preceding a quotation, be guided by the length and formality of the quotation.

No Punctuation	He yelled "Stop!" and grabbed the wheel.
Punctuation with a Comma	The old man said very quietly, "Under no circumstances will I tell you where my money is hidden."
Punctuation with a Colon	The speaker rose to his feet and began: "The party in power has betrayed us. It has not only failed to keep its election promises but has sold out to the moneyed powers."

26l Use a comma to separate an opening quotation from the rest of the sentence unless the quotation ends with a question mark or an exclamation point.

"The man is dead," he said with finality.
"Is the man dead?" he asked.
"Oh, no!" he screamed hysterically. "My brother can't be dead!"

26m When a quotation is interrupted by explanatory words (*he said,* or their equivalent), use a comma after the first part of the quotation. In choosing the proper punctuation mark to place after the explanatory words, apply the rules for punctuating clauses and phrases.

"I am not unaware," he said, "of the dangers of iceboat racing."

"I have always worked hard," he declared. "I was peddling newspapers when I was eight years old."

"John has great capacities," the foreman said; "he has energy, brains, and personality."

EXERCISE 26 Supply the appropriate punctuation in each of the following sentences.

1 The letter said tartly, The fault is not with our product but with your skin; it appears to be supersensitive.

2 Perhaps you might like to do a study of the sexual imagery in Shakespeare the professor suggested.

3 How long have you noticed this condition the doctor asked.

4 As the history professor said in class yesterday There is no real evidence that Marie Antoinette ever said Let them eat cake!

5 He said, When the policeman asked me Where's the fire? I felt like giving him an equally sarcastic answer.

6 The song Aquarius is from the musical *Hair.*

7 Arthur Schlesinger, Jr., says John Stuart Mill wrote a century ago, The greatness of England is now all collective; individually small, we appear capable of anything great only by our habit of combining.

8 The salesclerk said, Sir I would exchange this sweater, but he added, it has already been worn.

9 One day, just as I was going out to Rahul's house, I heard her shouting outside the door of the study. The director is a busy man! she was shouting. She had her back against the door and held her arms stretched out; M. stood in front of her and his head was lowered. Day after day you come and eat his life up! she said.

R. PRAWER JHABVALA, "My First Marriage"

10 I climbed up in the bar yelling, Walsh, I'm shot. I'm shot. I could feel the blood running down my leg. Walsh, the fellow who operated the fish-and-chips joint, pushed me off the bar and onto the floor. I couldn't move now, but I was still completely conscious. Walsh was saying, Git outta here, kid. I ain't got no time to play. A woman was screaming, mumbling something about the Lord, and saying, Somebody done shot that poor child.

CLAUDE BROWN, *Manchild in the Promised Land*

26m

27

27a

27–30   Word Punctuation WORD P

Italics, capitals, apostrophes, and hyphens identify words that have a special use or a particular grammatical function in a sentence.

> Our two-week reading program, assigned in Wednesday's class, is Shakespeare's *King Lear.*

Here the italics set off the words *King Lear* as a single title. The capitals identify *Wednesday, Shakespeare, King,* and *Lear* as proper names. The apostrophes indicate that *Shakespeare* and *Wednesday* are singular possessives and not plurals. The hyphen between *two* and *week* makes the two words function as a single adjective.

27   Italics

Strictly speaking, italics are typefaces that slope toward the right. In typed or handwritten manuscript, italics are indicated by underlining.

On the printed page: *italics*
In typewritten copy: italics

In handwritten copy: *italics*

27a   Italicize the titles of books, newspapers, magazines, and all publications issued separately.

"Issued separately" means published as a single work and not as an article or story in a magazine, nor as a chapter or section of a book. (For the proper punctuation of such titles, see **26d.**)

The New York Times	*Commentary*
The Lord of the Flies	*Death of a Salesman*
Webster's New Collegiate Dictionary	

Be careful not to add the word *The* to titles unless it belongs there and not to omit it if it does belong.

Not	*The Reader's Digest*	Not	the *Red Badge of Courage*
But	the *Reader's Digest*	But	*The Red Badge of Courage*

27b Italicize the names of ships and aircraft, and the titles of works of art, movies, television and radio programs, and record albums.

27b

The Titanic	*The Spirit of St. Louis*
The Sistine Madonna	*Earthquake*
Charlie's Angels	*New Orleans Jazz*

27c Italicize letters, words, and numbers used as words.

Your *r*'s look very much like your *n*'s.

I can't tell your *7*'s from your *1*'s.

The early settlers borrowed Indian words like *moccasin, powwow,* and *wigwam.*

Note: Quotation marks are also used to set off words as words in typewritten or handwritten manuscripts (see **26e**). However, if the subject you are writing about requires you to set off frequent words as words, underlining (italics) will give you a less cluttered looking manuscript.

27d Italicize foreign words and phrases that have not yet been accepted into the English language.

She graduated *magna cum laude.*

Many of the works of the *fin de siècle* that seemed so sensational when they were written appear to us now as innocent.

You may sometimes feel that a foreign word or phrase expresses your meaning more aptly or concisely than an English one. If you are sure that your readers will understand the expression, use it. But to overuse such words is pedantry. Many foreign words have been accepted into the English language and need no longer be italicized. The following words, for example, do not require italics:

bourgeois   milieu   denouement   liqueur

To determine whether a foreign word should be italicized, consult a good dictionary. (See discussion on spelling under "The Uses of a Dictionary," pp. 284–91.)

27e Use italics to give a word special stress.

The idea that knowledge follows interest is a scandalous half-truth; it is a better-than-half-truth that *interest follows knowledge.*

I heard him say once that in a democracy (a *democracy,* mind you) a division of opinion cannot be permitted to exist.

27f Avoid the overuse of italics.

Distinguish carefully between a real need for italicizing and the use of italics as a mechanical device to achieve emphasis. The best way to achieve emphasis is to write effective, well-constructed sentences. The overuse of italics will only make your writing seem immature and amateurish, as in the following:

27e

27f

Any good education must be *liberal.*

America is a *true* democracy, in every sense of the word.

This book has what I call *real* depth of meaning.

EXERCISE 27 Italicize words and phrases where necessary in the following sentences.

1 James Earl Jones, the eminent black actor, received a Tony award for his Broadway performance in The Great White Hope.
2 H.M.S. Queen Elizabeth, for years the flagship of the Cunard Line, was finally retired from service.
3 Are you supposed to pronounce the p in coup de grâce?
4 Some Americans use the word simpatico as though it meant sympathetic, but its meaning is really closer to that of the English word charming.
5 Is T. S. Eliot's The Wasteland included in The Oxford Book of English Verse?
6 His travels had brought him greater understanding of himself and just a touch of savoir-faire.
7 Webster's Third New International Dictionary lists more than half a dozen pronunciations of lingerie.
8 I am constantly forgetting what eclectic means.
9 New Englanders tend to add an r to words that end in a and to omit the r in words that do end in r.
10 Thus, in Boston, Cuba becomes Cuber, while river becomes riva.

28 Capitals

Modern writers capitalize less frequently than did older writers, and informal writing permits less capitalization than formal writing. Two hundred years ago, a famous author wrote:

Being ruined by the Inconstancy and Unkindness of a Lover, I hope a true and plain Relation of my Misfortune may be of Use and Warning to Credulous Maids, never to put much Trust in deceitful Men.   JONATHAN SWIFT, "The Story of the Injured Lady"

28a

28b

A modern writer would eliminate all capitals but the initial *B* and the pronoun *I*.*

28a   Capitalize the first word of a sentence and the first word of a line of poetry.

Education is concerned not with knowledge but the meaning of knowledge.

True ease in writing comes from art, not chance.
As those move easiest who have learned to dance.

> ALEXANDER POPE, *Essay on Criticism*

Some modern poets ignore the convention of capitalizing each line of poetry, perhaps because they feel that an initial capital letter gives a word unwanted emphasis.

a man who had fallen among thieves
lay by the roadside on his back
dressed in fifteenthrate ideas
wearing a round jeer for a hat

> e. e. cummings, "a man who had fallen among thieves"

28b   Capitalize the pronoun *I* and the interjection *O*.

Do not capitalize the interjection *oh* not unless it is the first word of a sentence.

---

*The practice of capitalizing nouns persisted long after Swift. The nineteenth-century poet Byron wrote:

> Near this spot are deposited the remains of one who possessed Beauty without Vanity, Strength without Insolence, Courage without Ferocity, and all the Virtues of Man without his Vices. This Praise, which would be meaningless Flattery if inscribed over human ashes, is but a just tribute to the Memory of Boatswain, a Dog.

Some modern humorous or satiric writers sometimes capitalize nouns as a way of personifying abstractions and pointing up irony:

> "Well," she said hesitatingly, "the idea is to reduce all employees to a Curve."
> STEPHEN LEACOCK, *Frenzied Fiction*

28c Capitalize proper nouns, their derivatives and abbreviations, and common nouns used as proper nouns.

1. Specific persons, races, nationalities.

William	Bob	George A. Smith	Negro
Asiatic	American	Mongolian	Cuban
Canadian	English	Latin	Zulu

2. Specific places.

Dallas	Jamestown	California	Lake Erie
Newfoundland	Iran	Jerusalem	Ohio River

3. Specific organizations, historical events, and documents.

Daughters of the American Revolution   the French Revolution
the Locarno Pact   NAACP
             Declaration of Independence

4. Days of the week, months, holidays.

Thursday   April   Christmas   Sunday   Labor Day

5. Religious terms with sacred significance.

the Virgin   Allah   Holy Ghost   the Saviour

6. Titles of books, plays, magazines, newspapers, journals, articles, poems.
Capitalize the first word and all others except articles, and conjunctions and prepositions of fewer than five letters. (See also **26d** and **27a**.)

Gone with the Wind	*The Country Wife*	*Pippa Passes*
Paradise Lost	*Atlantic Monthly*	*War and Peace*
Ebony		*Much Ado About Nothing*

7. Titles, when they precede a proper noun.
Such titles are an essential part of the name and are regularly capitalized.

Professor Wilson	Secretary Hawkins
Dr. Natalie Spence	Mr. Gottschalk
President Carter	Judge Paul Perry

When titles follow a name, do not capitalize them unless they indicate high distinction:

       Robert F. Jones, president of the National Bank
       J. R. Derby, professor of English

But   Abraham Lincoln, President of the United States
       John Marshall, Chief Justice, United States Supreme
       Court

"High distinction" is, however, becoming more and more broadly interpreted. Some people write*

       Robert F. Jones, President of the National Bank
       J. R. Derby, Professor of English

8. Common nouns used as an essential part of a proper noun. These are generic names such as *street, river, avenue, lake, county, ocean, college.*

28d

Vine Street Fifth Avenue	Pacific Ocean	Lake Huron
General Motors Corporation	Penn Central Railroad	
Hamilton College	Mississippi River	

When the generic term is used in the plural, it is not usually capitalized.

       Vine and Mulberry streets   Hamilton and Lake counties
            the Atlantic and Pacific oceans

28d Avoid unnecessary capitalization.

A good general rule is not to capitalize unless a specific convention warrants it.

1. Capitalize *north, east, south, west* only when they come at the beginning of a sentence or refer to specific geographical locations.

       Birds fly south in the winter.
But   She lives in the western part of the Old South.

2. The names of seasons need not be capitalized.

fall   autumn   winter   midwinter   spring   summer

---

*This practice is a variance with the trend toward less capitalization, but is perhaps explained by (1) a writer's desire to seem polite, and (2) copying the style of capitalization used in formal letters, as

   Robert F. Jones
   President of the National Bank
   West Third Avenue
   Kokoma Hills, Georgia

3. Capitalize nouns indicating family relationships only when they are used as names or titles or in combination with proper names. Do not capitalize *mother* and *father* when they are preceded by possessive adjectives.

| | I wrote to my father. | | My uncle has ten children. |
| But | I wrote Father | But | My Uncle Ben has ten children. |

4. Ordinarily, do not capitalize common nouns and adjectives used in place of proper nouns and adjectives.

28d

	I went to high school in Cleveland.
But	I went to John Adams High School in Cleveland.
	I am a university graduate.
But	I am a Columbia University graduate.
	I took a psychology course in my senior year.
But	I took Psychology 653 in my senior year.

EXERCISE 28 Capitalize words as necessary in the following sentences. Remove unnecessary capitals.

1 After leaving detroit, we turned North toward Mackinac island for our Summer vacation with uncle Jim.
2 The reverend Martin Luther King, jr., first came to public attention as a leader of the Civil Rights sit-ins in the south.
3 The late Robert Kennedy had been attorney general of the United States before being elected senator from the state of New York.
4 It has been predicted that power in the un will eventually shift from the security council to the general assembly.
5 The Boston symphony orchestra is not to be confused with the Boston pops orchestra.
6 All Math Majors who were preparing to teach Elementary School students were required by the math department to take courses in the New Math.
7 The organization of American states is designed to encourage cooperation and understanding among the nations of the western hemisphere.
8 Michael O'hara, president of the student congress, addressed the meeting.
9 Many of the aberdeen angus cattle come from the state of Nebraska.
10 It was the fall of the Roman empire which ushered in the middle ages.

29 Apostrophe

29a Use an apostrophe to show the possessive case of nouns and indefinite pronouns.

1. If a word (either singular or plural) does not end in _s_, add an apostrophe and _s_ to form the possessive.

the woman's book   the women's books
the child's book   the children's books
the man's book   the men's books
someone's book   people's books

2. If the singular of a word ends in _s_, add an apostrophe and _s_ unless the second _s_ makes pronunciation difficult; in such cases, add only the apostrophe.

         Lois's book   James's book
But   Moses' leadership   Sophocles' dramas

(The addition of a second _s_ would change the pronunciation of _Moses_ to _Moseses_ and _Sophocles_ to _Sophocleses_.)

3. If the plural of a word ends in _s_, add only the apostrophe.

the girls' books
the boys' books
the Smiths' books (referring to at least two persons named Smith)

4. In compounds, make only the last word possessive.

father-in-law's book (_singular possessive_)
mothers-in-law's books (_plural possessive_)
someone else's book

5. In nouns of joint possession, make only the last noun possessive; in nouns of individual possession, make both nouns possessive.

John and Paul's book (_joint possession_)
John's and Paul's books (_individual possession_)

Here is a list of standard spelling forms:

Singular	Possessive Singular	Plural	Possessive Plural
child	child's	children	children's
man	man's	men	men's
lady	lady's	ladies	ladies'
father-in-law	father-in-law's	fathers-in-law	fathers-in-law's
passer-by	passer-by's	passers-by	passers-by's

29b

29c

29d

29b   Use an apostrophe to indicate the omission of a letter or number.

doesn't   can't   won't   o'clock   the blizzard of '89

In reproducing speech, writers frequently use an apostrophe to show that a word is given a loose or colloquial pronunciation.

"An' one o' the boys is goin' t' be sick," he said.

A too-frequent use of the apostrophe for such purposes, however, clutters up the page and annoys the reader.

29c   Use an apostrophe and *s* to form the plurals of letters, numbers, and words used as words.

(In such cases, the letters, numbers, and words are also italicized, but the *s* is not.)

Cross your *t*'s and dot your *i*'s.
Count to 10,000 by *2*'s.
Tighten your sentence structure by eliminating unnecessary *and*'s.

Note that these are the only situations in which the apostrophe is used in forming plurals. It is <u>never</u> used in forming the plurals of proper names or other nouns.

29d   Do not use the apostrophe with the possessive form of personal pronouns.

The personal pronouns *his, hers, its, ours, yours, theirs,* and the pronoun *whose* are possessives as they stand and do not require the apostrophe.

his father; a book of *hers;* a friend of *theirs*

Be particularly careful not to confuse the possessive pronoun *its* with the contraction *it's* (it is).

We couldn't find *its* nest.
We know *it's* a robin.

EXERCISE 29 Insert apostrophes or apostrophes plus *s* as necessary in the following sentences.

1 One of my most prized possessions is the Supremes first record album.
2 Its hard to believe that in a country as rich as ours, some people still go to bed hungry every night.
3 The chairmans secretary has assured all members of the department that theyll have their class schedules in two weeks time.
4 Most modern cities havent the resources with which to keep up with their expanding populations.
5 He had asked for a months leave of absence, but he was allowed to take only the three days sick leave that were due him.
6 Hers was the better way, mine was the quicker.
7 Whats the point of experimenting with mind-expanding drugs when they can do terrible damage to ones mind?
8 A rock groups career, as show business goes, is relatively short.
9 The greatest years of *The New Yorker* were those under Harold Ross editorship.
10 Its hard to keep up with the Joneses when you dont have Mr. Jones income.

30   Hyphen

The hyphen has two distinct uses: (1) to form compound words, and (2) to indicate that a word is continued from one line to the next.

Convention in the use of the hyphen for (2), commonly called "syllabication," is arbitrarily fixed. (See "Syllabication," Section 18.) But convention in the use of hyphens with compounds not only shifts rapidly, but is unpredictable. As a noun, *short circuit* is spelled as two words; but the verb *short-circuit* is hyphenated. *Shorthand, shortstop,* and *shortwave* are spelled as single words, but *short cut* is spelled as two words, and *short-term* as in *short-term loan* is hyphenated.

In such a rapidly changing and unpredictable matter, the writer's only safe recourse is to consult a good up-to-date dictionary. The following uses of the hyphen in forming compound words are widely accepted.

30a Use a hyphen to form compound words that are not yet accepted as single words.

The spelling of compound words that express a single idea passes through successive stages. Originally spelled as two separate words, then as a hyphenated word, a compound word finally emerges as a single word.

base ball became *base-ball* became *baseball*
post man became *post-man* became *postman*

There is no way of determining the proper spelling of a compound at any given moment, but your dictionary is your most authoritative reference.

30b Use a hyphen to join two or more words serving as a single adjective before a noun.

Do not hyphenate such an adjective if it follows the verb as a predicate adjective.

	a well-known speaker
But	The speaker was well known.
	a grayish-green coat
But	The coat was grayish green.

Omit the hyphen when the first word is an adverb ending in *-ly*.

	a slow-curving ball		a quick-moving runner
But	a slowly curving ball	But	a quickly moving runner

30c Use a hyphen to avoid an ambiguous or awkward union of letters.

Not	belllike	Not	recreate
But	bell-like	But	re-create (create anew)

In commonly used words, the hyphen is omitted.

coeducational   coordinate   readdress

30d Use a hyphen to form compound numbers from twenty-one through ninety-nine, and to separate the numerator from the denominator in written fractions.

twenty-nine   fifty-five   two-thirds   four-fifths

30e Use a hyphen with the prefixes *-self, all-, ex-,* and the suffix *-elect.*

self-important   all-Conference   ex-mayor   governor-elect

Do not capitalize the prefix *ex-* or the suffix *-elect,* even when used in titles that are essential parts of a name.

ex-Mayor Kelley   Governor-elect Jones   ex-President Truman

EXERCISE 30 Insert hyphens as needed.

1 The editor in chief owns a well designed house.
2 He boasts that he is self made and self educated, but he forgets that he is also self centered.
3 My father in law once ran in the hundred meter relay; his team went as far as the semi finals.
4 The life long dream of many Americans is a four bedroom home with a two car garage.
5 He changed a twenty dollar bill into five dollar bills.

30e

"WORD PUNCTUATION" REVIEW EXERCISE (Sections 27–30) Supply the necessary italics, capitals, apostrophes, and hyphens in the sentences below.

1 magazines such as yankee and vermont life are popular with readers who idolize old time country life.
2 The item appeared in last mondays new york times.
3 its a well known fact that most old age pensions are inadequate for present day needs.
4 sarahs exhusband had been well meaning enough but too self effacing for an out going girls taste.
5 hes got too many ands in his sentences.
6 barbra streisands first big break in show business was in the broadway play i can get it for you wholesale.
7 the four american delegates carefully prepared proposal was rejected by the soviet unions spokesman.
8 although eighteen year olds can now vote, my brothers friend didn't vote until he was twenty-one.
9 the four cylinder sixty horse power car wasnt able to pull Jones custom built limousine out of the ditch.
10 roots, an eight part dramatic series based on alex haleys search for his long buried past, topped all previous tv programs in the nielson ratings.

PUNCTUATION

EXERCISE A   Make all necessary corrections in internal punctuation and in the use of capitals, italics, apostrophes, and hyphens in the following sentences.

1 Her favorite writers joyce carol oates and james dickey are both contemporary.
2 His faults are an uncontrollable temper inexperience and indifference to his work.
3 Since we had driven the car 87,000 miles we decided to turn it in.
4 If siege is spelled with an ie why is seize spelled with an ei?
5 What we need said mr. blevin the union spokesman is a good days pay for a good days work.
6 Many people perhaps most people do not know from what materials their cereals plastics and clothing are made.
7 The government was faced with a difficult task it had to persuade a skeptical frustrated people that the energy shortage was real.
8 Her camera her new dress and her books all of which she had left in her car had been stolen.
9 I have just received an un-expected letter from the director of the bureau of internal revenue.
10 Ruth wanted a pontiac francis a ford donna a chrysler and alice a raleigh bicycle.
11 The late will rogers favorite saying was ive never met a man i did'nt like.
12 Judy garland is best remembered for her role in the 1930s film the wizard of oz.
13 Does anyone remember who said absolute power corrupts absolutely?
14 I make it a point to read the new york times every day and the new yorker every week only rarely however do i get around to time or newsweek.
15 You can't do that, she cried hysterically, you can't you can't.

EXERCISE B   Make all necessary corrections in the passage below.

trip describes the psychedelic experience very well it is gratuitous an extra day in the week one saying goes and the sense of this experience being unearned is perhaps the common feature of all the attitudes that have grown up around it it shapes the disbelief of those who have not experienced it and paradoxically it confirms the belief that something quite so rich in life experience must somehow always be a gift and unmerited the view of ordinary life is nearly always altered after a trip but this does not mean the style of post psychedelic life is set or naturally follows egos are still distinct twins in their variety and the egoless the genuine lsd head cant really be said to have returned from his trip you cant bring the universe home with you perhaps all you can do is choose your home.

PAUL VELDE, "Psychedelics: You Can't Bring the Universe Home"

EXERCISE C In the following sentences determine which marks of punctuation are used correctly, which marks are used incorrectly, and what additional punctuation is needed. Be prepared to give reasons for your decisions.

1 I've seen the play *Hello Dolly* twice, but I still find it's plot fascinating.

2 We like to think that the spoils system went out with Andrew Jackson, but actually it's still in effect: in federal, state, and municipal government.

3 Is'nt it time we all ignored our own personal problems and cooperated with one another in making this world a better place to live in

4 She watches television all day long; and in the evening too.

5 Should one judge a candidate from the speeches he makes? from the printed matter he distributes? or from the ideas he generates?

6 Blacks and whites must learn to live and work together; otherwise, this country is doomed.

7 The Presidents daughters activities are always reported in the press, so are his wifes.

8 I think I recognize that actor, wasn't he on the television show *My Three Sons?*

9 I wanted to make that perfectly clear, the President said, Have I made it so?

10 As one pundit once observed of Senator Humphrey, He certainly couldn't be accused of using any greasy kid stuff!

LARGER ELEMENTS

If you wish to be a writer, write.
EPICTETUS

Anyone who wishes to become a good writer should endeavor, before he allows himself to be tempted by the more showy qualities, to be direct, simple, brief, vigorous, and lucid.
H. W. FOWLER

31 The Whole Composition PLAN

Whatever our intention in a specific piece of writing, we face two difficulties as writers: Can we say what we really mean, and can we make that meaning clear to our readers? There are no pat solutions to this double problem, no series of writing steps that guarantee success. It is fairly certain, however, that we will get nowhere unless we make some hard decisions: We must decide <u>what</u> we want to write. We must decide <u>whom</u> we are writing it for. We must decide <u>how</u> we want to write it. Then, having written it, we must stand off and look at the results of our labor and make a judgment. Is our writing readable and clear? Does it have a sense of direction and purpose? Does it engage the reader in the way we want it to?

Many writers, professional as well as amateur, follow the "writing process" suggested in this chapter. Some writers manage to discover a shortcut or two; and perhaps your instructor will suggest the elimination of a step (for example, the complete outline), or the addition of a step (for example, a separate page describing the type of reader you are addressing). It is probably safe to say, however, that the following outline of writing steps can be useful to most student writers:

1. Decide what you are going to write about (See **31a** on selecting a subject and **31b** on limiting the subject.)

2. Decide on your purpose and frame a specific thesis statement. (See **31c** on determining your purpose and your thesis.)

3. Think carefully about the kind of reader you are writing for. (See **31d** on considering your audience.)

4. Make a rough but full list of ideas, assertions, facts, and illustrations that may have some bearing on your subject. (See **31e** on making a preliminary outline.)

5. Consider the kind of organization that will best serve your purpose. (See **31f** on deciding on a pattern of organization.)

6. Sort out the items in your rough outline, putting together all the ideas that belong together and eliminating all those that seem irrelevant. (See **31g** on making an outline.)

7. Try to find a concrete instance, illustration, anecdote, or example for a good opening statement. If you can think of nothing appropriate to your purposes, proceed to the next step immediately. (See **31h** on beginning the paper.)

8. Begin to write. Don't let problems of wording and phrasing slow you down, or you will lose momentum and direction. (See **31i** on writing a first draft.)

9. Once you have finished the first draft, go back over it and polish your words, sentences, and paragraphs. Check the ending to make sure that it gives the impression of finality and completeness. (See **31j** on ending the paper and **31k** on writing a second draft.)

31a

10. If possible, put your paper aside for a few days before making final revisions. You will gain perspective in this way and will spot errors in logic and presentation more readily. (See **31l** on making final revisions.)

In brief, the writing process consists of two basic steps: (1) planning what you are going to say, and (2) writing and rewriting it. Remember that the first step is fully as important as the second. Good writing requires careful planning.

31a   Select a subject that interests you.

In a college writing course, some assignments prescribe your subject, and some even the specific method of handling it. Others give you either complete freedom or a range of choice. If you are given a choice, select a subject that captures your interest and about which you have or want to have ample knowledge. Begin by reviewing your own experience, abilities, and beliefs. Can you repair an automobile, put together a hi-fi set, make a dress? What interesting people have you known? Which have you liked or disliked and why? What sports do you enjoy playing or watching? What books have you read recently? What was your reaction to them? What social problems do you think need to be solved? Which do you feel strongly about? How do you think your education can be improved? What kind of work have you done?

The principal problem most of us have is that we fail to recognize how rich in possibilities for writing or discussion our daily experience is. Almost everything we do, or read, or are involved in is material for explanation, analysis, and controversy if we examine it. We read the daily newspaper and are provoked by or approving of the story or editorial on the proposed regulation of energy. We watch TV and are frustrated by commercials or by unexpected shifts in the scheduling of our favorite detective shows. We believe or do not believe that Archie Bunker is overdrawn, or representative. We are annoyed or not annoyed by the failure of the college to provide adequate parking and security for bicycles. If we keep our eyes open and our mind alert, and are willing to make our mind's eye move over our experiences and ideas, we will find a thousand topics waiting for us.

31a

Such subjects, close to your everyday experience, make interesting writing if you dig for the details that really describe them. Indeed, no writing will be interesting or useful unless you do dig for the details that will make it concrete, and you are much more likely to dredge up the material for a paper describing your own house than for one describing a South Sea sunrise you have never seen.

Many times you may be asked to write on a particular kind of topic—an explanation of a process or a description of a place, for example. Or you may be asked to write on a more specific topic—an assigned reading selection that has been assigned, a comparison of two short stories. Note that even in such assignments you still have choices to make. Only in some very special kinds of assignments are you told exactly what your topic is to be. If you are asked to describe a process or give a set of directions, you must still turn to your own experience and select within it. If you are asked to write on a particular reading selection, you must not only accumulate details from the selection itself, but also explore your own responses to, and observations about, that selection, and define a precise topic growing out of those responses and observations.

No matter what your assignment or topic, remember always that good writing is not made up of great billowing generalizations unsupported by details, examples, illustrations, and explanations. You can't say much that is meaningful about prejudice, for instance, without tying your paper down to examples; and examples bring you back to your own experience. This approach is likely to lead you to some such topic as "Racial Prejudice in My Home Town," "My Prejudice against Dentists," or "My Roommate's Prejudices."

The list below may be helpful, not only for the specific subjects it gives, but also for those it brings to mind.

General	Specific
1. Controlling Pollution	Cleaning up the Charles River
2. Technology Today	The Gadgets in My Home
3. Television	The Cereal War on TV
4. Parents and Children	Getting Along with Father
5. Advertising	The Well-Dressed Man in *Esquire*
6. Fashions in Clothes	Casual Dress on _____ Campus

7. Science Fiction — Themes in Ray Bradbury's Novels

8. College Administration — The Role of the College Senate

9. Moms and Momma's Boys — Homesickness in College

10. The College Newspaper — Student Editorials

11. Women Think for Themselves — Women's Lib on _____ Campus

12. Will Americans Pay for Education? — Teachers' Salaries in My Hometown

13. Nathaniel Hawthorne — "The Ambitious Guest"

14. Are We Progressing Backward? — Six New Ways of Being Sick

15. Abortion — The Position of My Church on Abortion

16. The U.S. Space Effort — Did We Have to Go to Mars?

17. Racial Prejudice in the U.S. — Black Militancy and the White Backlash

18. Changing Sexual Mores in the U.S. — The Pill and Its Effects on Teenage Morality

19. Drug Addiction — If Dad Drinks Gin, Why Can't I Smoke Pot?

20. Urban Congestion — Riding the Subway during Rush Hour

EXERCISE 31a(1) Make a list of five titles suggested by your taste in television, movies, or sports—for example, "Why Are Police Dramas So Popular?" "My Reaction to X-Rated Movies," or "The Home Run and the Touchdown Pass."

EXERCISE 31a(2) List five titles suggested by your hobbies or your work—for example, "Collecting Old Jazz Records," or "A Day in the Life of a Stockboy."

EXERCISE 31a(3) List five titles suggested by your reading—for example, "Imagery in Robert Frost's 'Design,'" or "Why I Read _____ Magazine Every Month."

31b Limit the subject you have chosen so that you can handle it in the time and space at your disposal.

Don't try to do too much in a paper of 300 to 500 words, or you will end up with a series of vague and half-supported generalizations that never come into focus. It is attempts to solve world problems such as "NATO and Soviety policy," "United States Involvement in the Far East," "The Future of Mass Media," or "Public Education, Past and Present" that lead to difficulties.

Experienced writers are constantly aware of the limitations dictated by the time and space at their disposal. They will reject a subject like "The Problems of Television" for something like "My Nights with Mary Hartman," or "The Superbowl in Your Living Room," and a subject like "Swimming" for "How to Swim the Backstroke," or "Developing Speed in Swimming."

31b

Five hundred or even 1,000 words do not provide much space. Consider that a page of a magazine such as *Harper's* or *The Atlantic* carries 700 words or more. A typical newspaper column runs to 1,000 words. Clearly these lengths are not sufficient for such topics as "The Role of Women in the 1970's," "The Problem of Equality," "World Peace," and "Drugs in Modern Medicine." Such topics can provide only meaningless generalizations and commonplace judgments. If you are tempted to tackle these or similar topics, discipline yourself to <u>trim them down to the size required.</u>

For example, let us suppose you have decided on the general subject of "Education." <u>Your task for a brief theme is, then, to find a single aspect of this subject that you can deal with in terms of your experience.</u> Since you probably know little or nothing about education in the Middle Ages or even in your grandmother's day, your first narrowing will almost surely be to "Present-Day Education." This may momentarily seem reasonable until you realize that you will certainly not be able to talk about elementary, secondary, and higher education in a single paper. You then might narrow your subject to "Education at My University." That seems plausible until you examine the catalog and discover that the university has 16 schools, 97 departments, 150 programs, and more than 3,500 courses. At this point, you may wish to move to "My College Courses." But that will involve you in several courses, several different faculty, and a variety of texts, assignments, and scholastic problems.

You decide to try a simple course and select biology, in which you are having certain troubles. But in biology you have both lectures and laboratory work, as well as a variety of assignments, tests, and the like. Even at this point, you have too much material for a 500-word theme. You try confining your theme to the laboratory work in the course. That, you believe, will finally do. But you have had a whole range of experiments, slides, and reports—still perhaps too much material. At the end, you decide upon "My Difficulty with the Microscope in Biology Laboratory."

At this point you have something simple, completely within your own experience, concrete, actual—and most important, something which is <u>one</u> thing. And, we might add, it is something upon which you are the world's supreme authority. No one knows better than you the trouble you have seeing the slide at all, the strange things you see that you're not supposed to see, and the remarkably inaccurate representation you manage to produce on paper of what you do—or do not—see.

Your own thinking will usually be less involved and more rapid than that we have just illustrated. But some similar procedure is almost inescapable if you are to arrive finally at a topic you can fully manage in a single theme of typical length.

Finally, be sure that when you have narrowed your topic adequately, the title of the paper accurately reflects the limitations you have set yourself. Don't call a paper on the care of tropical fish "Tropical Fish," a personal paper on working out your quarrels with your roommate "Roommates," or an analysis of a tale by Nathaniel Hawthorne "Nathaniel Hawthorne."

31c

EXERCISE 31b(1)   List five topics that would be appropriate for themes of several thousand words. Select a single aspect of each of these topics that would make an appropriate title for a theme of 300 to 700 words. For one of the topics, trace through explicitly the steps in successive limiting as we did above for the topic "Education."

EXERCISE 31b(2)   Refer to the topics suggested on pages 150–151. Choose five items from the *general* list and devise another more *specific* topic for each.

EXERCISE 31b(3)   Write specific titles for five of the general topics listed below.

1 Photography	6 Dishonesty
2 Mass Media	7 The U.S. Supreme Court
3 Experimental Education	8 Hockey
4 Autumn	9 Ecology
5 Censorship	10 Political Conventions

31c   Determine your purpose and your thesis.

When you have selected a subject and narrowed it to manageable size, you have made real progress. But a subject is not a purpose. You still must decide exactly what you want to <u>do</u> with that subject, and exactly what you want to <u>say</u> about it. You must, in other words, (1) determine your overall purpose, and (2) decide upon a thesis.

1. Determining a purpose. If you have decided to write about your difficulties with the microscope in biology, you must then decide whether you mean to <u>describe</u> the difficulties, <u>explain</u> their causes, or <u>persuade</u> the reader that they are an example of bad laboratory instruction. If you have decided to write about violence on TV, you must next decide whether you mean to <u>explain</u> the kinds of violence we find, the percentage of programs which have such violence, and the like. Or do you mean to <u>describe</u> the violence in such a way that the reader reacts to it as you do. Or is your overall purpose neither of these, but rather to <u>persuade</u> your reader that such violence is harmful?

Whatever our purpose, it is likely to correspond to one of the four main types of writing: *exposition* or explanation (the giving of information); *argument* or persuasion; *description;* and *narration.* These overlap, to be sure; and most good writing intertwines two or more of them. But even when this is so, a given piece of writing usually has a single main, dominant purpose which the writer has in mind.

31c

A. Exposition. Here our purpose is to inform, to explain, to clarify, to make our readers know or understand something about a subject. Often, expository prose does more than that: it appeals to our emotions, to our moral and aesthetic sense. The subject itself sometimes transcends the expository presentation. A report on the detonation of a hydrogen bomb or on heroin addiction will for most readers be something more than an exposition of process or cause and effect.

Still, if our purpose in writing on these subjects is primarily to inform, we are writing expository prose. Whether our subject is an automobile engine, a social problem, a law, a poem, a hobby, or a city, what we are saying to our reader in effect is this: "I'm going to tell you something. I'm not trying to persuade you to believe what I believe or to lead you to value judgments, although there is the possibility that may happen. What I want to do is to make you know or understand something you didn't know or understand before—at least not so well or clearly."

B. Argument. Here our purpose is to persuade our readers that what we believe or do is right and just, or that what others do is not right or just. If we wish to persuade our readers, we may choose to present our case as fully and objectively as we can, appealing to our readers' reason and common sense. Or we may choose to appeal to their emotions by choosing emotional language and by playing upon their beliefs. But whatever evidence, reasons, or appeals we use, what we are saying to our readers in effect is this: "I know what I believe. You may find what I have to say interesting and informative. But my main purpose is not to inform. My main purpose is to persuade you to believe as I do or act as I want you to."

C. Description. Here our purpose is to share with our readers the impression something has made upon us. We wish to make our readers see, feel, or hear as vividly as we can what we have seen or felt or heard. Such description is sometimes called SUGGESTIVE DESCRIPTION, to distinguish it from TECHNICAL DE-

SCRIPTION, the purpose of which is mainly to explain. If we write a technical description of a building for a course in architecture, we will need to explain as exactly as possible its design, the materials used in its construction. But if we write a suggestive description of the same building, we will be trying rather to communicate our impression of it as ugly or beautiful, simple or grand, cramped or spacious. In this kind of description, we say in effect: "I know the impression what I am describing has made upon me. I want you to have the same impression."

D. Narration. Here our purpose is to tell the readers about something that happened; we wish to share with them the real or imagined events. In fact, we rarely narrate events with the sole intention of narrating them. Even the novelist or short story writer usually tells his or her story as a way of explaining how people behave, or ought to behave. And if we recount some part of our own lives, more often than not we tell our story in such a way that it reveals something about us or explains something about our own behavior.

31c

More often, we use narration as a part of exposition or argument. We retell a historical event to clarify a current political situation. We tell the story of a friend's fatal car crash to illustrate the dangers of high-speed driving. But whatever use we may put it to, we are always saying to our readers: "I know about or have experienced an event. I want to tell you what happened."

2. Writing a Thesis Statement. A THESIS STATEMENT is a sentence that sums up the controlling idea and purpose of a paper. It answers the question, "What is the point I am making, the opinion I am supporting, the stand I am taking?" A carefully formed thesis sentence is an introductory summary of the paper that follows.

Like any other sentence, a thesis sentence consists of a subject and a predicate. If you have successfully limited your subject (see **31b**) so that it is narrow and specific enough to manage in your paper, you have already defined the subject of your thesis sentence. Writing a thesis sentence for a paper on that subject is a matter of writing a predicate to go with that subject, a matter of deciding what assertion about that subject you wish to make.

Let us suppose that, starting with the general subject "Mass Media," you have progressively limited your topic first to "Television," and finally to "Television Commercials." The obvious question is: What about television commercials? Your next step clearly is to state what your central idea about television commercials is, what you wish to assert about them. The number of different assertions we can make about this topic, or any other, is of course almost endless. The following examples suggest some typical possibilities.

> Television commercials are thoroughly entertaining.
>
> Television commercials appeal to our desires for good health, good looks, and good living.
>
> Television commercials make us endlessly dissatisfied with our health, our appearance, and our income.
>
> Television commercials are at best misleading, and at worst downright dishonest.
>
> Television commercials make financially possible a far greater range of entertainment than would otherwise be practical.

31c

Each of these thesis sentences gives its writer a clearly stated controlling idea and gives direction to the whole paper. Note that the first two thesis sentences suggest an overall expository purpose also—to explain in what ways commercials are entertaining, or how they appeal to certain desires. The remaining three sentences suggest an overall persuasive purpose—to convince the readers that commercials make them dissatisfied, are dishonest, or make possible something very desirable, whatever their limitations.

Such well-formed thesis sentences not only give a paper a clear purpose, they can also help keep a paper unified, provided of course the writer sticks to the purpose he has defined. With a good thesis sentence, you commit yourself. Your purpose is clearly to support your thesis, to back it up with details and evidence, to explain what you mean by it, to convince your readers it is true and valid. It helps you in organizing your paper, and particularly in deciding what to include and what to exclude. What sponsors pay for TV advertising is crucial to your cause if the point of your paper is that such payments support a broad range of entertainment. It is just as clearly entirely irrelevant if your point is that commercials are entertaining.

Most important, perhaps, the thesis sentence can give your paper an "argumentative edge," a kind of dramatic interest. Even in a paper in which your general purpose is to explain or describe, a thesis sentence is a kind of commitment on your part, a promise to make your point clear, to convince the reader that commercials in fact _are_ entertaining, and not, as the reader thought, boring and frustrating.

A good thesis sentence which defines your central idea clearly and precisely, and which gives your paper confident direction, must meet three tests. It must be (1) unified, (2) limited, and (3) specific.

1. A good thesis sentence is unified. A thesis sentence expresses one and only one idea. Although it may include a secondary idea, it must clearly subordinate any secondary idea to the central idea. We should be suspicious of any thesis statement that is a compound sentence. Such sentences can sometimes commit the writer to explaining or defending two central ideas and defeat the purpose of the thesis. Each of the following sentences, for example, commits its writer to two major ideas, either of which will require a full paper to be supported adequately.

31c

> TV commercials are entertaining and they help support a great range of programs.
>
> Science fiction often anticipates new scientific developments, but it has never had as much appeal as detective stories.
>
> The new curriculum revisions provide increased opportunities for students, but they also restrict the students' choices.
>
> Intercollegiate football costs a disproportionate amount of money, and involves many fewer students than other sports.

2. A good thesis sentence is limited. Just as we need to narrow down any general subject to a limited topic, so we need to narrow down our assertion about it. In other words, just as the subject of our thesis sentence must be limited, so must the predicate. A good thesis must deal with a narrow enough assertion so that we can support it in the space and time we have.

Weak	Good teachers have several different things in common.
Better	Good teachers are competent in their subjects, fair in their grading, and imaginative in presenting their materials.
Weak	Magazine advertising varies from magazine to magazine.
Better	Magazine advertising reflects the tastes of a magazine's readers.
Weak	The selfishness of people can be seen in many ways.
Better	The selfishness of people is at its worst in a crowded subway.

3. A thesis sentence must be specific. A thesis sentence can be unified and restricted and yet not define a central idea usefully because the predicate is too vague and imprecise to give the paper any clear direction. Predicates that consist of *is* or *are* plus a vague complement such as *good, interesting, a serious problem* are too imprecise to be useful. A sentence such as *The rising cost of higher education is a serious problem,* for example, does not help indicate for whom or in what ways the "problem" is "serious." A thesis sentence such as *The characters in Faulkner's stories are interesting* may mean anything from interestingly realistic to interestingly remote from real life.

31c

Vague	The rising cost of higher education is a serious problem.
Specific	The rising cost of higher education seriously restricts the kind of student who can hope to go to college.
Specific	The rising cost of higher education is making it increasingly impossible for private colleges to remain open.
Vague	The neighborhood I grew up in was a good place to live.
Specific	Although the neighborhood I grew up in was crowded and noisy, it was always friendly.
Specific	Although the neighborhood I grew up in was open and quiet, it was oppressively lonely.
Vague	My difficulties in the biology lab are interesting.
Specific	My difficulties in the biology lab are amusing to my fellow students, confusing to my instructor, and frustrating to me.
Specific	My difficulties in the biology lab are so serious that they provide a strong argument against requiring a laboratory science of all students.

The more unified, limited, and specific we can make our thesis sentences, the more clearly and usefully we will have focused on the central idea, the controlling purpose of our paper. And the more clearly we have that purpose stated, the more prepared we are to determine what materials should go into the paper to support that idea, and how we may best organize those materials to serve our purpose.

EXERCISE 31c(1) Some of the following thesis sentences define a unified, limited, and specific central idea. Others are not unified, or are too broad or vague to be useful. Indicate which ones you think are satisfactory and explain why. Suggest revisions for those you think are unsuccessful.

1 Government regulation of business causes difficulties.
2 Cigarette smoking is disgusting to those who don't smoke, and dangerous to those who do, and should be prohibited.
3 Professor Winslow is a real human being.
4 Welfare is a necessary evil.
5 Mathematics ought to be a required course for everyone.
6 A good coach has many different qualities.
7 Objective examinations are limited because they give undue weight

to memory and not enough weight to ability to relate facts to one another.

8 Birth control is urgently needed today, but it has dangerous side effects.

9 The Women's Liberation movement is an important movement.

10 Poverty is the most serious problem in the United States today.

EXERCISE 31c(2) Make a thesis statement for two or three of the titles you listed in Exercise 31a.

EXERCISE 31c(3) Write a thesis statement for an essay or a chapter assigned to you as outside reading.

EXERCISE 31c(4) Write thesis statements for paragraphs 2, 5, 8, 11, and 14 on pages 227–233.

31d

EXERCISE 31c(5) Write two brief themes covering roughly the same subject but with different aims. For example, write a factual, informative theme describing a dormitory room or an apartment; then write a persuasive theme in which your aim is to convince the reader that he should live in the dormitory room or rent the apartment. Or, write an objective narrative report of an incident, and then write a report of the same incident in which your aim is to entertain the reader.

31d Consider your reader.

Unless you are taking notes for yourself or writing a diary, your writing always assumes at least one reader. And you must keep your readers in mind as you write, because they—your audience—always influence the way you write, even your choice of specific subject. Always try to focus on specific readers, or some specific kind of reader. Then ask yourself whether the best presentation for them will be simple or complex, popular or technical, general or specific. If you are honestly trying to communicate, you must adjust your subject matter, your point of view, the kind of detail and explanation you use, and even the words you choose to the reader or readers you are writing for.

Except for your mother, your uncle, your sister, your boy-friend, and other friends whose interest and language you know very well, your readers may seem difficult to pin down. Even so, you probably do more adjusting for different readers than you realize. You write a report on the football game for the college newspaper differently than you write an angry letter to the president of student government. If you write both your uncle and the financial aid office asking them for a loan, you do not use the same letter. In each instance, you adjust to your idea of the reader.

Specialized and general audiences

In most of your writing, both for college classes and later, it is useful to think of two broadly different kinds of readers: specialized and general.

The SPECIALIZED READER is one who already knows a good deal about a subject. The psychologist writing for a professional journal does not have to define technical terms; his readers already understand them. He does not have to get his readers' attention; the subject matter will do that. Specialists do not necessarily have to be scholars or doctors or engineers. They can be enthusiasts for almost anything—drag racing, photography, country music, astrology, pottery making, or football. If you and a friend to whom you are writing a letter are both lifelong photography enthusiasts, your letters will be an exchange between specialists, at least as long as they are about photography.

The GENERAL reader is the reader that most writing is addressed to. Such readers may have specialized interests, but when they turn to the *Sunday Magazine,* the *Saturday Review, People, Ebony,* or *Psychology Today,* they are general readers. They doubtless have varied backgrounds and interests, but they all share a common broad interest in events, ideas, and interpretations. In writing for them, the psychologist, for example, will make an effort to interest them. He will avoid technical terms whenever he can, and when he must use such terms, he will be careful to define them. He will take care to provide examples and explanations his readers can follow. In short, he will use standard, nontechnical language, being careful neither to talk down to his readers or be condescending. In the same way, when you write a paper describing to your fellow students the rewards of amateur photography, you will want to avoid technical details, perhaps directing your paper to some subject of broad interest such as the pleasures your general readers can get from an inexpensive and simple camera combined with the right choice of subjects for their pictures.

Some special advice

One word of warning to you in your college writing: Do not waste time trying to "write what the instructor wants." There will be requirements and standards in all your courses, but most instructors try their best to serve as sympathetic general or specialized readers, according to the circumstances. They try to judge how well a paper has met the needs of the readers to whom it was directed. Their criticisms are aimed at explaining to you how to put your papers together more clearly, sharpen your writing, adjust more appropriately to your readers. But they want your explanations, your ideas, your reasons. They want you to be able to speak your own piece so that others will listen, not to ape someone else.

A word about the reader you want to persuade

If your principal purpose is to explain a process, a mechanism, or an idea, or to tell a story, or to describe, it is probably enough to decide whether you are writing for a specialized or a general reader. But if you are writing to convince your readers to believe in one way or another, or to act in one way or another, you will do well to ask first whether they are likely to (1) agree with you, or (2) disagree with you.

31d

1. Readers likely to agree with you. If your audience already agrees with you, your problem is clearly not to convince them further. It is rather to persuade them to act. When Thoreau delivered his address "Civil Disobedience," he knew his audience was already opposed to slavery; his task was not to convince them of the evils of slavery but to inspire them to act on behalf of the antislavery cause. Thoreau's essay is full of emotionally charged language, passionate in its call for action. How much emotion you can effectively communicate to your reader will depend on your topic and the intensity of your and your reader's beliefs.

Clearly, you do not need a fist-shaking, tear-streaming appeal to vote down a proposed $2 increase in club dues. On the other hand, if you fail to express deep feeling when the occasion demands you will be just as ineffective. "Move us," the audience says to you, "don't talk about a serious problem as if it were a minor inconvenience."

2. Readers likely to disagree with you. No matter how strongly you believe that abortion is wrong, that welfare should be increased, or that writing courses should not be required in college, there are nonetheless persuasive arguments for believing the opposite. And you will be pretty safe in assuming that many of your readers will start out disagreeing with your point of view. If you want those readers to listen to your position, you will do well to start out by recognizing theirs. If you begin by acknowledging their arguments, and even admitting the strength of their arguments, you can then move on to suggest their weaknesses, and finally to set your own arguments against them.

If you go about your task of persuading with knowledge of and respect for your readers' convictions, you will be much more likely to get them to listen. Your purpose is, after all, to persuade. If you tell your readers they are ignorant, stupid, or ridiculous to believe as they do, you can only antagonize them. You will never persuade them.

31e Gather materials and make preliminary notes.

31e

Your next job is to get together the rough materials for your paper. A good many inexperienced writers make the mistake of thinking that once they have decided upon a topic such as "The Qualities of a Good Teacher" they should be able to sit down and dash off 400 or 500 words. No one can do this. Any writer needs a kind of incubation period for even the simplest subject. For some writers, the work of incubation goes on half subconsciously. They think about their topic over a cup of coffee, while they are walking between classes, while they are brushing their hair or shaving. For others it goes on with much chewing of pencils over a blank piece of paper. However it does go on, for few people have on the top of their minds the kind of specific detail out of which a solid piece of writing, even about personal experiences, is made.

The material you need for a solid paper can come from a variety of sources, depending on the topic. For papers based on your own experience, you will need to dig around in your memory. A paper on the qualities of teachers whom you considered good will require you to ask such questions as: What teachers did you like? Why? What did they do that others did not? Were they more friendly? To everyone? To you in particular? In what ways? Did they know their subject matter better than other teachers? How did you know? What specific things did they do that made you like them? For papers based on observation you will need to do some closer looking and thinking than you are accustomed to. Indeed, one part of the value of a composition course is that it encourages you to look more closely, to see more than you ordinarily do. All of us think we know our own neighborhoods, or know what our best friends look like, until we try to describe them on paper. Only then do we find how hard we have to work to remember all the specific details we assumed we knew well.

Most inexperienced writers discover that the best way to get their observations and ideas in order is to put them on paper. Making written notes is a way of finding out what you have to say on a subject. Notes help you select and evaluate your material and put it in order. Suppose you decide to write a paper on "The Scene," the discotheque where you usually go on Saturday nights. As a start, you might jot down the following:

1. Good selections of records
2. More exciting than fraternity dances
3. Very crowded dance floor
4. Good coffee
5. Psychedelic decor
6. Cheaper than a night club
7. Food badly prepared and selection limited
8. Waitresses pleasant, especially Liz
9. Good place to meet people
10. Makes a change from movies or TV
11. See some people you don't meet around college
12. Close to the center of town and the college
13. No alcoholic drinks
14. Owner keeps place clean
15. Too small
16. Customers always shouting above music

31e

Or suppose you decide to write a paper on "Buying a Second-Hand Car." Your preliminary notes might consist of the following:

1. Used-car dealers in town
2. Down payment from Dad
3. Sources of used cars
4. Advantages of car loan over personal loan
5. Condition of car
6. Choosing the car
7. Price
8. Trade-in allowance for old car
9. Newspaper used-car ads
10. Comparison shopping
11. Criteria for choice

If you are writing argument, your task will be to gather the evidence necessary to persuade your reader. For example, the student who wrote Specimen Paper 2, at the end of this section, made the following preliminary notes:

1. Condemnation of motion picture violence in editorial
2. Claim that TV is less violent
3. Example of motion picture violence—*The Dirty Dozen*—"violent" characters, *Bonnie and Clyde*—does audience approve of their actions?
4. Violence in *B & C* justified—necessary to bring out audience reaction
5. TV violence—*Garrison's Gorillas*

6. *GG* follows *Dirty Dozen* pattern
7. Characters in *GG* unsympathetic
8. Situation in *GG* absurd
9. Violence in *GG* cannot be justified
10. If anything, TV violence worse

The first two of these lists are just preliminary jottings of ideas, without logical order and arrangement. It is clear that the writer will have to spend more time thinking about his topic and then work out a more coherent outline. The third list comes closer to a workable outline and, with a few additions and changes, can serve as a guide for the writing of the first draft. In either case, making a list is a valuable first step. It gets your ideas down on paper and shows you how much you have to work with and how much more you have to get.

EXERCISE 31e(1) Make preliminary notes for two of the theme titles you prepared for Exercises 31a(1)–31a(3).

31f

EXERCISE 31e(2) Which of the suggested topics listed on pages 150–151 could you use for a 300- to 500-word theme without any further study or research? Make preliminary notes for three of them, to see whether you know as much about them as you think you do.

EXERCISE 31e(3) Make preliminary notes of one subject you can write about from personal experience (for example, "Problems of an Oldest Child") and one you know about only from hearsay or guesswork (for example, "The Life of a Ranch Hand").

31f Decide on a pattern of organization and development.

If you have successfully limited your topic and determined your purpose and thesis, you have set the general limits of your theme. And as you have gathered the materials for your paper and made your preliminary notes, your sense of the paper has become more clear. You must now think about organization and development.

Organization. The difference between a composition that is not planned and one that is well planned is the difference between a collection of parts for a motor, and a working motor. The collection of parts has no organization; it is a small chaos. The motor has organization; the parts are in place according to a design and they function together as a whole. Good organization comes from keeping your purpose and thesis statement clearly in mind and from arranging your ideas and facts in an orderly way. What is an orderly sequence, and more particularly, what is good order, given your subject and purpose? There is no one answer to this question, for there are different ways of organizing any given composition. But there are standard patterns, and a particular subject and aim are very likely to follow one or a combination of a number of them.

Broadly, there are two kinds of order: NATURAL ORDER and LOGICAL ORDER. NATURAL ORDER is the order inherent in the thing itself. That is, a narrative will normally lead us to tell things in time sequence, to arrange our materials chronologically; a description will normally lead us to arrange things spatially. LOGICAL ORDER, in contrast, is imposed; the writer must determine by reason the order in which he will arrange his material to gain the greatest clarity and effectiveness.

1. Natural order. The two natural orders are (A) time, or chronological order, and (B) space order. They are the common orders of most narrative and descriptive writing.

A. Time order. Time or chronological order will almost certainly be the appropriate order if your purpose is narrative. The report of an athletic contest, an autobiographical narrative, an account of an incident in history, all naturally and effectively fall into time sequence. Similarly, the description of a process such as setting up a campsite, the stages in the development of a frog, or the process of selecting a college program falls naturally into time order.

31f

B. Space order. Some form of spatial organization will almost certainly be appropriate if your purpose is descriptive. The description of a geographical area—your neighborhood, for instance—will fall naturally into a pattern which takes your residence as center and moves outward first in one direction, then in another. The description of a car may move from the external appearance to the internal appearance; and the outside appearance itself might move from a head-on view, to a side view, to a rear view.

2. Logical order. When we are giving reasons to persuade a reader, or examples to explain an idea, there is no natural order to guide us as there is when we tell a story or describe a scene. We must decide on an order for our reasons or examples on the basis of what will be clearest for the reader and most effective for our purpose. The most common and useful orders for such material are (A) the order of climax, and (B) general to particular, or its reverse, particular to general. Thus if we present three reasons to persuade a reader, we will be more effective if we arrange those reasons so that we begin with our weakest reason and conclude with our most persuasive. If we are explaining an idea, we most often state our general idea first—in our thesis sentence, for example—and then move from this statement to the particular details and examples which clarify our idea.

In many papers we are very likely, of course, to draw upon

some combination of natural and logical orders. Thus in a paper with the thesis that TV commercials are misleading if not dishonest, our overall organization will probably move from general to particular—from our thesis to the examples supporting it. But in choosing our order for those examples, we may arrange them in the order they occur during a typical Sunday evening (time), or may choose to arrange them in an order moving from the least misleading to the most misleading (climax).

Development. No matter how clearly we organize a paper, if we are to make it clear, convincing, and complete, we must give the reader ample relevant specifics. That is, we must <u>develop</u> it. Most papers can be developed by one of the following methods or some combination of them: (A) detail and example, (B) comparison and contrast, (C) classification, and (D) cause and effect. Note that although we separate the processes of organizing and developing in order to explain them, the two go hand in hand. How we develop an idea affects how we may best organize it. And both depend in part on our purpose and our thesis.

A. Detail and example. A great many brief themes consist basically of a thesis and supporting specific details, examples, and reasons. This is an appropriate pattern of development for such topics as "The Value of Studying History," "College Should Develop Courses in Women's Studies," and "The Problem of Sharing an Apartment." It is essentially the method of development followed by the writer of the paper entitled "How Do You Want Your Violence?" (Specimen Paper 2).

Such a method of development imposes two special requirements upon the writer. <u>First</u>, he must have a very clearly stated thesis focused upon a limited point. The thesis may not simply set out a general topic such as "Apartments make for good living," "There is violence on TV," or "Buying a used car is time consuming." The thesis must be sharply enough defined to exert real control over the details, examples, or reasons that will support it. <u>Second</u>, the writer must be certain that all details, examples, or reasons with which he develops his thesis bear directly upon it, and he must arrange them in a clear order.

B. Comparison and contrast. This is the kind of development most clearly invited by such topics as "The Demands of College vs. High School Education," "My Preference for Carter," or "Why Nineteenth-Century Women were Happier [Less Happy] Than Women Today." This is a subsidiary kind of development in the paper on "How Do You Want Your Violence?" (Specimen Paper 2).

31f

C. Classification. Classification and its sister process, analysis, provide useful clues to the development of many topics. Analysis takes apart things usually thought of as a unit. Thus if we wish to develop a paper on the federal government, one kind of development would divide that government into the legislative, judicial, and executive functions. If we wished to describe a television set, it would be useful to analyze its components.

The opposite side of this process is classification, which consists of grouping things we habitually think of as existing separately. Thus you might develop a theme describing the student body at your university by dividing the students into several classes—those who are seriously devoted to their studies, those who want to work hard enough to stay in college but are not genuinely serious, and those who have no serious purpose and expect to be asked to leave. Notice that, depending on the purpose of your paper, you might set up a wide variety of classifications. One thesis might invite a classification of students by age groups; another by place of residence—dormitory, apartment, home; another by choice of career—prospective teachers, engineers, journalists, and computer technicians. The important principle to note is that no one classification is "right" and that the classification you decide on will be dictated by your purpose.

31f

D. Cause to effect or effect to cause. We often explore the nature of a thing by asking either its causes or its effects. Thus if you explore as a possible topic the fact that you have unusual difficulty with mathematics, you may discover that your discussion easily falls into the pattern of (1) stating the problem and then explaining the causes (effect to cause), or (2) following through the effects on your choice of career that result from your difficulty in coping with mathematics (cause to effect).

EXERCISE 31f As we have noted, there is no one "right" organization or development for a given topic. Suitable patterns of organization and kinds of development depend upon the particular purpose and thesis of a paper. Even given a particular purpose, there are often several possible ways of organizing and developing a paper.

Below is a list of general topics for papers. Select three or four and be prepared to discuss (1) at least two different purposes you might define for each, and (2) the kind of organization and development that seems most appropriate for each different purpose.

For example, for the general topic "purchasing a camera," your purpose might be to describe the process of selecting a camera. In that case, your organization might be chronological, and your development by details and examples making specific each step in the process. Or your purpose might be to explain the criteria for selecting a camera. In that case, you might develop your ideas by classifying or grouping the kinds of criteria, and organize your paper by presenting the different kinds of criteria in the order of their increasing importance.

Living in a mobile home
The effects of inflation
The view from _____
My life and hard times
The women's movement at _____
Selecting a college program
Owning a car (bicycle, boat)
Kinds of students
Abolishing examinations
How to build (or make) _____
Living with a roommate
Cheating in college (or life)
Safety in today's cars
Arguments for (or against) birth control
The limits of equality
My current slang vocabulary

31g Make an outline or plan for your paper.

31g

Make it a habit to construct a complete outline for every piece of writing you do. An outline provides you with a working plan for organizing your paper. It insures that your development of the subject will be logical and orderly, and enables you to distinguish clearly between important ideas and less important ones.

Outlines may vary from simple, informal notes for your own guidance, to carefully worked out topic or sentence outlines for longer and more complex papers. The kind of outline you choose will depend upon your writing assignment. For a brief class paper on your high school preparation in English, for example, you might have time only for such scratch notes as the following:

1. More literature than composition
2. Emphasis on grammar in 10th grade
3. Wrote most papers on literature
4. Research papers in 11th and 12th grades
5. Enjoyed literature more than papers
6. Lack of contemporary literature
7. Not much comment on papers except 11th grade.

Even such a limited set of notes as this provides a guide for your paper. It suggests immediately two major divisions into composition and literature, and clarifies the fact that the main emphasis in high school was on literature. A glance at the notes suggests a scheme in which topics 1, 3, 5, and 6 go in one paragraph, and 2, 4, and 7 in another. The whole suggests some such thesis statement as *My high school preparation in English included work in both composition and literature, but the latter was the more thorough as well as the more enjoyable.* With this kind of start and your notes before you as you write, even a brief paper is likely to go more smoothly and logically. Such preliminary outlines are, of course, especially valuable in writing examinations.

The greater the number of notes you have to begin with, the greater the probability that a more formal outline will be useful. *ordering* In constructing your outline, follow some consistent principle of organization—chronological, general to specific (deductive), specific to general (inductive), spatial, and so on. Bring together all related ideas in one place and do not repeat them in other parts of the outline.

In the preliminary outline for "Buying a Second-Hand Car" **(31e)**, notice that two of the items stand out as general headings: "Sources of used cars" and "Choosing the car." Notice too that a third general heading, "Financing," must be added; otherwise there would be no place to put such items as "Down payment from Dad" and "Advantages of car loan over personal loan." If we arrange all the details under these three major headings, we come up with the following outline:

31g

BUYING A SECOND-HAND CAR

   I. Sources of used cars
      A. Used-car dealers in town
      B. Newspaper used-car ads
  II. Choosing the car
      A. Comparison shopping
      B. Criteria for choice
         1. Condition of car
         2. Price
         3. Trade-in allowance for old car
 III. Financing
      A. Down payment from Dad
      B. Advantages of car loan over personal loan

Such an outline will help you keep your plan in mind as you write your paper (adherence to purpose). It will indicate the order in which you want to discuss each idea (logical development) and the relative importance of each (proportion of material).

If you are to do an efficient job of organizing your material, you must know something of the formal mechanics of outlining, and the various types of outlining that your instructor may require.

1. Use a consistent method for numbering and indenting major headings and subheadings. For most outlines, it is unnecessary to divide subheadings more than two degrees. Here is a conventional system of outline notation:

```
   I. . . . . . . . . . . . . . .
      A. . . . . . . . . . . . . . .
         1. . . . . . . . . . . . . . .
            a. . . . . . . . . . . . . . .
            b. . . . . . . . . . . . . . .
         2. . . . . . . . . . . . . . .
      B. . . . . . . . . . . . . . .
  II. . . . . . . . . . . . . . .
```

2. Be sure that your outline is logically clear and consistent. Do not use single headings or single subheadings in your outline. Any category of heading or subheading must have at least two parts. If you have a I, you must also have a II. If you introduce an A under a Roman numeral, you must also have a B under that Roman numeral. If you put a 1 under an A, you must also put a 2. And so on for any division. The reason for this procedure is sheer logic. Each breakdown of the outline is a division of a foregoing bigger point, and you cannot logically divide something into just one part. A single subheading reflects poor organization; it should be incorporated into the heading of which it is logically a part.

We might illustrate the principle mathematically as follows:

TWO DOLLARS

```
   I. One dollar
      A. Fifty cents
      B. Fifty cents
         1. Twenty-five cents
         2. Twenty-five cents
  II. One dollar
```

The same principle requires that each group of subheadings be logically equal to the larger heading under which they fall. If we wish, for instance, to divide the general heading "dogs," we can do so with the subheadings "house dogs" and "working dogs," or "large dogs" and "small dogs," or "poodles," "collies," "spaniels," and the like. But each one of these groups represents a different principle of classification, and if we mix them we will have an illogical outline.

3. Use either the topic, the sentence, or the paragraph form throughout your outline. In a topic outline the separate headings are expressed by a noun, or a word or phrase used as a noun, and its modifiers. In a sentence outline, which has the same structure as the topic outline, the separate headings are expressed in complete sentences. The sentence outline is more informative than the topic outline, because it states ideas more fully; but the topic outline is easier to read. The paragraph outline gives a summary sentence for each paragraph in the theme. It does not divide and subdivide headings into subordinate parts.

Before you start to outline, decide which of the three types of outline you are going to use and then follow it consistently. If, for example, you choose to make a sentence outline, remember that every statement in the outline must be expressed as a complete sentence. Remember, too, to make all parts of the outline parallel in structure (see "Parallelism," Section 35), as in the following models.

ADVERTISEMENTS OF THE PAST

31g

Topic Outline

I. Colonial period
   A. Benjamin Franklin's advertisements
   B. Advertisements in newspapers
      1. Products and services
      2. Personal
II. Nineteenth century
   A. Mass circulation publications
      1. General audience newspapers and magazines
      2. Women's magazines
   B. Frequently advertised products
      1. Soap and cosmetics
      2. Patent medicines
      3. Bicycles
III. Analysis of P. T. Barnum advertisements

Sentence Outline

I. Advertisements were printed during the colonial period.
   A. Benjamin Franklin both wrote and published advertisements.
   B. Advertisements appeared frequently in newspapers.
      1. A variety of products and services were advertised.
      2. Personal advertising was also very common.
II. In the nineteenth century advertising flourished.
   A. Mass circulation publications made their appearance.

1. Some newspapers and magazines appealed to general audiences.
2. Some magazines appealed especially to women.

B. A number of products were advertised frequently.
   1. Soap and cosmetics advertisements proliferated.
   2. Patent medicines sold to millions as the result of mass advertising.
   3. As bicycles became popular toward the end of the century, competitive advertisements appeared by the hundreds.

III. An analysis of P. T. Barnum advertisements shows how sensational material promoted sales.

Paragraph Outline

1. A variety of advertisements appeared frequently in newspapers of the colonial period.
2. With the development of mass circulation publications in the nineteenth century, advertisements proliferated in general audience and women's magazines.
3. An analysis of P. T. Barnum advertisements shows how sensational material promoted sales.

31g

4. Cast all items in the outline in parallel grammatical constructions. Consistency of grammatical form emphasizes the logic of the outline and gives it clarity and smoothness. Inconsistency of form, on the other hand, makes a perfectly rational ordering of items seem illogical.

THE GAME OF TENNIS	THE GAME OF TENNIS
Nonparallel	*Parallel*

I. The playing court
  A. The surface materials for it
    1. Made of clay
    2. Grass
    3. The asphalt type
  B. Measuring the court
    1. For singles
    2. Doubles
  C. Net
  D. Backstops necessary

II. Equipment needed
  A. Racket
  B. The tennis balls
  C. The wearing apparel of players

III. Rules for playing tennis
  A. The game of singles
  B. Doubles

I. Playing court
  A. Surface materials
    1. Clay
    2. Grass
    3. Asphalt
  B. Measurements
    1. Singles
    2. Doubles
  C. Net
  D. Backstops

II. Equipment
  A. Racket
  B. Ball
  C. Wearing apparel

III. Playing rules
  A. Singles
  B. Doubles

IV. Principal strokes of tennis
   A. Serving the ball
   B. The forehand
     1. Drive
     2. Lobbing the ball
   C. The backhand stroke
     1. The drive
     2. Lob
	IV. Principal strokes
	   A. Serving stroke
	   B. Forehand stroke
	     1. Drive
	     2. Lob
	   C. Backhand stroke
	     1. Drive
	     2. Lob

5. Avoid vague outline headings such as *introduction, body, and conclusion*. Not only does the outline serve as a guide in your writing; submitted with your paper, it may also serve as a table of contents for your reader. To use such words as *introduction, body,* and *conclusion* as outline headings is meaningless, for they give no clue to what material is to come. If your paper is to have an introduction, indicate in the outline what will be in it. If your paper is to have a formal conclusion, indicate in the outline what conclusion you will draw.

EXERCISE 31g(1) Study the following outlines. Are they consistently organized? Do you find any single headings or subheadings? Are all items in parallel grammatical construction? Be prepared to suggest appropriate revisions for each. Choose one and revise it so that it will be fully consistent with the principles of outlining.

31g

THE ADVANTAGES AND DISADVANTAGES OF A CITY UNIVERSITY

I. Convenience of location
   A. Transportation
   B. Hotels
   C. People
   D. Stores
   E. Theaters

II. Advantages
   A. Center of travel
   B. Students learn to be more independent
   C. More types of people
   D. Those who have never been in city get new view
   E. Opportunities for work

III. Disadvantages
   A. Tendency to become too interested in other things
   B. Too much for some to cope with
   C. Too close to other schools

THE VALUE OF PUBLIC OPINION POLLS

I. Introduction
   A. Operation of public opinion polls
     1. Selection of an important issue

2. Constructing a set of questions
   a. Scientific nature of this construction
3. A cross section of the population is selected
  B. Replies are tabulated and results summarized
II. Importance of polls' results
  1. Attitudes of public revealed to lawmakers
  2. Power of present groups revealed
  3. Polls are a democratic process
   a. Polls reveal extent of people's knowledge

BAKING YOUR OWN BREAD

  I. Introduction—Delicious taste, look, and feel of good bread
 II. Breadmaking in the past
  A. More difficult than now
  B. Necessary to make own yeast
  C. Kneading difficult
III. Breadmaking today is popular
  A. Much easier
   1. Can make a few loaves at a time
   2. Gas and electric ovens easier to control
  B. Making bread is enjoyable
   1. Sense of satisfaction in kneading own dough
   2. Bread baking in oven smells good
   3. More tasty than most bought breads
IV. Three easy recipes
  A. White-flour bread
  B. Sweetened breads
   1. Raisin
 V. Conclusion—Pleasure of sitting down to eat a slice of your own baked bread

31h

EXERCISE 31g(2) Construct a complete outline for one of the titles suggested on pages 150–151. Use each of the three forms just described: (1) topic, (2) sentence, (3) paragraph.

EXERCISE 31g(3) Write a topic outline for one of the theme titles you prepared for Exercises 31a(1) to 31a(3).

31h   Begin your paper effectively.

A good beginning serves as a springboard into your subject. It can also attract the reader's interest. Of the two, getting started is more important than devising a catchy opening.

Important as your opening sentences may be in your final draft, don't waste time over them in the early drafts. After you have written a first draft, you will often find that your purpose has become clearer and that it is much easier to write good opening sentences. Indeed you may frequently discover that the first few sentences you wrote were really useless warming-up and that with slight revision the fourth or fifth sentence is in fact a good beginning.

How long your beginning should be depends on the length and complexity of your subject. A 1,000- or 1,200-word paper on the relative merits of business and journalism as possible careers may deserve a paragraph stating your thesis and indicating the general plan of your paper. But briefer papers of 500 or 600 words usually need no more than a sentence or two to get started effectively.

Although the kind of beginning you choose will depend upon your topic and the length of your paper, some advice about the kinds of beginnings to avoid, and some suggestions about effective beginnings may be helpful.

Beginnings to Avoid

1. Avoid beginnings that are not self-explanatory. Do not make your reader refer back to your title to find out the meaning of your opening sentence. Do not begin a paper entitled "Nuclear Energy" with *Everyone is against it;* or a paper giving instructions for building a model airplane with *The first thing to do is to lay all the parts on the table.*

2. Avoid beginnings that start too far back. If you are writing a paper describing last Saturday's football game, get directly to the description; don't begin by explaining how you happened to go to the game. The writer of the following paragraphs meant well, but should have begun with the second paragraph.

31 h

FATHER KNOWS BEST

You probably wonder from my title what I am going to write about. Well, it's a long story. It started way back in 1955 when I was born. My mother announced to my father that I was a boy! "We're going to send him to State University!" my father exclaimed. So here I am at State, a member of the freshman class.

It was my father's idea from the first that I should come to State. He had been a student here in 1948 when he met my mother. . . .

3. Avoid beginnings that complain or apologize. If you want to complain about the assigned topic, or apologize for what you have written, do so in a note attached to your paper. Do not use your opening paragraph to do so. The first opening below is a typical complaint beginning; the second, a typical apology beginning.

psychological impact

Describing a building accurately is a very difficult task. Though it is a good assignment because it makes you look closely and observe details you would not otherwise notice, it takes considerable time and does not leave the student enough time to write the actual paper. I discovered this when I tried to observe and describe the university chapel.

After trying unsuccessfully to write a paper describing my roommate, and then attempting to gather some new ideas on books I had read during the summer, I gave up and decided to write on my experience in reading *The Grapes of Wrath* by John Steinbeck. I hope this fits the assignment.

Effective Beginnings

If you have finished your first draft and are still having trouble writing a good beginning, try one of the following.

1. Begin with a statement of fact, or an unusual detail.

Mrs. Gardner didn't drink tea; she drank beer.

My grandmother believed in ghosts.

Ninety-two percent of the students at State College live at home and commute.

Lonepine is a little place in Sanders County in western Montana. The people there are farmers.

The world does not much like curiosity. The world says that curiosity killed the cat.

EDMUND S. MORGAN, "What Every Yale Freshman Should Know"

31h

2. Begin with a firm statement of opinion, or a directly stated proposition.

I do not believe in composition courses.

Cats are a nuisance. They should be exterminated.

Television made Alex Haley's book *Roots* into an interesting drama, but the book itself is more compelling.

Because people who rarely talk together talk differently, differences in speech tell what groups a man belongs to.   JAMES SLEDD,
"Bi-Dialectalism: The Linguistics of White Supremacy"

Every culture develops some kind of art as surely as it develops language.

SUSANNE K. LANGER, "The Cultural Importance of Art"

3. Begin with a brief anecdote or incident that leads directly into your main topic.

I had a job interview several weeks ago. Friends warned me not to be too aggressive. During the interview, I tried to present myself as a competent candidate, able to "think like a man" and yet not to be a "masculine" female. After fielding several questions relevant to the job, I suddenly heard, "Miss Stern, are you in love?"

PAULA STERN, "The Womanly Image"

When Mark Twain left home at an early age, he had no great respect for his father's intelligence. When he returned a few years later, he was astounded at how much his father had learned in the meantime. I have been similarly astonished at how much both my father and mother have learned in the time I have been away from home.

4. Begin with a quotation that illustrates or leads into your thesis.

"Courage is what it takes to stand up and speak," Winston Churchill once said, and then added, "Courage is also what it takes to sit down and listen." Churchill was talking about politics. But the advice is sound advice for college students, who often have the courage to stand up and speak, but lack the courage to sit down and listen. If we are to learn all we can, we need a lot of both kinds of courage.

I heartily accept the motto, "That government is best which governs least"; and I should like to see it acted up to more rapidly and systematically. HENRY DAVID THOREAU, "Civil Disobedience"

EXERCISE 31h(1) Choose three titles from the list of suggested topics on pages 150–151. Then write a beginning for each, using a different technique each time.

31h

EXERCISE 31h(2) Comment upon the following beginnings.

1 One of the characters in *The Moon and Sixpence* remarked that he had faithfully lived up to the old precept about doing every day two things you heartily dislike; for, said he, every day he had got up and he had gone to bed. CHRISTOPHER MORLEY, "On Going to Bed"

2 There is something to be said for a bad education.

PHYLLIS MCGINLEY, "The Consolations of Illiteracy"

3 Come what may, I change my razor blade each Saturday morning, and as I did so on a hot one not long ago, I found myself worrying about the Civil War.

ROBERT HENDERSON, "The Enamelled Wishbone"

4 There is nothing more alone in the universe than man.

LOREN EISELEY, "The Long Loneliness"

5 The School System has much to say these days of the virtue of reading widely, and not enough about the virtues of reading less but in depth. JOHN CIARDI, "Robert Frost: The Way to the Poem"

EXERCISE 31h(3) Comment on the beginnings of the specimen papers at the end of this chapter.

31i   Always write a preliminary rough draft of your paper.

Having completed your outline and having phrased an opening statement, you are ready to proceed with the actual writing of your paper. <u>Be sure to allow time to write your papers at least twice</u>. The first—or rough—draft gives you an opportunity just to <u>write</u>. In this draft you need not concern yourself with spelling, punctuation, mechanics, or grammar. Rather, you can devote your attention to getting your ideas, as directed by the outline, down on paper.

Remember that your paper is more than an outline. No matter how unified, clear, and coherent a paper is, it will be thin and weak unless it is adequately developed. Good writing is not made by orderly outlines alone. It is packed with specific detail, example, and illustration. The real failure of a great many student papers lies not in their lack of essential unity or coherence, but in their thinness. They say little or nothing because their writers have contented themselves with generalizations and have not been willing to dig for the sort of facts and examples that will make the subjects alive for a reader. The papers make good sense as far as they go; but they do not go far enough or deep enough to make good reading. Since the ways of developing papers are the same as the ways of developing paragraphs, which are their principal units of thought, this problem is considered in more detail in Section 32, "Effective Paragraphs."

31i

31j

31j   End your paper effectively.

Just as a good opening gets your paper off to a good vigorous start, <u>so an intelligent conclusion lends a finished note to</u> your paper. An <u>effective ending may bring your paper to a logical conclusion or tie it all together</u>. A paper titled "How to Build a Model Airplane" might end with this statement:

> If you have followed all the directions given here, you should now have an assembled model ready to be put in the family room.

Here are some ideas to help you end your papers effectively.

1. <u>**Conclude with a restatement of your thesis statement.**</u> In the paper "Father Knows Best" this sort of ending might be effective:

> Now that I have been here and have seen the school for myself, I am convinced that Father *does* know best. I have decided to enroll for the next term at State.

2. Summarize the major ideas you have brought out in the paper. A summary serves the double purpose of bringing your paper to a good conclusion and of reminding your readers once more of the major points you have made. The paper called "Buying a Second-Hand Car" could effectively employ this sort of ending:

> Thus, it is clear that buying a second-hand car is a complex process. But anyone who investigates the sources of used cars carefully, chooses his car intelligently, and finances it soundly will have a car that lasts for years.

3. Draw a conclusion from the facts you have presented. This sort of conclusion is especially effective if you have set out to defend a point of view. For example, if you have been exploring a topic such as "Should Political Conventions Be Abolished?" your conclusion might be a call for action to reinforce whichever side you have defended.

4. Avoid weak endings.

A. Don't end your paper with an apology. Such endings as *This is only my opinion, and I'm probably not really very well qualified to speak* or *I'm sorry that this isn't a better paper, but I didn't have enough time* spoil the effect of whatever you have written. If you feel that you have failed, your reader will probably think so too.

B. Don't end your paper by branching off into another aspect of the topic or by introducing new material. The end of your paper should conclude what you have already said. It is disconcerting to a reader to find new ideas introduced that are not explored further. Avoid such endings as: *There is a lot more I could say about this if I had more time* or *Another aspect of buying a second-hand car is convincing your parents you should have a car in the first place, but it would take another paper to tell about it.* This type of ending leaves the reader with the feeling that you have led him to no definite conclusion.

31k

31k   Prepare a finished second draft.

After a cooling-off period of several hours, you are ready to check, revise, and rewrite. Test the overall organization of your first draft by asking yourself the following questions:

1. Does the title fit the discussion?
2. Is the material divided into distinct sections?
3. Are these sections arranged in logical order? (Is there an orderly sequence of thought from one section to the next, and from the beginning to the end?)

4. Is all the material relevant to the central purpose of the paper?

5. Is the topic of each paragraph clear-cut and adequately developed (see Section 32)?

6. Is every generalization supported by sufficient evidence—details, facts, illustration, examples, reasons? If you find an opinion or assertion that lacks support, supply that support—or discard the opinion entirely.

7. Is the beginning direct and pertinent?

8. Does the ending give an impression of finality and completeness, or does it trail off in a cloud of minor details?

Once you have answered these questions to your own satisfaction, you can proceed with your actual rewriting. Recast clumsy sentences, repair faulty phraseology, make the diction more exact and precise. Supply needed transitions and check existing transitions for accuracy. Scrutinize every mark of punctuation and look up all questionable spellings. Then recopy or retype the whole paper in the required format (see "Manuscript Form," Section 15).

31l Make final revisions.

If possible, set your manuscript aside for a day or two before making final revisions. Then you can go back to it with some of the objectivity of a reader. Make minor revisions—punctuation, spelling, word substitution—directly (but neatly) on the manuscript. If you find that more fundamental revisions—paragraph and sentence structure—are needed, you may have to recopy one or more pages. Usually the reaction of an unofficial reader—a roommate, a friend, a parent, even a well-disposed stranger—is helpful. Ask whether or not your paper communicates clearly. The revisions your reader suggests may be minor: a word here, a punctuation mark there. If he spots more fundamental flaws, you may have to rewrite the whole paper. One final proofreading—if possible, aloud to yourself—is good insurance against handing in an imperfect paper. Good writers are patient, with an infinite capacity for revision.

31l

Specimen papers 1 and 2: Critical Commentary

Both "Government Censorship of TV Violence" and "How Do You Want Your Violence?" are attempts to persuade the reader to the point of view of the writer. In both papers the sentence structure is competent, the spelling and punctuation correct, and the manuscript mechanics faultless. The second paper, however, succeeds in its main intention; the first one does not.

"Government Censorship of TV Violence" is not a good paper. The author's announcement of his subject in the title is all but forgotten in the process of the actual writing. The paper obviously was written without a preconceived plan, or even a tentative outline.

The first three sentences of the paper are concerned not with television violence, but with movie heroes of the 1930's, nor is any attempt made by the writer to connect this in any way with the stated subject of the paper. The concluding sentence of the first paragraph, instead of providing a transition to the next, is an unsupported generalization that marks a further digression from the topic.

The second paragraph, without any transition from the one preceding it, launches finally into the subject with which, according to the title, the paper was to be concerned. But again the author's digressive tendencies prevail. Instead of discussing violence on TV, or government censorship, the paragraph veers into a consideration of psychiatric studies of the effects of TV violence on young children.

Paragraph 3 begins with an attempt to provide a transition between the effects of mass media on children and their effects on adults. The second sentence, however, leaps to another subject, violence in the society, and is furthermore an unsupported generalization. Only with the third sentence of this paragraph is the idea of government interest in TV introduced—and even then there is no indication that that interest is taking any form other than that of investigation and study.

The fourth paragraph, instead of tying up all the many loose ends of the paper, brings in a few more of its own. The author has forgotten that the paper was supposed to have been about government censorship. Instead, he is now attempting to fix the blame for the violence, a subject which could be done justice to only in a paper of its own. Thus, although strong and provocative, the concluding paragraph does not fulfill its proper function here. When a paper ends, the reader wants to feel that a certain area has been covered thoroughly. In this paper, the end serves only to add to the haphazard selection of topics, and to the constant lack of connection among them.

"How Do You Want Your Violence?" is a much better paper. The title is well-chosen, and the topic is limited and reasonably developed within the length limitation of the assignment.

The opening paragraph clearly presents the position of the

311

writer and the argument he is going to develop. There are effective transitions between sentences and a link is provided to connect the first paragraph to the second.

The second paragraph is also unified and coherent. It is developed around a clear-cut topic sentence ("Violence serves as an integral part of the story. . . ."). The concluding sentence is short and emphatic.

The third paragraph moves smoothly ("By way of contrast") to a discussion of television violence. It provides information about the plot and characters of *Garrison's Gorillas* as well as the writer's opinion of the program.

The fourth paragraph continues the argument and shows how the program compares unfavorably to *Bonnie and Clyde*.

The final paragraph effectively summarizes the views of the writer and makes a concluding generalization based on the evidence presented in the paper.

EXERCISE: Specimen Papers 3 and 4   The assignment for Specimen Papers 3 and 4 was to write a brief narration-description. "Hunting Alone" is a narration which makes use of some descriptive detail; "Vagrants" is a description which includes narrative passages.

1 Allowing for the difference in main intention, which is the more successful paper?
2 To what extent is "Hunting Alone" arranged chronologically? Would the paper have been better organized if the writer had started with the second paragraph? Explain why or why not. Describe the organization of "Vagrants."
3 What is the dominant impression in "Vagrants"? How does the narrative contribute to it?
4 What "happens" in "Hunting Alone"? Are you satisfied with the ending? If not, what would you change or add?
5 Do you think the beginnings and endings of the two papers are effective? If so, why? If not, how would you improve them?
6 List some descriptive details that you think could be incorporated into "Hunting Alone."

EXERCISE: Specimen Paper 5   The assignment for Specimen Paper 5 was to write a brief explanation or analysis of the skills or qualities necessary for some task—that of being a teacher, a student, a parent, a pianist, a swimmer, or the like. The writer chose to explain the skills and qualities needed by a football quarterback.

How successful do you think the writer has been? Can you tell clearly from the paper what skills the quarterback must have? Is there a well-stated thesis sentence? Does the paragraph organization of the paper follow the pattern suggested by the thesis? Is the transition from the first to the second paragraph effective? From the second to the third? How does the author support his thesis? Are the beginning and ending of the paper effective? Explain.

311

Specimen Paper 1

GOVERNMENT CENSORSHIP OF TV VIOLENCE

In the 1930's, America acquired a new pantheon of heroes. Among them were James Cagney, Edward G. Robinson, and Humphrey Bogart. But the real heroes were the gangsters they portrayed, men beyond the reach of the law (except in the final scenes) and addicted to violence as a way of life. In a way, violence has always been a way of life in America.

There is an alarming amount of violence on TV. Most of us are too used to it to really notice it anymore, but it is there. Psychiatrists are increasingly concerned with the effect of TV violence on young children. Recent studies have shown that children tend, to a large extent, to adopt behavior patterns they have observed on the TV screen. It has been noted that children who are exposed to large doses of TV-watching exhibit more aggressive characteristics than children whose exposure to TV is more severely limited.

It is impossible to estimate how much effect the mass media have on adult behavior. But it is a well-known fact that crimes of violence are relatively far more frequent in the United States than in any other of the so-called civilized countries of the world. Several Senate subcommittees have already begun investigating the various causes of the continuing rise in violent crime in this country.

TV, with its constant access to the American home, is the greatest offender. The fault lies with the producers, with the networks, with the sponsors. But most of all it lies with the American public, which continues to watch it.

Specimen Paper 2

HOW DO YOU WANT YOUR VIOLENCE?

A recent review of current films is filled with complaints about the violence in motion pictures. The reviewer insists that this exploitation of brutality is "unnecessary," and that if it continues he will stop going to movies and instead stay home and watch television. It seems to me that to do so is to jump out of the frying pan into the fire. Night after night, TV offers violence in more variation, for longer periods of time, and for cheaper cost than any motion picture I have seen.

In regard to motion picture violence, the reviewer's most poisonous arrows are directed at <u>Bonnie and Clyde</u>. My own feeling is that this picture needs its particular amount of violence. Violence serves as an integral part of the story which the film tries to convey. The most disputed scene in <u>Bonnie and Clyde</u> --when the pair is ambushed and killed by lawmen who for some thirty seconds machine-gun their dead bodies--is the main scene in the film. The audience has become so involved with Bonnie and Clyde that for a time morality is upended and spectators feel like cheering whenever the two shoot their way out of police traps. Bonnie and Clyde have gotten almost everyone in the audience on their side, even believing in the immortality of the two killers, when the final ambush takes place. The bullets shatter the audience's dream-world with shocking reality. Justice triumphs, but few are glad--brutality has served its intended purpose of convincing the audience that Bonnie and Clyde got what was coming. It was the only means possible.

By way of contrast, let us look at TV violence, excessive style. A program, highly publicized, premiered this year with the title Garrison's Gorillas. It is an illegitimate offspring of the film, The Dirty Dozen. The plot is simple: an American officer, young and clean-cut, is picked to lead a gang of assorted brigands on commando missions behind German lines. The Gorillas are stereotyped in such a way as to increase the show's chances of attracting viewers of all tastes. There is a young, cool thug; an older, suave thug; a thug of all trades; and, for comic relief, the moronic, English thug. All in all they are the sorriest candidates for an audience's sympathy and interest ever created. The entire show seems to be filmed through a mental wad of gauze. Why this officer was picked for such a rotten job is never explained. Why the Gorillas agree to leave their nice, safe prisons--where they are serving terms for minor felonies--and risk their lives every week is never explained. Watching for five minutes convinces the viewer they do it for reasons other than patriotism.

In case these questions pop up in the mind of the viewer, they are quickly brushed aside by the excitement generated by the most wanton displays of carnage ever filmed. One expects a war story to show plenty of enemy deaths, but Gorillas does so to a disgusting degree. Unlike Bonnie and Clyde, there is little, if any, justification for the excess of killing. In the weekly climaxes anyone foolish enough to stroll onto the screen in a German outfit is promptly cut to pieces. The Gorillas, of course, remain unscathed. This How-We-Won-the-War tale goes on the screen at 7:30 p.m. every Tuesday.

Bonnie and Clyde and *Garrison's Gorillas* are of course
not typical of all motion pictures and television programs. But a
comparison of the two shows that motion pictures have no monopoly
on violence. Of course there is violence in motion picture films.
The question the viewer must answer is whether it serves a legitimate
purpose. So too with television. It seems to me that those who
enjoy watching nasty people doing nasty things can find such entertainment either at home or in the theatre. Those who look for good
entertainment, violent or nonviolent, must be not only selective
but also intelligent in their critical judgments.

Specimen Paper 3

HUNTING ALONE

The day was beautiful and full of sunshine as I started, rifle in hand, on one of the many exciting days of my life. This was to be my first deer-hunting trip alone. Before I had always gone with my father, who was never very trusting.

Living in a little town on the Olympic Peninsula, where hunting is a way of life, didn't mean that I could go deer hunting by myself. My father figured that I might trip and fall on the rifle, thus suffering one of the many hazards of hunting. This time I had to prove that I could handle a rifle and compass properly. I took a course given by the Game Department, which taught me the proper use of and basic rules for handling of firearms. It was very educational.

When the deer season opened and I asked my father about going alone, he said, to my surprise, "OK," adding, without a trace of a smile, "Just be sure to bring back a deer so we'll have steaks this winter." So here I was, jogging along the highway. The birds sounded more cheerful than I did.

After turning off an old logging road, I took a bearing with my compass. I listened as I walked, trying to get any sound or sight that a deer had been this way. Suddenly, I spotted a hoofprint in the mud beside the road. But on closer examination, I found it to be at least two days old.

Then I noticed a berry bush that had been stripped of its berries. Could it have been a bear? No, there are no bears here, I thought. Then I saw the tracks--two, three, four sets of deer tracks beyond the bush. Then, through the bushes I saw them in a clearing, a watchful doe, her timid offspring, and a magnificent buck. I stood frozen to the ground. They caught my scent and were gone in the flicking of an eye.

Specimen Paper 4

VAGRANTS

A small, dark shape drifted out of the thunderclouds piled erratic-ally over the city. Sinking down to the river the strange object rapidly gained speed and just above the metal-gray water exploded into a dozen pieces. The twelve birds gave off brittle cries as they made wide, food-seeking circles. Occasionally dipping heads and fluttering soaked wings, they kept on moving, around and around.

A few yards from them lay a silty beach, spreading its wet green around a few, elongated trees. From this beach struggled a crumbling brick wall which, in a loose way, held out of the river a railroad siding. A small, dark figure slipped out the door of one of the box-cars lined neatly along the track. Dropping to the roadbed, the figure began to trot clumsily along, and suddenly slipping, toppled down the pile of gravel, rolling down to the brick wall. The man gave off a low grunt, and dragged himself up onto the wall. He glanced around several times, his purple lips moving silently while he stretched and rubbed himself.

The birds had drifted closer to the beach, still searching, still crying out. The man suddenly noticed them and stared emptily at their actions. Soon one of the birds, pulling its quick head from the water, displayed a thick, pallid fish before gulping it down. The man blinked, swallowed a mouthful of spittle and began, in a slowly-rising growl, to curse. The birds answered with louder cries, and flew off, stitching the water's surface with the droplets falling from their feathers. The man's spittle ran from his pursed mouth, splashing on the slime of the beach.

Specimen Paper 5

THE QUARTERBACK

The quarterback must be an exceptional athlete. Not only must he be strong and speedy but he must also be an intelligent and inspiring leader.

The main task of a quarterback is to move the football down field for a score. First, he must "read" the defense of the opposing team, evaluate it, find a weakness in it, and then decide on the best offensive play. Usually he will mix up his plays in order to keep the defense off guard; he must not become predictable. On one set of downs he may call for two running plays and then a pass play; on another set he may pass three times in a row. And sometimes he calls a play that catches the opposition completely by surprise. Steve Grogan, for example, made a big gain for the New England Patriots in an important game when he fooled the opposition with a daring run around end with no blocking. He faked to fullback Sam Cunningham running to the right, had the whole line pulling right, and with no blockers in front of him he took off on the left side for a big gain. Whether or not he practiced this play is beside the point; the decision to use the play at a particular time was made in a few seconds. A quarterback who can make these quick decisions, sometimes in a split second, can inspire his teammates to play to their fullest potential.

Inspired, a team can sometimes move from what seems to be certain defeat to a dramatic victory. With less than a minute to play, the

Dallas Cowboys were losing to the Minnesota Vikings 14-10. The Vikings kicked off to the Cowboys. In spite of poor field position, an inspired Dallas team, led by quarterback Roger Staubach, played perfect football. Every man did exactly what he was expected to do; every man executed flawlessly. In five plays the Cowboys moved from one end of the field to the other for a winning touchdown.

Football is a game played by very strong men and very fast men. Some are paid to be strong and some to be fast. But these physical attributes are not enough to win games unless there is an intelligent leader to bring out the best in every man. This leader is the quarterback.

32   Effective Paragraphs ¶

A good paragraph has (1) unity, (2) coherence, and (3) adequate development.

UNITY requires that the paragraph have a single, clear controlling idea, and that all the details introduced into the paragraph contribute to that controlling idea. The controlling or central idea will usually be stated in a single sentence of the paragraph, called the TOPIC SENTENCE; this sentence often, though not always, is the first sentence of the paragraph. COHERENCE requires that all the sentences in a paragraph be connected in an orderly, clear way so that the reader can easily see how each sentence follows from the previous one, and how all relate to the controlling idea. ADEQUATE DEVELOPMENT requires that there be enough details, facts, examples, evidence, or reasons included in the paragraph to make the controlling idea clear and meaningful to the reader.

For convenience, we discuss these three elements of a good paragraph separately, but all three are interrelated. A coherent paragraph is also unified and adequately developed. In other words, to support a topic sentence clearly and persuasively, you must develop a paragraph adequately and connect its sentences in an orderly way. Making a good paragraph calls for all three skills; no one is sufficient in itself.

Unity in the Paragraph ¶ UN

A unified paragraph is one that has a single, clear purpose, and one in which all sentences clearly relate to that purpose.

32a   Be sure that the central idea is stated in a single sentence.

Most paragraphs have a TOPIC SENTENCE—a sentence that sums up the central idea of the paragraph. Topic sentences in paragraphs serve the same purpose as thesis sentences in papers. They insure that you have defined, both for yourself and your reader, the controlling idea of the paragraph. And by so doing, they serve as a guide to you in developing that idea.

The following paragraphs illustrate various ways of placing the topic sentence.

32a

1. The topic sentence may be the first sentence of the paragraph.
Such paragraphs state their central idea first and then add details supporting it. This kind of paragraph is the most common in expository writing, but it also occurs in persuasive and descriptive writing as well.

> *The tea-plant, a native of Southern China, was known from very early times to Chinese botany and medicine.* It is alluded to in the classics under the various names of Tou, Tseh, Chung, Kha, and Ming, and was highly prized for possessing the virtues of relieving fatigue, delighting the soul, strengthening the will, and repairing the eyesight. It was not only administered as an internal dose, but often applied externally in the form of paste to alleviate rheumatic pains. The Taoists claimed it as an important ingredient of the elixir of immortality. The Buddhists used it extensively to prevent drowsiness during their long hours of meditation.
>
> OKAKURA KAKUZO, *The Book of Tea*

Note that the initial sentence may combine a transition from the preceding paragraph with the statement of the new paragraph, as in the following example.

> Although it lay in the shadow of the Arctic Circle, more than four thousand miles from civilization, and although it was the only settlement of any size in a wilderness area that occupied hundreds of thousands of square miles, *Dawson was livelier, richer, and better equipped than many larger Canadian and American communities.* It had a telephone service, running water, steam heat, and electricity. It had dozens of hotels, many of them better appointed than those on the Pacific Coast. It had motion-picture theaters operating at a time when the projected motion picture was just three years old. It had restaurants where string orchestras played *Cavalleria Rusticana* for men in tailcoats who ate pâté de fois gras and drank vintage wines. It had fashions from Paris. It had dramatic societies, church choirs, glee clubs, and vaudeville companies. It had three hospitals, seventy physicians, and uncounted platoons of lawyers. Above all, it had people.
>
> PIERRE BERTON, *The Klondike Fever*

2. The topic sentence may be the last sentence of the paragraph.
Such paragraphs give details first and lead up to the main point in the final sentence.

> The true problem of city planning and rebuilding in a free society is how to cultivate more city districts that are free, lively and fertile places for the differing plans of thousands of individuals—not planners. Nothing could be farther from the aims of planners today. They have been trained to think of people as interchangeable statistics to be pushed around, to think of city vitality and mixture

as a mess. Planners are the enemies of cities because they offer us only the poisonous promise of making every place in a city more like dull and standardized Morningside Heights. They have failed to pursue the main point: to study the success and failure of the real life of the cities. With their eyes on simple-minded panaceas, they destroy success and health. *Planners will become helpful only when they abandon what they have learned about what "ought" to be good for cities.*   JANE JACOBS, "How City Planners Hurt Cities"

32a

Not until 1894 did Japan feel strong enough for a real test of arms. In that year she precipitated a war with China over control of Korea. The Japanese easily seized Korea, destroyed the Chinese naval forces, overran Southern Manchuria, and even captured the port of Wei-hai-wei in China proper. The war ended in 1895. In the peace treaty China agreed to pay a large indemnity to Japan, recognized the full independence of Korea, and ceded to Japan the rich island of Formosa, the strategically placed Pescadores Islands between Formosa and the coast of China, and the Liaotung Peninsula at the southern tip of Manchuria. *Japan had demonstrated that she had indeed become a modern military power, and had made a successful start in building an empire.*

EDWIN O. REISCHAUER, *Japan Past and Present*

3. The topic sentence may appear first and last. In such paragraphs the last sentence repeats the idea of the first, frequently restating it with some amplification or a slight difference in emphasis in the light of the intervening details or discussion.

Another principle underlying communicative writing is that clarity is a prerequisite to validity. It is to be considered that statements that flow beautifully and are grammatically superb may be, also, utterly devoid of factual meaning, or meaningful but vague, or precise but invalid. For writing to be effective, in the sense in which I am using this term, it may or may not be grammatically correct, but it must be both clear and valid. It can be clear without having validity, but if it is unclear its validity cannot well be determined. It must, then, first of all, be clear; it must be that before the question of its validity can even be raised. We ask the writer, "What do you mean?" before we ask, "How do you know?" *Until we reach agreement as to precisely what he is writing about, we cannot possibly reach agreement as to whether, or in what degree, his statements are true.*   WENDELL JOHNSON, "You Can't Write Writing"

The second meaning of thinking limits it to things not sensed or directly perceived, to things not seen, heard, touched, smelt, or tasted. We ask the man telling a story if he saw a certain incident happen, and his reply may be, "No, I only thought of it." A note of invention, as distinct from faithful record of observation, is present. Most important in this class are successions of imaginative incidents and episodes that have a certain coherence, hang together on

32a

a continuous thread, and thus lie between kaleidoscopic flights of fancy and considerations deliberately employed to establish a conclusion. The imaginative stories poured forth by children possess all degrees of internal congruity; some are disjointed, some are articulated. When connected, they simulate reflective thought: indeed, they usually occur in minds of logical capacity. These imaginative enterprises often precede thinking of the close-knit type and prepare the way for it. *In this sense, a thought or idea is a mental picture of something not actually present, and thinking is the succession of such pictures.*   JOHN DEWEY, *How We Think*

4. The topic sentence may be implied. Narrative and descriptive paragraphs sometimes do not state a topic sentence directly; instead, the topic may be implicit in the details given. The implied topic of the paragraph below, for example, is *a description of the Grand Ball at Bath, England, in the late eighteenth century.*

The hour is just on nine. At six, with the playing of a minuet, the dancing had started; now there is the usual pause for the gentlemen to hand tea to the ladies, and for the musicians to wet their tired throats. Tonight being something of an occasion there will be supper as well, and behind screens footmen are busily laying a long table with cold ham and pheasant, biscuits, sweetmeats, jellies and wine. And now the Master of Ceremonies in plum satin and paste buckles offers his arm to the ranking lady present, Her Grace the Duchess of Marlborough, and together they swing across the room. Behind them rustle the others, her Grace's inferiors. Countesses and ladyships, wealthy tradesmen's wives and daughters, the mothers and mistresses of bone-setters and shipbuilders and swindling gamesters, all come to Bath to taste the salubrious "Spaw" waters at the Pump Room, to take the cure, to ogle their partners at balls at the Assembly Rooms—and best of all, to be stared at themselves in return.   ALICE GLASGOW, *Sheridan of Drury Lane*

EXERCISE 32a What is the topic sentence, expressed or implied, in each of the following paragraphs?

1 One aspect of participatory democracy is the idea of parallel structures. The F[reedom] D[emocratic] P[arty] is a parallel political party, prompted by the conclusion that registration of Negroes in the regular Democratic Party of Mississippi is presently impossible. Freedom Schools were parallel schools, although delegates to the Freedom School Convention decided they would return to the public schools and seek to transform them rather than continue into the winter a parallel school system. In the North, neighborhood unions organized by SDS represent parallel antipoverty agencies, challenging the legitimacy of the top-down middle-class "community organizations" sponsored by urban renewal and anti-poverty administrators.   STAUGHTON LYND,
"The New Radical and 'Participatory Democracy'"

2 The discomfort a woman feels each time she tells her age is quite independent of the anxious awareness of human mortality that everyone has, from time to time. There is a normal sense in which nobody, men and women alike, relishes growing older. After thirty-five any mention of one's age carries with it the reminder that one is probably closer to the end of one's life than to the beginning. There is nothing unreasonable in that anxiety. Nor is there any abnormality in the anguish and anger that people who are really old, in their seventies and eighties, feel about the implacable waning of their powers, physical and mental. Advanced age is undeniably a trial, however stoically it may be endured. It is a shipwreck, no matter with what courage elderly people insist on continuing the voyage. But the objective, sacred pain of old age is of another order than the subjective, profane pain of aging. Old age is a genuine ordeal, one that men and women undergo in a similar way. Growing older is mainly an ordeal of the imagination—a moral disease, a social pathology—intrinsic to which is the fact that it afflicts women much more than men. It is particularly women who experience growing older (everything that comes *before* one is actually old) with such distaste and even shame.

SUSAN SONTAG, "The Double Standard of Aging"

3 The bright and serious students in this group are the ones who demand the most from the university. They get good grades, although they often feel cynical about the system. Many of them are genuinely more concerned with putting knowledge of the past to work in the present than regurgitating it on a final. In a sense they are always putting administrators on the spot, because they believe that the educational process should provide a continuum between ideas and social and political action. For instance, when these students sit in for Negro rights in San Francisco or go off to register Negro voters in Mississippi, they are convinced that they are only carrying out a literal application of the democratic ideals they are supposed to memorize in the classroom. Such behavior unnerves the administration, which has to soothe the ruffled feelings of taxpayers and their representatives who grow anxious about the threats their sons and daughters are posing to the Established order.

MICHAEL VINCENT MILLER, "The Student State of Mind"

4 The poor who came to America—the majority of the settlers—had fewer illusions to shed than had the gentry. They took a rationally pessimistic view of the world and did not expect to get anything for nothing. Whether they were solvent enough to pay their way (the mere cost of transportation was relatively very high indeed in those days), or sold themselves as indentured servants to earn, by seven years' serfdom, the passage to America, or were transported, free, by a vigilant government for offenses ranging from taking the wrong side in a rebellion to plain and fancy felonies, the move to America was important and final. They did not expect to go back; if they were religious or political refugees they did not want to. And the new world into which they came had to be made habitable by them.

D. W. BROGAN, *The American Character*

32b   Be sure that every sentence in a paragraph bears on the central subject.

Not only must you have a clear purpose in writing a paragraph, you must also hold to that purpose throughout the paragraph. The writer of the following paragraph, for example, changes his purpose three times in the first three sentences; and he tacks on the last sentence as a kind of afterthought:

> Henry James's extensive travel during his early years greatly influenced his later writings. Born in New York in 1843, Henry was destined to become one of the first novelists of the world. He received a remarkable education. His parents took him abroad for a year when he was only an infant. He was educated by tutors until he was twelve, and then taken abroad for three more years by his parents. His father wanted him to absorb French and German culture. His older brother, William, received the same education.

One way of revising this paragraph would be to restrict its subject matter to the one major topic of James's childhood.

> Henry James, the novelist, had an unusual childhood. In 1844, while still an infant, he was taken abroad by his parents for a year. Upon his return, he and his older brother, William, were given private tutoring until Henry was twelve. At that time both boys were taken abroad to spend three years absorbing French and German culture.

Be careful not to violate the principle of unity by introducing new topics or points of view at the end of a paragraph. Notice in the following example how the last sentence, in which the writer deserts his earlier objectivity and takes sides in the argument, breaks the unity.

> In the years following World War II there was much discussion on the question of lowering the minimum voting age to eighteen. Among those people who believed that the age limit should be lowered, the favorite statement was "If a boy is old enough to die for his country, he's old enough to vote in it." Those people who wanted the age limit to remain at twenty-one thought eighteen-year-olds would be unduly influenced by local wardheelers who would urge them to vote a "straight ticket." But the young voter who had not had a chance to become a "dyed-in-the-wool" party member tended to weigh the merits of the individual candidate rather than those of the party itself.

Revised, the paragraph might read:

> In the years following World War II there was much discussion on the question of lowering the minimum voting age to eighteen. Among those people who believed that the age limit should be lowered, the favorite statement was, "If a boy is old enough to die for his country, he's old enough to vote in it." Those people who wanted the age limit to remain at twenty-one thought eighteen-year-olds would be unduly influenced by the promises of dishonest politicians.

32b

EXERCISE 32b(1) Each of the following paragraphs opens with a topic sentence, but each violates unity by introducing information not related to the topic. Which sentences in each paragraph are not related to the topic of the paragraph? Could any of the sentences you identify as not related to the topic actually contribute to the topic if their position in the paragraph were changed? For example, in paragraph 4, sentence 6 clearly seems tagged on as a final sentence. But would it seem unrelated if it followed the first sentence?

1 (1) Racial discrimination has existed in the United States for many years. (2) It began when the first white settler decided that the Indians were an inferior breed. (3) It was given impetus by the arrival of the first Negro slaves. (4) A civil war was fought largely because the spokesman of the North, Abraham Lincoln, believed that all men are created equal. (5) Slavery was abolished and the Negro set free by act of Congress.

2 (1) The life of Thomas A. Edison illustrates the truth of the old saying "Genius is ten percent inspiration and ninety percent perspiration." (2) Edison was born in Milan, Ohio, and was expelled from school because his teachers thought he was a moron. (3) So Edison was educated at home by his mother, who helped him build a laboratory in the basement. (4) Edison spent long hours here, sometimes working as long as sixteen hours a day.

3 (1) Hardy's *The Return of the Native* is one of the finest novels I have ever read. (2) I was amazed to see how Hardy makes his major and minor episodes culminate in a great climax, and how inextricably he weaves the fortunes of his chief characters with those of his lesser characters. (3) Moreover, his handling of the landscape—gloomy Egdon Heath—is masterful. (4) He makes it a genuine, motivating force in the story. (5) My favorite character, however, was Diggory Venn.

4 (1) Many people who use the word *fascism* in discussing current world problems confuse it with *communism*. (2) Both fascism and communism are totalitarian, but fascism is the economic antithesis of communism. (3) Fascism uses military force to sustain capitalism; communism uses force to suppress capitalism. (4) Obviously, no two systems of government could be more different. (5) But there has never been a clear explanation of the two systems. (6) The popular information media—newspapers, radio, and television—refer indiscriminately at times to communism and fascism in the same terms.

5 (1) The advantages of modern transportation are many. (2) An enormous amount of time is saved by the great speeds at which vehicles of today travel. (3) Cross-country trips are much more comfortable than they were, and they can be made in days rather than months. (4) For land travel today the automobile, motorcycle, and bus have taken the place of the horse and wagon, stage coach, and mule. (5) The railroad has been developed and extended since the use of the diesel. (6) Sailing ships are now chiefly a hobby and few consider them seriously as a means of transportation.

32b

6 (1) If you intend to plant a strawberry bed, there are several things that you should consider. (2) Strawberries do best in a sandy loam or sandy clay that has been enriched with humus. (3) Blueberries and blackberries are better in acid soils. (4) Strawberries should be set out in an area that receives adequate drainage. (5) Too much moisture in the soil will kill them or interfere with their growth. (6) Other kinds of plants do better in marshy soils. (7) On account of frost dangers it is better to plant strawberries on a hillside or on a relatively high level area. (8) The effects of frost are rather peculiar; in general, plants in low-lying areas are more likely to be harmed by frost than those on hills. (9) The growth of young strawberries is actually increased if one pinches off the runners from the plants.

EXERCISE 32b(2) Following are three topic sentences, each accompanied by a set of statements. Some of the statements are relevant to the topic, some are not. Eliminate the irrelevant ones, and organize the rest into a paragraph.

1 Given my choice I would sooner be in the Air Force than any other service branch.
   1. I am more interested in flying than in any other military occupation.
   2. Opportunities for advancement are greater in the Air Force.
   3. Wages in certain brackets of the Air Force are higher than in other branches.
   4. There are many opportunities to travel.
   5. The Navy gives one travel opportunities too.
   6. My cousin has been in the Navy for two years, and has sailed around the whole world.
   7. I think, though, that I still like the Air Force better.

2 The wreck on Route 64 at Mt. Nixon was caused entirely by careless and reckless driving by the driver of the Buick.
   1. When the wreck occurred the lights were green for the cars coming off the side road.
   2. A heavy truck loaded with hay was pulling out to cross the highway.
   3. The Buick came speeding down the main road, went through the stoplight, and crashed into the truck.
   4. You could hear the screeching of the tires and then the crashing and grinding of metal a quarter of a mile away.
   5. You could hear it in our house up the road.
   6. Both drivers were killed, and I will never forget how awful the accident was.

3 We owe some of our notions of radar to scientific observation of bats.

1. Most people hate bats.
2. Bats are commonly considered unattractive, ugly creatures.
3. They really look more like mice with wings than anything else.
4. Scientists noticed that bats rarely collided with anything in their erratic flight.
5. Keen eyesight could not be the reason for their flying the way they do, since bats are blind.
6. It was found that bats keep sending out noises inaudible to people and that they hear the echoes of those noises.
7. This principle whereby they fly safely was found to be similar to the main principle of radar.

32c

Coherence in the Paragraph ¶ COH

A paragraph may be unified without being coherent. Unity depends upon selecting details and ideas relevant to the paragraph topic. Coherence depends upon organizing these details and ideas so that the reader can easily see how they are relevant. Even though all the sentences of a paragraph bear upon a single point, unless they are knit together and flow into one another so that their relation to that single point is clear, they will not be coherent. A coherent paragraph leads the reader easily from sentence to sentence. An incoherent paragraph confronts him with puzzling jumps in thought, events out of sequence, facts illogically arranged, or points in a discussion omitted. Coherence requires that sentences be logically arranged and clearly connected.

32c Arrange the sentences in a clear order.

To insure coherence in a paragraph, arrange all sentences within the paragraph in some pattern that will make for an orderly, natural flow of ideas. The arrangement we choose for a particular paragraph will depend on our materials and our purpose in that paragraph. The common ways of ordering sentences are (1) time order, (2) space order, (3) order of climax, and (4) general to particular or particular to general.

   1. Time order. Narrative paragraphs naturally arrange themselves in the order in which the events occur. The following simple paragraph recounts the death of a female eagle as observed by the author.

On her own, one of the female's bold hunting trips was to prove fatal. The male saw from high above that she was making an attack on a ground squirrel in a dry arroyo. Her path would take her over an embankment at low altitude. Hidden from her view were two hunters walking close to the bluff. The male tensed as he saw his mate approach the men. As her black form swept over the hunters, they whirled and raised their guns. The female saw, but too late. As she banked sharply, two shots sang out and one slug tore through her body, sending her crashing in a crumpled mass. Helpless and distraught, the male watched from above as the hunters stretched out the wings of his mate and examined their prize. With the fear of man reinforced in his mind, he turned away and mounted up to return to the safety of the back country.

KENT DURDEN, *Flight to Freedom*

32c

Specific directions and explanations of processes also arrange themselves naturally in time order. The following directions for mixing powdered clay proceed step by step through the process.

Clay purchased in powder form is mixed with water to make it a plastic mass. To mix, fill a large dishpan or small tub about one-third full of water, sift clay over [the] water, one handful at a time, until [the] clay settles on top of the water to make a coating about 1 inch thick. Cover [the] pan with paper or cloth and let the unstirred mixture set overnight. On the following day mix and stir it thoroughly. If [the] mass is too thick to knead, add more water. If too thin, add dry clay. Clay is in a state to store when it is soft and pliable but does not stick to the hands. Since clay improves with aging in a damp condition, mix as far ahead of time of use as you can. Wrap [the] clay in damp cloth and store in a covered crock for at least one week before using.

HERBERT H. SANDERS,
"How to Make Pottery and Ceramic Sculpture"

2. Space order. Many descriptive paragraphs arrange themselves easily according to some spatial order, from east to west, from bottom to top, from near to far, from the center outward, and the like. In the following paragraph, the author is standing at a high point overlooking a valley. The description moves first to the right, then to the left, then straight ahead (*before me*), and then farther and farther into the distance ahead (*beyond that,* and still *beyond that*).

On my right a woods thickly overgrown with creeper descended the hill's slope to Tinker Creek. *On my left* was a planting of large shade trees on the ridge of the hill. *Before me* the grassy hill pitched abruptly and gave way to a large, level field fringed in trees where it bordered the creek. *Beyond the creek* I could see with effort the vertical sliced rock where men had long ago quarried the mountain under the forest. *Beyond that* I saw Hollins Pond and all its woods and pastures; then I saw in a blue haze all the world poured flat and pale between the mountains.

ANNIE DILLARD, "Pilgrim at Tinker Creek"

3. Order of climax. Many paragraphs can be made coherent as well as more effective by arranging details or examples in order of increasing importance. The following paragraph moves from the kinds of a composition in which the subject, skill in expressing yourself, is least important to those kinds in which it is most important.

> If you work as a soda jerker you will, of course, not need much skill in expressing yourself to be effective. If you work on a machine your ability to express yourself will be of little importance. But as soon as you move one step up from the bottom, your effectiveness depends on your ability to reach others through the spoken or the written word. And the further away your job is from manual work, the larger the organization of which you are an employee, the more important it will be that you know how to convey your thoughts in writing or speaking. In the very large business organization, whether it is the government, the large corporation, or the Army, this ability to express oneself is perhaps the most important of all the skills a man can possess.
>
> PETER F. DRUCKER, "How to Be an Employee"

32c

4. General to particular or particular to general order. A great many paragraphs begin with a topic sentence that makes a general statement. Sentences that follow support that statement with details, examples, evidence, and the like. Other paragraphs reverse this order, presenting first a series of details or reasons and concluding with a general statement which summarizes.

In the following paragraph the author begins with a general statement—that readers generally get lost through a writer's carelessness, which can take "any number of forms." The five successive sentences beginning with "perhaps" list five different forms that carelessness can take.

> If a reader is lost, it is generally because the writer has not been careful enough to keep him on the path. This carelessness can take any number of forms. Perhaps a sentence is so excessively cluttered that the reader, hacking his way through the verbiage, simply doesn't know what it means. Perhaps a sentence has been so shoddily constructed that the reader could read it in any of several ways. Perhaps the writer has switched pronouns in mid-sentence, or has switched tenses, so the reader loses track of who is talking or when the action took place. Perhaps Sentence B is not a logical sequel to Sentence A—the writer, in whose head the connection is clear, has not bothered to provide the missing link. Perhaps the writer has used an important word incorrectly by not taking the trouble to look it up. He may think that "sanguine" and "sanguinary" mean the same thing, but the difference is a bloody big one. The reader can only infer (speaking of big differences) what the writer is trying to imply. WILLIAM ZINSSER, "On Writing Well"

EXERCISE 32c(1) Write a coherent paragraph that incorporates, in your own words, all the following information about Thomas Hardy.

1 He was an English novelist, short story writer, and poet.
2 He died in 1928, at the age of eighty-eight.
3 He is considered one of the most important of the writers who revolted against Victorian tradition at the end of the nineteenth century.
4 He is known for the pessimism of his ideas.
5 His most important prose works are novels of character and environment.
6 *The Return of the Native, Tess of the D'Urbervilles,* and *Jude the Obscure* are among his most important novels.
7 His best novels are studies of life in the bleak English countryside.
8 In his best novels individuals are defeated in their struggle against their physical and social environment.
9 Individuals in his best novels also struggle against the caprices of chance.

32c

EXERCISE 32c(2) We can see how the order of sentences in a paragraph contributes to its coherence if we examine a paragraph in which the original order has been changed. The following paragraphs were coherent as they were originally written, but their order has been changed. Rearrange each group of sentences to make a coherent paragraph.

1 (1) Landing a space capsule on Mars is technically complicated. (2) In 1971 one Soviet lander crashed and another stopped sending signals back after 20 seconds. (3) One of the Soviet 1974 attempts just flew past Mars. (4) Descending through Martian atmosphere is much trickier than landing on the airless moon. (5) The Soviets tried to land on Mars four times, twice in 1971 and twice in 1974. (6) Instruments on the second 1974 flight failed during descent, after transmitting usable signals for a few seconds.

2 (1) Language is full of symbols, but we also use signs or images that are not strictly descriptive. (2) Such things are not symbols. (3) We use spoken and written language to express the meaning we want to convey. (4) Although meaningless in themselves, signs have acquired a recognizable meaning through common usage or deliberate intention. (5) Some of these signs are mere abbreviations or strings of initials such as UN or UNESCO. (6) They are signs and do no more than denote the object to which they are attached. (7) Other signs are things such as familiar trademarks, badges, flags, and traffic lights.

3 (1) Juvenile delinquency is a major problem in this country. (2) This problem became more serious after World War II. (3) The war itself is one of the causes. (4) Parents of youngsters born during these years either avoided their responsibility or were unable to maintain it. (5) Everywhere we read about the vicious crimes committed by young people. (6) During the war the newspapers and the movies depicted violence, cruelty, and bloodletting as heroic rather than vicious. (7) The war inspired brutality by distorting and twisting

humane values. (8) It is no wonder that the younger generation has made a problem of itself. (9) During the war many of them had fathers who were in the service; their mothers were working in war plants. (10) Consequently, they were unhappy and undisciplined. (11) Many of them are now organized in gangs and proud of their devotion to a life of crime.

32d   Make clear the relationships among sentences.

Coherence requires not only that the sentences within a paragraph be related to each other, but also that their relationship be made clear. You can achieve clear relationships among sentences by: (1) being consistent in point of view, (2) using parallel grammatical structure, (3) repeating words or ideas, and (4) using transitional words or phrases.

32d

1. Maintain a consistent point of view. Avoid unnecessary shifts in person, tense, or number within a paragraph.

Unnecessary Shift in Person

A pleasant and quiet place to live is essential for a serious-minded college student. If possible, you should rent a room from a landlady with a reputation for keeping order and discipline among her renters. Moreover, a student ought to pick a roommate with the same temperament as his own. Then you can agree to and keep a schedule of study hours.

Unnecessary Shift in Tense

Last summer I finally saw the movie *Around the World in 80 Days,* based on the novel by Jules Verne. I particularly enjoyed the main character, who is played by David Niven. He gives an excellent performance and really seemed intent on winning the wager he has made with his friends. His personal servant was played by the Mexican actor Cantinflas, who is very able in his part, too.

Unnecessary Shift in Number

Of great currency at the moment is the notion that education should prepare students for "life." A college graduate no longer goes out into the world as a cultivated gentleman. Instead students feel obliged to prepare themselves for places in the business world. Consequently, we are establishing courses on how to get and keep a mate, how to budget an income, and how to win friends and influence people—that is, how to sell yourself and your product. The study of things not obviously practical to a businessman is coming to be looked upon as unnecessary.

2. Use parallel grammatical structure. Using parallel grammatical structure in successive sentences is one of the most important ways of connecting them. Just as parallel grammatical form in coordinate parts of a single sentence emphasizes the coordinate relation of the ideas, so parallel structure from sentence to sentence within a paragraph emphasizes the relation of these sentences to the single idea of the paragraph. Note the following examples:

> We Americans have a strange—and to me disturbing—attitude toward the subject of power. <u>We don't like</u> the word. <u>We don't like</u> the concept. <u>We are suspicious</u> of people who talk about it. <u>We like to feel that</u> the adjustment of conflicting interests is something that can be taken care of by juridical norms and institutional devices, voluntarily accepted and not involving violence to the feelings or interests of anyone. <u>We like to feel that</u> this is the way our own life is arranged. <u>We like to feel that</u> if this principle were to be understood and observed by others as it is by us, it would put an end to many of the misunderstandings and conflicts that have marked our time.
>
> GEORGE F. KENNAN, "Training for Statesmanship"

> What crucial elements in the American experience gave it this quality [of dynamism]? <u>There was the fact of a fresh start</u>, with rich resources, by men who carried with them a passion for freedom and an aversion to authoritarianism. <u>There was the vast expanse of a continent</u>, lending a largeness of outlook to those who lived on it. <u>There was the richness of racial and ethnic mixture</u> which is part of a larger pluralism in American life—a pluralism not only of stock but of regional environments, of Federal political units, of economic forms, and of religious sects. <u>There was a system of opportunity</u> that gave scope to the energies of its young people and managed tolerably to give work its opportunity, aspiration its outlet, talent its stimulus, and ability its reward. <u>There was an optimistic view of American prospects</u> and a tough concreteness of outlook that judged ideas and values by their results. <u>There was, finally, the idea of equality</u> which, in spite of economic obstructions, educational discriminations, and the distorting hatreds of racism, was kept alive as the ruling passion of American life.
>
> MAX LERNER, *America as a Civilization*

3. Repeat key words and phrases. Many well-constructed paragraphs depend heavily upon the repetition of key words and phrases, often with slight modification, to emphasize major ideas and carry the thought from sentence to sentence. Pronouns referring back to clearly established antecedents in the previous sentence function in the same way. In the following paragraphs the words and phrases that are repeated to provide clear links from sentence to sentence and produce a closely integrated whole are underlined.

In discussing the pre-Civil War South, it <u>should be remembered</u> that the large plantation owners constituted only a small part of the total Southern population. By far the greater part of that population was made up of small farmers, and of course the Negro slaves themselves. Some small farmers had acquired substantial acreage, owned three or four slaves, and were relatively prosperous. But most of the small farmers were terribly poor. They rented their land and worked it themselves, sometimes side by side with the slaves of the great landowners. In everything but social position they were worse off than the Negro slaves. But it must also be remembered that they were as jealous of that superior social position as the wealthy landowner himself.   Student paragraph

Nobody has succeeded in explaining the connection between the private sources and the public functions of art. But art does have its public functions, though we often lose sight of them. In primitive agricultural societies, and even in Western Europe until the Renaissance, the functions were more clearly defined. It was the duty of the artist to celebrate the community in its present oneness, in its divine past, and in its glorious future. Thus he invented dances and rituals for the group, he retold the stories of its gods and heroes, he fashioned their images, and he persuaded the "people"—his own tribe that is, the only genuine persons—that they were reenacting the lives of the gods, who would some day return and reinstitute the golden age. Thus the artist played a recognized part in the daily life of the people.

MALCOLM COWLEY, "Artists, Conscience, and Censors"

Nonconformity is not only a desirable thing, it is an actual thing. One need only remark that all art is based upon nonconformity—a point that I shall undertake to establish—and that every great historic change has been based upon nonconformity, has been bought either with the blood or with the reputation of nonconformists. Without nonconformity we would have had no Bill of Rights nor Magna Carta, no public education system, no nation upon this continent, no science at all, no philosophy, and considerably fewer religions. All that is pretty obvious.

But it seems to be less obvious that to create anything at all in any field, and especially anything of outstanding worth, requires nonconformity, or a want of satisfaction with things as they are. The creative person—the nonconformist—may be in profound disagreement with the present way of things, or he may simply wish to add his views, to render a personal account of matters.

BEN SHAHN, *The Shape of Content*

4. Use transitional markers. A transitional marker is a word or a phrase placed at or near the beginning of a sentence to indicate its relation to the preceding sentence. The coordinating conjunctions *and, but, or, nor, so,* and *yet* are often used this way, particularly in informal writing, for they provide easy bridges from one sentence to another. But English provides a wide variety of transitional markers, as suggested in the lists below. Good modern writing uses the more formal markers

32d

sparingly, and we should be wary of cluttering our writing with unnecessary *however*'s, *moreover*'s, and *consequently*'s. But we should be equally careful to know them and to use them when they make for clarity.

Here is a list of many of the common transitional words and phrases:

To Indicate Addition

again, also, and, and then, besides, equally important, finally, first, further, furthermore, in addition, last, likewise, moreover, next, second, third, too

To Indicate Cause and Effect

accordingly, as a result, consequently, hence, in short, otherwise, then, therefore, thus, truly

32d

To Indicate Comparison

in a like manner, likewise, similarly

To Indicate Concession

after all, although this may be true, at the same time, even though, I admit, naturally, of course

To Indicate Contrast

after all, although true, and yet, at the same time, but, for all that, however, in contrast, in spite of, nevertheless, notwithstanding, on the contrary, on the other hand, still, yet

To Indicate Special Features or Examples

for example, for instance, incidentally, indeed, in fact, in other words, in particular, specifically, that is, to illustrate

To Indicate Summary

in brief, in conclusion, in short, on the whole, to conclude, to summarize, to sum up

To Indicate Time Relations

after a short time, afterwards, as long as, as soon as, at last, at length, at that time, at the same time, before, earlier, immediately, in the meantime, lately, later, meanwhile, of late, presently, shortly, since, soon, temporarily, thereafter, thereupon, until, when, while

Transitional words and phrases are underlined in the following:

As I have remarked, the pilots' association was now the compactest monopoly in the world, perhaps, and seemed simply indestructible. And yet the days of its glory were numbered. First, the new railroad stretching up through Mississippi, Tennessee, and Kentucky, to Northern railway-centers, began to divert the passenger travel from the steamboats; next the war came and almost entirely annihilated the steamboating industry during several years, leaving most of the pilots idle and the cost of living advancing all the time; then the treasurer of the St. Louis association put his hand into the till and walked off with every dollar of the ample fund; and finally, the railroads intruding everywhere, there was little for steamers to do, when the war was over, but carry freights; so straightway some genius from the Atlantic coast introduced the plan of towing a dozen steamer cargoes down to New Orleans at the tail of a vulgar little tugboat; and behold, in the twinkling of an eye, as it were, the association and the noble science of piloting were things of the dead and pathetic past!   MARK TWAIN, *Life on the Mississippi*

Sometimes a question may be made still more clear or precise by an indication of the circumstances in which it occurs. Let us take an example. I ask, "How wide is this bookcase?" This certainly appears to be a straightforward question that could be answered simply enough by specifying the number of inches across its front. But when one undertakes to find the answer, several perplexing considerations may arise. What dimension is wanted: the length of the shelf? the outside dimension? at the widest point? or at some other typical point? Again, how accurate a measure is wanted?—for no measurement is entirely accurate; all we can expect is greater or less accuracy. All these questions could be more or less cleared up by indicating the circumstances under which the problem arose. It might be, for example, that I contemplate placing the bookcase against a certain wall and desire to know whether or not it is too wide to fit into the position under consideration. At once I realize that the widest outside dimension is the one required, and that a relatively high degree of accuracy is necessary only if the width of the wall and that of the bookcase are found to be nearly the same.

HENRY S. LEONARD, *Principles of Right Reason*

Charles, however, had one advantage, which, if he had used it well, would have more than compensated for the want of stores and money, and which, notwithstanding his mismanagement, gave him, during some months, a superiority in the war. His troops at first fought much better than those of the Parliament. Both armies, it is true, were almost entirely composed of men who had never seen a field of battle. Nevertheless, the difference was great. The parliamentary ranks were filled with hirelings whom want and idleness had induced to enlist. Hampden's regiment was regarded as one of the best; and even Hampden's regiment was described by Cromwell as a mere rabble of tapsters and serving-men out of place. The royal army, on the other hand, consisted in great part of gentlemen, high-spirited, ardent, accustomed to consider dishonor as more terrible than death, accustomed to fencing, to the use of firearms, to bold riding, and to manly and perilous sport, which has been well called the image of war. Such gentlemen, mounted on their favorite horses, and commanding little bands composed of their younger brothers, grooms, gamekeepers, and huntsmen, were, from the very first day on which they took the field, qualified to play their part with credit in a skirmish. The steadiness, the prompt obedience, the

32d

mechanical precision of movement, which are characteristic of the regular soldier, these gallant volunteers never attained. <u>But</u> they were at first opposed to enemies as undisciplined as themselves, and far less active, athletic, and daring. <u>For a time</u>, <u>therefore</u>, the Cavaliers were successful in almost every encounter.

THOMAS MACAULAY, The History of England

EXERCISE 32d(1) Make a coherent paragraph of the following statements. First, put them in logical order. Second, give them a consistent point of view and link them smoothly with transitional words or phrases. Revise the wording of the statements if necessary, but use all the information given.

32d

1 This attitude shows a naïve faith in the competency of secretaries.
2 Practicing engineers and scientists say they spend half their time writing letters and reports.
3 Many of us foolishly object to taking courses in writing.
4 College students going into business think their secretaries will do their writing for them.
5 A student going into the technical or scientific fields may think that writing is something he seldom has to do.
6 Young businessmen seldom have private secretaries.
7 Our notion that only poets, novelists, and newspaper workers have to know how to write is unrealistic.
8 Other things being equal, a man in any field who can express himself effectively is sure to succeed more rapidly than a man whose command of language is poor.

EXERCISE 32d(2) Arrange the following statements into a coherent paragraph, revising if necessary as in 32d(1).

1 It takes a considerable amount of equipment to operate a ham radio.
2 There are 260,000 licensed amateur stations in the United States.
3 My cousin, Glenn Wade, had DRT as his signal code which he used to broadcast as Dirty Rotten Tomatoes.
4 Radio amateurs or hams send messages on their home radio stations to people all over the world.
5 The Federal Communications Commission has often praised these hams for their voluntary aid in times of emergencies such as floods or storms.
6 There are four types of licenses a ham may obtain from the FCC: (1) novice, (2) technician, (3) general class, and (4) extra class.

EXERCISE 32d(3) The following paragraphs and paragraph parts are marred and made incoherent by shifts in person, tense, and number. Rewrite the paragraphs to insure consistency and coherence throughout.

1 Literature is a medium through which a person can convey his ideas toward or protests against different norms of society. Those works that deal with a moral issue are of particular importance in literature; they are written with a particular purpose in mind. A literary work such as Shakespeare's plays with a moral issue will live on to

be reinterpreted by different generations. These works involve the reader for he forms his own moral judgment toward the issue. Arthur Miller's *Death of a Salesman* is a play which deals with moral issues.

2 It is difficult to feel compassion for people who do not deserve it. My neighbor, John Carroll, is a poor little rich boy who just can't find happiness and love. He had never been deprived of anything. The one thing he really wanted, a girl who had gone to high school with him, he couldn't get. His mother tells the story in such a way that you feel pity for this man because of this one thing that he couldn't attain. The people who least deserve compassion get more than their share of it.

3 Every time a nation is involved in a war it must face problems about its ex-soldiers after that war. The veteran is entitled to some special considerations from society, but how to treat them with complete fairness is a baffling problem. Livy reports that grants to the former soldier caused some troubles in the early history of Rome. There were many disagreements between them and the early Roman senators.

32e

4 Preparing a surface for new paint is as important a step in the whole process as the application of paint itself. First, be sure that the surface is quite clean. You should wash any grease or grime from the woodwork. The painter may use turpentine or a detergent for this. One must be careful to clean off whatever cleanser they have used. Then sand off any rough or chipped paint.

5 One of the books I read in high school English was Dickens's *Tale of Two Cities*. In it the author tells of some of the horrors of the French Revolution. He spent several pages telling about how the French aristocrats suffered. The climax part of the book tells how a ne'er-do-well who had failed in life sacrifices himself for another. He took his place in a prison and went stoically to the guillotine for him.

Paragraph Development ¶ DEV

32e   Develop every paragraph adequately.

If you do not pay attention to unity and coherence in writing your paragraphs (and your papers), you will lose your reader. No matter how willing he may be to stay with you, he will soon give up if you include details and reasons that he can't relate to your controlling ideas. And he will give up if he can't follow you from sentence to sentence. Paying attention to unity and coherence helps insure that your thinking is clear and orderly both to yourself and to your readers.

But no matter how careful you are not to introduce irrelevant details, or to insure that one sentence follows another with shining clarity, you must develop your central ideas with details, examples, evidence, and reasons if you are to inform, persuade, or simply interest your readers. Good topic sentences, no matter how carefully they are constructed to state the controlling ideas of the paragraphs, are relatively general statements. To make the reader understand what those statements mean and to keep the reader interested in them, you must explain or support them.

The following paragraph does not go far beyond its topic sentence.

> It is not always true that a good picture is worth a thousand words. Often writing is much clearer than a picture. It is sometimes difficult to figure out what a picture means, but if a writer is careful he can almost always explain it.

32e

The writer of this paragraph has given us no details that explain why it is not true that pictures are worth more than words, or any reasons for believing his topic sentence. His second sentence merely restates his topic sentence, and the third and final sentence does very little more.

Compare the following paragraph built on the same topic sentence.

> It is not always true that a picture is worth a thousand words. Sometimes, in fact, pictures are pretty useless things. Far from being worth more than words, they can be downright frustrating. If you buy a new typewriter, would you rather have a glossy picture of it, or a 1000-word booklet explaining how it works? If your carburetor is clogged, do you need a picture of the carburetor, or an explanation of how to unclog it? If you can't swim and you fall in the river and start gulping water, will you be better off to hold up a picture of yourself drowning, or start screaming "Help!"?

In contrast to the first writer, this writer has given us three concrete examples of how words may in fact be worth more than pictures. We may object that pictures of both the typewriter and the clogged carburetor would be helpful along with the words. But we understand what the writer means. And we've been kept interested.

Each of the following sample paragraphs begins with a satisfactory topic sentence stating the writer's central idea. But each fails to give enough details or reasons to explain that idea to the reader, to make the idea concrete and clear. In short, these paragraphs are not adequately developed.

The president should be elected for an eight-year term. In a four-year term the president has to spend too much of his time being a politician. He therefore can't carry out his plans.

A reader who is not already convinced that one eight-year presidential term is wiser and safer than two four-year terms is not likely to be persuaded by the two very general reasons the writer gives here.

Work as a physical therapist is rewarding financially, but more important it provides the satisfaction of helping others. For example, physical therapists can help handicapped children. They can also help others.

The reader expects more concrete details about the kind of work the physical therapist does, perhaps examples of the kinds of improvement brought to handicapped children, and certainly some more concrete information about who "others" are. He expects, too, some clearer explanation of the idea of "satisfaction" which the topic sentence promises.

32f

EXERCISE 32e Choose two of the following topic sentences and develop each into a meaningful paragraph by supporting it with details, examples, evidence, and reasons.

1 A first impression is not always a reliable basis for judgment.
2 A book that is one man's meat may be another man's poison.
3 The first day of college is a nerve-shattering experience.
4 Making homemade furniture is less difficult than it appears.
5 Words are the most powerful drugs used by mankind.
6 There are three great advantages to air travel—speed, comfort, and thrills.
7 Harmony seldom makes the headlines.
8 Keeping a detailed budget is more trouble than it's worth.
9 A good hitter is far more valuable to a baseball team than a good fielder.
10 Fashions in clothes (books, drama, hairdress, slang, etc.) change from one year (decade, century) to the next.

32f Avoid excessively long and excessively short paragraphs.

The length of a paragraph is determined by the nature of the subject, the type of topic sentence, the intention of the writer, and the character of the audience. Ultimately, the length of a paragraph is a matter that you must determine for yourself. In general, however, avoid paragraphs that contain less than four or more than eight sentences. Too short a paragraph may indicate that you are not developing your topic sentence adequately. Too long a paragraph may indicate that you are permitting excessive detail to obscure your central aim.

Excessively long paragraphs may be revised either by a rigorous pruning of details or by division into two or more paragraphs. Insufficiently developed paragraphs usually show lack of attention to detail and an imperfect command of the full idea of the paragraph. The paragraphs below, for example, are all insufficiently developed. The arguments are undirected, and the generalizations are inadequately supported by reasons, examples, and details. Simply stitching these fragments together would not produce a coherent, unified statement; instead, the entire statement would have to be thought through again and then rewritten.

> I am in favor of lowering the minimum voting age to eighteen. I think the average eighteen-year-old has more good judgment to put to use at the polls than the average middle-aged person.
>
> Among the members of the two major parties there is too much straight-ticket voting. I think the candidate himself and not his party should be voted on. The young voter would weigh the virtues of the candidate and not his party.
>
> It is unlikely that the young voter would be influenced by corrupt politicians. The majority of eighteen-year-olds are high school graduates and would surely have learned enough about current affairs to use good judgment.
>
> If the question of lowering the voting age were put to a nationwide vote, I am sure it would pass.
>
> In conclusion I say give young Americans a chance. I am sure they will make good.

32f

EXERCISE 32f Group the following sentences into two or three paragraphs. You need not rewrite the sentences, even though they may need revision.

Frederick Winslow Taylor was born in 1856. His mother was a cultured Easterner. She took the family abroad for three years. Fred's father was a lawyer. While at Exeter, Fred was a star baseball player and head of his class. Fred began work as a machinist. He liked the men he worked with. He was short, heavily built, and sharp-tongued. When he became a foreman he forgot about his working pals. He thought up new ways of doing things. The idea of producing things efficiently went to his head. He divided up jobs. When he was thirty-four, he married. In six years he became chief engineer. Then he went to work for Bethlehem steel. This job did not last long. He began to play golf and entertain. He lectured on production techniques at various colleges. The reason he lost his job was that he was more interested in production than in profit.

32g Choose a method of paragraph development suitable to your subject matter and your purpose.

Paragraphs are clear, convincing, and complete in proportion as they are packed with relevant specifics which put flesh on their general controlling ideas, that is, in proportion as those ideas are developed. There are many ways of developing paragraphs, and the best way of course depends on the paragraph topic and the way it is related to the other paragraphs in the paper. Most paragraphs can be developed by one of the following methods: (1) by using details, examples, or illustration, (2) by comparing or contrasting, (3) by defining, (4) by explaining causes and effects, or (5) by analyzing or classifying.

1. Details, examples, and illustrations. One of the most common and convincing ways to develop a general statement is to provide concrete and specific details or illustrations that will convey to the reader a clear impression of what the general statement really means to the writer. In fact, a good many of the other methods of development depend more or less on the use of detail and example, for these are virtually indispensable to clear and lively writing.

32g

A writer may support his topic sentence either by amassing a variety of specific details, by providing a few examples, each stated in a sentence or two, or by describing at greater length a single extended illustration of his topic.

The author of the following paragraph gives us his controlling idea in the first and last sentences: the freedom of Americans today is a limited and licensed freedom. If you don't believe me, he says in effect, look at this list of thirty or forty different things you must have certificates or licenses for. Note how the writer gains coherence in his long list of details by ordering them roughly in the sequence in which they occur from birth to death.

Americans are still born free but their freedom neither lasts as long nor goes as far as it used to. Once the infant is smacked on the bottom and lets out his first taxable howl, he is immediately tagged, footprinted, blood-tested, classified, certificated, and generally taken in census. By the time that squawler has drawn the breath of adulthood he must have some clerk's permission to go to school or stay away, ride a bike, drive a car, collect his salary, carry a gun, fish, get married, go into the army or stay out, leave or re-enter the country, fly a plane, operate a power boat or a ham radio, buy a piece of land, build a house or knock one down, add a room to the house he has bought, burn his trash, park his car, keep a dog, run his business, go bankrupt, practice a profession, pick the wildflowers, bury the garbage, beg in the streets, sell whiskey in his store, peddle magazines from house to house, walk across a turnpike from one of his fields to another now that the state has divided him—the list is endless. Even in death his corpse must be certified and licensed before the earth may swallow him legally. Freedom is no longer free but licensed.

JOHN CIARDI, "Confessions of a Crackpot"

The central idea of the following paragraph is that in all civilizations intellectuals have been allied to those in power and have been indifferent to the fate of the masses. The idea is supported by five examples of different civilizations in which one finds this to be true. Note that the paragraph gains coherence by the arrangement of the five examples in chronological order, and by the parallelism of the constructions with which each is introduced. (These constructions have been underlined in the paragraph.)

32g

In almost every civilization we know of the intellectuals have been either allied with those in power or members of a governing elite, and consequently indifferent to the fate of the masses. In ancient Egypt and Imperial China the literati were magistrates, overseers, stewards, tax-gathers, secretaries, and officials of every kind. They were in command, and did not lift a finger to lighten the burden of the lower orders. In India the intellectuals were members of the uppermost caste of the Brahmins. Gautama, who preached love of service for others and the mixing of castes, was by birth not an intellectual but a warrior; and the attempt to translate Buddha's teaching into reality was made by another warrior—Emperor Asoka. The Brahmin intellectuals, far from rallying to the cause, led the opposition to Buddhism, and finally drove it out of India. In classical Greece the intellectuals were at the top of the social ladder: philosophers and poets were also legislators, generals, and statesmen. This intellectual elite had an ingrained contempt for the common people who did the world's work, regarding them as no better than slaves and unfit for citizenship. In the Roman Empire, the intellectuals, whether Greek or Roman, made common cause with the powers that be, and kept their distance from the masses. In medieval Europe, too, the intellectual was a member of a privileged order—the Church—and did not manifest undue solicitude for the underprivileged.   ERIC HOFFER, *The Ordeal of Change*

The following paragraph supports its central idea with a discussion of nine brief examples, each consisting of a quotation. All are selected to support the general assertion that popular magazine biographies of celebrities overflow with superlatives.

We can hear ourselves straining. "He's the greatest!" Our descriptions of celebrities overflow with superlatives. In popular magazine biographies we learn that a <u>Dr. Brinkley</u> is the "best-advertised doctor in the United States"; <u>an actor</u> is the "luckiest man in the movies today"; <u>a Ringling</u> is "not only the greatest, but the first real showman in the Ringling family"; <u>a general</u> is "one of the best mathematicians this side of Einstein"; <u>a columnist</u> has "one of the strangest of courtships"; <u>a statesman</u> has "the world's most exciting job"; <u>a sportsman</u> is "the loudest and by all odds the most abusive"; <u>a newsman</u> is "one of the most consistently resentful men in the country"; <u>a certain ex-King's mistress</u> is "one of the unhappiest women that ever lived." But, despite the "supercolossal" on the label, the contents are very ordinary. The lives of celebrities which we like to read, as Leo Lowenthal remarks, are a mere catalogue of "hardships" and "breaks." These men and women are "the proved specimens of the average."   DANIEL J. BOORSTIN, *The Image*

The central idea of the paragraph below is that scientists who experiment with the world's living space take irresponsible risks with our future. Here the author does not offer several relatively brief examples to support his assertion. Rather he describes more fully a single illustration—an experiment with the little understood Van Allen Belt—in which scientists have acted without any foreknowledge of the consequences.

32g

When the mad professor of fiction blows up his laboratory and then himself, that's O.K., but when scientists and decision-makers act out of ignorance and pretend it is knowledge, they are using the biosphere, the living space, as an experimental laboratory. The whole world is put in hazard. And they do it even when they are told not to. During the International Geophysical Year, <u>the Van Allen Belt was discovered</u>. <u>The Van Allen Belt</u> is a region of magnetic phenomena. <u>Immediately the bright boys decided</u> to carry out an experiment and explode a hydrogen bomb in the Belt to see if they could produce an artificial aurora. The colorful draperies, the luminous skirts of the aurora, are caused by drawing cosmic particles magnetically through the rare gases of the upper atmosphere. It is called ionization and is like passing electrons through the vacuum tubes of our familiar neon lighting. It was called the Rainbow Bomb. Every responsible scientist in cosmology, radio-astronomy, and physics of the atmosphere protested against this tampering with a system we did not understand. They exploded their bomb. They got their pyrotechnics. We still do not know the price we may have to pay for this artificial magnetic disturbance.

LORD RITCHIE-CALDER, *Polluting the Environment*

A special kind of illustration is ANALOGY. An analogy draws a parallel between two things that have some resemblance, on the basis of which we infer other resemblances. When we draw comparisons, for example, between a large city and an anthill, or between a college and a factory, or between the human nervous system and a telephone system, we are using analogy. Parallels of this sort, although they may be quite inexact in many respects, enable us to visualize ideas or relations and therefore to understand them better. Note that the first paragraph below uses analogy to explain, while the second uses it to argue.

> Having a manuscript under Ross's scrutiny was like putting your car in the hands of a skilled mechanic, not an automotive engineer with a bachelor of science degree, but a guy who knows what makes a motor go, and sputter, and wheeze, and sometimes come to a dead stop; a man with an ear for the faintest body squeak as well as the loudest engine rattle. When you first gazed, appalled, upon an uncorrected proof of one of your stories or articles, each margin had a thicket of queries and complaints—one writer got a hundred and forty-four on one profile. It was as though you beheld the works of your car spread all over the garage floor, and the job of getting the thing together again and making it work seemed impossible. Then you realized that Ross was trying to make your Model T or old Stutz Bearcat into a Cadillac or Rolls-Royce. He was at work with the tools of his unflagging perfectionism, and, after an exchange of growls or snarls, you set to work to join him in his enterprise.
>
> JAMES THURBER, *The Years with Ross*

32g

> But the tendency of the time is much better illustrated by a group of professors of education who have just recently proposed that the list of "required reading" in schools should be based upon a study which they have just sponsored of the tastes of school children. . . . Would any pediatrician base the diet which he prescribed for the young submitted to his care simply on an effort to determine what eatables they remembered with greatest pleasure? If he knew that the vote would run heavily in favor of chocolate sodas, orange pop, hot dogs and bubble gum, would he conclude that these should obviously constitute the fundamental elements in a "modern" child's menu? JOSEPH WOOD KRUTCH,
> "Should We Bring
> Literature to Children, or Children to Literature?"

2. Comparison and contrast. Some controlling ideas naturally suggest development by comparison and contrast. Consider these topic sentences:

> My brother is a natural student; I am a natural nonstudent.

> Women have a long way to go before they have genuinely equal opportunity and recognition, but they have gone some of the distance since my mother finished high school.

> Foreign small cars may have virtues, but if we compare them carefully to their American counterparts, we'll choose the American.

Such sentences either directly assert or imply a contrast and almost require the writer to fill out the details of that contrast. The author of the following two paragraphs is comparing Roosevelt and Churchill. Note that he is careful to keep the order the same within the two paragraphs; in each he speaks first of Roosevelt, then of Churchill; in each he moves back, at the end of the paragraph, to a telling final point of comparison. The careful ordering of the paragraphs helps keep them coherent.

Roosevelt, as a public personality, was a spontaneous, optimistic, pleasure-loving ruler who dismayed his assistants by the gay and apparently heedless abandon with which he seemed to delight in pursuing two or more totally incompatible policies, and astonished them even more by the swiftness and ease with which he managed to throw off the cares of office during the darkest and most dangerous moments. Churchill too loves pleasure, and he too lacks neither gaiety nor a capacity for exuberant self-expression, together with the habit of blithely cutting Gordian knots in a manner which often upsets his experts; but he is not a frivolous man. His nature possesses a dimension of depth—and a corresponding sense of tragic possibilities, which Roosevelt's lighthearted genius instinctively passed by.

Roosevelt played the game of politics with virtuosity, and both his successes and his failures were carried off in splendid style; his performance seemed to flow with effortless skill. Churchill is acquainted with darkness as well as light. Like all inhabitants and even transient visitors of inner worlds, he gives evidence of seasons of agonized brooding and slow recovery. Roosevelt might have spoken of sweat and blood, but when Churchill offered his people tears, he spoke a word which might have been uttered by Lincoln or Mazzini or Cromwell but not Roosevelt, greathearted, generous, and perceptive as he was.   ISAIAH BERLIN, "Mr. Churchill"

32g

The paragraph that follows compares poetry and advertising, developing the assertion that they are alike in many ways by giving three examples of their similarity. The parallel constructions which mark the successive points of comparison and help give the paragraph coherence have been underlined.

Nevertheless, poetry and advertising have much in common. To begin with, they both make extensive use of rhyme and rhythm ("What's the word? Thunderbird!"). They both use words chosen for their affective and connotative values rather than for their denotative content ("Take a puff . . . it's springtime! Gray rocks and the fresh green leaves of springtime reflected in a mountain pool. . . . Where else can you find air so refreshing? And where can you find a smoke as refreshing as Salem's?"). William Empson, the

English critic, said in his *Seven Types of Ambiguity* that <u>the best poems are ambiguous</u>; they are richest when they have two or three or more levels of meaning at once. <u>Advertising, too</u>, although on a much more primitive level, <u>deliberately exploits ambiguities</u> and plays on words: a vodka is advertised with the slogan "Leaves you breathless"; an automobile is described as "Hot, Handsome, a Honey to Handle."

S. I. HAYAKAWA, Language in Thought and Action

The pattern may be used to clarify a principal topic by comparing and contrasting it with others. In the paragraph below Whitehall sharpens our understanding of the care we must exercise in writing by contrasting the written language with the wide range of expressive features in the spoken language.

Even a moment's reflection will show that the <u>spoken American language</u> is backed by expressive features lacking in the written language: the rise or fall of the voice at the ends of phrases and sentences; the application of vocal loudness to this or that word or part of a word; the use of gesture; the meaningful rasp or liquidity, shouting or muting, drawling or clipping, whining or breaking, melody or whispering imparted to the quality of the voice. <u>Written English</u>, lacking clear indication of such features, must be so managed that it compensates for what it lacks. It must be more carefully organized than speech in order to overcome its communicative deficiencies as compared with speech. In speech, we safeguard meaning by the use of intonation, stress, gesture, and voice qualities. In writing, we must deal with our medium in such a way that the meaning cannot possibly be misunderstood. In the absence of an actual hearer capable of interrupting and demanding further explanation, a clear writer is always conscious of "a reader over his shoulder." All this despite the fact that writing, being permanent, as compared with speech, which is evanescent, allows not only reading but also rereading.

HAROLD WHITEHALL, Structural Essentials of English

3. Definition.* The logic of a paragraph sometimes requires that key objects or terms be defined. Definition is necessary to set the limits within which a topic or a term is used, especially when we are dealing with abstract matters. Full and exact paragraphs of definition are frequently important parts of papers, essays, and articles. Note that paragraphs of definition many times make use of details and examples, of comparison and contrast, and of restatement in order to insure clarity.

The following definition first states the two basic elements of the fairy story—"a human hero and a happy ending." The au-

---

*For a discussion of the indispensability of clear definition, and the requirements of formal definition, see **37a.**

32g

thor develops the paragraph by describing the kind of hero and the kind of story pattern that are the special marks of the fairy tale. Our underlining marks the movement of the paragraph, a movement basically controlled by the progress of the hero from beginning to end of the tale.

A fairy story, as distinct from a merry tale, or an animal story, is a serious tale with a human hero and a happy ending. The progression of its hero is the reverse of the tragic hero's: at the beginning he is either socially obscure or despised as being stupid or untalented, lacking in the heroic virtures, but at the end, he has surprised everyone by demonstrating his heroism and winning fame, riches, and love. Though ultimately he succeeds, he does not do so without a struggle in which his success is in doubt, for opposed to him are not only natural difficulties like glass mountains, or barriers of flame, but also hostile wicked powers, stepmothers, jealous brothers, and witches. In many cases indeed, he would fail were he not assisted by friendly powers who give him instructions or perform tasks for him which he cannot do himself; that is, in addition to his own powers, he needs luck, but this luck is not fortuitous but dependent upon his character and his actions. The tale ends with the establishment of justice; not only are the good rewarded but also the evil are punished.

W. H. AUDEN, Introduction to *Tales of Grimm and Andersen*

32g

In the two paragraphs below, John Holt is developing his definition of intelligence. Holt relies upon contrast to develop his definition: intelligence is not, Holt tells us, what it is often said to be—an ability to score well, or do well. Rather, it is a "way of behaving" in certain situations. We might call the development here a not-this-but-that development.

The three-sentence first paragraph sets the general contrast between the two definitions. The second moves initially to the more specific but quickly returns to the basic pattern. The underlined phrases will help you follow the controlling not-this-but-that flow of the definition. Notice that the two paragraphs here could be combined without excessive length. By using two paragraphs, however, Holt is better able to draw our attention to his description of how a person acts in a new situation—a description that is very important in clarifying his definition.

When we talk about intelligence, we do not mean the ability to get a good score on a certain kind of test, or even the ability to do well in school; these are at best only indicators of something larger, deeper, and far more important. By intelligence we mean a style of life, a way of behaving in various situations, and particularly in new, strange, and perplexing situations. The true test of intelligence is not how much we know how to do, but how we behave when we don't know what to do.

The intelligent person, young or old, meeting a new situation or problem, opens himself up to it; he tries to take in with mind and senses everything he can about it; he thinks about *it,* instead of about himself or what it might cause to happen to him; he grapples with it boldly, imaginatively, resourcefully, and if not confidently at least hopefully; if he fails to master it, he looks without shame or fear at his mistakes and learns what he can from them. This is intelligence. Clearly its roots lie in a certain feeling about life, and one's self with respect to life. Just as clearly, unintelligence is not what most psychologists seem to suppose, the same thing as intelligence only less of it. It is an entirely different style of behavior, arising out of an entirely different set of attitudes.

JOHN HOLT, Why Children Fail

4. Causes and effects. (See also p. 167.) Some kinds of central ideas invite development by an examination of causes or effects. Pollution and poverty exist. What causes them? What are their effects? What are the effects of television? Of the widespread use of computers? What are the causes behind the movements for equality of women, the popularity of football, the high rate of unemployment?

32g

The initial topic sentence of the following paragraph by Margaret Mead states a general *effect*—that in our society women suffer from lack of stimulation, from loneliness, dullness. Mead then develops the paragraph by detailing specific causes. Notice that the paragraph gains clarity and order by the author's division of detailed causes into two main groups—those associated with the pattern of relationships with children and husbands, and those associated with certain "conditions of modern life."

Women in our society complain of the lack of stimulation, of the loneliness, of the dullness of staying at home. Little babies are poor conversationalists, husbands come home tired and sit reading the paper, and women who used to pride themselves on their ability to talk find on the rare evening they can go out that their words clot on their tongues. As the children go to school, the mother is left to the companionship of the Frigidaire and the washing machine. Yet she can't go out because the delivery man might come, or a child might be sent home sick from school. The boredom of long hours of solitary one-sided communication with things, no matter how shining and streamlined and new, descends upon her. Moreover, the conditions of modern life, apartment living, and especially the enormous amount of moving about, all serve to rob women of neighborhood ties. The better her electric equipment, the better she organizes her ordering, the less reason she has to run out for a bit of gossipy shopping at the corner store. The department stores and the moving-picture houses cater to women—alone—on their few hours out. Meanwhile efficient mending services and cheap ready-made clothes have taken most sensible busy work out of women's hands and left women—still at home—listening to the radio, watching television.   MARGARET MEAD, "What Women Want"

The central idea of the paragraph by Kosinski below is that television has turned today's students into spectators. Television is the cause, says Kosinski; I have just described the effects. Note that here the topic sentence—the statement of *cause*—comes in the middle of the paragraph. Kosinski leads up to it by detailing the *effects* he has observed, and follows it with his speculative explanation.

During the last four years, I have taught at Wesleyan, Princeton, and at Yale University. I have often lectured at many schools throughout the country. I am appalled by what I think emerges as the dominant trait of the students of today—their short span of attention, their inability to know or believe anything for more than half an hour. I feel it was television which turned them into spectators, since by comparison with the world of television, their own lives are slow and uneventful. When they first believed that what they saw on TV was real, they overreacted, only to feel cheated when the next program demanded a new emotion. Later, they felt simply manipulated by whatever drama they witnessed. By now, they have become hostile, and so they either refuse to watch the TV altogether or they dissect the medium and throw out all that upsets them.   JERZY KOSINSKI, NBC *Comment*

32g

5. Analysis and classification. (See also p. 167.) Analysis takes things apart. Classification groups things together on the basis of their differences or similarities. We use them both every day. We break our days into morning, noon, and night; in the supermarket we look for the pepper among spices and the hamburger in the meat department, because we know that's the way they're classified. Similarly in our writing, both in individual paragraphs and in entire essays, analysis and classification frequently serve as guides to development and to organization.

In the paragraph below the author divides language into three classes on the basis of three different functions which language performs. From such a paragraph, the author could clearly develop successive paragraphs illustrating each function by example, or by further subdivision.

Language has more than one purpose. We might say that language operates on different levels, except that the word "levels" suggests higher and lower planes in a scale of value, and this is not intended here. We shall deal with three functions: the informative, the expressive, and the directive. To say that language has these three functions is to say that there are three different reasons for speaking. One reason, or purpose, is to communicate factual information. This is the informative function. We speak also in order to express our feelings, to "blow off steam," or to stir the feelings and attitudes of the person we are talking to. We shall call this the expressive or "emotive" function. And, finally, we speak in order to get people to act. This is the directive function.

LIONEL RUBY, *The Art of Making Sense*

In the following paragraph, Lynes develops his explanation of bores by setting up three different classes: the Crashing Bore, the Tinkling Bore, and the Still Waters Run Deep Bore. Note that he also suggests two broader classes, the militant to which the first two kinds belong, and the passive. The classification provides the pattern for the development of his paragraph and serves as a guide to the kind of detail he will select in describing each.

32g

The common variety of bores is well known to everyone. Ambrose Bierce said that a bore is "a person who talks when you want him to listen," but as apt as the definition is, the species is a good deal more complicated than that. There are, for example, many gradations of boredom, such as the Crashing Bore whose conversation weighs on you like an actual physical burden that you want to throw off because it is stifling you, and quite a different kind, the Tinkling Bore whose conversation bothers you in the way that an insistent fly does, annoying but not dangerous. There are such types as the Still Waters Run Deep variety who defy you to say anything that will change the expression on their faces much less elicit an encouraging word from them. There you are on the sofa with them, their intense eyes peering at you with something between hopelessness and scorn, impressing on you the deep reservoir of their self-sufficiency and challenging you to ruffle the waters that lurk there. I cite this merely as an example of the passive as opposed to the militant type (both the Crashing and the Tinkling are militant), for it is those who make you feel like a bore who are the most boring of all.   RUSSELL LYNES, *Guests: or How to Survive Hospitality*

EXERCISE 32g(1) Which of the methods of paragraph development discussed in **32g** seems to be the most appropriate method of developing each of the following topic sentences into a paragraph? Why? After you have answered this question briefly, choose one of the topics and write a paragraph around it. Is your paragraph developed according to your original notion?

1 Attending a small college has disadvantages as well as advantages.
2 To watch a college "mixer" is to see every type of human being.
3 Wit and humor are not the same thing.

4 Athleticism focuses its attention on doing good for boys who least need it.

5 Contemporary society places too much emphasis on test scores.

6 The rapidly rising population of the world creates problems of future survival.

7 The civil rights issue is a continuum of the Civil War.

8 Good government begins at the local level.

9 Fraternities have to watch carefully the line between fellowship and snobbishness.

10 Some people come to college wanting to learn, but refusing, at the same time, to change a single idea they came with.

11 To know how to suggest is the great art of teaching.

12 The notion that women are poor automobile drivers is not supported by any real evidence.

13 A distinction should be drawn between liberty and license.

14 Campus slang is a puzzle to the uninitiated.

15 The differences in education and social conditioning for boys and girls in our society make for an enormous waste of female talent.

16 If we must reduce the amount of energy we use, we must expect to change greatly the way we live.

17 A dormitory is not an ideal place for study.

18 A child who has learned to live and love in the movies will suffer when he enters a world in which there is odor as well as sight and sound.

19 We are too much inclined to measure progress by the number of television sets rather than by the quality of television programs.

20 The people you see at a patriotic rally are not very likely to be the ones that move you to love your country.

EXERCISE 32g(2) *You cannot do wrong without suffering wrong.* Write two separate paragraphs to develop this topic sentence. In the first paragraph, define as clearly as you can what you think is meant by *wrong* and *suffering wrong*. In the second, demonstrate the truth or falsity of the statement by giving examples.

EXERCISE 32g(3) *My reading tastes have changed since I came to college.* Write three separate paragraphs to develop this topic sentence. In the first paragraph, show <u>why</u> your tastes have changed. In the second, demonstrate <u>how</u> they have changed. In the third, contrast specifically your reading tastes in high school with your reading tastes in college.

Consistency of Tone in the Paragraph ¶ CON

When we read effective writers we are often struck by the fact that what seems to hold their sentences together is more than mere adherence to an organizational principle. There is about their writing some inner consistency which unites everything they say into an authoritative whole. What we are responding to is a kind of consistency of TONE that pervades the whole of a passage of good writing.

Tone is one of those matters that is clear enough to us until we try to define it. We know well enough what we mean when, if our neighbor has complained about our barking beagle, we remark that we don't mind his complaining but we don't like his tone. But when we try to describe exactly what it is we don't like, we find it extremely difficult. For tone is produced by an interplay of many elements in speech and writing. Sentence structure, diction, the mode of organization and development we choose, the kinds of examples, illustrations, and details we draw on—these and many other factors are involved.

The best way to increase our awareness of tone in writing is to study carefully a variety of effective paragraphs, asking ourselves how we would describe their tone and then trying to determine how the writer has conveyed that tone to us. A writer's tone can be impersonal or personal, formal or informal, literal or ironic, sentimental or sarcastic, sincere or insincere, enthusiastic or indifferent, dogmatic or doubtful, hostile or friendly, condescending or respectful, modest or authoritative, serious or humorous, and the like. Obviously it can be a level in between any of these extreme pairs, or it can be a complex quality which can be adequately described only by a combination of several of these terms. Only by careful study of good writing can we increase our awareness of the many factors that contribute to the control of tone.

32h   **Choose an appropriate tone and maintain it consistently.**

1. Appropriate tone. An appropriate tone is one that reflects the writer's understanding of and respect for the needs and feelings of his audience. It is not easy to state what will make for such appropriateness in any particular paragraph or paper; but some things are generally to be avoided. Among them the most important are: talking down to your audience by repeating the obvious; talking over the heads of your audience, merely to impress them, by using words or allusions or examples they are unlikely to understand; being excessively dogmatic or sarcastic; and being excessively or falsely enthusiastic.

This opening sentence of a student paper illustrates an extreme of inappropriate tone: *No one can tell me that people who vote for the characters on the Democratic ticket aren't putting their own selfish interests ahead of the true good of the country.* Whatever we may think of the thesis of the writer, his expression of it offends us. The language is emotional, his attitude dogmatic. We have the immediate feeling that there is no point in reading further, since we cannot hope, apparently, for any sort of balanced or reasoned discussion of the sort appropriate to the topic.

2. Consistent tone. Consistency requires that once we have set a particular tone, we maintain it. A jarring shift in tone may ruin the effect of a paragraph even though it otherwise meets the tests of unity, coherence, and adequate development. The following paragraph from a student theme illustrates the point:

> Curiosity has developed ideas that have been vastly beneficial to mankind. We have seen mankind emerge from the age of great darkness into the age of great light. Today every hotrod artist profits from the ideas of past inventors and every housewife has a kitchen full of push-button gadgets that she couldn't have without ideas. Above all, modern scientific theory leads us to a clearer and deeper comprehension of the universe. So we see curiosity is really a helpful tool.

The principal fault of this paragraph is its jarring shifts of tone. The first two sentences and the next to last sentence set a serious, somewhat formal tone by such phrases as *vastly beneficial, we have seen mankind emerge,* the parallel phrases *great age of darkness* and *great age of light,* and *clearer and deeper comprehension of the universe.* But the language of both the third and the last sentences, and the examples cited in the third sentence depart completely from this tone of seriousness and formality. Having been prepared for comment about the great concepts of religion, politics, education, or science, we are offered *hotrod artists* and *push-button gadgets.* The effect is something like that of a cat meowing in a church service.

32h

EXERCISE 32h Study the following paragraphs. Describe the tone of each and discuss the factors that contribute to it.

1 We are at that point in our moral history as a people at which we have failed, for the first time in a moment of decision, to assert our moral purpose. We have not yet denied that purpose—the cock has not crowed for the second time—but we have failed to assert it. We have not yet changed the direction of our national life but we have lost our momentum, we have lost our initiative. We have not yet rejected our role as a revolutionary people moving with the great revolutionary current of history but we have ceased to move, we have begun to resist, to oppose. It does not require a prophet to see that we have come to a moment of critical decision—a decision which is none the less critical because it may be taken unaware.

ARCHIBALD MACLEISH, "The Conquest of America"

2 It is not easy to live in that continuous awareness of things which alone is true living. Even those who make a parade of their conviction that sunset, rain, and the growth of a seed are daily miracles are not usually so much impressed by them as they urge others to be. The faculty of wonder tires easily and a miracle which appears every day is a miracle no longer, no matter how many times one tells oneself that it ought to be. Life would seem a great deal longer and a great deal fuller than it does if it were not for the fact that the human being is, by nature, a creature to whom *"O altitudo"* is much less natural than "So what!" Really to see something once or twice a week is almost inevitably to have to try—though, alas, not necessarily with success—to make oneself a poet.

JOSEPH WOOD KRUTCH, *The Desert Year*

3 For we're always out of luck here. That's just how it is—for instance in the winter. The sides of the buildings, the roofs, the limbs of the trees are gray. Streets, sidewalks, faces, feelings—they are gray. Speech is gray, and the grass where it shows. Every flank and front, each top is gray. Everything is gray: hair, eyes, window glass, the hawkers' bills and touters' posters, lips, teeth, poles and metal signs—they're gray, quite gray. Cars are gray. Boots, shoes, suits, hats, gloves are gray. Horses, sheep, and cows, cats killed in the road, squirrels in the same way, sparrows, doves, and pigeons, all are gray, everything is gray, and everyone is out of luck who lives here.

WILLIAM H. GASS, "In the Heart of the Heart of the Country"

32 h

4 Even though large tracts of Europe and many old and famous States have fallen or may fall into the grip of the Gestapo and all the odious apparatus of Nazi rule, we shall not flag or fail. We shall go on to the end. We shall fight in France, we shall fight in the seas and oceans, we shall fight with growing confidence and growing strength in the air; we shall defend our Island, whatever the cost may be. We shall fight on the beaches, we shall fight on the landing grounds, we shall fight in the fields and in the streets, we shall fight in the hills; we shall never surrender; and even if, which I do not for a moment believe, this Island or a large part of it were subjugated and starving, then our Empire beyond the seas, armed and guarded by the British Fleet, would carry on the struggle, until, in God's good time, the New World, with all its power and might, steps forth to the rescue and liberation of the Old.

WINSTON CHURCHILL, Speech at Dunkerque

5 At first they had come in wagons: the guns, the bedding, the dogs, the food, the whiskey, the keen heart-lifting anticipation of hunting; the young men who could drive all night and all the following day in the cold rain and pitch a camp in the rain and sleep in the wet blankets and rise at daylight the next morning and hunt. There had been bear then. A man shot a doe or a fawn as quickly as he did a buck, and in the afternoons they shot wild turkey with pistols to test their stalking skill and marksmanship, feeding all but the breast to the dogs. But that time was gone now. Now they went in cars,

driving faster and faster each year because the roads were better and they had farther and farther to drive, the territory in which game still existed drawing yearly inward as his life was drawing inward, until now he was the last of those who had once made the journey in wagons without feeling it and now those who accompanied him were the sons and grandsons of the men who had ridden for twenty-four hours in the rain or sleet behind the steaming mules. They called him "Uncle Ike" now, and he no longer told anyone how near eighty he actually was because he knew as well as they did that he no longer had any business making such expeditions, even by car.

WILLIAM FAULKNER, Delta Autumn

Paragraphs for study

We cannot learn to write well simply by following general prescriptions. One of the best ways to develop skill in writing is to develop skill in observing how others write. Reading is an integral part of the process of learning to write, not something entirely separate from it. Test your understanding of the principles of good paragraphs by a close study of as many of the following paragraphs as possible. Analyze each to determine the main points, the topic sentence, the transitions from sentence to sentence, the method or methods of paragraph development and organization, and the tone.

32 h

1. What people do not seem to realize is that the editors of the various "digests" do not simply delete a word here and there. They do not cut only extraneous material. Instead, they "blue pencil" paragraphs and pages. We depend upon the discretion of these editors, and what seems of importance to them becomes the text we read. We have no idea what has been cut. What we do read may be so removed from its original context that the remainder of the article is completely distorted. The reader, however, has no way of knowing of this distortion and thus reads his digest version in good faith. Consequently, when he tries to discuss his mutilated concept with someone who has taken the time to read the unabridged version, he may find himself unfamiliar with a point that was the basis of the entire thesis. STUDENT PARAGRAPH

2. Any sort of problem can start us thinking: a stuck door, a rainy day, or a kiss. But the problems that require hard and sustained thinking nearly always come to our attention through *language*. The most perplexing problems we face, as citizens or as members of a family or as people doing some kind of job, are problems that require us to handle words. A paragraph in a newspaper, an announcement over the air, a quarrel, a letter, a chapter in a book: these may be the occasion of thinking, or may turn up to be reckoned with before the thinking has reached its goal. There is still a good deal of mystery about the exact relation between words

and thoughts, but we know that the connection is intimate, and we can't talk very fruitfully about the one without talking about the other. MONROE C. BEARDSLEY, *Practical Logic*

3. In the old anthropology there was an important proposition about how a tribe took on culture from its neighbors: If the cultural trait had to do with a new utility or technique, e.g. better seeds, a new plough, or making vessels out of clay, it was picked up readily and it diffused rapidly; but if the trait was moral, psychological, or religious, e.g. a change in tabu, kinship, child-rearing, or music, then its adoption was resisted and it diffused slowly. People want what is useful and lightens labor, but they refuse what makes them anxious and seems to threaten their moral integrity. Sometimes there may be an odd compromise: basket-weavers will pick up fired pottery, but they paint the old basket design on the new pots, for people are conservative about esthetics.

PAUL GOODMAN, *Confusion and Disorder*

4. The world does not much like curiosity. The world says that curiosity killed the cat. The world dismisses curiosity by calling it idle, or *mere* idle, curiosity—even though curious persons are seldom idle. Parents do their best to extinguish curiosity in their children, because it makes life difficult to be faced every day with a string of unanswerable questions about what makes fire hot or why grass grows, or to have to halt junior's investigations before they end in explosion and sudden death. Children whose curiosity survives parental discipline and who manage to grow up before they blow up are invited to join the Yale faculty. Within the university they go on asking their questions and trying to find the answers. In the eyes of a scholar, that is mainly what a university is for. It is a place where the world's hostility to curiosity can be defied.

EDMUND S. MORGAN, "What Every Yale Freshman Should Know"

32 h

5. As man proceeds toward his announced goal of the conquest of nature, he has written a depressing record of destruction, directed not only against the earth he inhabits but against the life that shares it with him. The history of the recent centuries has its black passages—the slaughter of the buffalo on the western plains, the massacre of the shorebirds by the market gunners, the near-extermination of the egrets for their plummage. Now, to these and others like them, we are adding a new chapter, and a new kind of havoc—the direct killing of birds, mammals, fishes, and indeed practically every form of wildlife by chemical insecticides indiscriminately sprayed on the land. RACHEL CARSON, *Silent Spring*

6. On the east, England is bounded by the North Sea, which is really nothing but an old depression which has gradually run full of water. Again a single glimpse at the map will tell you more than a thousand words. There on the right (the east) is France. Then we get something that looks like a trench across a road, the British Channel and the North Sea. Then the great central plain of England with London in the deepest hollow. Then the high mountains

of Wales. Another depression, the Irish Sea, the great central Irish plain, the hills of Ireland, a few lonely rocks further toward the west, rearing their tops above the shallow sea. Finally the rock of St. Kilda (uninhabited since a year ago as it was too hard to reach) and then suddenly down we go, down, down, down, for there the real ocean begins and the last of the vast European and Asiatic continent, both submerged and semi-submerged, here comes to an end.   HENDRIK WILLEM VAN LOON, *Van Loon's Geography*

7. By day it [the kitchen] was the scene of intense bustle. The kitchen-maid was down by five o'clock to light the fire; the laborers crept down in stockinged feet and drew on their heavy boots; they lit candles in their horn lanthorns and went out to the cattle. Breakfast was at seven, dinner at twelve, tea at five. Each morning of the week had its appropriate activity: Monday was washing day, Tuesday, ironing, Wednesday and Saturday baking, Thursday "turning out" upstairs and churning, Friday "turning out" downstairs. Every day there was the milk to skim in the dairy—the dairy was to the left of the kitchen, and as big as any other room in the house. The milk was poured into large flat pans and allowed to settle; it was skimmed with horn scoops, like toothless combs.

HERBERT READ, *The Eye of Memory*

8. The whole aim of good teaching is to turn the young learner, by nature a little copycat, into an independent, self-propelling creature, who cannot merely learn but study—that is, work as his own boss to the limit of his powers. This is to turn pupils into students, and it can be done on any rung of the ladder of learning. When I was a child, the multiplication table was taught from a printed sheet which had to be memorized one "square" at a time— the one's and the two's and so on up to nine. It never occurred to the teacher to show us how the answers could be arrived at also by addition, which we already knew. No one said, "Look: if four times four is sixteen, you ought to be able to figure out, without aid from memory, what five times four is, because that amounts to four more one's added to the sixteen." This would at first have been puzzling, *more* complicated and difficult than memory work, but once explained and grasped, it would have been an instrument for learning and checking the whole business of multiplication. We could temporarily have dispensed with the teacher and cut loose from the printed table.   JACQUES BARZUN, *Teacher in America*

32h

9. He [Wagner] was a monster of conceit. Never for one minute did he look at the world or at people, except in relation to himself. He was not only the most important person in the world, to himself; in his own eyes he was the only person who existed. He believed himself to be one of the greatest dramatists in the world, one of the greatest thinkers, and one of the greatest composers. To hear him talk, he was Shakespeare, and Beethoven, and Plato, rolled into one. And you would have had no difficulty in hearing him talk. He was one of the most exhausting conversationalists that ever lived. An evening with him was an evening spent in listening to a mono-

logue. Sometimes he was brilliant; sometimes he was maddeningly tiresome. But whether he was being brilliant or dull, he had one sole topic of conversation: himself. What *he* thought and what *he* did.

DEEMS TAYLOR, *Of Men and Music*

10. The words we choose to define or suggest what we believe to be important facts exert a very powerful influence upon civilization. A mere name can persuade us to approve or disapprove, as it does, for example, when we describe certain attitudes as "cynical" on the one hand or "realistic" on the other. No one wants to be "unrealistic" and no one wants to be "snarling." Therefore his attitude toward the thing described may very well depend upon which designation is current among his contemporaries; and the less critical his mind, the more influential the most commonly used vocabulary will be. JOSEPH WOOD KRUTCH,

Human Nature and the Human Condition

32 h

11. The pyramids were built with sheer muscle-power. Holes were bored in stone in the quarries of the Mokattam Mountains, wooden sticks were driven into them, and these, swelling when soaked with water, cracked apart the rock. On sledges and rollers the resulting blocks were dragged to the site. The pyramids rose layer by layer. Candidates for a doctorate in archaeology write theses on the question of whether one construction plan was used or several. Lepsius and Petrie occupy diametrically opposed positions on this controversy, but modern archaeology inclines to support the Lepsian point of view. Apparently there were several plans of construction, drastic changes being necessitated by suddenly conceived additions. The Egyptians, forty-seven hundred years ago, worked with such precision that mistakes in the lengths and angles of the great pyramids can, as Petrie says, "be covered with one's thumb." They fitted the stone blocks so neatly that "neither needle or hair" can, to this day, be inserted at the joints. The Arab writer, Abd al Latif, remarked on this in wonder eight hundred years ago. Critics point out that the old Egyptian master builders misjudged their stresses and strains, as for example, when they made five hollow spaces over the burial-chamber ceiling to reduce the downward pressure, when one would have sufficed. But these fault-finders forget, in our own day of electronically analyzed T-beams, that it was not so long ago that we used to build with a safety factor of five, eight, or even twelve.

C. W. CERAM, *Gods, Graves, and Scholars*

12. Science is not merely a collection of facts and formulas. It is preeminently a way of dealing with experience. The word may be appropriately used as a verb: one *sciences,* i.e., deals with experience according to certain assumptions and with certain techniques. Science is one of two basic ways of dealing with experience. The other is art. And this word, too, may appropriately be used as a verb; one may *art* as well as science. The purpose of science and art is one: to render experience intelligible, i.e., to assist man to adjust

himself to his environment in order that he may live. But although
working toward the same goal, science and art approach it from
opposite directions. Science deals with particulars in terms of universals: Uncle Tom disappears in the mass of Negro slaves. Art
deals with universals in terms of particulars: the whole gamut of
Negro slavery confronts us in the person of Uncle Tom. Art and
science thus grasp a common experience, or reality, by opposite but
inseparable poles.   LESLIE A. WHITE, *The Science of Culture*

13. What men, in their egoism, constantly mistake for a defi-
ciency of intelligence in woman is merely an incapacity for master-
ing that mass of small intellectual tricks, that complex of petty
knowledges, that collection of cerebral rubber-stamps, which constitute the chief mental equipment of the average male. A man
thinks that he is more intelligent than his wife because he can add
up a column of figures more accurately, or because he is able to
distinguish between the ideas of rival politicians, or because he is
privy to the minutiae of some sordid and degrading business or
profession. But these empty talents, of course, are not really signs
of intelligence; they are, in fact, merely a congeries of petty tricks
and antics, and their acquirement puts little more strain on the
mental powers than a chimpanzee suffers in learning how to catch a
penny or scratch a match.   H. L. MENCKEN, *In Defense of Women*

14. In the first place, any language is arbitrary. This means that
there is nothing—or at most very little—in the nature of the things
we talk about that dictates or controls the language we use to talk
about them. When we are children we do not know this. We believe
that the connection between an act or an object and the word
which refers to it is somehow a natural and inevitable one. If you
ask a child why he calls a certain object a *clock,* he will probably
answer, "Because it *is* a clock." We can see the error of this belief in
this childlike form. But it is likely to persist in a somewhat more
sophisticated form in the minds of those who have not thought or
studied about language. All of us have heard people make statements like "The real name for these things is *crullers,* but I call
them *doughnuts* because everybody else around here does." Note
the assumption that there is a *real*—natural or inevitable—name
for something, even though nobody uses it. Only when we learn a
foreign language do we become completely disabused of this notion.
When we discover that *horloge* and *Uhr* seem to other people just
as natural names for a timepiece as *clock,* we come to realize that
none of them is really natural, but all are arbitrary.

W. NELSON FRANCIS, *The English Language*

32h

15. A sign is anything that announces the existence or the im-
minence of some event, the presence of a thing or a person, or a
change in a state of affairs. There are signs of the weather, signs of
danger, signs of future good or evil, signs of what the past has been.
In every case a sign is closely bound up with something to be noted
or expected in experience. It is always a part of the situation to

which it refers, though the reference may be remote in space and time. In so far as we are led to note or expect the signified event we are making correct use of a sign. This is the essence of rational behavior, which animals show in varying degrees. It is entirely realistic, being closely bound up with the actual objective course of history—learned by experience, and cashed in or voided by further experience.   SUSANNE K. LANGER, "The Lord of Creation"

16. Only twice in literary history has there been a great period of tragedy, in the Athens of Pericles and in Elizabethan England. What these two periods had in common, two thousand years and more apart in time, that they expressed themselves in the same fashion, may give us some hint of the nature of tragedy, for far from being periods of darkness and defeat, each was a time when life was seen exalted, a time of thrilling and unfathomable possibilities. They held their heads high, those men who conquered at Marathon and Salamis, and those who fought Spain and saw the Great Armada sink. The world was a place of wonder; mankind was beauteous; life was lived on the crest of the wave. More than all, the poignant joy of heroism had stirred men's hearts. Not stuff for tragedy, would you say? But on the crest of the wave one must feel either tragically or joyously; one cannot feel tamely. The temper of the mind that sees tragedy in life has not for its opposite the temper that sees joy. The opposite pole to the tragic view of life is the sordid view. When humanity is seen as devoid of dignity and significance, trivial, mean, and sunk in dreary hopelessness, then the spirit of tragedy departs. "Sometime let gorgeous tragedy in sceptred pall come sweeping by." At the opposite pole stands Gorki with *The Lower Depths.*

32 h

EDITH HAMILTON, *The Great Age of Greek Literature*

17. My boyhood was spent in a world made tranquil by two invisible catastrophes: the Depression and World War II. Between 1932, when I was born, and 1945, when we moved away, the town of Shillington changed, as far as I could see, very little. The vacant lot beside our home on Philadelphia Avenue remained vacant. The houses along the street were neither altered nor replaced. The high-school grounds, season after season, continued to make a placid plain visible from our rear windows. The softball field, with its triptych backstop, was nearest us. A little beyond, on the left, were the school and its boiler house, built in the late 1920's of the same ochre brick. In the center a cinder track circumscribed the football field. At a greater distance there were the tennis courts and the poor farm fields and the tall double rows of trees marking the Poorhouse Lane. The horizon was the blue cloud, scarred by a gravel pit's orange slash, of Mount Penn, which overlooked the city of Reading.   JOHN UPDIKE, *Five Boyhoods*

18. He saw, facing him across the spring, a man of undersize, his hands in his coat pockets, a cigarettee slanted from his chin. His suit was black, with a tight, high-waisted coat. His trousers were rolled once and caked with mud above mud-caked shoes. His face

had a queer, bloodless color, as though seen by electric light; against the sunny silence, in his slanted straw hat and his slightly akimbo arms, he had that vicious depthless quality of stamped tin.

WILLIAM FAULKNER, *Sanctuary*

19. It was all over though. The big cat lay tangled in the willows: his head and shoulder raised against the red stems, his legs reaching and his back arched downward, in the caricature of a leap, but loose and motionless. The great, yellow eyes glared balefully up through the willows. The mouth was a little open, the tongue hanging down from it behind the fangs. The blood was still dripping from the tongue into the red stain it had already made in the snow. High behind the shoulder, the black pelt was wet too, and one place farther down, on the ribs. Standing there, looking at it, Harold felt compassion for the long, wicked beauty rendered motionless, and even a little shame that it should have passed so hard.

WALTER V. T. CLARK, *The Track of the Cat*

32 h

EFFECTIVE SENTENCES
EF

Every sentence is the result of a long probation [and] should read as if its author, had he held a plough instead of a pen, could have drawn a furrow deep and straight to the end.

HENRY DAVID THOREAU

33

A sentence may be perfectly clear and grammatical without being <u>effective</u>. Most effective sentences not only communicate simple facts and ideas, they bring together a number of facts and ideas in ways that show the relationship among them. Such sentences enable the writer to knit into the basic subject-verb-object pattern of a sentence the modifiers that give interest and full meaning to ideas. And the skillful use of such sentences together, in carefully thought out sequence, allows us to express our meaning more exactly.

<u>Unity</u>, <u>coherence</u>, and <u>emphasis</u> are the basic qualities of effective sentences. The "rules" of sentence writing on the succeeding pages are statements about the specific qualities of effective sentences. They will often tell you where your sentences go wrong. But they are also guides to building strong sentences. Effectiveness is not a simple mechanical matter achieved by avoiding "error." It is an active welding of our thought to the means we have for expressing it. There is no way of divorcing a sentence from the idea it expresses. The idea constructs the sentence, the two go hand in hand. A clumsy sentence is likely to be a badly thought-out idea. To revise it means, first, to rethink it.

33   Subordination SUB

Most effective sentences bring together two or more ideas which they relate to one another by COORDINATION and SUBORDINATION. Broadly, COORDINATION expresses equality: two things that are coordinate have roughly the same importance, the same rank, the same value. SUBORDINATION expresses some sort of inequality: when one thing is subordinate, or dependent, upon another, it is in some way of lesser importance or rank, or value.

Grammatically, words and groups of words joined by *and, but, or,* and other coordinating words are said to be coordinate. Groups of words and whole sentences that have the same construction are also coordinate. When we put our ideas in coordinate constructions, we indicate that they are roughly equal in weight and meaning. Modifying words, phrases, and clauses are grammatically subordinate. Though they are frequently vital to the full meaning of a sentence, we indicate by subordinating them that they are less important to our meaning than other parts of the sentence. Effective sentences depend heavily upon the careful arrangement of both coordination and subordination, for these are the means by which we knit together major and minor ideas into clear and coherent units.

33a

33a Do not use coordinating conjunctions to join subordinate ideas and main ideas.

Coordinating conjunctions such as *and* should be used to join only words and ideas that are of equal importance and deserve equal emphasis. If you use them carelessly, your sentences will be inexact and poorly unified. In such a sentence as *He was late and I was angry,* there are two statements, both clear enough. We suspect, however, that the lateness caused the anger, yet we can't be certain. But we can be certain in the sentence *Because he was late, I was angry.*

Inexact	Sometimes violent storms arose and then the workers sought shelter in the huts.
Revised	When violent storms arose, the workers sought shelter in the huts.
Revised	Because violent storms sometimes arose, the workers sought shelter in the huts.
Inexact	The treaty was signed at Panmunjon in 1953, and Korea was still not a united country.
Revised	After the treaty was signed at Panmunjon in 1953, Korea was still not a united country.
Revised	Although the treaty was signed at Panmunjon in 1953, Korea was still not a united country.
Unrelated	My Uncle Bert was a golf instructor and moved here from New Mexico in 1959.
Revised	My Uncle Bert, a golf instructor, moved here from New Mexico in 1959.
Revised	My Uncle Bert, who moved here from New Mexico in 1959, was a golf instructor.

Notice that in each of the above examples, there is more than one possible revision. In the first two examples, the alternate revisions indicate different kinds of relations between the subordinate and the main clause. In the third, the alternate revisions subordinate different information. All the revisions bring what were two main clauses in the original sentences into more exact and unified relation to each other.

Sometimes a series of sentences consisting of clauses joined by *and* results if a writer strings together miscellaneous facts as though they were all equally important.

33a

"Light-Horse Harry" Lee lived from 1756 to 1818 and was an officer in the Revolutionary War. His army was responsible for quelling the Whiskey Rebellion in Pennsylvania, and he also served his country as governor of Virginia and as member of Congress. It was "Light-Horse Harry" who described Washington as "first in war, first in peace, and first in the hearts of his countrymen," and was the father of Robert E. Lee.

There is usually little reason for such a collection of ill-assorted facts except in a reference book. But, if they are all necessary, be sure that you subordinate the less important to the more important ones.

The author of the description of Washington as "first in war, first in peace, and first in the hearts of his countrymen," was "Light-Horse Harry" Lee, father of Robert E. Lee. "Light-Horse Harry," having made a reputation as an officer in the Revolutionary War, later became governor of Virginia and led the army which quelled the Whiskey Rebellion.

Sometimes poor coordination occurs when writers omit important information that is evident to them but not to their readers.

Unrelated	He was in the army, but he didn't have enough money to finish college.
Revised	Although his service in the army entitled him to some schooling under the GI Bill, he didn't have enough money to finish college.

Note that items joined in a coordinate series should be of the same kind. When we join items that are not of the same kind or class, the result is confusing.

Confusing	Entered in the pet show were several dogs, a parrot, a monkey, and one rather mangy cocker spaniel. (The *mangy cocker spaniel* clearly belongs among the dogs, but the construction of the sentence makes it appear that there are four classes of things. There are only three classes: dogs, a parrot, and a monkey.)
Revised	Entered in the pet show were a parrot, a monkey, and several dogs, one of which was a rather mangy cocker spaniel.

EXERCISE 33a Eliminate weak coordination in the following sentences by subordinating less important ideas.

1 I didn't see the traffic light and I didn't stop.
2 The city's sanitation workers are striking and the garbage has not been collected for two weeks.
3 The Indian Highway was formerly an Indian trail, but now it is a major highway, and it is a scenic as well as an important route.
4 Her grandfather's will left her a collection of old glass, three clocks, an antique car, and several broken bottles.
5 Pollution and overpopulation are our most serious problems, and we are spending billions on new weapons.
6 His father was an accountant and worked for the City Bank and had moved to New York in 1967.
7 Olson bought his new car only three months ago and he has already had two accidents.
8 James Dickey was born in 1923 and he has written the novel *Deliverance* and several books of poems.
9 He had dropped out of high school but he decided to get a job and when he couldn't find one he decided to go back to school and later went on to college.
10 *Funny Girl* had a long run on Broadway and broke many box office records and was later made into a movie and Barbra Streisand played the leading role.

33b

33b Avoid the "primer style" unless you want to achieve a specific effect.

The primer style consists of a series of short, simple sentences of similar structure (e.g., subject is followed immediately by predicate, clauses are joined by *and*). (See "Variety," Section 34.) This style tends to give all actions and ideas equal weight and importance. Although skilled narrative writers sometimes use the primer style deliberately and effectively, beginning writers will do well to avoid it.

Choppy   He stood on a street corner. The wind was blowing. He peered into the darkness. He was a stranger. He realized that he had no place to go.

Revised   Standing on a windy street corner and peering into the darkness, the stranger realized that he had no place to go.

Choppy   A plane far off broke the sound barrier. Several windows on the avenue were shattered. The landlords were angry. They complained to the authorities.

Revised   When several windows on the avenue were shattered by a distant plane breaking the sound barrier, the angry landlords complained to the authorities.

Joining a series of short clauses by *and* to make them into a longer sentence only compounds the error of the primer style.

Ineffective   We approached the river and we looked down from the bluff, and we could see the silvery stream and it wound below in the valley.

Revised   When we approached the river and looked down from the bluff, we could see the silvery stream winding below in the valley.

33c

EXERCISE 33b Revise the following sentences by making one idea the main clause and subordinating other ideas.

1 We drove onto a gravel road. It led into the woods. It was narrow. We wondered whether it was safe.
2 The house was very old. It was painted yellow. The paint was faded. In some places was cracked.
3 The bookshelves were too expensive. I went to a lumber yard. I bought some boards. I bought some brackets. I put them up myself.
4 I got up late this morning. I had to wait for a bus. I was late to class.
5 One of the early experimenters with submarines was Robert Fulton. He built the first successful steamboat. He also experimented with torpedoes.
6 He had never smoked marijuana before. He was invited to a pot party. He went. Someone offered him a joint. He took it. The effect was not quite what he had expected. He didn't finish it. He left the party.
7 Late-night TV talk shows are very popular. The host is usually very funny. The guests are from many walks of life. Some of them are politicians. Some are show-business celebrities. They talk about various things. The mixture makes for interesting conversation.
8 TV documentaries are very interesting. One showed the plight of the migrant workers. Another showed conditions in the ghetto. Still another showed the helplessness of our neglected senior citizens. The one I like best was entitled "Birth and Death."
9 She decided to take the subway. She didn't know the way. She asked directions. The train agent was very helpful.
10 I studied hard. I read the textbook. I read outside sources. I wrote a 15-page paper. I bought the instructor a Christmas present. I flunked the course.

33c Do not subordinate your main idea.

In many sentences, determining which ideas to place in a main clause and which to subordinate depends entirely on context. In one context, we may wish to write, *While Lincoln was still President, he was shot,* thus emphasizing the assassination itself. In another, we may wish to write, *When he was shot,*

Lincoln was still in office, thereby making more prominent the fact that he was still in office. There is no way of determining, aside from context, which of these versions is the better sentence.

But in many sentences, the logic of normal expectation works on the reader. A sentence such as *He happened to glance at the sidewalk, noticing a large diamond at his feet,* contradicts our sense of the relative importance of glancing at the sidewalk and noticing a diamond. Except in a very unusual situation, we would normally take the finding of a diamond to be the logically more important fact and would expect the sentence to read *Happening to glance at the sidewalk, he noticed a large diamond at his feet.* Sentences that subordinate what we would normally expect to be more important ideas to lesser ideas are said to have "upside-down" subordination.

33d

Ineffective	The octopus momentarily released its grip, when the diver escaped.
Revised	When the octopus momentarily released its grip, the diver escaped.
Ineffective	He was playing his first major league game, being a better first baseman than some who had been playing for years.
Revised	Although he was playing his first major league game, he was a better first baseman than some who had been playing for years.
Ineffective	I visited my home town after being away twenty years, when I was astonished at the change in its appearance.
Revised	When I visited my home town after being away twenty years, I was astonished at the change in its appearance.
Revised	After being away twenty years, I visited my home town and was astonished at the change in its appearance.

33d Avoid excessive subordination.

Unessential details in your sentences make your reader lose sight of the points you are trying to make.

Excessive Subordination	My fishing equipment includes a casting rod *which Uncle Henry gave me many years ago* and which is nearly worn out, and an assortment of lines, hooks, and bass flies, which make good bait *when I can get time off from work to go bass fishing* at Hardwood Lake.

Revised
My fishing equipment includes an old casting rod and an assortment of lines, hooks, and bass flies. The flies make good bait when I am bass fishing at Hardwood Lake.

In the particular ineffective kind of construction that is called the "house-that-Jack-built" sentence, one dependent clause is tacked on after another, each seeming to be an afterthought:

The heroine thought the hero was a gambler while he was really a government agent who was investigating the income tax frauds of gamblers who concealed the larger part of their winnings which they took in violation of laws of the state which would arrest them if they made their activity public, which is why she wouldn't marry him, which is why I was disgusted with the movie.

33d

EXERCISE 33c–d Some of the following sentences subordinate their more important ideas. Others contain excessive subordination. Rewrite them, using both coordination and subordination to make them more effective.

1 She pulled the emergency cord, averting a train wreck.
2 According to the popular ballad, Casey Jones attempted to arrive on schedule, being prevented by a head-on collision with another train.
3 The reporters, many of them wearing their press cards pinned to their lapels, flocked to the launch site, where the technicians were giving a last check to the spaceship that was to carry three astronauts, who were just then walking up the ramp, to the moon.
4 Ralph Waldo Emerson was an individualist because he said, "Whoso would be a man must be a noncomformist."
5 *A Clockwork Orange,* which was written by Anthony Burgess, and which was a best seller for many months, was made into a motion picture, directed by Stanley Kubrick, which was very well received by film critics who thought it was one of the year's best movies.
6 Although his salary remained the same, prices continued to rise.
7 Mrs. Wood opened the door of the cage, when her pet parrot escaped.
8 My sports car, which I bought from a friend of mine, a car enthusiast who buys old cars and then rebuilds them as a hobby, had developed a rumble in the engine which has begun to worry me for I know nothing about repairing cars and haven't the money to go to a mechanic.
9 He fell seven stories and broke eight ribs, puncturing one lung, although he lived to tell the tale.
10 Although Marion graduated with honors, she had to pay most of her own expenses.

33e   Use all connectives (*but, as, while,* etc.) accurately and clearly.

Careless use of such conjunctions as *and, as, but, so,* and *while* conceals the exact relationship or shade of meaning that you intend to convey.

1. Do not use the conjunction *as* in sentences where it could imply either time or cause.

Ambiguous	As the river rose to flood stage, many people fled to higher ground. (Time or cause intended?)
Revised	*When* the river rose to flood stage, many people fled to higher ground. (Time intended.)
Revised	*Because* the river rose to flood stage, many people fled to higher ground. (Cause intended.)

2. Do not use the conjunction *as* in the sense of *whether* or *that*.

Faulty	I do not know *as* I want to go tomorrow.
Revised	I do not know *whether* (or *that*) I want to go tomorrow.

3. Use the conjunction *but* to connect contrasted statements.

Faulty	He was an All-American in college, *and* today he is in poor physical condition.
Revised	He was an All-American in college, *but* today he is in poor physical condition.

The misuse (intended, of course) of *but, and though,* and *under it all* in the sentence below shows how baffling an illogical transition can be.

> [Pittsburgh millionaires] are rough but uncivil in their manners, and though their ways are boisterous and unpolished, under it all they have a great deal of impoliteness and discourtesy.
>
> O. HENRY

4. Do not use the preposition *like* as a substitute for the conjunctions *as if* or *as though* in formal writing.

Informal	He looks *like* he is exhausted.
Formal	He looks *as if* (or *as though*) he were exhausted.

34

5. Do not use the conjunction *while* in the sense of *and* or *but*.

Ineffective	John is a doctor, *while* Ray is an engineer.
Revised	John is a doctor *and* Ray is an engineer.
Ineffective	Monday was a cool day, *while* Tuesday was warmer.
Revised	Monday was a cool day, *but* Tuesday was warmer.

6. Do not use the conjunction *while* in cases where it is not clear whether time or concession is intended.

Ambiguous	*While* I was working at night in the library, I saw Jane often. (Time or concession intended?)
Revised	*When* I was working at night in the library, I saw Jane often. (Time intended.)
Revised	*Although* I was working at night in the library, I saw Jane often. (Concession intended.)

EXERCISE 33e In the following sentences replace any connectives that are used weakly or inaccurately.

1 Ann likes her coffee black, while I like cream in mine.
2 I did not feel as I was qualified for the job.
3 My parents bought a new car and they still liked the old one.
4 She was dead tired, but she lay down to rest.
5 While it was very cold, he continued to work.
6 I don't really feel like I should go out in this weather—not with the cold I have.
7 As the ship struck the rocks, several people jumped overboard.
8 He talks like he is happy.
9 I don't know if I could paint, as I have never tried.
10 As the furnace broke down, the manager closed the offices.

34 Variety VAR

Variety in length and structure of our sentences helps us avoid monotony. But a series of well-written sentences is more than a mere absence of monotony. It reflects the careful molding of sentence form to the writer's thought, and the careful choice of sentence structure and length to gain emphasis where the writer wants it (see Section 36). A long series of sentences identical in structure and similar in length, unless they are consciously planned for coherence and emphasis, is not only tiresome and ineffective, but also symptomatic of muddy thinking.

34a Avoid the overuse of short simple sentences. ✳

Ineffective	Jack approached the mare warily. She saw the bridle in his hand. He stood still. The mare waited. Jack tried to toss the reins over her head. But she galloped away.
Revised	Jack warily approached the mare, who saw the bridle in his hand. He stood still and the mare waited. But when he tried to toss the reins over her head, she galloped away.

34a

34b

34c

See **33b** for a discussion of "primer" sentences, and for exercises in combining short sentences by subordinating less important ideas.

34b Avoid the overuse of long compound sentences. ✳

(See "Subordination," **33d.**)

Ineffective	He was chief of the volunteer fire company, and he was the town's grocer, but he was never too busy in his store to attend a fire.
Revised	The chief of the volunteer fire company, who was also the town's grocer, was never too busy in his store to attend a fire. (The first coordinate clause becomes a noun phrase, the subject of the main clause in the revised sentence; the second coordinate clause becomes a subordinate clause; the third coordinate clause becomes the predicate of the main clause.)
Ineffective	She carefully powdered her nose, and then she applied her lipstick, and then she smiled at her reflection in the mirror.
Revised	She carefully powdered her nose, applied her lipstick, and then smiled at her reflection in the mirror. (The compound sentence is revised to make a simple sentence with a compound predicate.)

See **33a** for discussion and exercises on the use of subordination to improve faulty and excessive coordination.

34c Use various sentence structures to avoid monotony and increase effectiveness.

It is easy to fall into monotonous and poorly controlled patterns of sentences. Effective variety can be achieved with relatively simple modifications of word order. Remember, however, that word order is closely associated with meaning and emphasis and that shifts in order will lend slightly different shades of meaning to the whole sentence. The decision about what, if any, variation to use in a particular context must depend upon the total meaning you wish to express and upon the relation of the individual sentence to the sentences that stand before and after (see "Paragraph Coherence" in Section 32). The principal ways of varying sentences are outlined below.

1. Vary the beginnings of sentences. *

34c

Deer grazed peacefully in the valley and were unaware of the advancing hunter.

Beginning with a Prepositional Phrase
In the valley the deer grazed peacefully and were unaware of the advancing hunter.

Beginning with a Verbal Phrase
Grazing peacefully, the deer in the valley were unaware of the advancing hunter.

Beginning with an Expletive
There were deer grazing peacefully in the valley, unaware of the advancing hunter.

Beginning with a Subordinate Clause
As they grazed peacefully in the valley, the deer were unaware of the advancing hunter.

Beginning with a Coordinating Conjunction
And the deer, grazing peacefully in the valley, were unaware of the advancing hunter.
But the deer, grazing peacefully in the valley, were unaware of the advancing hunter.

A sentence beginning with a coordinating conjunction usually depends for meaning on the preceding sentence.

2. Vary the normal subject-verb-object pattern of sentences. The subject-verb-object pattern of the English sentence is so strongly established that shifts in its order are likely to produce heavy emphasis. They must therefore be used with caution. Note the following:

---

* Note that slightly more than half the sentences in most good writing begin with the subject—a great deal more than any other structure. It is the exclusive or excessively heavy use of subject beginnings that should be avoided, not the frequent use.

Subject-Verb	Verb-Subject
Henry leaped over the hedge.	Over the hedge leaped Henry.
An empty bottle stood on the table.	On the table stood an empty bottle.

Subject-Verb-Object	Object-Subject-Verb
I never said that.	That I never said.
Helen adores Siamese cats.	Siamese cats Helen adores.

Subject-Verb-Complement	Complement-Subject-Verb
We shall never be wealthy.	Wealthy we shall never be.
Einstein was surely a genius.	A genius Einstein surely was.

34c

3. Vary the usual declarative statement by using interrogative or imperative sentences when it is effective to do so.

Interrogative — What is a civilized man? By derivation of the word, he is one who lives and thinks in a city.
BERNARD IDDINGS BELL

Imperative — Observations indicate that the different clusters of galaxies are constantly moving apart from each other. To illustrate by a homely analogy, think of a raisin cake baking in an oven.

EXERCISE 34c Rewrite each of the following sentences twice, varying the structure in two of the ways suggested above.

1 We came home sullen and irritable after fighting traffic for an hour and a half.
2 The child had lost her way but was brought home by a thoughtful neighbor.
3 The coach rushed out on the field to protest the umpire's decision.
4 He knew his hangover had begun because his head ached and his mouth felt dry.
5 The upholsterer, his mouth full of tacks and his magnetic hammer swinging like a piece of machinery, stretched and fastened the chair cover with amazing speed.
6 The Surgeon General has determined that cigarette smoking is dangerous to your health, and that warning is printed on every package of cigarettes.
7 The earthquake caused much loss of life and devastation in the villages and cities of Nicaragua, and the United States quickly offered assistance.
8 Black writers have made important contributions to American literature for more than 150 years, but many educated people are still not aware of it.
9 They wanted to dance and the record player was broken.
10 They bought only old furniture which they refinished themselves, and were able to furnish their new home at relatively little cost.

35

Mark felt better as he slammed the front door. He did not even glance over his shoulder to see if his parents were watching him. He walked to a nearby park. He sat down on a bench. He knew why his parents had yelled at him. He didn't blame them. They had both worked hard at their restaurant to keep him in comfort. They wanted him to have the opportunities that they had missed. They wanted him to be a doctor. But he couldn't seem to concentrate at school. He wanted to sleep in class. He liked most of his teachers but he didn't really hear them. He brought home very poor marks. He wanted to work with automobiles. He didn't want to be a doctor. The smell of gasoline, the sound of the motor, the shine of the chrome all fascinated him. He would have to face them and tell them that he couldn't be something he didn't want to be. He delayed returning home to tell them and he did not look forward to the scene they would make and the lack of understanding they would show.

35 Parallelism ||

Parallel structure puts similar ideas into the same kinds of grammatical constructions. If one idea in a sentence is expressed by a phrase, other equal ideas should be expressed by phrases. If one idea is expressed by an infinitive, a gerund, or a clause, other equal ideas should be expressed by duplicate grammatical constructions. Parallelism helps make sentences grammatically clear by keeping elements of the same grammatical rank and function in the same kind of grammatical construction. But it is also an important device for organizing sentences, or groups of sentences, so as to emphasize their close relation in thought.

Suppose we are trying to get together our ideas about the things necessary for good writing, and that we have written the following in a first draft:

Logical thinking is one of the things necessary for good writing. Good writers also have to organize their ideas coherently. And finally, anyone who wants to write well must express his ideas clearly.

If we look at this closely, we will see that *thinking, organizing,* and *expressing* are the main related processes we are talking about. Parallel structure can help us knit these together tightly and emphasize them clearly. Compare the following single sentences with our original three sentences.

| Thinking logically,
organizing ideas coherently,
and
expressing ideas clearly | are three requirements of good
writing. |

or

| Logical thought,
coherent organization,
and
clear expression | are the major ingredients of good
writing. |

or

| Anyone who wishes to write well must
learn | to think logically,
to organize ideas
coherently,
and
to express them
clearly. |

Any of these three versions of our original first draft pulls our ideas together into a single economical unit and gives emphasis to the three major items we have in mind.

Notice how parallelism helps to keep the following sentences clear and to emphasize the relation between the ideas.

| Strikes, though sometimes necessary,
mean | loss of wages for
workers,
interference with
production for
managers,
and
disruption of services
for consumers. |

| Students can be successful if
they | buy the assigned books,
do the required reading,
and
take careful notes. |

| Political language is
designed | to make | lies sound truthful
and
murder respectable |

and
to give an appearance of
solidity to pure wind.

Note how parallelism can keep a complicated sentence from getting out of hand, as in the following from Thomas Wolfe.

And always America is | the place of deathless and enraptured moments,

		the eye	that	looked,
		the mouth	that	smiled
				and
				vanished,

and
the word;
the stone,
the leaf,
the door we | never found
and
never have
  forgotten.

Just as the judicious use of parallelism can be an aid to effective sentences, violations of grammatically required parallelism can throw the reader off and make for particularly ineffective sentences. The following three sections call attention to three situations in which we are most likely to violate required parallelism.

35a Use parallel structure for sentence elements joined by coordinating conjunctions.

For balance and smoothness in your writing let the structure of the first of two or more coordinate elements set the pattern for the structure of the remaining coordinate elements.

Awkward	She likes to sew and cooking.
Parallel	She likes to sew and cook.
Awkward	Sam is tall, with blue eyes, and has a congenial manner.
Parallel	Sam is tall, blue-eyed, and congenial.

Note: You may point up the parallel structure by repeating a strategic word or words (see also **36d**).

Ambiguous	He wants to write stories that describe the South and study the habits of the Creoles. (Stories that study the habits of the Creoles?)
Revised	He wants *to* write stories that describe the South and *to* study the habits of the Creoles.
Ambiguous	Mr. Gray helps his wife by cooking and ironing his own shirts.
Revised	Mr. Gray helps his wife *by* cooking and *by* ironing his own shirts.

EXERCISE 35a In the following sentences, express the coordinate ideas in parallel structure.

1 His work consisted of planning the menus, purchasing of the food, and supervision of the employees.
2 He bought a new Volvo having a standard transmission and with a radio and heater.
3 The lecture was long, tiresome, and could not be easily understood.
4 The biography of Stilwell is interesting, lively, and also an informative piece of writing.
5 Being too early, even if it wastes valuable time, is better than to arrive late.
6 Mary has a full-time job, is a member of the school committee, and doing her own housework.
7 The student was told to obtain a transcript of his grades and that then he could apply for admission.
8 To be a good teacher, one must have patience, liking to help others, and to show an infinite capacity for learning.
9 The policeman told us to drive very slowly and that we should not put on our bright lights.
10 Marcia moved to a new apartment with more space and having air-conditioning.

35b

35c

35b Avoid faulty parallelism with *and who, and which.*

Do not use an *and who* or an *and which* clause in a sentence unless you have already used a parallel *who* or *which* clause.

Faulty	We met Abner Fulton, a brilliant biologist and who is also an excellent pianist.
Revised	We met Abner Fulton, who is a brilliant biologist and who is also an excellent pianist.
Revised	We met Abner Fulton, who is both a brilliant biologist and an excellent pianist.
Faulty	She likes a romantic novel with exciting action and which keeps her guessing.
Revised	She likes a romantic novel which has exciting action and which keeps her guessing.

35c Use parallel constructions after correlatives.

The correlatives are *either–or, neither–nor, not only–but also, both–and, whether–or.* When the correlatives *whether–or* are used, *or* is often followed by *not.* (*I wondered whether he would come or not.*) In such sentences, of course, a parallel construction is unnecessary.

Faulty	You are either *late* or *I am early.* (An adjective made parallel with a clause.)

Revised	Either *you are late* or *I am early.* (Two parallel clauses.)
Faulty	Jim not only *has been* outstanding in athletics, but also *in* his studies. (A verb made parallel with a preposition.)
Revised	Jim has been outstanding not only *in athletics,* but also *in his studies.* (Two parallel phrases.)

EXERCISE 35c Correct the faulty use of correlatives in the following sentences.

1 A good politician not only works well with people but also he does not compromise his ideals.
2 Hemingway was both a good writer and he influenced other writers.
3 The reviewer couldn't decide whether he should ignore the book or to write an unfavorable review.
4 Either Congress will repeal the law or I think the Supreme Court will declare it unconstitutional.
5 He was both intelligent as well as courteous.

36 Emphasis EMP

Effective sentences emphasize our main ideas. We control emphasis by using subordination, parallelism, and variety carefully. But we can also emphasize ideas in other ways discussed in the following sections.

36a Place important words at the beginning or at the end of the sentence.

Generally, the most emphatic place in a sentence is its ending; the next most emphatic, its beginning; the least emphatic, its middle.

| Weak | Such matters as incorrect spelling and unconventional punctuation sometimes distract a reader from otherwise good writing. |
| More Emphatic | Incorrect spelling and unconventional punctuation sometimes distract a reader from otherwise good writing. |

Phrases such as *in my opinion, by and large, for the most part,* and the like often weaken emphasis when they come at the beginning or end of a sentence. Often the sentence will be stronger if they are simply omitted.

If qualifying phrases are necessary for accuracy, it is usually better to place them carefully inside the sentence.

| Weak | The history of English vocabulary is the history of English civilization, in many ways. |
| More Emphatic | The history of English vocabulary is, in many ways, the history of English civilization. |

36b

EXERCISE 36a Revise the following sentences by putting important words in an emphatic position.

1 He is an overbearing, egotistical bore, in my opinion.
2 The results of the flood were disastrous, by and large.
3 Women are more perceptive and far more sensitive than men are, as a rule.
4 Tolstoy had a profound understanding of people and of the passions that drive them, for the most part.
5 This university would be closed and its faculty fired, if I had my way.
6 Teddy Roosevelt was dynamic and full of life, I have read.
7 Test results prove that smoking seriously impairs the health, in most cases.
8 The lawyer shirked his responsibility and the judge was biased, it seems to me.
9 The day was clear, the sun was shining, and the snow was packed hard; it was a great day for skiing, in my opinion.
10 With its superior technology and its single-minded determination, the U.S. will definitely win the space race, if everything goes right.

36b   Use the periodic sentence for emphasis.

A PERIODIC SENTENCE holds its main idea until the end. A LOOSE SENTENCE begins with its main idea and adds subordinate details.

| Periodic | The poor, housed in crowded and run-down neighborhoods, always fighting debt, and now constantly harried by rising prices, merely survive. |
| Loose | The poor merely survive, housed in crowded and run-down neighborhoods, always fighting debt, and now constantly harried by rising prices. |

Of the two kinds of sentences, the loose is the more informal, the more natural, and by far the more common. But exactly because the periodic sentence is uncommon and unexpected, it is emphatic; and by holding its central idea until the end, it creates suspense.

Because it creates suspense, be careful not to use the periodic sentence when your subject matter does not warrant it.

| Periodic and Ineffective | At the end of a dark alley, three flights down in a dark basement full of grim and evil-looking sailors, I ate my lunch. |

Often periodic and loose constructions are more or less equally effective. Your choice must be guided by the particular emphasis you want, and by the relation of your sentence to those before it and after it.

36c

Loose	Balboa reached the Pacific after a long, hazardous journey.
Periodic	After a long, hazardous journey, Balboa reached the Pacific.
Loose	He will be a good physician, if enthusiasm is a guarantee of success.
Periodic	If enthusiasm is a guarantee of success, he will be a good physician.

EXERCISE 36b   Change these loose sentences into periodic ones.

1 She began seeing a psychiatrist regularly after her marriage broke up.
2 He started a new business and made a million dollars after his first business failed.
3 The wine turned to vinegar, although we tried to keep it in a cool place.
4 The boat neared the finish line, the rowers bending rhythmically and the oars flashing in the sun.
5 They stood the cold for an hour, stamping their feet and blowing on their fingers.
6 I saw two cars crash head-on several years ago on a three-lane highway in Minnesota.
7 Her doctor insisted that she take a vacation after she suffered a severe depression.
8 Your research paper will be accepted if, after you have finished typing it, the footnotes are in good order.
9 Norma had still not balanced her accounts, although she had checked her figures and added again.
10 Three miles of rough water lay between the ship and the shore.

36c   Arrange items in a series in order of importance as well as in parallel form.

When words or ideas are in a series, readers generally assume that they are arranged in order of increasing importance. Thus if you say *She is young, wealthy, and intelligent,* you suggest to a reader that you value intelligence most highly. The meaning for your reader will be different if you say *She is intelligent, young, and wealthy.* Note the following examples. In each, items are arranged in order of their importance.

His life was brief and tragic.
He was broke, lonely, and thoroughly discouraged.
The city is famous for clear signs, wide clean streets, beautiful parks, and well-planned museums.

ANTICLIMAX—the arrangement of ideas in reverse order of importance—is sometimes used for its humor.

If once a man indulges himself in murder, very soon he comes to think little of robbery; and from robbing he next comes to drinking and Sabbath-breaking, and from that to incivility and procrastination.   THOMAS DE QUINCEY

36d

EXERCISE 36c Revise the following sentences by arranging ideas in more logical order.

1 He moved away from the city because he was ill, his rent was high, and he wanted to let his dog run.
2 Most students get bored with school after years of college, high school, and elementary school.
3 She inherited a million dollars, a house, and some jewelry.
4 The play closed after the first week and received terrible reviews.
5 The candidate promised a guaranteed income for all, mingled with men in the street, and smiled at children.
6 Charles is a capable gardener, a famous doctor, and a poker player.
7 We find similar psychological reactions in frogs, in guinea pigs, in men, and in rats.
8 During his vacation David acquired some souvenirs, a wife, and a bad sunburn.
9 The earthquake caused 100 deaths and toppled several of the buildings in the area.
10 Laurence Olivier is one of the great Shakespearean actors of all time and a director and producer as well.

36d   Repeat key words and ideas for emphasis.

Careless and awkward repetition of words makes sentences weak and flabby (see **41d**), but careful repetition of key words can be an effective way of gaining emphasis, as in the following sentences.

A *moderately* honest man with a *moderately* faithful wife, *moderate* drinkers both, in a *moderately* healthy home: that is the true middle class unit.   G. B. SHAW

Don't *join* too many gangs. *Join* few if any. *Join* the United States and *join* a family—but not much in between, unless a college.

ROBERT FROST

It is the *dull* man who is always *sure,* and the *sure* man who is always *dull.*

H. L. MENCKEN

Note: For a discussion of ways in which repetition of words and ideas link sentences within a paragraph, see **32d.**

EXERCISE 36d Discuss the effectiveness of the repetition of words and phrases in each of the sentences below. (Note how frequently effective repetition and effective parallelism reinforce each other.)

1 No one can be perfectly free till all are free; no one can be perfectly moral till all are moral; no one can be perfectly happy till all are happy.   HERBERT SPENCER

2 There is no mistake; there has been no mistake; and there shall be no mistake.   DUKE OF WELLINGTON

3 To know how to say what others only know how to think is what makes men poets or sages; and to dare to say what others only dare to think makes men martyrs or reformers or both.

ELIZABETH CHARLES

4 It is true that you may fool all the people some of the time; you can even fool some of the people all the time; but you can't fool all of the people all the time.   ABRAHAM LINCOLN

36e   Prefer the active to the passive voice.

The ACTIVE VOICE puts the subject (the actor), first, and follows it with the active verb, and then the object (the receiver of the action): *The cat killed the rat.* The PASSIVE VOICE turns things around, putting the receiver in front, then the verb, and finally the subject: *The rat was killed by the cat.*

The passive voice has its uses (see below), and when you need it, you should of course use it. But the active is almost always more direct, more forceful, and more economical. Always prefer it to the passive unless you have good reason not to. When you find yourself using the passive, check yourself to be sure you really need it, that what you want to say cannot in fact be better said in the active voice. More often than not, you will find that you gain both economy and emphasis with the active voice. Note the following examples:

Passive   The pump has been installed in several medical centers and will be tested next week. (15 words)

Active   Several medical centers have installed the pump and will test it next week. (13 words)

Passive	Two devices for insuring safety are shown in the accompanying illustrations. (11 words)
Active	The accompanying illustrations show two safety devices. (7 words)
Passive	It was voted by the faculty that all students should be required to take mathematics. (15 words)
Active	The faculty voted to require mathematics. (6 words)
Passive	Your request has been received and reviewed by the department, but it has been decided that it does not meet the requirement as stated by departmental rules. (27 words)
Active	We have reviewed your request; it does not meet requirements stated by the department. (14 words)

Careless and unnecessary use of the passive sometimes leads to a shift in voice which makes your sentences inconsistent. (See **10a.**) Note the following:

36e

Faulty	He boiled the water, and then the spaghetti was added.
Revised	He boiled the water, and then added the spaghetti.
Faulty	When a weasel sucks eggs, the meat is sucked out of the egg.
Revised	When a weasel sucks eggs, he sucks the meat out of the egg.

There are two situations in which the passive voice is useful and natural.

1. When the subject is not known. Consider the following:

Peter L. Little was attacked and badly beaten while walking through Eastern Park about 11:15 last night.

The play was first performed in 1591.

In the first of these, since the writer presumably does not know who attacked Peter L. Little, he is forced to use the passive or to resort to some much less economical alternative such as *Some person or persons unknown attacked and badly beat. . . .* The second sentence suggests that though there is a record of the play's performance, there is none of its performers.

2. When the receiver of the action is more important than the actor. Consider the following:

The new bridge was completed in April.

The experiment was finished on June 16; on June 17 the conclusions were reviewed by the advisory board and reported immediately to the Pentagon.

In such sentences as these, we have little interest in <u>who</u> completed the bridge, or <u>who</u> performed the experiment and reported the results; the important things are the bridge and the experiment.

EXERCISE 36e In the following sentences replace the passive voice with the active.

1 A boomerang can be made to do amazing stunts by a skillful thrower.
2 My ankles were snapped at by an angry dog.
3 The radiator of her car became frozen during the cold spell.
4 Extreme caution is needed if we are to experiment with genetic change.
5 Police procedures were scrutinized by the press.
6 An addition to the house was planned by my parents.
7 The returned astronauts were interviewed by reporters.
8 The menu was selected by the chairman of the refreshments committee.
9 Many major accidents are caused by drunken drivers.
10 Polio vaccine is distributed by the local Department of Health.

36e

"EFFECTIVE SENTENCES" REVIEW EXERCISE (Sections 33–36) Indicate what strikes you as the principal error from the standpoint of effectiveness in each of the following sentences (faulty subordination, lack of emphasis, lack of parallelism, etc.) and then revise the sentence.

1 While Mario was still deeply in debt, he felt that the bargain was too good to let pass.
2 The child was terrified and confused and he fell exhausted on the wet leaves.
3 Robert Frost was a poet. He wrote about rural New England. He also wrote about the human condition.
4 After reading the book, Susan decided to change her way of life, and her plans for the future also changed.
5 The fighter was very strong and in excellent condition and he was knocked out in the fifth round.
6 Poverty still exists in the United States, and it's a shame because we are the wealthiest nation on earth, and there is no excuse for it, and it's about time we eradicated it.
7 Many countries are suffering badly from overpopulation, and India and Pakistan are but two examples.
8 Some college students regard their education as irrelevant, and not being useful.
9 After working in the Peace Corps for two years, Elizabeth returned to school after refusing several job offers.
10 He leaned back in his chair, closed his eyes, rested his hands on his lap, and sleep came to him.
11 While Chekhov was the principal support of his family, he attended medical school and wrote short stories.
12 The substitute teacher was a married woman with a good sense of

humor and who loved science ardently and conveyed this to her classes.

13 To a naughty child, a scolding parent seems like a giant standing seven feet tall with a large mouth, and having eyes that glared in the dark.

14 Our love of Colonial arts and crafts is reflected in our homes and in our home magazines but our love of modern technological skills is also reflected in our homes and magazines.

15 Arizona has the largest United States Indian population and the Hopi, Navajo, and Apache are the names of the Indian tribes there.

16 To become a responsible voter you should know the issues. You should listen to the candidates. You should become familiar with their views. You should also learn their weaknesses. You should also come to know their strengths. Then you can make a wise choice.

17 Rachel Carson wrote a great deal about the problems that arise when insecticide is used and she was vigorously opposed by insecticide companies and some people who find insecticides helpful but what about the people who have been poisoned by them?

18 Harlem is reached by walking up Fifth Avenue, the most glamorous street in the richest city in the world, and it is infested with rats and disease.

19 Terror gripped the city of Boston when the Boston Strangler roamed free, and later a movie was made that recalled those days.

20 The space trip was an unqualified success, and the astronauts had been kept in seclusion for weeks before it to guard them against infection.

LOGIC
LOG

37

In answering he states the question, and expoundeth the terms thereof. Otherwise the disputants shall end, where they ought to have begun, in differences about words, and be barbarians each to the other, speaking in a language neither understand.

THOMAS FULLER (1642)

I come from a state that raises corn and cotton and cockleburs and democrats, and frothy eloquence neither convinces nor satisfies me. I am from Missouri. You have got to show me.

WILLIAM DUNCAN VANDIVER

Clear and grammatical structure is not an end in itself, but a means for communicating facts and ideas clearly. Clear and purposeful writing reflects clear and logical thinking. People who complain "My ideas are good, but I can't express them clearly in writing" are usually fooling themselves. Vague and undirected writing is likely to reflect vague and undirected thinking.

The treatment of logic that follows is brief and oversimplified. It is limited to those matters that have a direct relationship to your writing.

37a   Define terms whose exact meaning is essential to clear communication.

Clear-cut definition is central to clear thinking and writing. Your reader must know what you mean by your terms before he can understand you. Much senseless argument arises because people fail to agree on meanings. Your writing will be clearer and stronger if you are always sure to define important terms that you use. To do so, you need to understand what a sound definition requires.

1. Definition by word substitution. To define *education* as *learning,* or *freedom* as *liberty* serves little purpose. But many times concrete terms can be quite satisfactorily defined merely by offering a synonym that the reader is likely to know. This is particularly true with technical or other little-known terms. Often an APPOSITIVE—that is, another noun, or a group of words used as a noun—placed immediately after the term will be useful for such a definition.

> the cardiac heart muscle, or principal heart muscle
> the meerkat, or South African mongoose
> the mongoose, a small animal that feeds on snakes and rodents
> cannikin, an old New England word for a wooden basket

2. Formal definition. We learn about something new by finding out if it resembles things we already know and then noting how it differs from them. The steps in constructing a formal definition are exactly the same. We first explain the class of things—the genus—to which it belongs, and then explain how it differs from the other things in that class.

A. First put the term into the class of objects (*genus*) to which it belongs. This process is called CLASSIFICATION.

Term		Genus
A saw	is	a *cutting tool.*
A carpet	is	a *floor covering.*

In general, the narrower the classification, the clearer the eventual definition.

Not	A rifle is a *weapon.*
But	A rifle is a *firearm.*

Though *weapon* is a legitimate classification for *rifle,* for purposes of definition it includes more than is necessary (*knives, spears, bows and arrows, clubs,* etc.).

B. Next, distinguish the term from other objects in its class. This process is called DIFFERENTIATION.

Term		Genus	Differentiation
A saw	is	a *cutting tool*	*with a thin, flat blade and a series of teeth on the edge.*
A carpet	is	a *floor covering*	*of woven or felted fabric, usually tacked to the floor.*

C. Use parallel form in stating the term to be defined and its definition. Do not use the phrases *is when* or *is where* in making definitions.

Not	A debate *is when* two people or sides argue a given proposition in a regulated discussion.
But	A *debate is a regulated discussion* of a given proposition between two matched sides.

D. Be sure that the definition itself does not contain the name of the thing defined or any derivative of it. Nothing is achieved when words are defined in terms of themselves.

Not	A rifle is a firearm with *rifling* inside its barrel to impart rotary motion to its projectile.
But	A rifle is a firearm with *spiral grooves* inside its barrel to impart rotary motion to its projectile.

Whenever possible, define a term in words that are more familiar than the term itself. The complexity of Dr. Samuel Johnson's definition of the simple word *network* is notorious:

Network: anything reticulated or decussated, at equal distances, with interstices between the intersections.

Ordinarily, of course, you will define terms without being aware of giving them a genus and a differentiation. But it is always possible to check your definition against the criteria given above. Consider the following example from a student paper:

> Finally, college is valuable to a person interested in success. By *success* I don't mean what is usually thought of when that word is used. I mean achieving one's goals. Everybody has his own goals to achieve, all of them very different. But whatever they are, college will give one the know-how and the contacts he needs to achieve them successfully.

This definition is obviously unsatisfactory; but the specifications for definition will help clarify why and how it breaks down. If the statement which this paragraph makes about *success* is isolated, it comes out like this: *Success is the successful achievement of goals which know-how and contacts gained at college help one achieve.* First, this statement violates one of the principles of definition because it defines the word in terms of itself—*success is the successful achievement. . . .* Next, the writer does not make it clear what he means by *goals,* and the qualifying clause *which know-how and contacts gained at college help one achieve* does nothing to help us grasp his intended meaning because we do not know what his definition would be for *know-how* and *contacts.* Hence he has failed in both aspects of good definition. He has neither put the terms into an understandable class nor made a real differentiation. What he says is that success means being successful, which is not a definition.

3. Extended definition. A good many words, particularly abstract words like *propaganda, democracy, virtue, religion, freedom,* and *justice,* require considerably more than a formal definition if their meaning is to be very clear.

We may define a *representative democracy,* for instance, as a *form of government in which political power resides in the people and is given by them to elected representatives.* That is a sound logical definition. But clearly democracy as we understand it in the United States will not be contained in such a sentence. Nor is a person unacquainted with the United States likely to derive much understanding of our government from such a definition. If we are going to clarify the meaning of the term for ourselves and others, we shall need to provide illustrations, to make comparisons, not only with other forms of government, but perhaps also with "democracy" as it exists in other countries, or as it has been used in the past. Such an expansion, or extension, of our basic formal definition is what we mean by EXTENDED DEFINITION. Extended definitions may be one paragraph long, or may take an entire article or even a book.

The following paragraph illustrates a simple extended definition. (For further examples see pages 219–220.) Note that the initial topic sentence in this definition gives us a kind of dictionary definition of induction. It belongs to a class of things—in this case reasoning. It differs from other things in that class—in this case by being that kind of reasoning in which we first examine particulars and then draw a conclusion from them. That general definition is then developed in two parts: (1) by explaining the kind of scientific reasoning that is inductive, and (2) by explaining, through a series of specific examples, how our everyday reasoning is inductive.

37a

> Induction is the kind of reasoning by which we examine a number of particulars or specific instances and on the basis of them arrive at a conclusion. The scientific method is inductive when the scientist observes a recurrent phenomenon and arrives at the conclusion or hypothesis that under certain conditions this phenomenon will always take place; if in the course of time further observation supports his hypothesis and if no exceptions are observed, his conclusion is generally accepted as truth and is sometimes called a law. In everyday living, too, we arrive at conclusions by induction. Every cat we encounter has claws; we conclude that all cats have claws. Every rose we smell is fragrant; we conclude that all roses are fragrant. An acquaintance has, on various occasions, paid back money he has borrowed; we conclude that he is frequently out of funds but that he pays his debts. Every Saturday morning for six weeks the new paper boy is late in delivering the paper; we conclude that he sleeps on Saturday mornings and we no longer look for the paper before nine o'clock. In each case we have reasoned inductively from a number of instances; we have moved from an observation of some things to a generalization about all things in the same category.
>
> NEWMAN AND GENEVIEVE BIRK,
> *Understanding and Using English*

EXERCISE 37a(1)   Examine the following definitions and be prepared to answer the following questions about each. Is the class to which the term belongs clearly named? Is the class narrow enough to be satisfactory? Does the definition clearly differentiate the term from other things in the class? Does the definition repeat the term it is defining? Is it stated in parallel form?

1 An expert is a man who guesses right.
2 A pot party is where everyone is smoking pot.
3 A thermometer measures temperature.
4 Religion is emotion seasoned with morality.
5 A touchdown pass is when the player throws the ball for a touchdown.

6 Analysis means to break something down into its parts.
7 Passive resistance is when people simply refuse to follow orders.
8 A frying pan is a cooking utensil which is large and flat.
9 Inflation is rising prices.
10 "Home is the place where, when you have to go there, they have to take you in."

37b

EXERCISE 37a(2)   Write formal definitions of two of the following.

1 rain check
2 guerilla
3 jukebox
4 chair
5 examination

EXERCISE 37a(3)   Select one of the following and write a paragraph of extended definition. Use your first sentence to state a formal definition of the term and then clarify it in the rest of the paragraph.

1 mass media
2 radical
3 women's liberation movement
4 propaganda
5 the term "turned on"

37b   Support or qualify all generalizations.

A generalization is an assertion that what is true of several particulars (objects, experiences, people) of the same class (genus) is true of most or all of the particulars of that class. For example, the statement *Drinking coffee in the evening always keeps me awake all night* is a generalization based on several particular experiences on separate evenings. Generalization is an essential process in thinking; without it, there could be no evaluation of experience—only the accumulation of isolated facts. Yet generalization has its dangers, as the following examples reveal.

1. Base all generalizations on adequate evidence.   We all tend to generalize on the basis of a few striking examples, especially when they accord with what we want to believe.

The hasty generalization—leaping to conclusions on the basis of insufficient evidence—is especially dangerous in that it can lead you to make absurd assertions. Test the soundness of this generalization:

Particular A	Mrs. Jones's son never gets home when his mother tells him to.
Particular B	Sally, the girl down the street, won't go to college though her father wants her to.

Particular C	My brother keeps telling his daughter not to go out with that boy, but she keeps right on doing it.
Hasty Generalization	Young people today don't obey their parents (or are a bad lot, or rebel against authority).
	(Does this generalization include Henry and John and Mike, who are always home on time? Or Katie who is in college though she doesn't want to be? Or the brother's other daughter, who married the son of her father's best friend?)
Particular A	I know an Italian who is a bookie.
Particular B	The Italian who runs our neighborhood grocery once short-changed my neighbor.
Particular C	A man named Valenti was a gangster.
Hasty Generalization	Italians are crooks.

37b

Generalizations of this sort are particularly dangerous. They make statements about groups that contain millions of individuals, on the basis of three or four examples. And they more often than not exclude other examples with which the speaker is equally familiar, but which don't fit the generalization.

To protect yourself, as well as to be fair to your readers, never advance a generalization unless you are prepared to support it with ample evidence. How much evidence you need depends on the purpose of your writing. Sometimes you will need to list only three or four examples; sometimes you will need to analyze the evidence itself in detail. Generalizations often take the form of topic sentences in paragraphs (see **32a**).

2. Be cautious in using such words as *always, never, all, none, right, wrong* **in generalizations.** Broad generalizations are as pernicious as hasty generalizations. In fact, the two usually spring from the same desire—to reach a conclusion without going through the effort of collecting evidence. A generalization is often rendered unreasonable by the careless use of *never* instead of *seldom,* of *always* instead of *usually.*

Overstated	Students who study regularly always do better in their courses than those who do not.
Qualified	Students who study regularly usually do better in their courses than those who don't.
Or	Other things being equal, students who study regularly do better in their courses than those who don't.

(Clearly, how well one does in a course depends upon previous experience, native ability, and other factors as well as the amount of study. Unhappily, some students who study a great deal do not do well.)

Overstated People who are excessively radical in their youth always become conservative when they acquire power and property.

Qualified Even the most radical youths are likely to grow conservative when they acquire power and property.

37c

Note that an overstated generalization does not necessarily specifically state that it applies to all people. By not making a qualification, it clearly implies all.

EXERCISE 37b Discuss the following sentences as generalizations. Restate those that seem hasty or too broad.

1 Women who have children cannot work and still care properly for their children.
2 Television is responsible for much of the violence of today.
3 No intelligent person can believe in religion in the twentieth century.
4 A college education increases one's earning power.
5 Inflation is caused by a small number of greedy corporations.
6 Women who support women's liberation are those who are frustrated and unsuccessful.
7 Anyone who gets to be head of a large corporation has to be ruthless and materialistic.
8 Lobbies discourage honest legislation.
9 Welfare discourages people from seeking employment.
10 Students who earn their own way through college are more successful.

37c **Base your arguments on honest evidence and present them fairly.**

Consciously or unconsciously, in our desire to be right, we tend to falsify, suppress evidence, call names, cheat, and hit below the belt in our arguments.

1. Base your judgment on what you know, not on what you want to believe. Prejudice (PREJUDGMENT, or judgment before the facts are examined) is the commonest type of unfairness. Notice in the examples below that a judgment is passed although no facts pertinent to that judgment have been stated.

I heard that Steve didn't get in until 2 A.M. last night, *and you can bet that he was spending his time with some other woman.*

(How does the speaker know Steve wasn't working until 2 A.M.? Or that he wasn't involved in an accident? Or that he wasn't with his brother who was ill?)

Did you know that someone said Peggy stole money? We must ask her to resign immediately.
(Who is "someone"? Where did the information come from originally? What does Peggy say?)

37c

Unhappily, such leaps in logic, often in less easily recognizable form, make up much of everyday talk, and the careless thinking that goes with it. Too often, our generalizations rest upon vague feelings; we have actually made up our minds. We fit the facts to our conclusions, not our conclusions to the facts. Since our neighbor strikes us as unfriendly, we don't like him. We have made our judgment. Then we notice that various people frequently come to his home but leave quite quickly. He is a bookie, we conclude, paying off his bets.

Out of the same kind of prejudgments come far more serious conclusions—that Jews are not to be trusted, that Greeks are surly, that Italians are noisy, that blacks are lazy, that Republicans are bad and Democrats good, that corporations are greedy, and so on.

2. Do not try to dismiss an argument or an opponent by appealing to general prejudice. If we are to argue soundly and fairly, we must try to examine the issues in question, and to appeal to reason. Arguments that divert attention from the actual question by trying to appeal to the prejudices and emotions of the audience may succeed; but they do so, at best, at the expense of avoiding the real questions, and at worst, by being irresponsible and dishonest.

Many appeals to emotion and prejudice make use of the connotations of words (see Section 40). Today, for example, words like *radical, permissive* and *cover-up* can be counted on to bring an unfavorable response from many audiences. Words like *faith, democratic tradition, freedom,* and *efficiency* can be counted on to bring favorable responses from most audiences. The calculated—or careless—use of such words therefore tends to evoke an emotional rather than a reasonable response.

Much irresponsible argument consciously or unconsciously relies on such words. Candidate Jones is thus described as standing for "free, honest, and effective government," a description which leaves us with a pleasurable feeling that Jones is the right man for the job, but with no specific information about what programs he will or will not support. If, in contrast, Candidate Smith is described to us as "a radical with strong leftist ideas" we are likely to end up voting for Candidate Jones without ever having the faintest idea whether either Jones or Smith supports lower or higher taxes, slum clearance, or funds for new roads—all questions we are vitally interested in.

A. Do not sidestep an argument by trying to discredit the man who proposed it. This is known as ARGUMENT TO THE MAN (*argumentum ad hominem*). It fails to take into account that even though discredited for one thing, the man might be right about others.

37c

> Why should you believe what Hartwell says about the needs of our schools? He is suspected of taking bribes.
> (Quite aside from the fact that Hartwell is only "suspected of taking bribes," what he has to say about school needs may be based upon extensive study and analysis.)
> Don't listen to Collins's arguments for abortion. He doesn't even like children.
> (That Collins doesn't like children says something about him. But his arguments for abortion may stem from deep conviction reached after long experience as a doctor.)

B. Do not associate an idea with a great name or movement in the hope of imbuing your idea with borrowed prestige. This is the erroneous technique of TRANSFER (*argumentum ad verecundiam*). This method usually involves associating an idea with a great name or movement (or, particularly, with an attractive face or figure, as in advertising) in the hope that its prestige or glamour will be transferred to the proposal being argued. The transfer device also works in reverse: If a proposal or person can be associated with a movement or name in general disfavor (communism, economic-royalism, and so on), it or he has very little chance of being objectively and logically judged. The technique clouds the issue, for the associations made usually have no real bearing on the conclusions drawn.

> If Abraham Lincoln were alive today, I am sure he would devote his full energies to seeing our policy made the law of the land.
> She's lovely! She's engaged! She uses X!
> He believes in a high income tax, just as do the Marxists.

C. Do not sidestep an argument by appealing to the instincts and ideas of the crowd. This is known as ARGUMENT TO THE PEOPLE (*argumentum ad populum*) or the "bandwagon" approach. It assumes that what the crowd thinks or believes is right. Thus, to be right, one must go along with the crowd. Obviously this is not true, as many incidents of mob rule would bear out. Nonetheless it is a favorite approach among advertisers, who are masters of this appeal:

Drink X! For 75 years *it has been the favorite drink of the man in the street, You'll like it too.*

Decent, upright citizens will not be interested in anything he says.

EXERCISE 37c Discuss the "fairness" of the statements below.

1 How can movie stars have happy marriages? They're too good-looking.

2 Just as an individual would be in trouble if he spent more than he earned, so must the government keep its expenditures in line with its revenue.

3 It says in the Bible that a woman taken in adultery must be stoned to death, and what was good enough for the Bible is good enough for us.

4 The reason that Congress doesn't investigate corruption is that the members of Congress are themselves corrupt.

5 How can Mr. Barry be a competent philosophy teacher? It is clear that he is a complete atheist.

6 What's wrong with our college students today is that they are pampered children.

7 He knew how to run the lathe, but I didn't hire him because he spent a year in reform school and once a criminal always a criminal.

8 The French take advantage of tourists; the Paris hotel I stayed at padded my bill.

9 Black people are born with a natural sense of rhythm.

10 Draft resisters are just afraid to die for their country.

37d   **Be sure that statements involving cause-and-effect relationships are logically sound.**

Some of the defects of thinking arise, not from prejudice, unfairness, or ignorance of the facts, but from lack of training in logical processes. The two major logical processes are INDUCTION and DEDUCTION.

In the process of INDUCTION, thinking proceeds from the particular to the general. This means, for example, that when particular facts are shown time after time to be true, or when a particular laboratory experiment time after time yields the same result, or when a wide and varied sampling of people gives the same type of answer to a given question, <u>then</u> a general conclusion based on the facts in question may be drawn. Repeated experimentation and testing led to the conclusion that the Salk vaccine would help prevent polio. The scientist uses induction when he tests and retests his hypothesis before stating it as a general truth. The whole "scientific method" proceeds by inductive processes.

In the process of DEDUCTION, thinking proceeds from the

general to the particular. This means that from a general conclusion other facts are deduced. Obviously, then, if deduction is to be valid, the conclusion from which you operate must be true. Given sound and valid conclusions from which to draw, deduction is a shrewd and effective logical technique. Knowing that penicillin is an effective weapon against infection, we wisely seek a doctor to administer it to us if we have infections.

Notice that there is an induction-deduction cycle of reasoning. The sound conclusions reached through induction may in turn serve as the bases for deduction. For example, over many years the National Safety Council has kept careful records of holiday highway accidents and has reached the valid conclusion that accidents increase greatly on holiday weekends. From this conclusion, you can deduce that it is safer not to travel on holiday weekends.

37d

The intricacies of induction and deduction as systems of logic would take many pages to explore. The foregoing is designed merely to give a working definition of each, from which we can now proceed to examine a few of the most common errors in reasoning. Such errors are called LOGICAL FALLACIES.

1. Do not assume that there is a cause-and-effect relationship between two facts merely because one follows the other in time. This fallacy is known as *post hoc, ergo propter hoc* ("after this, therefore because of this").

> We did not begin to have great increases in the cost of living until Nixon was in office. Clearly, his actions caused our present inflation.
> (Inflation is the product of complex forces. The mere fact that it became serious <u>after</u> Nixon took office may or may not have been related to the policies while he was President.)
> I won't say he's to blame, but Jane certainly wasn't an alcoholic before she married him.
> (The statement clearly implies that the drinking was caused by the marriage since it followed the marriage. But equally clearly, many other events have occurred in the meantime. Is Jane's life lonely? Is her husband away a great deal? Alcoholism is a slow-growing disease; did Jane not drink at all before she was married?)

2. Do not mistake a mere inference for a logically sound conclusion. This fallacy is known as *non sequitur* ("it does not follow").

> This is the best play I have seen this year and it should win the Pulitzer Prize.
> (Have you seen *all* the plays produced this year? Are you qualified to judge the qualities that make a Pulitzer Prize play? Does it

follow that just because a play is the best you have seen this year, it should therefore win the Pulitzer Prize?)

State College has a new athletic program, a new science building, and many new faculty. Clearly, more and more students will enroll. (The conclusion takes for granted that improved facilities and new faculty will cause enrollments to increase. But are these necessarily the things which lead students to select State College? And what if college-age population decreases? Or the costs of higher education become prohibitive?)

3. Do not assume the truth of something you are trying to prove. This fallacy is known as BEGGING THE QUESTION.

37d

His handwriting is hard to read because it is illegible.

I like Buicks because they are my favorite automobiles.

(In the first of these, since *illegible* means "difficult or impossible to read," the writer has said only that *the writing is hard to read because it is hard to read.* In the second, the writer has said *I like Buicks because I like Buicks.*)

I don't care what he's done; if he's in jail he's done *something* wrong. Good people don't go to jail.

(The writer here is really trying to defend the generalization that *Good people don't go to jail.* But he asserts, to begin with, his conviction that all people in jail have done something wrong—in other words *cannot be good.* Thus this statement amounts to merely repeating what he intends to prove.)

4. Do not assume that because two circumstances or ideas are alike in some respects, they are alike in all other respects. This is the fallacy of FALSE ANALOGY—and perhaps the principal cause of shoddy political thinking.

Of course he'll make a good Secretary of Agriculture—hasn't he lived on a farm all his life and hasn't he succeeded in making a profitable business of raising livestock!

(Undoubtedly, the Secretary of Agriculture should have experience with farmers' problems, and undoubtedly he should be a competent man. But a farming background and success in raising livestock are not in themselves proof that a man will be a good administrator or know what is best for all farmers.)

5. Do not assume that there are only two alternatives when actually there are several. Truth is sometimes an either/or sort of thing. Jones either went to New York or he didn't. You either passed the examination or you failed to pass it. Bill either voted Republican or he didn't. But most of the things about which we argue are not as clear-cut as this.

Courses, or governments, are not simply "good" or "bad"; the in-between possibilities are many. Arguing as if there were only two possibilities when the facts justify a variety of possibilities is known as the ALL-OR-NOTHING FALLACY, or the FALSE DILEMMA.*

> Students come to college either to work or to loaf. You must admit that John hasn't been working very much. Clearly, therefore, he came to college for an easy four years.
> (Most of us would probably agree that some students work a great deal, some not much at all. But clearly there are all kinds of in-between combinations of working and not working.)

> There's no sense talking further. Mustangs are better than Datsuns or they are not. All we have to do is get the facts and buy the better car.
> (Choices between cars are, unfortunately, not as neat and simple as this writer would like.)

37d

6. Avoid contradicting yourself. This fallacy occurs when you are unwilling or unable to establish a clear conclusion or opinion—when you want to have your cake and eat it too.

> Democracy and communism are widely different political systems, although communism is really an economic system.

EXERCISE 37d Discuss the validity of the reasoning in the following sentences. Point out which rules of logic are violated.

1 The government must cut spending because economy in government is essential.
2 World War I started during Wilson's term, World War II started during Roosevelt's term, and the Vietnam War escalated during Johnson's term; if we elect another Democratic president he'll start another war.
3 I knew Dwight Eisenhower would make a good president because he had led the Allied forces to victory in World War II.
4 Anyone who argues for increased contacts with the Soviet Union must be a communist himself.
5 Students are like machines: they should be oiled regularly with recreation and given frequent rests or they'll wear out.
6 I'd make a good movie critic because I love going to the movies.
7 The Rockefellers make good governors because they're used to handling large sums of money.
8 He made very good grades in college so he's bound to do well in the business world.
9 That girl my brother's seeing is a very bad influence on him; he met her at Christmas time and within a year he had grown a beard and dropped out of college.

*These two fallacies are frequently distinguished from each other, but both involve ignoring alternative possibilities.

10 An old remedy for nosebleed is to tie a piece of red yarn around the person's throat. I didn't believe it would work until I tried it the other day when John had a nosebleed. His nose stopped bleeding just a few minutes after. The old remedies are really wonderful.

"LOGIC" REVIEW EXERCISES (Section 37)

EXERCISE A Examine the reasoning in the following conversation. What generalizations does Jones make? What evidence does he offer to support them? When Smith says, "You don't want progress," is he really addressing himself to Jones's statements? What have automobiles got to do with the question? Smith says anyone can read and understand a newspaper today. Would you qualify that generalization? Smith makes an assumption about the reason that more people can read newspapers today than in the past. What is the assumption? What, if any, error in reasoning is he making?

37d

MR. JONES: Newspapers today coddle and spoon-feed the public by such devices as cheesecake, one-syllable words, clichés, jargon, etc. Don't you think it's about time that the public did something about this? It seems to me that our standards of literacy are getting lower and lower. Newspapers used to have a higher standard. They stood for something. Now they depend almost exclusively on cheap devices and sensationalism. All papers must follow this policy if they are to survive.

MR. SMITH: What you're saying is, "Let's go back to the covered wagon era." You don't want to progress. Don't you think automobiles are a sign of progress? I do. Similarly, with newspapers. Today they reach many more people than they used to. Anyone can read and understand a newspaper today. That's more than they could do a hundred years ago. If that isn't progress, then nothing is.

EXERCISE B Discuss in one or two paragraphs the reasoning in the following selection. What generalizations are made? Are they reasonable? Do you find any common errors in reasoning in the selection? If so, what are they?

SPORTS VERSUS THE SPORTSWRITER

The trouble with sports is the sportswriters. These tin-horn sports, these semiliterate dealers in clichés, cram the daily newspapers with misinformation and moronic opinions about atheltes, coaches, and sports themselves. The day after a sports contest sees the poor sports lover once again a victim in another of the eternal successions of "mornings-after"—when sportswriters begin again their assault on the English language, good taste, and common sense.

One would think that people who pretend to know so much about the secret workings and inside strategy of sports would be able to report on a football or baseball game with some objectivity and penetration. But no! The sportswriter goes to great pains to tell us what we already know: that Old Siwash won. He tells us further that it is his considered opinion that Old Siwash played the better game. He then proceeds to indulge in assorted bits of irrelevancy and viciousness, according to the state of his ulcers. He gives us the startling news that Old Siwash's supporters were eager to win the game; that Halfback Haggerty would not have fumbled the kickoff if he had caught it instead.

But a sportswriter in front of a typewriter is only an idiot; a sportswriter in front of a microphone is a jabbering idiot. The next time you listen to a radio broadcast of a football game, force yourself to listen to the half-time interviews. Listen to the sportswriters gather to tell one another, in their own substandard idiom, what marvelous jobs they had done in "bringing you the game." Listen to them inform you, in voices choked with emotion and borrowed Scotch, that the game isn't over until the final gun sounds—"that anything can happen." This is undoubtedly what sportswriters mean when they speak of "inside dope."

37d

EXERCISE C The following problems are designed to direct your attention to some of the violations of logic that we encounter every day.

1 Analyze several automobile advertisements, several cosmetic or drug advertisements, and several cigarette advertisements in current magazines or on television on the basis of the following questions:

   a What specific appeals are made? (E.g.: automobile advertising makes wide use of the "bandwagon" approach; cosmetic advertising often uses "transfer" methods.) How logical are these appeals?

   b Are all terms clearly defined?

   c What kinds of generalizations are used or assumed? Are these generalizations adequately supported?

   d Is evidence honestly and fairly presented?

   e Are cause-and-effect relationships clear and indisputable?

2 Look through copies of your daily newspaper and bring to class letters to the editor or excerpts from political speeches that contain examples of fallacious reasoning. Look for false analogies, unsupported generalizations, name-calling, and prejudices.

3 Read an opinion article in a popular magazine and write a report analyzing the logic underlying the opinions and conclusions stated.

WORDS
WDS

Dictionaries are like watches; the worst is better than none, and the best cannot be expected to go quite true.

SAMUEL JOHNSON

38   The Dictionary

The study of words begins with the dictionary. A good dictionary is a biography of words. It records spelling, pronunciation,
word history, meaning, part of speech, and, when necessary,
principal parts, or plurals, or other forms. Frequently it records
the level of current usage. Very often the dictionary includes
other information as well—lists of abbreviations, rules for punctuation and spelling, condensed biographical and geographical
information, the pronunciation and source of many given names,
and a vocabulary of rhymes. For writers and readers a dictionary
is an indispensable tool.

Unabridged Dictionaries

For English the great standard work is the *New English Dictionary,* sometimes called the NED, consisting of ten volumes
and a supplement issued between 1888 and 1933 by the Claren-
don Press, Oxford, England, and reissued in 1933 as the *Oxford
English Dictionary* (OED). A historical work, this dictionary
traces the progress of a word through the language, giving dated
quotations to illustrate its meaning and spelling at particular
times in history. Many pages may be devoted to a single word.
Set, for example, receives twenty-three pages of closely printed
type. Under one of the 150-odd definitions of *set*—"to fix or
appoint (a time) for the transaction of an affair"—there are
illustrative sentences taken from writings dated 1056, 1250, 1290,
1300, 1387, 1470–85, 1548–77, 1633, 1693, 1753, 1810, 1890, and
1893.

The unabridged dictionary most familiar to Americans is
*Webster's New International Dictionary of the English Lan-
guage,* first published in 1909, reissued in a second edition in
1934, and again thoroughly revised and published as *Webster's
Third New International Dictionary* in 1961 by the G. & C.
Merriam Company of Springfield, Massachusetts, the legal in-
heritor of Noah Webster's copyright. The Merriam-Webster entries are scholarly and exact, though by no means as exhaustive
as the OED's. Other unabridged dictionaries are the *New
Standard Dictionary of the English Language,* published by
Funk and Wagnalls, and the *Random House Dictionary of the*

English Language, published by Random House. The latter is
the only entirely new unabridged dictionary of English to have
been published in recent years.

The wide resources of an unabridged dictionary are suggested
by the specimen entry below. Since dictionaries must say much
in little space, they use a great number of abbreviations and
seemingly cryptic entries. You will find these troublesome unless
you take time to read the explanatory pages and acquaint yourself with the symbols used. It will be useful to follow through
our sample entry.

38

¹**howl** \'haùl, *esp before pause or consonant* -aùəl\ *vb* -ED/-ING/
-S [ME *houlen;* akin to MD *hūlen* to howl, MHG *hiulen,
hiuweln* to howl, OHG *hūwila* owl, Gk *kōkyein* to shriek,
wail, lament, Skt *kauti* he cries out] *vi* **1 :** to utter or emit a
loud sustained doleful sound or outcry characteristic of dogs
and wolves ⟨wolves ~*ing* in the arctic night⟩ ⟨the only sound
is a melancholy wind ~*ing* —John Buchan⟩ **2 :** to cry out or
exclaim with lack of restraint and prolonged loudness through
strong impulse, feeling, or emotion ⟨the scalded men ~*ing* in
agony⟩ ⟨the hungry mob ~*ed* about the Senate house, threaten-
ing fire and massacre —J.A.Froude⟩ ⟨proctors ~*ing* at the
blunder⟩ **3 :** to go on a spree or rampage ⟨this is my night
to ~⟩ ~ *vt* **1 :** to utter or announce noisily with unrestrained demonstrative outcry ⟨newsboys ~*ing* the news⟩
2 : to affect, effect, or drive by adverse outcry — used esp.
with *down* ⟨supporters of the Administration . . . ready to ~
down any suggestion of criticism —*Wall Street Jour.*⟩ **syn** see
ROAR
²**howl** \"\ *n* -s **1 :** a loud protracted mournful rising and
falling cry characteristic of a dog or a wolf **2 a :** a prolonged
cry of distress **:** WAIL **b :** a yell or outcry of disappointment,
rage, or protest **3 :** PROTEST, COMPLAINT ⟨raise a ~ over high
taxes⟩ ⟨set up a ~ that he was being cheated⟩ **4 :** something
that provokes laughter ⟨his act was a ~⟩ **5 :** a noise produced in an electronic amplifier usu. by undesired regenera-
tion of alternating currents of audio frequency **:** OSCILLATION
— called also *squeal*

By permission. From *Webster's Third New International Dictionary.* © 1976 by G. & C. Merriam Co., Publishers of the
Merriam-Webster Dictionaries.

In our specimen from *Webster's Third New International* we
find two main boldface entries preceded with the superscripts [1]
and [2]. The first we find labeled *vb* for *verb,* the second *n* for
noun. The *-ed/-ing/-s* in the first entry and the *-s* in the second
tells us that the endings of *howl* as verb and as noun are regular.
The pronunciation is indicated between slant lines (called RE-
VERSE VIRGULES) as follows: \ haùl or haùəl \. The note before
the second tells us that this pronunciation occurs especially
when the word is pronounced before a pause (at the end of a
sentence, for example) or before a word beginning with a consonant. If we refer to the inside front cover or to the prefatory
material of the dictionary, we find that *aù* is pronounced like the
ow in *now* or the *ou* in *loud,* and that ə is a symbol representing
the sound of the first and last *a* in *banana.*

The material between the brackets shows us the origin or
etymology of the word: *howl* comes from a word in Middle
English (ME) spelled *houlen,* and is related to Middle Dutch

38

(MD) *hūlen* and Middle High German (MHG) *hiulen* or *hiuweln,* all meaning *to howl;* to the Old High German (OHG) word *hūwila* meaning *owl;* to the Greek (Gk) *kōkyein* meaning *to wail* or *lament;* and to the Sanskrit (Skt) word *kauti* meaning *he cries out.*

The definitions that follow are divided into various senses by boldface numerals 1, 2, etc. The first group of these senses under ¹*howl* is preceded by the label *vi,* indicating that these are senses in which the verb is intransitive; that is, it is not followed by an object. The second group of two meanings is preceded by the label *vt,* indicating that these are meanings in which the verb is transitive; that is, it is followed by an object. For each sense we find enclosed in angle brackets (⟨ ⟩) quotations typical of the contexts in which the word occurs in the meaning given. These verbal illustrations become a major part of the definition itself by showing us an actual context for the word. Those labeled by authors' names or by sources are actual quotations; those not so labeled are typical phrases offered by the dictionary editors. Under meaning 2 as a transitive verb, we are given a usage note telling us that in this meaning *howl* is used especially with *down* in the phrase *howl down.* A swung dash (~) replaces the word itself in all such verbal illustrations of the word. Finally we are referred to the word *roar* for a discussion of the synonyms of *howl.* (See pp. 296–299 for illustration and discussion.)

If we turn to the second boldface entry, ²*howl,* we find the pattern repeated for the senses in which *howl* occurs as a noun. Since there is no separate pronunciation or etymology given, we know that each of these is the same as for the verb. Under *a* and *b* of meaning 2, two different but related senses of that meaning are given. The words in small capitals (*wail* in meaning 2; *protest* and *complaint* in meaning 3, and *oscillation* in meaning 5) refer us to other boldface entries at the appropriate alphabetical point in the dictionary where further related definitions are given.

We may see something of the ways in which dictionaries must change if they are to be contemporary by comparing with the entry reproduced above the following entry for the noun *howl* from an earlier edition of the same dictionary, an edition first issued in 1934.

> **howl,** *n.* **1.** The loud, protracted, mournful cry of a dog or a wolf, or other like sound.
> **2.** A prolonged cry of distress; a wail; also, a wild yell of disappointment, rage, or the like; as, *howls* of derision.
>
> By permission. From *Webster's New International Dictionary.* Second Edition, copyright 1959 by G. & C. Merriam Co., Publishers of the Merriam-Webster Dictionaries.

As we see at a glance, the two meanings offered here are very close to those numbered 1 and 2 in the *Third New International.* But meanings 3, 4, and 5 listed in the *Third International* are all missing. They probably have developed since this earlier entry was compiled. As we might expect, neither would we find in earlier editions the intransitive verbal meaning of *to go on a spree.*

Desk Dictionaries

Unabridged dictionaries are useful as reference works. For everyday purposes a good abridged or desk dictionary is more practical. Here is a list that may help you in selecting a good desk dictionary:

    1. ***Webster's New Collegiate Dictionary,* G. & C. Merriam Company, Springfield, Massachusetts.** Based upon the *Third New International,* this desk dictionary profits from the extensive scholarship which marks the *Third.* Insofar as possible, the order of definitions under any one word is historical: The original meaning is given first, the second meaning next, and so on. It is characterized particularly by relatively full etymologies, a wide range of synonymies, and full prefatory material. Abbreviations, biographical names, and place names are listed separately at the end of the dictionary. Some users may find inconvenient the fact that the editors have followed the *Third New International* in not using the label *colloquial* or its approximate equivalent *informal,* and in using the label *slang* rather sparingly.

> **howl** \\'hau̇(ə)l\\ *vb* [ME *houlen;* akin to MHG *hiulen* to howl, Gk *kōkyein* to shriek] *vi* **1 :** to emit a loud sustained doleful sound characteristic of dogs **2 :** to cry loudly and without restraint under strong impulse (as pain or grief) **3 :** to go on a spree or rampage ~ *vt* **1 :** to utter with unrestrained outcry **2 :** to affect, effect, or drive by adverse outcry — used esp. with *down* <~ed down the speaker> — **howl** *n*

> By permission. From Webster's New Collegiate Dictionary. © 1977 by G. & C. Merriam Co., Publishers of the Merriam-Webster Dictionaries.

    2. ***Webster's New World Dictionary,* Second College Edition, 1978, William Collins + World Publishing Company, Inc. Cleveland, Ohio.** This dictionary emphasizes simplified definitions even of technical terms and includes a large number of words and phrases which are relatively informal. Usage labels are generously used. Synonomies and etymologies are full and thorough. Common meanings are placed first in the definitions. All words are contained in the main alphabetical list. Identification of Americanisms and attention to the origin of American place names are special features.

38

howl (houl) *vi.* [ME. *hulen*, akin to G. *heulen* < IE. echoic base **kāu-*, whence Sans. *kāuti*, (it) cries, OHG. *hūwila*, owl] **1.** to utter the long, loud, wailing cry of wolves, dogs, etc. **2.** to utter a similar cry of pain, anger, grief, etc. **3.** to make a sound like this *[a howling wind]* **4.** to shout or laugh in scorn, mirth, etc. —*vt.* **1.** to utter with a howl or howls **2.** to drive or effect by howling —*n.* **1.** a long, loud, wailing cry of a wolf, dog, etc. **2.** any similar sound **3.** [Colloq.] something hilarious; joke —**howl down** to drown out with shouts of scorn, anger, etc. —**one's night to howl** one's time for unrestrained pleasure

With permission. From *Webster's New World Dictionary,* Second College Edition. Copyright © 1978 by William Collins + World Publishing Company, Inc.

3. *The American Heritage Dictionary of the English Language,* **American Heritage Publishing Company, Inc., New York, and Houghton Mifflin Company, Boston.** This is the most recent of the desk dictionaries. Its most immediately distinguishing features are a large page (8 × 11 inches), great generosity of illustrations and drawings, and the incorporation of usage notes based upon a consensus of a panel of some 100 writers, editors, poets, and public speakers. The large page, with illustrations in wide margins, makes the book readable but bulky to handle. The number of entries compares with that in the *Random House Dictionary.* Definitions are arranged in what the editors believe is a logical order, with the initial definition being that which offers the central meaning and serves as the base for the most logical arrangement of other senses of the word. Synonymies seem generous; etymologies are made somewhat more readable by avoidance of all abbreviations. The single alphabetical listing incorporates abbreviations and biographical and geographical entries. Among the several special articles within the front matter, those on usage, on grammar and meaning, and on spelling and pronunciation are particularly clear and helpful summaries reflecting current scholarship. The inclusion of an appendix of Indo-European roots in the back of the dictionary is a special feature.

howl (houl) *v.* **howled, howling, howls.** —*intr.* **1.** To utter or emit a long, mournful, plaintive sound characteristic of wolves or dogs. **2.** To cry or wail loudly and uncontrollably in pain, sorrow, or anger. **3.** *Slang.* **a.** To laugh uproariously. **b.** To go on a carousal or spree. —*tr.* **1.** To express or utter with a howl or howls. **2.** To effect, drive, or force by or as if by howling. —*n.* **1.** The sound of one that howls. **2.** *Slang.* Something uproariously funny or absurd. [Middle English *houlen, howlen,* perhaps from Middle Dutch *hūlen.* See **ul-** in Appendix.*]

© 1969, 1970, 1971, 1973, 1975, 1976, Houghton Mifflin Company. Reprinted by permission from *The American Heritage Dictionary of the English Language.*

4. *The American College Dictionary,* **Random House, New York.** This is convenient in format and type. Meanings of words are arranged so far as possible in order of frequency of occurrence. Synonym studies are particularly strong, and technical words tend to be treated rather fully. All words—general words, proper names, and abbreviations—are combined in the main alphabetical listing. Prefaces contain especially good discussions of synonyms and antonyms, and of usage levels, and have a rather thorough guide to usage.

howl (houl) *v.i.* **1.** to utter a loud, prolonged, mournful cry, as that of a dog or wolf. **2.** to utter a similar cry in distress, pain, rage, etc.; wail. **3.** to make a sound like an animal howling: *the wind is howling.* —*v.t.* **4.** to utter with howls. **5.** to drive or force by howls. —*n.* **6.** the cry of a dog, wolf, etc. **7.** a cry or wail, as of pain or rage. **8.** a sound like wailing: *the howl of the wind.* **9.** a loud scornful laugh or yell. [ME *houle.* Cf. G *heulen;* imit.]

From *The American College Dictionary.* Copyright © 1970 by Random House, Inc. Reprinted by permission.

5. *The Random House Dictionary of the English Language,* **College Edition, Random House, New York.** Based on the unabridged *Random House Dictionary of the English Language,* this is another recent addition to available desk dictionaries. It offers a great number of entries—155,000—yet maintains a pleasant type size and format. Definitions are arranged with the most common given first. Synonymies are full, and recent technical words receive careful attention. A single alphabetical listing incorporates all biographical and geographical as well as other entries. Illustrations appear to be used at least somewhat more generously than in most of the other desk dictionaries. Among its prefaces, that by Raven I. McDavid, Jr., on usage, dialects, and functional varieties of English is a particularly valuable summary.

howl (houl), *v.i.* **1.** to utter a loud, prolonged, mournful cry, as that of a dog or wolf. **2.** to utter a similar cry in distress, pain, rage, etc.; wail. **3.** to make a sound like an animal howling: *The wind howls through the trees.* **4.** *Informal.* to laugh loudly. —*v.t.* **5.** to utter with howls. **6.** to drive or force by howls (often fol. by *down*): *to howl down the opposition.* —*n.* **7.** the cry of a dog, wolf, etc. **8.** a cry or wail, as of pain, rage, protest, etc. **9.** a sound like wailing: *the howl of the wind.* **10.** a loud, scornful laugh or yell. **11.** something that causes a laugh or a scornful yell, as a joke or funny or embarrassing situation. [ME *hul(en),* c. D *huilen,* G *heulen,* LG *hülen,* Dan *hyle;* with loss of *h,* Icel *ȳla*]

From *The Random House College Dictionary,* Revised Edition. Copyright © 1975 by Random House, Inc. Reprinted by permission.

6. *Funk & Wagnalls Standard College Dictionary,* **Funk & Wagnalls, New York.** This is a relatively recent addition to the list of excellent available desk dictionaries. Though without the illustrious background of the *Webster's Collegiate,* its reliability is insured by an impressive advisory board, many members of which are among the leading linguists today. It is marked by a

38

convenient type size, by relatively simple and natural definitions, and by particular attention to usage labels for words judged to be *informal* (which replaces the term *colloquial*) and *slang*. Material on usage is incorporated in some 260 notes, especially valuable for the student, though the bulk of the same material is in *Webster's Collegiate* under the main entry for a word. Common meanings are placed first in each entry. The *Standard* runs biographical names and place names into the main body of the dictionary rather than listing them separately. Introductory material in the text edition includes valuable summaries of the history of the language, English grammar, and regional variations in American pronunciation.

> **howl** (houl) *v.i.* **1.** To utter the loud, mournful wail of a dog, wolf, or other animal. **2.** To utter such a cry in pain, grief, or rage. **3.** To make a sound similar to this: The storm *howled* all night. **4.** To laugh loudly: The audience *howled*. — *v.t.* **5.** To utter or express with howling: to *howl* one's disapproval. **6.** To condemn, suppress, or drive away by howling: often with *down*. — *n.* **1.** The wailing cry of a wolf, dog, or other animal. **2.** Any howling sound. [ME *houlen.* Cf. G *heulen.*]

From *Funk & Wagnalls Standard College Dictionary.* Copyright © 1977 by Harper & Row Publishers, Inc. Reprinted by permission of the publisher.

The Uses of a Dictionary

1. Spelling. The spelling entry of a word in the dictionary divides the word into syllables, showing how to separate it properly at the ends of lines (see "Syllabication," Section 18). It also gives the proper spelling of compound words—properness depending on whether the editors found them more often written as two single words (*half brother*), as a hyphenated compound (*quarter-hour*), or as one word (*drugstore*). Dictionaries also indicate foreign words that require italics (in manuscript, underlining). The *American Heritage,* the *Standard,* and the *American College* all label such words or phrases as Latin, German, etc.; *Webster's New World* uses a double dagger (‡). *The Random House Dictionary* indicates such words by printing the main entry word in boldface italic type. All dictionaries also indicate whether a word is always or usually capitalized in a particular meaning.

All good modern dictionaries list variant spellings of many words, though not all by any means list the same variants or give the same comments about them. Four recent desk dictionaries, *Webster's New Collegiate,* the *Random House,* the *Standard,* and the *American Heritage,* for example, all list *centre* and *theatre* as well as the more common *center* and *theater.* But while the *Standard* indicates that *centre* is "Brit-

ish" and that *theatre* is "more commonly British," and the *Random House* cites both as "chiefly British," *Webster's* and the *American Heritage* cite *centre* as "chiefly British" and add no limiting label to *theatre*. All four cite *tendentious* and *tendencious* as possible spellings, and agree that the former is the more common. The *Standard*, the *American Heritage*, and the *Random House* list *adduceable* and *adducible*, indicating that they have equal standing; *Webster's* does not contain either form.

Such variation among dictionaries is common, and we must be careful to examine the explanatory material at the front of a dictionary if we wish to know exactly what policy is followed. Frequently, though by no means always, if variant spellings are listed, the first will be somewhat more common; the most carefully edited dictionaries sometimes adopt some means of indicating that this is so. *Webster's New Collegiate*, for example, indicates that two variants are equally common by joining them with *or* (*caddie* or *caddy*) but joins variants the second of which is less common by *also* (*woolly* also *wooly*). In general, if there is a question about spelling, choose the first listed variant unless there is a special reason for choosing the second.

Whatever dictionary you choose, it will be your authority on all questions of spelling. Cultivate the habit of referring to it whenever you have any doubt about a correct spelling.

EXERCISE 38(1) Give the preferred spelling of each word.

aesthetic	daemon	liquorice
catalogue	enclose	modeled
catsup	favour	Shakspere
criticise	judgement	theatre

EXERCISE 38(2) Rewrite the following compounds, showing which should be written as they are, which hyphenated, and which written as two or more separate words.

bookshop	jazzmen	supermarket
castoff	passkey	uptodate
easygoing	selfgovernment	wellmarked
horserace	showdown	worldwide

EXERCISE 38(3) Copy the following foreign words, underlining those that require italics and supplying accents where needed.

bon voyage	dramatis personae	resume
coup d'etat	matinee	sine qua non
creche	nouveau riche	Weltschmertz
debutante		

2. Pronunciation. Dictionaries indicate the pronunciation of words by respelling them with special symbols and letters.

Explanation of the symbols is given either at the bottom of the page on which the entry appears or in the prefatory pages or both.

Indicating pronunciation is the most difficult of all the tasks of dictionary editors. <u>Correct pronunciation</u> is a very flexible term. Generally speaking, it is the standard of pronunciation prevailing among educated people, but often correctness is a theory rather than a reality. Does a Southerner mispronounce *I* when he says *Ah?* Is a Bostonian incorrect in saying *pa'k* for *park?* Dictionaries do not even attempt to list all the variant pronunciations in use.

The pronunciation of words, moreover, is influenced by the situation. In formal speech, syllables are likely to be more deliberately sounded than in informal speech. Further, the pronunciation of a word is affected by its position in the sentence and by the meaning it carries. Yet dictionary editors have no choice but to deal with each word as an individual entity. They record its formal, or full, pronunciation—what may be referred to as "platform" pronunciation. Certainly, to pronounce every word in our conversation as deliberately as the dictionary recommends would make our speech stilted and pompous.

Dictionaries do, however, attempt to show frequently occurring variant pronunciations as they do variant spellings. We have seen, for example, in our sample entry from *Webster's Third New International* that an unabridged dictionary may even show variant pronunciations for such a simple word as *howl.* Again, as with variant spellings, though the first listed is sometimes said to be "preferred" the statements about pronunciation in most carefully edited modern dictionaries do not bear this out. Usually, unless there is a limiting label or comment attached to one or more variants, they are all equally "correct." In the last analysis, your preference will be determined by the pronunciation you hear in the cultivated conversation around you.

EXERCISE 38(4)   What is the pronunciation of the following words? If usage is divided for any, which pronunciation seems more acceptable to you? Why? Copy the dictionary pronunciation for each.

adult	exquisite	impotent
alias	formidable	mischievous
cerebral	genuine	research
despicable	greasy	route

3. Etymology.   The ETYMOLOGY of a word—that is, its origin and derivation—often helps clarify its present meaning and spelling. Etymological information is sometimes interesting or amusing in its own right. Because the course of history changes, restricts, or extends the meanings of words, however, many original meanings have been lost completely. *Presently,* for example, formerly meant *at once, immediately;* it now usually means *shortly, in a little while.*

EXERCISE 38(5) Trace the etymology of each of the following:

assassin	familiar	neighbor	shirt
bedlam	fedora	organization	skirt
draggle	incisive	priest	slogan
egg	lampoon	sandwich	squelch

EXERCISE 38(6) From what specific names have the following words been derived?

ampere	gardenia	shrapnel
boycott	macadam	ulster
chauvinism	quisling	watt
dunce		

EXERCISE 38(7) From what language did each of the following words come?

almanac	dory	jute	mukluk	trek
cherub	goulash	kerosene	piano	tulip
cockatoo	huckster	moccasin	squadron	typhoon

4. Meaning. Strictly speaking, dictionaries do not <u>define</u> words; they record the meaning or meanings that actual usage, past and present, has attached to words. When more than one meaning is recorded for a single word, the Merriam-Webster dictionaries list them in order of historical use. Most other dictionaries list the more general and present meaning first. Special and technical meanings are clearly labeled. Choosing the appropriate meaning out of the many that are offered is not difficult if you read them <u>all</u> and understand their order of arrangement as indicated in the prefatory pages of the dictionary.

EXERCISE 38(8) How many different meanings can you find for each of the following words?

call	land	run
get	light	set
go	out	turn
high		

38

Trace the changes in meaning that have taken place in each of the following words:

bounty	gossip	machine
complexion	humor	manufacture
engine	intern	sincere
fond	knave	starve
generous	lozenge	virtue

EXERCISE 38(10) Distinguish between the meanings of the words in each of the following groups.

ambitious, aspiring, enterprising	eminent, celebrated
apt, likely, liable	enormous, immense
common, mutual	equanimity, composure
deface, disfigure	restive, restless
diplomatic, politic, tactful	voracious, ravenous

5. Synonyms and antonyms. A SYNONYM is a word having the same or almost the same general meaning as the vocabulary entry. An ANTONYM is a word having approximately the opposite meaning. In dictionaries, for practical reasons, not all entries show synonyms and antonyms. Well-edited desk dictionaries include paragraph-length discussions of groups of synonyms, defining the different shades of meaning associated with each member of the group. These discussions are located usually at the end of certain entries and cross-referenced at related entries. (For full illustration of synonym entries from various dictionaries, see pp. 296–299.)

6. Grammar. Grammatically, dictionaries are helpful in several ways. Good dictionaries indicate what part of speech each word is; or, if the word serves as more than one part of speech, the dictionaries will usually list each possibility and give illustrative sentences for each. Dictionaries also list the principal parts of verbs, the plurals of nouns, and the comparative and superlative degrees of adjectives and adverbs, but only when these forms are irregular or present spelling difficulties. Frequently, the past tense and present participle of a verb are not given when they are regularly formed by adding -ed and -ing (walked, walking). Similarly, plurals ending in -s or -es (cats, dishes) are often not given. And comparatives and superlatives formed by adding more, most, or less, least, or -er, -est are not given, unless the addition of the -er, -est endings presents a spelling difficulty (heavy, heavier, heaviest).

EXERCISE 38(11) What are the past tense and the present participle of each of these verbs?

broadcast	get	set
focus	lend	teach
dive	shrink	wake

EXERCISE 38(12)   What is the plural (or plurals) of each of the following?

38

alumnus	crisis	index
bear	daisy	madame
court-martial	fish	stratum

EXERCISE 38(13)   Write the comparative and superlative forms of each of the following:

bad	lengthy	red
ill	much	shyly
little	often	well

7. Labels. Dictionaries do not label words that belong to the general vocabulary. The absence of a label therefore means that the word is proper for formal and informal speaking and writing. Other words may have one of two kinds of labels:

SUBJECT LABELS, indicating that the word belongs to a special field: law, medicine, baseball, finance, and so on.

USAGE OR STATUS LABELS, indicating that a word is restricted in some special way in its occurrence, either in time, geographical range, or style. The following labels are in common use, but note that dictionaries vary both in their application of such labels and in the exact ways in which their editors define them. To be certain of the precise meaning of labels in your dictionary, be sure to read the explanatory material at the front of the dictionary.

The labels *obsolete* and *archaic* indicate that the word is restricted in time. *Obsolete* means that the word has passed out of use entirely, as *absume* and *enwheel,* which are not known to have been used for some two hundred years. *Archaic* means that although the word has passed out of general use, it appears occasionally or in special contexts, as *belike* and *eftsoons.*

Dialectal, and various labels such as *New England, Southern U.S., British, Australian,* and *Canadian,* all indicate restrictions in the geographical occurrence of the word. Dictionaries vary in the exact labels they apply, but as a general rule words that have a restrictive geographical label should not be used in writing unless a special purpose requires it. The term *dialectal* usually suggests a rather specialized local or provincial word, frequently rural or traditional. *Corn pone,* labeled *Southern U.S.* in the *American College Dictionary,* and *larrup* as a noun meaning a *blow,* labeled *dialect* by *Webster's New Collegiate,* are examples.

Slang, colloquial, informal, illiterate, substandard, and other similar labels are level, or style, labels. Dictionaries have their greatest variation both in the selection and the application of such labels.

Slang indicates that a word has not yet been dignified by inclusion in the general vocabulary; it frequently suggests that the word is used in a humorous way, often within a particular and limited group of people. *Hangup* (a fixation, an intense preoccupation), *shades* (sunglasses), and *snow* (cocaine or heroin) are typical examples. Of the dictionaries listed above, *Webster's Collegiate* is by far the most sparing in its use of this label, allowing many entries labeled <u>slang</u> by other dictionaries to pass without any label.

Colloquial and *informal* indicate that a word is more characteristic of cultivated speech or quite informal writing than of the more formal levels of writing. These terms are in much debate currently, particularly because *Webster's Third New International* applies no label of this kind to any word, nor does *Webster's Collegiate*. In the opinion of many, the failure of the latest Merriam-Webster dictionaries to use such labels limits their usefulness for students and others seeking guidance to determine the appropriateness of many words for particular writing contexts. The *Standard* substitutes the label *informal* for the more conventional label *colloquial,* used by both the *American College* and by *Webster's New World.* Thus the *Standard* labels *fizzle* as *informal;* the *American College Dictionary* labels it *colloquial; Webster's Collegiate* gives it no label.

Illiterate, substandard, and some other similar terms are labels indicating that a word is limited to uneducated speech, as *drownded* for the past tense of *drown.* Though dictionaries vary somewhat in the particular labels they use (the *Standard* uses *illiterate* to mean about the same thing as *Webster's substandard,* for example), their agreement in classifying a word as being limited to uneducated speech is much greater than their agreement in labeling a word as slang, colloquial, and so on.

It will be clear from the comments above that if you are to use your dictionary wisely as a guide to usage, you will have to examine the explanatory notes in it carefully to determine exactly what labels are applied and how they are interpreted by the editors.

EXERCISE 38(14)   Which of the following are standard English, which colloquial or informal, and which slang, according to your dictionary? If possible, check more than one dictionary to determine if they agree.

corny	goof	moll
cool	hipster	snollygoster
flap	jerk	wise-up
foul-up	kibitzer	yak

EXERCISE 38(15) In what areas of the world would you be likely to hear the following?

billabong	hoecake	potlatch
chuckwagon	laager	pukka
coulee	petrol	sharpie

EXERCISE 38(16) The following questions are designed to test your ability to use the whole dictionary, not only its vocabulary entries, but also its various appendices. Any of the desk dictionaries discussed in this section will help you find the answers. In the first seven questions, you may have to look up the meaning of the underlined words before answering the questions.

1 What is the <u>orthography</u> of the word *embarrass?*
2 What is the preferred <u>orthoepy</u> of the noun *envelope?*
3 What is the <u>etymology</u> of the word *precise?*
4 What are two <u>homonyms</u> for the word *reign?*
5 What are some <u>antonyms</u> for the word *concise?*
6 What is the <u>syllabication</u> of the word *redundant?*
7 What are some <u>synonyms</u> for the adjective *correct?*
8 Give the meanings of these abbreviations: *syn., v. mus., R.C.Ch.*
9 What do the following phrases mean: *finem respice, ars longa vita brevis, de profundis, honi soit qui mal y pense?*
10 What is the population of Birmingham, Michigan?
11 What is the meaning of the symbol B/E?
12 How long is the Cumberland River?
13 Who was the oldest of the Brontë sisters?
14 From what language does the proper name *Nahum* come?
15 List six words that rhyme with *mince.*

Special Dictionaries

When you need specialized information about words, check one of the following dictionaries:*

Dutch, Robert A., reviser of *The Original Roget's Thesaurus of English Words and Phrases.* 1965.
Goldstein, Milton. *Dictionary of Modern Acronyms and Abbreviations.* 1963.
Hayakawa, S. I. *Modern Guide to Synonyms and Related Words.* 1968.
Onions, C. T. *The Oxford Dictionary of English Etymology.* 1966.
Partridge, Eric. *Origins: A Short Etymological Dictionary of Modern English.* 1963.
————. *A Dictionary of Slang and Unconventional English.* 1961.
Webster's New Dictionary of Synonyms. 1968.
Wentworth, Harold, and Stuart B. Flexner. *Dictionary of American Slang.* 1967.

*See also the lists of reference books in "The Library," Section 45.

The difference between the right word and the almost-right word is the difference between lightning and the lightning bug.

Attributed to MARK TWAIN

39 Vocabulary

The English language contains well over a million words. Of these, about two-fifths belong almost exclusively to special fields: e.g., zoology, electronics, psychiatry. Of the remaining, the large dictionaries list about 600,000, the desk dictionaries about 150,000. Such wealth is both a blessing and a curse. On the one hand, many English words are loosely synonymous, sometimes interchangeable, as in *buy* a book or *purchase* a book. On the other hand, the distinctions between synonyms are fully as important as their similarities. For example, a family may be said to be living in *poverty,* or in *penury,* or in *want,* or in *destitution.* All these words are loosely synonymous, but only one will describe the family exactly as you see it and wish your reader to see it. In short, as a writer of English you must use your words carefully.

Passive and Active Vocabulary

In a sense, you have two vocabularies: a PASSIVE, or RECOGNITION, vocabulary, which is made up of the words you recognize in the context of reading matter but do not actually use yourself; and an ACTIVE vocabulary, which consists of "working" words—those you use daily in your own writing and speaking. In the passage below, the meaning of the italicized words is fairly clear (or at least can be guessed at) from the context. But how many belong in your active vocabulary?

> Has it been duly marked by historians that the late William Jennings Bryan's last *secular* act on this globe of sin was to catch flies? A curious detail, and not without its *sardonic overtones.* He was the most *sedulous* flycatcher in American history, and in many ways the most successful. His *quarry,* of course, was not *Musca domestica* but *Homo neandertalensis.* For forty years he tracked it with coo and bellow, up and down the *rustic* backways of the Republic. Wherever the *flambeau* of Chautauqua smoked and guttered, and the bilge of idealism ran in the veins, the Baptist pastors damned the brooks with the *sanctified,* and men gathered who were weary and heavy laden, and their wives who were full of Peruna and as *fecund* as the shad (*Alosa sapidissima*)—there the *indefatigable* Jennings set up his traps and spread his bait.
>
> H. L. MENCKEN, *Selected Prejudices*

Increasing Your Vocabulary

There are no shortcuts to word power. A good vocabulary is the product of years of serious reading, of listening to intelligent talk, and of seeking to speak and write forcefully and clearly. All this does not mean that devices and methods for vocabulary-building are useless. But it does mean that acquiring a good vocabulary is inseparable from acquiring an education.

1. Increasing your recognition vocabulary. English has many words based on a common root form, to which different prefixes or suffixes have been added. The root form *spec-*, for example, from the Latin *specere* (to look) appears in *specter, inspection, perspective, aspect, introspection, circumspect, specimen, spectator.* Knowing the common prefixes and suffixes will help you detect the meaning of many words whose roots are familiar.

A. Prefixes.

Prefix	Meaning	Example
ab-	away from	absent
ad-*	to *or* for	adverb
com-*	with	combine
de-	down, away from, *or* undoing	degrade, depart, dehumanize
dis-*	separation *or* reversal	disparate, disappoint
ex-*	out of *or* former	extend, ex-president
in-*	in *or* on	input
in-*	not	inhuman
mis-	wrong	mistake
non-	not	non-Christian, nonsense
ob-*	against	obtuse
pre-	before	prevent
pro-	for *or* forward	proceed
re-	back *or* again	repeat
sub-*	under	subcommittee
trans-	across	transcribe
un-	not	unclean

EXERCISE 39(1) Write words denoting *negation* from the following.

Example   moveable—able to be moved
immovable—*not* able to be moved

---

*The spelling of these prefixes varies, usually to make pronunciation easier. *Ad* becomes *ac* in *accuse,* *ag* in *aggregate,* *at* in *attack.* Similarly, the final consonant in the other prefixes is assimilated by the initial letter of the root word: *colleague* (*com* + *league*); *illicit* (*in* + *licit*); *offend* (*ob* + *fend*); *succeed* (*sub* + *ceed*).

39

accuracy	conformity	mutable
adorned	distinctive	rational
agreeable	explicable	workable

EXERCISE 39(2) Write words denoting *reversal* from the following.

Example accelerate—to move at increasing speed
decelerate—to move at decreasing speed

increase—to grow larger
decrease—to grow smaller

centralize	integrate	please
do	magnetize	qualify
inherit	persuade	ravel

B. Suffixes. These fall into three groups: noun suffixes, verb suffixes, adjectival suffixes.

(1a) Noun suffixes denoting *act of, state of, quality of.*

Suffix	Example	Meaning
-dom	freedom	*state of* being free
-hood	manhood	*state of* being a man
-ness	dimness	*state of* being dim
-ice	cowardice	*quality of* being a coward
-ation	flirtation	*act of* flirting
-ion	intercession	*act of* interceding
{ -sion	scansion	*act of* scanning
{ -tion	corruption	*state of* being corrupt
-ment	argument	*act of* arguing
-ship	friendship	*state of* being friends
{ -ance	continuance	*act of* continuing
{ -ence	precedence	*act of* preceding
{ -ancy	flippancy	*state of* being flippant
{ -ency	currency	*state of* being current
-ism	baptism	*act of* baptizing
-ery	bravery	*quality of* being brave

(1b) Noun suffixes denoting *doer, one who.*

Suffix	Example	Meaning
{ -eer (general)	auctioneer	*one who* auctions
{ -ess (female)	poetess	*a woman who* writes poetry
-ist	fascist	*one who* believes in fascism
{ -or	debtor	*one who* is in debt
{ -er	worker	*one who* works

(2) Verb suffixes denoting *to make* or *to perform the act of.*

Suffix	Example	Meaning
-ate	perpetuate	*to make* perpetual
-en	soften	*to make* soft

| -fy | dignify | *to make* dignified |
| -ize, -ise | sterilize | *to make* sterile |

(3) Adjectival suffixes.

Suffix	*Meaning*	*Example*
-ful	full of	hateful
-ish	resembling	foolish
-ate	having	affectionate
-ic, -ical	resembling	angelic
-ive	having	prospective
-ous	full of	zealous
-ulent	full of	fraudulent
-less	without	fatherless
-able, -ible	capable of	peaceable
-ed	having	spirited
-ly	resembling	womanly
-like	resembling	childlike

EXERCISE 39(3)   Write words indicating *act of, state of,* or *quality of* from the following words.

advance	deny	promote
calculate	helpless	rebel
disappear	judge	statesman

EXERCISE 39(4)   Write nouns indicating *doer* from the following.

advise	communicate	profit
boast	disturb	sail
command	preach	save

EXERCISE 39(5)   Write verbs indicating *to make* or *to perform the act of* from the following nouns and adjectives.

beauty	idol	moral
black	liquid	peace
captive	modern	victim

EXERCISE 39(6)   Make adjectives of the following words by adding a suffix.

humor	rest	thwart
irony	speed	wasp
mule	talk	whimsey

C. Combining forms. Linguists refer to these as BOUND FORMS. They appear generally, but not always, as prefixes.

Combining Form	*Meaning*	*Example*
anthropo	man	*anthropo*logy
arch	rule	*arch*duke, mon*arch*

39

auto	self	*auto*mobile
bene	well	*bene*ficial
eu	well	*eu*logy
graph	writing	*graph*ic, bio*graphy*
log, logue	word, speech	mono*logue*
magni	great	*magni*ficent
mal	bad	*mal*ady
mono	one	*mono*tone
multi	many	*multi*plication
neo	new	*neo*-classic
omni	all	*omni*bus
pan, pant	all	*pan*hellenic
phil	loving	*phil*osophy
phono	sound	*phono*graph
poly	many	*poly*gamy
pseudo	false	*pseudo*nym
semi	half	*semi*formal

2. Increasing your active vocabulary. Another way to increase word power is to keep transferring words from your <u>recognition</u> vocabulary to your <u>active</u> vocabulary. Make a conscious effort to introduce at least one new word a day into your active vocabulary. At the same time be alert to opportunities for increasing your recognition vocabulary. A good system is to enter each new word on a small card: Write the word on one side, the definition and a sentence illustrating its correct use on the other. Then you can quickly test yourself on the meaning of all the new words you collect.

EXERCISE 39(7)   Define each of the following words and use it correctly in a sentence.

compatible	malign	estrangement
demagogue	unscrupulous	promiscuous
intimidate	officious	euphoria
disparage	facetious	corpulent
ostentatious	incentive	transcend
altruistic	ambiguous	pompous
taciturn	pragmatic	finite

3. Strengthening your active vocabulary. Are you sure that *enthusiast, fanatic, zealot,* and *bigot* mean what you think they mean? You know that *deadly, mortal,* and *fatal* are very much alike in meaning—but do you know the exact distinctions among them? All the desk dictionaries listed in Section 38 group synonyms and point out their differences. Unabridged dictionaries carry quite exhaustive discussions of synonyms. And the

Merriam-Webster *Dictionary of Synonyms* is devoted exclusively to the grouping and differentiating of synonyms. The various editions of Roget's *Thesaurus* are valuable for the long lists of closely related words they provide, though they must be used cautiously because they give no discussion of distinctions in meaning and offer no guiding examples. **39**

One of the most valuable ways to strengthen your vocabulary is to cultivate the habit of studying dictionary discussions of synonyms. The extent of dictionary resources for this purpose is illustrated by the following sample entries.

From the *Random House:*

—**Syn. 1.** encourage, befriend; support, uphold, back, abet. HELP, AID, ASSIST, SUCCOR agree in the idea of furnishing another with something needed, esp. when the need comes at a particular time. HELP implies furnishing anything that furthers another's efforts or relieves his wants or necessities. AID and ASSIST, somewhat more formal, imply esp. a furthering or seconding of another's efforts. AID implies a more active helping; ASSIST implies less need and less help. To SUCCOR, still more formal and literary, is to give timely help and relief in difficulty or distress: *Succor him in his hour of need.* **4.** alleviate, cure, heal. **10.** support, backing. —**Ant. 4.** afflict. **8.** hinder.

From *The Random House College Dictionary,* Revised Edition. Copyright © 1975 by Random House, Inc. Reprinted by permission.

From *Webster's Third:*

syn HOWL, ULULATE, BELLOW, BAWL, BLUSTER, CLAMOR, VOCIFERATE: ROAR suggests the full loud reverberating sound made by lions or the booming sea or by persons in rage or boisterous merriment ⟨far away guns *roar* —Virginia Woolf⟩ ⟨the harsh north wind . . . *roared* in the piazzas —Osbert Sitwell⟩ ⟨*roared* the blacksmith, his face black with rage —T.B.Costain⟩ HOWL indicates a higher, less reverberant sound often suggesting the doleful or agonized or the sounds of unrestrained laughter ⟨frequent *howling* of jackals and hyenas —James Stevenson-Hamilton⟩ ⟨how the wind does *howl* —J.C.Powys⟩ ⟨*roared* at his subject . . . *howled* at . . . inconsistencies —Martin Gardner⟩ ULULATE is a literary synonym for HOWL but may suggest mournful protraction and rhythmical delivery ⟨an *ululating* baritone mushy with pumped-up pity —E.B.White⟩ BELLOW suggests the loud, abrupt, hollow sound made typically by bulls or any similar loud, reverberating sound ⟨most of them were drunk. They went *bellowing* through the town —Kenneth Roberts⟩ BAWL suggests a somewhat lighter, less reverberant, unmodulated sound made typically by calves ⟨a woman *bawling* abuse from the door of an inn —C.E.Montague⟩ ⟨the old judge was in the hall *bawling* hasty orders —Sheridan Le Fanu⟩ BLUSTER suggests the turbulent noisiness of gusts of wind; it often suggests swaggering and noisy threats or protests ⟨expressed her opinion gently but firmly, while he *blustered* for a time and then gave in —Sherwood Anderson⟩ ⟨swagger and *bluster* and take the limelight —Margaret Mead⟩ CLAMOR suggests sustained, mixed and confused noisy outcry as from a number of agitated persons ⟨half-starved men and women *clamoring* for food —Kenneth Roberts⟩ ⟨easy . . . for critics . . . to *clamor* for action —Sir Winston Churchill⟩ VOCIFERATE suggests loud vehement insistence in speaking ⟨was not willing to break off his talk; so he continued to *vociferate* his remarks —James Boswell⟩

By permission. From *Webster's Third New International Dictionary.* © 1976 by G. & C. Merriam Co., Publishers of the Merriam-Webster Dictionaries.

From *Webster's New Collegiate:*

syn WIT. HUMOR. IRONY. SARCASM. SATIRE. REPARTEE *shared meaning element* : a mode of expression intended to arouse amused interest or evoke attention and laughter or a quality of mind that predisposes to such expression. WIT suggests the power to evoke laughing attention by remarks showing verbal felicity or ingenuity and swift perception, especially of the incongruous <true *wit* is nature to advantage dressed, what oft was thought, but ne'er so well expressed —Alexander Pope> HUMOR implies an ability to perceive and effectively express the ludicrous, the comical, or the absurd, especially in human life <the modern sense of *humor* is the quiet enjoyment and implicit expression of the fun of things —Louis Cazamian> IRONY applies to a manner of presentation in which an intended meaning is subtly emphasized by appropriate expression of its opposite <*irony* properly suggests the opposite of what is explicitly stated, by means of peripheral clues — tone of voice, accompanying gestures, stylistic exaggeration . . . thus, for "Brutus is an honorable man" we understand "Brutus is a traitor" —Jacob Brackman> SARCASM applies to savagely humorous expression, frequently in the form of irony, intended to cut and wound <the arrows of *sarcasm* are barbed with contempt —Washington Gladden> SATIRE applies primarily to writing that holds up vices or follies to ridicule and reprobation often by use of irony or caricature <his dry wit and his easy, good-natured *satire* on the follies of the day —Eleanor M. Sickels> REPARTEE applies to the power or art of responding quickly, pointedly, and wittily or to an interchange of such response <as for *repartee*. . . , as it is the very soul of conversation, so it is the greatest grace of comedy —John Dryden>

From *Webster's New World:*

SYN.—**destroy** implies a tearing down or bringing to an end by wrecking, ruining, killing, eradicating, etc. and is the term of broadest application here *[* to *destroy* a city, one's influence, etc.*]*; **demolish** implies such destructive force as to completely smash to pieces *[* the bombs *demolished* the factories*]*; **raze** means to level to the ground, either destructively or by systematic wrecking with a salvaging of useful parts; to **annihilate** is to destroy so completely as to blot out of existence *[* rights that cannot be *annihilated]*

From the *American College:*

—**Syn. 3.** STOP, ARREST, CHECK, HALT imply causing a cessation of movement or progress (literal or figurative). STOP is the general term for the idea: *to stop a clock.* ARREST usually refers to stopping by imposing a sudden and complete restraint: *to arrest development.* CHECK implies bringing about an abrupt, partial, or temporary stop: *to check a trotting horse.* To HALT means to make a temporary stop, esp. one resulting from a command: *to halt a company of soldiers.* **17.** STOP, CEASE, PAUSE, QUIT imply bringing movement, action, progress, or conditions to an end. STOP is used in speaking of objects in motion or action: *the clock stopped.* CEASE, a more literary and formal word, suggests the coming to an end of that which has had considerable duration: *a storm ceases.* PAUSE implies the prospect of resumption after a short interval: *one pauses in speaking.* QUIT, in the sense of stop or cease, still very common in the U.S., is not used in England, though it survives in Scottish and Irish English (in England the term used is *leave off*): *make him quit.* —**Ant. 3, 17.** start, begin.

From the *Funk & Wagnalls:*

— **Syn. 4.** *Speech, address, talk, oration, harangue, lecture, discourse, sermon,* and *homily* denote something said to an audience. Any public speaking may be called a *speech.* An *address* is a formal *speech,* as on a ceremonial occasion. *Talk,* on the other hand, suggests informality. An *oration* is an eloquent *address* that appeals to the emotions, while a *harangue* is a vehement *speech,* appealing to the emotions and often intended to spur the audience to action of some sort. A *lecture* is directed to the listener's intellect; it gives information, explanation, or counsel. Any carefully prepared *speech* or writing is a *discourse. Sermon* and *homily* are concerned with religious instruction; a *sermon* is usually an interpretation of Scripture, and a *homily* gives ethical guidance.

From *Funk & Wagnalls Standard College Dictionary.* Copyright © 1977 by Harper & Row Publishers, Inc. Reprinted by permission of the publisher.

From the *American Heritage:*

Synonyms: *curious, inquisitive, snoopy, nosy, intrusive.* These adjectives apply to persons who show a marked desire for information or knowledge. *Curious* more often implies a legitimate desire to enlarge one's knowledge, but can suggest a less commendable urge to concern oneself in others' affairs. *Inquisitive* frequently suggests excessive curiosity and the asking of many questions. *Snoopy* implies an unworthy motive and underhandedness in implementing it. *Nosy* suggests excessive curiosity and impertinence in an adult; applied to a child, it may refer less unfavorably to habitual curiosity. *Intrusive* stresses unwarranted and unwelcome concern with another's affairs.

© 1969, 1970, 1971, 1973, 1975, 1976, Houghton Mifflin Company. Reprinted by permission from *The American Heritage Dictionary of the English Language.*

EXERCISE 39(8) Indicate the distinctions in meaning among the words in each of the following groups.

1 quality, property, character, attribute
2 neglect, omit, disregard, ignore, overlook
3 costly, expensive, valuable, precious, priceless
4 calm, tranquil, serene, placid, peaceful
5 eager, avid, keen, anxious
6 puzzle, perplex, bewilder, dumbfound
7 fashion, style, vogue, fad, rage, craze
8 conform, adjust, reconcile
9 correct, accurate, exact, precise
10 obstruct, hinder, impede, bar, block, dam
11 ghastly, grim, grisly, gruesome, macabre
12 design, plan, scheme, plot
13 mock, mimic, copy, ape
14 maudlin, mushy, sentimental
15 grudge, spite, malice

Care should be taken, not that the reader may understand, but that he must understand.   QUINTILIAN

40   Exactness EX

To write with precision, you must know both the denotation and the connotation of words. DENOTATION is the core of a word's meaning, sometimes called the "dictionary," or literal, meaning; for example, a *tree* is *a woody perennial plant having a single main axis or stem commonly exceeding ten feet in height.* CON-NOTATION refers to the reader's emotional response to a word and to the associations the word carries with it. Thus, *tree* connotes *shade* or *coolness* or *shelter* or *stillness.*

Obviously, the connotation of a word cannot be fixed, for individual responses differ. Some words have fairly standardized connotations (*flag* ⟩ *the emotion of patriotism; home* ⟩ *security, the sense of one's own place*). But even these words have other and less orthodox connotations. In fact, poets achieve many of their finest effects by avoiding standardized connotations. *Evening,* for example, connotes for most of us some quality of beauty, but T. S. Eliot jolts us out of our normal response by seeing

. . . the evening . . . spread out against the sky
Like a patient etherised upon a table.

If you ever decide to violate the generally accepted connotations of a word in your own writing, however, be very sure that you know exactly what you are doing. And always take pains to ensure that the connotations of your words reinforce and are consistent with their denotative meanings. For example, one of the denotative meanings of *smack* is *to give a hearty kiss,* but no one (unless he were trying to be funny) would write

He looked deep into her eyes, whispered endearing words, and *smacked* her on the ear.

Many words stand for abstractions: *democracy, truth, beauty.* Because the connotations of such words are both vague and numerous, you should state specifically what you mean when you use them, or ensure that the context clarifies their meaning. Otherwise, the reader will misunderstand, or—what is worse—will think he understands your terms when he does not. (See **37a.**)

40a Distinguish carefully among synonyms.

English is rich in synonyms, groups of words that have nearly the same meaning: *begin, start, commence; female, feminine, womanly; funny, comic, laughable.* Almost all synonyms differ in connotation, and exact writers choose carefully among them, observing their precise shades of meaning. Occasionally, the difference in meaning between two synonyms is so slight that it makes little difference which we choose: we can *begin a vacation* or *start a vacation*—either will do. But usually the differences will be much greater. To *commence a vacation,* for example, will not do; *commence* surely means *begin,* but it connotes far more formality than ordinarily goes with vacations. And it makes a much more important difference whether we describe a girl as *female, feminine,* or *womanly,* or a movie as *funny, comic,* or *laughable.*

Exact writing requires that we both increase the number of synonyms we can draw from in our writing (see pp. 296–299), and distinguish carefully among them. Knowing that *fashion* and *vogue* are synonyms for *fad,* or that *renowned* and *notorious* are synonyms for *famous,* gives us the chance to make our writing more exact. Choosing the synonyms that connote the precise shade of meaning we want makes it more exact.

The careless use of synonyms not only makes our writing inexact; it often actually distorts our meaning.

> Capone was a *renowned* gangster. (*Renowned* has favorable connotations that the writer probably did not intend. *Famous* would do, but it is not very exact. *Notorious* would be exact.)

EXERCISE 40a(1) Replace the italicized words in the following sentences with more exact ones. Explain why each italicized word is inappropriate.

1 His characters are *garish* and alive; they are people you will remember as old friends.
2 His *obstinacy* in the face of danger saved us all.
3 The ambassador, being treated like a common tourist, sputtered in *displeasure.*
4 We can't blame Margaret for leaving him; certainly she had an ample *pretext.*
5 The school's most honored professor was without fault: a wise mentor to his students, and in addition a scholar recognized as *pedantic* and profound.

EXERCISE 40a(2) Explain the differences in meaning among the italicized words in each of the following groups.

1 an *ignorant,* an *illiterate,* an *unlettered,* an *uneducated* person

2 a *detached,* a *disinterested,* an *indifferent,* an *unconcerned* attitude
3 to *codone,* to *excuse,* to *forgive,* to *pardon* a person's actions
4 an *insurrection,* a *mutiny,* a *rebellion,* a *revolution*
5 a *barbarous,* a *cruel,* a *fierce,* a *ferocious,* an *inhuman,* a *savage* character

40b

40b Do not confuse words with similar sound or spelling but with different meanings.

40c

Some words are HOMONYMS, that is, they have the same pronunciation but different meanings and different spellings (*idol, idle, idyll; aisle, isle*). Other words are sufficiently similar in sound and spelling to be confusing. You must treat all these words as you would any other unfamiliar term: Learn the correct spelling and meaning of each as an individual word.

EXERCISE 40b What are the differences in meaning in each of the following groups of words?

1 adapt, adept, adopt	16 confidently, confidentially
2 alley, ally	17 costume, custom
3 allude, elude	18 elicit, illicit
4 anecdote, antidote	19 epic, epoch
5 anesthetic, antiseptic	20 flaunt, flout
6 angel, angle	21 genteel, gentile
7 arraign, arrange	22 historic, historical
8 block, bloc	23 human, humane
9 borne, born	24 ingenious, ingenuous
10 Calvary, cavalry	25 marital, martial
11 cannon, canon	26 morality, mortality
12 canvas, canvass	27 prescribe, proscribe
13 carton, cartoon	28 receipt, recipe
14 chord, cord	29 statue, statute
15 climactic, climatic	30 waive, wave

40c Generally, avoid "invented" words.

A COINED word is a new and outright creation (like *gobbledegook, blurb*). A NEOLOGISM is either a new word or a new use of an old word or words (like Madison Avenue's *package plans*). A NONCE-WORD, literally ONCE-WORD, is a word made up to suit a special situation and generally not used more than once (*"My son," he said, "suffers from an acute case of televisionitis"*). Though the great majority of neologisms and nonce-words are short-lived, they are among the ways by which new words and new functions for old words are constantly working their way into a changing language.

English is relatively free in shifting words from one part of speech to another. The process is called FUNCTIONAL SHIFT and is one of the many ways in which our language grows. The noun *iron* is used as an adjective in *iron bar,* and as a verb in *iron the sheets.* The space age gives us *All systems are go,* using the verb *go* as a modifier. *River, paper,* and *sea* are clearly nouns in form (they make plurals with *-s*), but we commonly use them as modifiers in *river bank, paper bag,* and *sea water.*

But the fact that such changes are common in English does not mean that we can freely shift any word from one function to another. In *He opinioned that Edward was guilty, opinion* is used as a verb, a grammatical function to which it is entirely unaccustomed. The meaning may be roughly clear, but the use is not accepted. We *punish* a person. There is perhaps no good reason why we should not speak of *a punish.* But we don't; if we want a noun, we must use *punishment.*

40c

As an inexperienced writer you need to devote most of your attention to learning the meanings of words already established by usage, but you should not be afraid to try a new coinage if it seems to suit your purpose. As an experienced reader, your instructor will be able to judge whether the experiment is successful. Be careful, however, to avoid "unconscious" inventions—words that you "invent" because of spelling errors or an inexact knowledge of word forms (*understandment* for *understanding, multification* for *multiplication*). If you have any doubt about the accepted grammatical functions of a word, consult your dictionary.

EXERCISE 40c In the following sentences correct the italicized words that seem to you needlessly invented. Check your dictionary when necessary to determine whether a particular word is an accepted form or whether it is used in the way it appears in the sentence in the exercise.

1 One glimpse of the activities of the police or the mobs in urban riots reveals the *savagism* of human nature.
2 Teachers should be strictly *unpolitical;* they should not try to influence their students.
3 Even in our computer age, human behavior is largely *unpredictable.*
4 He displayed *liberalistic* tendencies in economic affairs.
5 That highway is *stoplighted* all the way to town; let's take the turnpike.
6 The cottage is nearly finished; we're going *to roof* it tomorrow.
7 Before we started building it, we had *to bulldoze* a clearing.
8 As each of the kids came out of the pool, I *toweled* him dry.
9 This year we're going *to holiday* in Bermuda.
10 Next summer we're going *to jeep* our way cross-country.

40d Be alert to changes in meaning from one suffixal form of a word to another.

A roommate whom you *like* is not necessarily a *likable* roommate, nor is a *matter of agreement* an *agreeable matter.* Many words have two, sometimes three, adjectival forms: e.g., a *changeable* personality, a *changing* personality, a *changed* personality. Be careful not to substitute one form for another.

Faulty	The cook served our *favorable* dessert last night.
Standard	The cook served our *favorite* dessert last night.
Faulty	He is a good student; he has a very *questionable* mind.
Standard	He is a good student; he has a very *questioning* mind.

40d

40e

EXERCISE 40d Point out the differences in meaning between the italicized words in each of the following groups.

1 an *arguable* point
  an *argued* point

2 a *practical* solution
  a *practicable* solution

3 a *hated* person
  a *hateful* person

4 a *liberal* foreign minister
  a *liberated* foreign minister

5 a *single* effect
  a *singular* effect

6 an *intelligible* writer
  an *intelligent* writer

7 a *godly* man
  a *godlike* man

8 an *informed* teacher
  an *informative* teacher

9 a *peaceful* nation
  a *peaceable* nation

10 a *workable* arrangement
   a *working* arrangement

11 an *amicable* woman
   an *amiable* woman

12 a *yellow* piece of paper
   a *yellowed* piece of paper

40e Avoid "elegant variation."

Often you will use a variety of synonyms and pronouns in order to avoid the awkward repetition of a word. That is a perfectly legitimate stylistic device. But when your desire to avoid repetition is so overwhelming that you dig up a synonym or epithet for almost every word you have used previously, you are guilty of "elegant variation."

Pee Wee Pearce, the Chicago second-baseman, got three hits yesterday. The tiny infielder came up in the first frame and lashed a one-base blow to right field. In the third inning the diminutive keystone sacker knocked a single through the box. In the seventh the little ballhawk reached first safely on a screaming drive to the outer garden.

Here, in the short space of four sentences, we have well over a dozen examples of elegant variation:

Pee Wee	*second-baseman*	*hits*
tiny	infielder	one-base blow
diminutive	keystone sacker	single
little	ballhawk	screaming drive
lashed	*right field*	*first frame*
knocked	box	third inning
reached first	outer garden	seventh

In the first of the examples below, the use of the simple pronoun *he* would have made unnecessary the frantic search for synonyms for *king*. In the second, *visitor* could be omitted and *Two of the other people in attendance* changed to *Two others.*

40e

The *King* appeared yesterday at the Navy Barracks. *His Majesty* was in full dress and escorted by the Home Guards. After inspecting the cadets, the *royal guest* was entertained at the Officers' Club.
I saw many of my old classmates at your garden party. Two of your *guests* were my fraternity brothers. Another *visitor* played on the same football team with me. *Two of the other people in attendance* were brothers of my old girl friend.

EXERCISE 40e(1) Find a specimen of elegant variation in a newspaper or popular magazine and rewrite it to show how the variation might be avoided.

EXERCISE 40e(2) Discuss in one or two paragraphs the elegant variation in the following passage.

The outcome of the game was a personal victory for All-American Marty Jerome. The diminutive halfback scored ten times for the Mustangs, five of these coming in the final frame. In the first quarter the pint-sized wingback ran 10 yards for one score, scampered 45 for another, and actually bulled his way over for a third from the two-yard stripe. In the second period the little fellow galloped half the length of the field for a marker after intercepting a Longhorn pass on his own fifty. In the third frame the mighty mite was held to one touchdown—that one coming on the last play of the period and featuring a series of fumbles. Lou Zamberg, Longhorn fullback, dropped the ball as he came through the line; Joe Harris, the Mustangs' giant tackle, picked it up, was hit from behind and fumbled. Like a streak of light the tiny Jerome grabbed it just before it hit the ground and dashed 85 long and magnificent yards to paydirt. The last frame was all Jerome's. In a display of ability seldom, if ever, seen, the little man ran for five tallies, one of them a 105-yard kickoff return. He scored again on an intercepted pass, then on a 20-yard rabbit-run through center, and twice more on bullet-like plunges from the 5-yard line to home base.

40f   Use accepted idioms.

An IDIOM is an expression that does not follow the normal pattern of the language, or that has a total meaning not suggested by its separate words: *to catch fire, strike a bargain, ride it out, lose one's head, hold the bag.** Such expressions are a part of the vocabulary of native speakers. In fact, we learn them in the same way we learn new words—by hearing them in the speech around us, and by reading them in context. For the most part they give us no more, and no less, difficulty than vocabulary itself gives us. Dictionaries usually give the common idiomatic expressions at the end of the definition of a word entry.

For many writers the most troublesome idioms in English are those which require a particular preposition after a given verb or adjective according to the meaning intended. The following list contains a number of such combinations which frequently cause trouble.

40f

absolved by, from	I was *absolved* by the dean *from* all blame.
accede to	He *acceded to* his father's demands.
accompany by, with	I was *accompanied by* George. The terms were *accompanied with* a plea for immediate peace.
acquitted of	He was *acquitted of* the crime.
adapted to, from	This machine can be *adapted to* farm work. The design was *adapted from* a previous invention.
admit to, of	He *admitted to* the error. The plan will *admit of* no alternative.
agree to, with, in	They *agreed to* the plan but *disagreed with* us. They *agreed* only *in* principle.
angry with, at	She was *angry with* me and *angry at* the treatment she had received.
capable of	He is *capable of* every vice of the ignorant.
compare to, with	He *compared* the roundness of the baseball *to* that of the earth. He *compared* the economy of the Ford *with* that of the Plymouth.

---

*The term *idiom* is also used to mean the characteristic expression or pattern of a dialect or language. In this sense of the word, we can speak of the *idiom* of speakers from South Boston, or we can compare English *idiom* with German or French.

concur with, in	I *concur with* you *in* your desire to use the revised edition.
confide in, to	He *confided in* me. He *confided to* me that he had stolen the car.
conform to, with conformity with	The specifications *conformed to* (or *with*) his original plans. You must act in *conformity with* our demands.
connect by, with	The rooms are *connected by* a corridor. He is officially *connected with* this university.
differ about, from, with	We *differ about* our tastes in clothes. My clothes *differ from* yours. We *differ with* one another.
different from*	Our grading system is *different from* yours.
enter into, on, upon	He *entered into* a new agreement and thereby *entered on* (or *upon*†) a new career.
free from, of	He was *freed from* his mother's domination and now he is *free of* her.
identical with	Your reasons are *identical with* his.
join in, with, to	He *joined in* the fun *with* the others. He *joined* the wire cables *to* each other.
live at, in, on	He *lives at* 14 Neil Avenue *in* a Dutch Colonial house. He *lives on* Neil Avenue.
necessity for, of, need for, of	There was no *necessity* (*need*) *for* you to lose your temper. There was no *necessity* (*need*) *of* your losing your temper.
object to	I *object to* the statement in the third paragraph.
oblivious of	When he held her hand he was *oblivious of* the passing of time.
overcome by, with	I was *overcome by* the heat. I was *overcome with* grief.
parallel between, to, with	There is a *parallel between* your attitude and his. This line is *parallel to* (or *with*) that one.
preferable to	A leisurely walk is *preferable to* violent exercise.

40f

---

* *Different than* is colloquially idiomatic when the object of the prepositional phrase is a clause:

Formal	This town looks *different from* what I had remembered.
Colloquial	This town looks *different than* I had remembered it.

† In many phrases, *on* and *upon* are interchangeable: *depend on* or *depend upon*; *enter on* or *enter upon*.

reason with, about	Why not *reason with* him *about* the matter?
variance with	This conclusion is at *variance with* your facts.
vary from, in, with	The houses *vary from* one another *in* size. People's tastes *vary with* their personalities.
worthy of	That woman is not *worthy of* your trust.

EXERCISE 40f Provide the idiomatic prepositions needed in the following sentences.

1 The students acceded _____ the increased need to conform _____ security regulations.
2 The men were acquitted _____ the charge and absolved _____ all blame for the damage to the building.
3 Price control seems preferable _____ excessive inflation but many businessmen differ _____ this conclusion.
4 Some critics argue that there was no necessity _____ the resumption of bombing North Vietnam, and that the United States could have entered _____ a ceasefire agreement earlier.
5 I agreed _____ his proposal, which had been adapted _____ one I had made previously.
6 Lois Bowers said she was angry _____ him because his actions did not conform _____ those of a gentleman.
7 The fence was built parallel _____ the street and connected _____ his neighbor's stone wall.
8 Having been freed _____ his parents' supervision, he saw no necessity _____ keep (*or* keeping) them informed of his whereabouts.
9 I am not capable _____ budget (*or* budgeting) my own income for I am unable to add 4 and 4 and get 8.
10 We entered _____ a contract to buy the house after Mr. Jones agreed _____ our request for a twenty-year mortgage.

40g

40g Use specific words rather than general words.

A general word stands for generalized qualities or characteristics, as *color, beast, vehicle*. A specific word singles out more definite and individual qualities, as *red, lion, tricycle*. The context determines whether a particular word is general or specific. For example, *man* is a general word in relation to *Leonard Chapman* and *Barney Rider,* but a specific word in relation to *mammal*. And *beast* is less specific than *lion* but more specific than *creature*.

No piece of writing can be vivid with generalized, abstract words. We can't always avoid using such words as *useful, democratic,* and *nice,* but we can submit them to a few down-to-earth questions: *useful* for what? *useful* how? *democratic* attitude as in a mob or *democratic* process as in an election for public office? *nice* as in prim? wealthy? fastidious? delicate? precise? agreeable? When we answer these questions, we are forced to be specific. And it is the writer's choice of particular, concrete words and phrases which arouses vivid responses in the reader's mind. When you use generalizations, be sure you illustrate or support them with concrete details: names, numbers, quotations, facts, and color words.

Try constantly to express your thoughts in concrete and unambiguous terms; search for the most specific words available.

General	The flowers were of different colors.
Specific	The chrysanthemums were bronze, gold, and white.
General	The cost of education has increased greatly.
More Specific	Tuition at many private universities has increased as much as 1000 percent in the past three decades.
Still More Specific	Tuition at Boston University was $300 in 1947; it was $3,800 in 1977.

40g

Specific	Mateo was a stocky man, with clear eyes and a deeply tanned face. His skill as a marksman was extraordinary, even in Corsica, where everyone is a good shot. He could kill a ram at one hundred and twenty paces, and his aim was as accurate at night as in the daytime.
More Specific	Picture a small, sturdy man, with jet-black, curly hair, a Roman nose, thin lips, large piercing eyes, and a weather-beaten complexion. His skill as a marksman was extraordinary, even in this country, where everyone is a good shot. For instance, Mateo would never fire on a wild ram with small shot, but at a hundred and twenty paces he would bring it down with a bullet in its head or shoulder, just as he fancied. He used his rifle at night as easily as in the daytime, and I was given the following illustration of his skill, which may seem incredible, perhaps, to those who have never travelled in Corsica. He placed a lighted candle behind a piece of transparent paper as big as a plate, and aimed at it from eighty paces away. He extinguished the candle, and a moment later, in utter darkness, fired and pierced the paper three times out of four.

PROSPER MÉRIMÉE, *Mateo Falcone*

41

In composing, as a general rule, run your pen through every other word you have written; you have no idea what vigor it will give your style.

SIDNEY SMITH

41a

41 Directness DIR

The challenge to directness comes from two fronts—wordiness and vagueness. A wordy writer uses more words than are necessary to convey his meaning.

Wordy	He attacks the practice of making a profitable business out of college athletics from the standpoint that it has a detrimental and harmful influence on the college students, and, to a certain degree and extent, on the colleges and universities themselves.
Improved	He attacks commercialization of college athletics as harmful to the students, and even to the universities themselves.

A vague writer fails to convey his meaning sharply and clearly.

Vague	The report asserts the danger from unguarded machines which may lessen the usefulness of workers in later life as well as reducing their life expectancy.
Improved	The report asserts that unguarded machines may severely injure or even kill workers.

Vagueness and wordiness are sometimes indistinguishable, as in the preceding examples. The weight of unnecessary words tends to obscure meaning. But very often wordiness is just awkwardness; the meaning is clear, but the expression is clumsy.

Awkward	The notion that Communists are people who wear long black beards is a very common notion.
Improved	The notion is common that Communists are people who wear long black beards.

41a   Eliminate words and phrases that do not add to your meaning.

Good writing says things in as few words as possible without losing clarity or completeness. It makes every word count. You can often make your writing more direct and economical by (1) cutting unnecessary words and phrases, and (2) reducing clauses to phrases, and phrases to single words.

1. **Cutting unnecessary words and phrases.** Often as you revise your writing you will be able to strike out words that are clearly unnecessary, or gain directness by slight changes.

Wordy	When the time to go had arrived, Molly left.
Revised	When it was time to go, Molly left.
Wordy	After the close of the war, Bob went to college.
Revised	After the war, Bob went to college.
Wordy	She is attractive in appearance, but she is a rather selfish person.
Revised	She is attractive, but rather selfish.

Words such as *angle, aspect, factor,* and *situation,* and phrases such as *in the case of, in the line of, in the field of* are almost never necessary. They are common obstacles to directness in much writing today.

Wordy	John is majoring in the field of biology.
Revised	John is majoring in biology.
Wordy	Another aspect of the situation that needs to be examined is the matter of advertising.
Revised	We should also examine advertising.

Be suspicious of sentences beginning with *there are, there is, it is.* They are often roundabout statements.

Wordy	There are many reasons why we have pollution.
Revised	Pollution has many causes.
Wordy	It is a fact that many students read very little.
Revised	Many students read very little.

Phrases such as *I believe, I think,* and *in my opinion* are usually unnecessary.

Wordy	In my opinion, we must reduce violence on television.
Revised	We must reduce violence on television.
Wordy	I believe that nuclear power plants are dangerous.
Revised	Nuclear power plants are dangerous.

2. **Reducing clauses to phrases and phrases to single words.** Wordiness often results from using a clause when a phrase will do, or a phrase when a single word will do.

| Wordy | There were instances of aggression on the country's frontier in many cases. |

41a

Revised	There were many instances of aggression on the country's frontier.
Revised	Aggression was frequent on the country's frontier. (In the first revision the phrase *in many instances* has been reduced to a single adjective modifying *instances*. But note that the second revision is made even more direct by eliminating the *there are* construction.)
Wordy	The shirt, which is made of wool, has worn well for eight years.
Revised	The woolen shirt has worn for eight years. (The clause *which was made of wool* has been reduced to the single modifier *woolen*.)
Wordy	The snow which fell yesterday is already melting.
Revised	Yesterday's snow is already melting. (The clause *which fell yesterday* has been reduced to the single modifier *yesterday's*.)
Wordy	The conclusions which the committee of students reached are summarized in the newspaper of the college which was published today.
Revised	The conclusions reached by the student committee are summarized in today's college newspaper. (The first *which* clause has been reduced to a participle phrase beginning with *reached*. The second *which* clause has become the single word *today's*. The phrases *of students, in the newspaper,* and *of the college* have all been reduced.)
Wordy	The football captain, who is an All-American player, played his last game today.
Revised	The football captain, an All-American, played his last game today. (The clause has been reduced to a descriptive noun phrase—an appositive.)

EXERCISE 41a Rewrite the following sentences to reduce their wordiness.

1 He is an expert in the field of labor relations.
2 The fastest kind of automobile requires the best quality of gasoline.
3 Most Congressmen spend a majority of the hours which they have in each working day attending committee meetings.
4 In my opinion, Dr. Mackenzie is of greater ability and of greater experience than Dr. Smith.
5 People have to be educated as to how to plan good, inexpensive menus that will meet their nutritional needs.
6 The rain, which has been coming down steadily for two weeks now, is washing away the seeds I planted in the ground at an earlier time.
7 Mr. Armstrong, who was my history teacher, had a classroom manner which was very dynamic.

8 There are two reasons that I have for not going: the first is that I have an examination to study for; the second is that I have no money.
9 Love and understanding of them are two of the most important things young children need.
10 After several hours of shopping around to buy my mother a gift, I finally decided to give her a check to buy whatever she decided she preferred.
11 After he finished his military service in the Navy, he decided to go on and enroll again in school.

41b

41c

41b   Prefer one exact word to two or more approximate words.

Many groups of words are simply roundabout ways of expressing what a single exact word expresses more directly.

Wordy	*Direct*
this day and age	today
of an indefinite nature	indefinite
at this point in time	now
by means of	by
call up on the telephone	telephone
destroy by fire	burn
was made the recipient of	was given

Often we can substitute one precise word for two or more approximate synonyms.

Wordy	His *temperament* and *disposition* are unpleasant.
Revised	His *disposition* is unpleasant.
Wordy	She described her *deeds* and *doings* as a foreign correspondent.
Revised	She described her *adventures* as a foreign correspondent.

41c   Avoid redundancy.

Expressions such as *visible to the eyes* and *audible to the ears* are said to be REDUNDANT. They say the same thing twice. Typical examples are:

Redundant	*Direct*
advance forward	advance
continue on	continue
refer back	refer
combine together	combine

circle around	circle
small in size	small
disappear from view	disappear
throughout the whole	throughout
basic fundamentals	fundamentals
important essentials	essentials

Sometimes sentences become wordy through the writer's careless repetition of the same meaning in slightly different words.

Wordy	As a rule, Susan usually woke up early.
Revised	Susan usually woke up early.
Wordy	We planned to go at 3 o'clock P.M. in the afternoon.
Revised	We planned to go at 3 P.M.
Wordy	In their opinion, they think they are right.
Revised	They think they are right.

41d   Avoid awkward repetition.

Repetition of important words is a useful way of gaining emphasis (see **36d**). But careless repetition is awkward and wordy.

Awkward	The investigation revealed that the *average teachers teaching* industrial arts in California have an *average* working and *teaching* experience of five years.
Revised	The investigation revealed that teachers of industrial arts in California have an average of five years experience.
Awkward	Gas mileage in the American car is being *improved* constantly in order to *improve* efficiency.
Revised	Gas mileage in the American car is being improved constantly to increase efficiency.
Awkward	The *important subject* on which I was going to speak is career opportunities, a *subject* of *great importance* to college students.
Revised	I am going to speak on career opportunities, a subject of great importance to college students.

EXERCISE 41b–d Eliminate redundancies and unnecessary repetition from the following sentences.

1 Because Jim believed exercise was a necessary requirement, his habitual custom was to jog every morning at 7 A.M.
2 This book is intended and designed to explain the basic fundamentals of English.

3 Barbara Linger's limousine sedan, black in color, has been seen a countless number of times parked in front of Blickels' market.
4 It was the consensus of opinion among the students that grades should be abandoned.
5 Teachers should provide several examples to illustrate the grammatical rules they are trying to teach.
6 So far as understanding his meaning is concerned, I would classify Joyce in the category of writers who are very difficult to read.
7 He is an industrial engineering student studying the principles of time-and-motion study.
8 As far as I'm concerned, government should keep out of intervening in private business, in my opinion.
9 A reckless driver is no better than a murderer who goes around killing people.
10 Last night we had to circle all around the block before finding a parking space in which to park the car.

41e Prefer simple, direct expressions to needlessly complex ones.

41e

Never be ashamed to express a simple idea in simple language. The use of complicated language is not in itself a sign of superior intelligence (see **42d**).

| Needlessly Complex | Not a year passes without some evidence of the fundamental truth of the statement that the procedures and techniques of education are more complicated and complex than they were two decades ago. |
| More Direct | Each year shows that methods of education are more complex than they were twenty years ago. |

If alternative forms of the same word exist, prefer the shorter. Choose *truth* and *virtue* rather than *truthfulness* and *virtuousness*. Choose *preventive* rather than *preventative*.

To prefer simplicity does not mean to make all writing simple. Naturally, highly complex or technical subjects call at times for complex and technical langauge.

One of the simplest ways of evolving a favorable environment concurrently with the development of the individual organism, is that the influence of each organism on the environment should be favorable to the *endurance* of other organisms of the same type. Further, if the organism also favors *development* of other organisms of the same type, you have then obtained a mechanism of evolution adapted to produce the observed state of large multitudes of analogous entities, with high powers of endurance. For the environment automatically develops with the species, and the species with the environment.

A. N. WHITEHEAD, *Science and the Modern World* [his italics]

EXERCISE 41e Find a paragraph or two of "needlessly complex" writing in one of your textbooks. Explain in one or two paragraphs how you think the writing might be made more direct.

41f   Use euphemisms sparingly.

Euphemisms substitute a more pleasant word or phrase for one that is, for any reason, objectionable. They express unpleasant things in less harsh and direct ways: *pass away* for *die, perspire* for *sweat, mortal remains* for *corpse, intoxicated* for *drunk*. Most common euphemisms are associated with the basic facts of existence—birth, age, death, sex, the bodily functions—and often seem necessary for politeness or tact. We are more comfortable describing a good friend as one who *is stout* and *likes to drink* than as a *fat drunk*. And in such contexts these terms are harmless.

41f

But the use of euphemisms to distract us from the realities of work, unemployment, poverty, and war is at best misleading and at worst dishonest and dangerous. Today we take for granted such terms as "sanitation engineer" (plumber), "funeral director" (undertaker), and "maintenance people" (janitors). Such terms perhaps help protect the feelings of individuals and give them status. But the individuals themselves still have to sweat pipes, prepare bodies for burial, and sweep floors—in short do work that is hard or unpleasant. And if the terms make us forget that reality, they are misleading. It is a short step further to language consciously intended to deceive. Such language gives us "protective reaction" (bombing), "pacification" (killing people and destroying their homes), "strategic withdrawal" (retreat), "visual surveillance" (spying), and "inoperative statements" (lies). Such phrases are downright dishonest. They are created for the sole purpose of distracting us from realities that we need to know about. Slums and ghettos are no less slums and ghettos because we call them the "inner city." And if you're fired, you're out of a job even if you've been "terminated" or "deselected."

Keep your own writing honest, and be alert to dishonesty in the writing of others. Use euphemism when tact and genuine respect for the feelings of your audience warrants it. Do not use it to deceive.

EXERCISE 41a–f Each of the sentences below violates a principal of directness. Find and then correct the error.

1 We of the United States cannot expect to spread peace throughout other nations and countries until we can teach and educate our own people to respect each other as equal individuals.

42

2 His capacity for hard work makes him capable of working long hours each day.

3 The integration of public schools is a major step forward toward complete equality of all groups.

4 During the entirety of his whole college career, Peter continually went on thinking about his plan to work his way around the world.

5 It has just been in the past couple of years that black Americans have begun to make clear that they wish to develop their own racial identity by themselves without outside interference.

6 The reason for Nixon's choice of Agnew as a running mate for vice-president stemmed from the fact that he wanted a Southern candidate as nominee.

7 The first settlers in the West were prospectors who explored the new land as they prospected for gold.

8 The actress acted very badly, but the play was played through to the very end and conclusion.

9 He was the handsomest-looking man I had ever seen before in my life.

10 The increasing filth in our waterways through pollution has bothered and troubled scientists for a period of one and a half decades.

A speech is composed of three things: the speaker, the subject on which he speaks, and the audience he is addressing.

ARISTOTLE, *Rhetoric*

42 Appropriateness APPR

Because the English language is constantly growing, it continues to be a useful vehicle for conveying thought accurately and effectively. Fortunately, words appear, disappear, or shift their meanings slowly so that there is always available a large core of stable, generally used words. Beyond this core are wide ranges of usage: slang, regional expressions, profanity, clichés, jargon, stilted diction. Words from these categories must be used sparingly if at all.

There are no words in the English language that cannot be used somewhere at some time. But when a piece of writing is overloaded with slang or clichés, the question of <u>appropriateness</u> arises. You may consider yourself such a casual, easy-going person that you think casual, easy-going language is appropriate to you. It may be—in a letter to a close friend about an exciting summer holiday. Even in letter-writing, however, you must also <u>consider your audience and your</u> subject: that letter to a friend would necessarily be different if you were expressing your sympathy for an illness in his family. But when you sit down to write papers for your courses, keep your eye on that core of stable, generally used and generally understood words. If you do depart from those words, have a good reason.

42a Ordinarily, avoid slang.

Slang consists of the rapidly changing words and phrases in popular speech that people invent to give language novelty and vigor. Slang often is created by the same processes we use to create most new words: by combining two words (*fishface, blockhead, sob-stuff*); by shortening words (*pro, prof, vet*); by borrowing from other languages (*kaput, spiel*); and by generalizing a proper name (*the real McCoy*). Often slang simply extends the meaning of phrases borrowed from other activities (*lower the boom* from sailing; *tune in, tune out* from radio; *cash in your chips* from poker). A great deal of slang gives a new range of meaning to existing words (*tough, cool, bread, heavy, crash, turned on, joint*).

Slang is a part of the current language. It is spontaneous and direct and helps give color and liveliness to the language. It often contributes directly to the growth of the language as slang terms move gradually into general use. Words like *rascal* and *sham* were originally slang terms; shortened forms such as *A bomb, ad, gym,* and *phone* are now appropriate to most informal writing. In informal writing, a carefully chosen slang word can be effective:

Has Harold Wilson *lost his cool?*   *New York Times* headline

Heaven knows there are large areas where a shrewd eye for the *quick buck* is dominant.

FREDERICK LEWIS ALLEN, *The Big Change*

But slang has serious limitations in writing, and even in much conversation. It is imprecise, is often understandable only to a narrow social or age group, and usually changes very rapidly. We may know *crazy, goof balls,* and *far out,* but how many of us know *lollapalooza, balloon juice,* or *twerp.* The fact that *hep* became *hip* in a little more than two years suggests how short-lived slang can be.

We can enjoy slang for the life it sometimes gives to speech. But even in conversation we need to remember that our slang expressions may not be understood, that at best a little of it goes a long way, and that if we rely on *hot, cool, lousy,* and *tough* to describe all objects, events, and ideas, we don't communicate much. In writing, we need to use slang only when it serves some special purpose. Except in carefully controlled contexts, slang and standard language make an inappropriate mixture.

> Persuading Mrs. McGinnis to be seated, the chairman of the committee on Indian Affairs asked her politely not to foul up the state's plans to hit pay dirt on Ishimago's claim.

EXERCISE 42a(1) Almost everyone has favorite slang terms. Make a list of your own slang expressions and compare the list with those of your classmates to see how "original" your own slang is.

EXERCISE 42a(2) Can you think of a situation or general context in which the following sentences might be appropriate? Explain.

1 We were invited to a party last night but we couldn't make the scene.
2 The trouble was that my boyfriend was all uptight about his car and I got hung up on a TV show I was watching.
3 I finally told him that he should do his thing and I'd do mine.
4 Anyway, I never got a chance to show off my crazy new hairdo and my really cool fur coat.
5 My boyfriend finally came when I was all decked out and he said I was a real ringading broad.
6 I asked him how he was making out with the car and he told me everything was coming up roses.
7 So we decided to blast off and go to a movie.
8 The movie was like dullsville so my boyfriend asked if I wanted to go and tie one on.

42b Avoid regional and nonstandard language.

REGIONAL words (sometimes called PROVINCIALISMS or LOCALISMS) are words whose use is generally restricted to a particular geographical area. Examples are *tote* for *carry, poke* for *bag, spider* for *frying pan, gumshoes* for *overshoes, draw* for *small valley,* and *woodpussy* for *skunk.* NONSTANDARD words and expressions generally occur only in the speech of uneducated speakers. Examples are *ain't, could of, he done,* and double negatives such as *can't never.* Dictionaries label such words as *nonstandard* or *illiterate.*

Regional	She *redded up* the house for our *kinfolk.*
General	She cleaned the house for our relatives.
Nonstandard	He *didn't ought to have* spent the money.
Standard	He shouldn't have spent the money.
Nonstandard	I wish Irving *had of drove more careful.*
Standard	I wish Irving had driven more carefully.

Of all nonstandard English forms, the double negative (*can't hardly, scarcely none, don't want no,* and so on) is perhaps the most controversial. In the eighteenth century, Englishmen, applying the mathematical principle that two negatives make a positive, ruled out the double negative in grammar. The argument was that a person who says *I don't want nothing to do with you* is really saying *I want something to do with you.* Actually the double (or triple) negative is a means of being emphatic. But since its use is generally frowned upon, you do well to avoid it.

42c

EXERCISE 42b(1) List at least five examples of regionalisms (as *The cat wants in*) and describe the circumstances under which they could be used appropriately.

EXERCISE 42b(2) If you are a native of the region in which your college is located, ask a classmate from another region to give you a list of ten words or expressions that strike him or her as being regionalisms in your speech. If you come from another region yourself, make up your own list of regionalisms of the college area and compare it with a classmate's.

42c Avoid trite expressions.

A trite expression, sometimes called a CLICHÉ, or a STEREOTYPED or HACKNEYED phrase, is an expression that has been worn out by constant use, as *burning the midnight oil, Father Time, raving beauties, man about town.* Words in themselves are never trite—they are only used tritely. We cannot avoid trite expressions entirely, for they sometimes describe a situation accurately. But the writer who burdens his language with clichés runs the risk of being regarded as a trite thinker. What would be your estimate of the person who wrote this?

A college education develops a *well-rounded personality* and gives the student an appreciation of *the finer things of life.*

Effectively used, triteness can be humorous. Note how the string of trite expressions in the example below explodes into absurdity when the writer transposes the words in the two clichés in the last clause.

A pair of pigeons were cooing gently directly beneath my window; two squirrels plighted their troth in a branch overhead; at the corner a handsome member of New York's finest twirled his night stick and cast roguish glances at the saucy-eyed flower vendor. The scene could have been staged only by a Lubitsch; in fact Lubitsch himself was seated on a bench across the street, smoking a cucumber and looking as cool as a cigar.

S. J. PERELMAN, *Keep It Crisp*

Watch for trite words and phrases in your own writing, and replace them with new, original ways of expressing yourself. As you proofread your manuscripts, be as sensitive to clichés as you are to misspellings.

EXERCISE 42c(1) The selection below contains a number of trite expressions. List as many as you can identify.

The wily Indians, wishing to strike while the iron was hot, converged on the wagon train at the break of dawn. The hardy pioneers, firing in unison, presented the attacking force with a veritable hail of bullets. Dozens of the pesky redskins keeled over and bit the dust. The rugged frontiersmen continued to give a good account of themselves until broad daylight. Then the Indians broke through the ramparts. The defenders, their backs against the wall, were slaughtered mercilessly. When the dust had risen from the battlefield and when the smoke had cleared away, the carnage was frightful. Every single white man had gone to meet his Maker.

EXERCISE 42c(2) Copy the following passage. Circle all clichés and all expressions that are longer or more involved than they need be. Suggest more appropriate wordings for each.

The American Way is the only feasible route for educational personnel to tread in our educational institutions of learning. Despite its humble origins, this child of adversity, born in a log cabin, has beyond a shadow of a doubt reached the summits in this fair country of ours.

There is too much of a tendency to view this great institution with alarm. But on the other hand people who live in glass houses, which is the type most inclined to cast aspersions and generally be wet blankets, are usually the ones by whom the criticisms are made.

Now I'm just an ordinary schoolteacher, and don't have any complicated ideas on how our schools should be run, but I know that Abe Lincoln, if he were alive, would disapprove of the newfangled techniques that are making a shambles of our educational system.

Foreigners are at the bottom of the attack on our American heritage and the American Way in education. These notorious radicals have wreaked havoc with our boys and girls.

42d   Avoid jargon in writing for a general audience.

The term JARGON has several meanings. In a famous essay, "On Jargon," Sir Arthur Quiller-Couch defined the term as vague and "woolly" speech or writing that consists of abstract words, elegant variation, and "circumlocution rather than short straight speech." Linguists often define jargon as hybrid speech or dialect formed by a mixture of languages. An example would be the English-Chinese jargon known as pidgin English.

To most people, however, jargon is the technical or specialized vocabulary of a particular trade or profession—for example, engineering jargon or educational jargon. Members of the profession, of course, can use their jargon when they are communicating with one another, for it is their language, so to speak. But the use of technical jargon is inappropriate when you are writing for a general audience.

Unfortunately, jargon impresses a great many people simply because it sounds involved and learned. We are all reluctant to admit that we do not understand what we are reading. What, for example, can you make of the following passage?

THE TURBO-ENCABULATOR IN INDUSTRY

42e

. . . Work has been proceeding in order to bring to perfection the crudely conceived idea of a machine that would not only supply inverse reactive current for use in unilateral phase detractors, but would also be capable of automatically synchronizing cardinal grammeters. Such a machine is the Turbo-Encabulator. . . . The original machine had a base plate of prefabulated amulite surmounted by a malleable logarithmic casing in such a way that the two spurving bearings were in a direct line with the pentametric fan. . . . The main winding was of the normal lotus-o-delta type placed in a panendermic semiboloid slot in the stator, every seventh conductor being connected by a non-reversible tremie pipe to the differential girdlespring on the "up" end of the grammeters. . . .*

This new mechanical marvel was a joke, the linguistic creation of a research engineer who was tired of reading jargon.

EXERCISE 42d Make a list of twenty words, terms, or phrases that constitute the jargon in a field that you know. Define these terms in a way that a general reader could understand; then justify the use of the terms among the people in your field.

42e Avoid artificial or stilted diction and "fine writing."

Artificiality is not inherent in words themselves but in the use that we make of them. State simple facts and assertions simply and directly, or else you will run the risk of making your writing sound pompous and self-conscious, as in the following examples.

Artificial	The edifice was consumed by fire.
Natural	The house burned down.

---

*Reprinted by permission of the publishers, Arthur D. Little, Inc., Cambridge, Mass.

| Artificial | We were unable to commence our journey to your place of residence because of inclement weather conditions. |
| Natural | We could not come because it was snowing. |

Many inexperienced writers believe, mistakenly, that an artificial diction makes for "good writing." They shift gears when they go from speaking to writing. They try to make their writing sound like the speech of Hollywood's version of a college professor, and once again the results sound stilted.

Artificial	The athletic contest commenced at the stipulated time.
Natural	The game began on time.
Artificial	I informed him that his advice was unsolicited.
Natural	I told him to mind his own business.

Your writing may become artificial simply because you are trying too hard to write effectively, because you have grown more concerned with <u>how</u> you write than with <u>what</u> you write. Writing marked by a continuously artificial diction is called "fine writing."

42f

| Fine Writing | Whenever the press of daily events and duties relaxes its iron grip on me, whenever the turmoil of my private world subsides and leaves me in quiet and solitude, then it is that I feel my crying responsibility as one of God's creatures and recognize the need to speak out loudly and boldly against the greed and intolerance that carry humanity into the terrible destruction of armed conflict. |
| Natural | I am a crusader for international peace. |

EXERCISE 42e Find an example of "fine writing" in a newspaper or magazine and explain in a short paper why you think it ineffective.

42f Avoid mixed and incongruous metaphors and other illogical comparisons.

One of the most effective means of reinforcing and enlivening communication is the use of comparison. An apt figure of speech can help make writing concrete and vivid, and by making one experience understandable in terms of another, it can help clarify an abstract idea.

The teacher shook her finger in my face as she might shake a clogged fountain pen.

When he tried to think of the future, he was like some blundering insect that tries again and again to climb up the smooth wall of a dish into which it has fallen.

ROBERT PENN WARREN, *Night Rider*

Figurative language, however, has pitfalls for the unwary writer. The student who wrote *We are snowed by a bunch of baloney* was colorful but confused. Unless the figure of speech is clear, logical, and vigorous, it may well obscure rather than clarify your meaning. The following examples suggest the need for care in using figurative language.

He had to be on the rocks before he would turn over a new leaf.

Grandmother's tiny fingers seemed to stitch the material with the speed of a pneumatic drill.

Socialists are snakes in the grass, gnawing at the roots of the ship of state.

42f

Unfortunately, the well-meaning search for fresh comparisons may betray a writer into using figures that are inappropriate to what he is trying to say.

The minister was not too proud to spend his days visiting the sick and the needy and those rejected by society. He was as little concerned with personal contamination as a pig in a mud puddle when the Lord's work was to be done.

The effective use of figures of speech in your writing is a real challenge. Nothing is more apt, more pointed, more expert than a good figure of speech. Nothing is flatter or more ludicrous than a poor one. Make a habit of reviewing the originality, congruity, logic, and appropriateness of every figure of speech you use.

EXERCISE 42f Replace the mixed or incongruous figures of speech in the following sentences with fresher, more appropriate comparison.

1 While he was battling his way through the sea of life, fate stepped in and tripped him up.
2 John brought his big guns to the debate and stifled his opponent.
3 The odor of the flowers on the table shouted a welcome.
4 The young teacher is rapidly gaining a foothold in the eyes of the student.
5 We're skating on thin ice and if anybody upsets the applecart we'll all lose our bread and butter.
6 The Senate wanted to plug the loopholes in the tax bill but they couldn't because too many important people had their fingers in the pie.

7 He worked as busily as a beaver but one day he got as sick as a dog and decided to turn over a new leaf.

8 I'm as blind as a bat without my glasses, even in my apartment which I know like the back of my hand.

9 She was head over heels in love with him but she kept her feet firmly on the ground.

10 He had his back to the wall when he finally hit the nail on the head.

EXERCISE 42a–f First assume an "audience" (English teacher, classmates, group of businessmen, parents, etc.); then comment on the appropriateness of the language in the following selection in terms of that audience.

Like many other just plain "guys," I just graduated from high school. Being like most of these other guys, I naturally didn't really accomplish much during my previous school years. Yes, I got fair grades, met lots of swell kids, played football. I guess I'm just one of those guys who had the run of the school and never bothered to study.

No, I'm not bragging. I'm just telling you why high school was never like college.

A lot of people graduate from high school every year. A good percentage go to college and the rest go out and get a job. Four years later, the college student graduates. Does that mean he's going to get a better job than the fellow who went from high school directly to a job?

42f

No. It doesn't mean a thing unless the guy in college really studied and hit the books. What I'm trying to bring out is that a person who goes to college and doesn't study is no better off than a guy who goes out and gets a job immediately after high school graduation.

So college for me is the "big jump." I fooled around in high school, and if I don't get right down and study now, I might as well quit school and start that $100.00 a week job.

Now, I don't have anything against a $100.00 a week job. It's just that twenty years from now, I'd probably still be there getting the same $100.00. This is it, so I guess it's time for me to bear down and study hard. I think this will be the "big jump."

"WORDS" REVIEW EXERCISE (Sections 40–42) Revise each of the following sentences according to what you have learned in the sections on "Exactness," "Directness," and "Appropriateness."

1 He was trying to keep abreast of company developments when the tide turned against him and his reputation ebbed.

2 A college student has to invest most of his time with studying if he is going to be a successful student.

3 C. B. Brown must have really been on the stick when he polished off six Gothic novels in less than four short years.

4 Many neophyte pedagogues in the area of bilingual education are substandard in instructional methodology of teaching.

5 The authorship of the novel has not been authenticated, but the

evidence of the extant material that survives points to one Joshua Fiddings.

6 The campus police opinionated that the burglary attempters had entranced through the caf.

7 Although my little sister is pretty as a picture, her face becomes red as a beet when my brother beats the stuffing out of her in table tennis.

8 Mr. Smith's frequent forgetfulness of his wife's shopping instructions was the bane of her existence.

9 It is our intention to supply all your wants, and we intend to make you so comfortable here that you will not be afraid to tell us what you want in the way of comforts.

10 Professor Caitlin's life was poor in terms of meager remunerative values, but more students in the college remember him than any other teacher.

11 Coaches are paid for the type of teams they produce or for the number of winning games per season.

12 The house was square in shape and blue in color, and he decided in his mind that price-wise it was a real good buy.

13 I thought I was doing the best thing when I signed up for the army.

14 I was filled with anger and rage when my precious and expensive stereo equipment was destroyed and ruined by the vandals.

15 By reading *Yachting* I am able to keep abreast with the tide of affairs in the sailing world.

"Awfully nice" is an expression than which few could be sillier: but to have succeeded in going through life without saying it a certain number of times is as bad as to have no redeeming vice.

H. W. FOWLER

43   Glossary of Usage GLOS

Choosing the right word—or not choosing the wrong one—is one of the most difficult problems for writers, particularly for less experienced writers. General guidelines—such as, be idiomatic, confine colloquial words to speech and very informal writing, avoid nonstandard words—can be helpful, but only if you know the idiom and know what is colloquial and nonstandard. And that knowledge often comes only slowly and with much reading and experience. This glossary is intended to help you with some of the most commonly troublesome words and phrases. But it is necessarily brief; you should keep a good college dictionary at hand and consult it both for words not listed here and for additional information about words that are listed.

For information about labels used in dictionaries, see pp. 289–90. The following two labels are used in this glossary.

COLLOQUIAL Commonly used in speech but inappropriate in all but the most informal writing.

NONSTANDARD Generally agreed not to be standard English.

In addition to specifically labeled words, some words and phrases are included here because, although widely used, they are wordy or redundant (e.g., *but that, inside of, in the case of*); vague and overused (e.g., *level, overall*); or objected to by many readers (e.g., *center around, hopefully* meaning *it is hoped, -wise* as a suffix). A few word pairs often confused (e.g., *imply, infer*) are included, but the reader should consult p. 302 for a more complete list of such pairs.

a, an *A* is used before words beginning with a consonant sound, even when the sound is spelled with a vowel (*a dog, a European, a unicorn, a habit*). *An* is used before words beginning with a vowel sound or a silent *h* (*an apple, an Indian, an hour, an uproar*).

above, below *Above* and *below* are standard ways of referring to material preceding or following a particular passage in writing (*the paragraph above, the statistics below*). Some readers object to the use as stilted and overly formal.

accept, except To *accept* is to receive. To *except* is to exclude. As a preposition *except* means "with the exclusion of." (*He accepted the list from the chairman. The list excepted George from the slate of candidates. He asked why it included all except George.*)

actually Like *really,* frequently overworked as an intensifier.

ad A shortened form of *advertisement* inappropriate in formal writing. Other clipped forms include *auto, exam, math, phone, photo.*

affect, effect As verbs, to *affect* is to influence; to *effect* is to bring about. *Effect* is more commonly used as a noun meaning "result." (*Recent tax reforms affect everyone. They are intended to effect a fairer distribution of taxes. The effects have yet to be felt.*)

aggravate To *aggravate* is to intensify, to make worse (*The hot sun aggravated his sunburn*). Colloquially it is often used to mean "to annoy, provoke" (*Her teasing aggravated him*).

agree to, agree with To *agree to* is to consent; to *agree with* means "to concur" (*I agree with John's opinion, and will therefore agree to the contract*).

43

ain't A contraction of *am not,* extended to *is not, are not, has not, have not.* Though often used in speech, it is strongly disapproved by the majority of speakers and writers.

all, all of Constructions with *all of* followed by a noun can frequently be made more concise by omitting the *of;* usually the *of* is retained before a pronoun or a proper noun; <u>*all of* Illinois,</u> but <u>*all* the money,</u> <u>*all*</u> *this confusion.*

allude, refer To *allude to* is to refer to indirectly; to *refer to* is to direct attention to (*When he spoke of family difficulties, we knew he was* <u>*alluding*</u> *to his wife's leaving him even though he did not* <u>*refer*</u> *directly to that*).

allusion, illusion An *allusion* is an indirect reference; an *illusion* is a false impression (*He was making an* <u>*allusion*</u> *to magicians when he spoke of people who were apt at creating* <u>*illusions*</u>).

alot Should be rendered as two words: *a lot.*

already, all ready *Already* is an adverb meaning "previously" (*We had* <u>*already*</u> *left*) or "even now" (*We are* <u>*already*</u> *late*). In the phrase *all ready, all* modifies *ready;* the phrase means "completely prepared" (*We were* <u>*all ready*</u> *by eight o'clock*).

alright, all right *All right* remains the only established spelling. *Alright* is labeled nonstandard in both the *New World* and *Random House* dictionaries, although *Webster's* lists it without a usage label.

also Not a substitute for *and* (*We packed our clothes, our food,* <u>*and*</u> [not <u>*also*</u>] *our books*).

altogether, all together *Altogether* means "wholly, completely"; *all together* means "in a group," "everyone assembled" (*She was* <u>*altogether*</u> *pleased with her new piano, which she played when we were* <u>*all together*</u> *for our reunion*).

alumnus, alumna An *alumnus* (plural *alumni*) is a male graduate. An *alumna* (plural *alumnae*) is a female graduate. *Alumni* is now usually used for groups including both men and women.

among, between *Among* implies more than two persons or things; *between* implies only two. To express a reciprocal relationship, or the relationship of one thing to several other things, however, *between* is commonly used for more than two. (*She divided the toys* <u>*among*</u> *the three children. Jerry could choose* <u>*between*</u> *pie and cake for dessert. An agreement was reached* <u>*between*</u> *the four companies. The surveyors drove a stake at a point* <u>*between*</u> *three trees.*)

amount, number *Amount* refers to quantity or mass; *number* refers to countable objects (*Large* <u>*numbers*</u> *of guests require a great* <u>*amount*</u> *of food*).

43

an See *a, an*.

and etc. *Etc.* (Latin *et cetera*) means "and so forth." The redundant *and etc.* means literally "and and so forth." See **17a(4)**.

and/or A legalism to which some readers object.

and which, and who Use only when *which* or *who* is introducing a clause that coordinates with an earlier clause introduced by *which* or *who* (*John is a man who has opinions and who often expresses them*).

ante-, anti- *Ante-* means "before," as in *antedate*. *Anti-* means "against," as in *anti-American*. The hyphen is used after *anti-* before capital letters, and before *i*, as in *anti-intellectual*.

anyone, everyone, someone Not the same as *any one, every one, some one*. *Anyone* means "any person" (*He will talk to anyone who visits him*). *Any one* means "any single person or thing" (*He will talk to any one of his students at a time, but not more than one at a time*).

anyplace Colloquial for *any place*.

anyway, any way, anyways *Anyway* means "nevertheless, no matter what else may be true" (*He's going to leave school anyway, no matter what we say*). Do not confuse it with *any way* (*I do not see any way to stop him*). *Anyways* is a colloquial form of *anyway*.

anywheres Colloquial for *anywhere*.

apt See *liable*.

around Colloquial as used in *stay around* meaning "stay nearby" and in *come around to see me*. As a synonym for the preposition *about, around* is informal and objected to by some in writing; write *about one hundred* rather than *around one hundred*.

as In introducing adverbial clauses, *as* may mean either "when" or "because." Thus it is best avoided if there is any possibility of confusion. See **33e(1)**. As a substitute for *that* or *whether* (*He didn't know as he could go*) or for *who* (*Those as want them can have them*), *as* is nonstandard. For confusion between *as* and *like*, see *Like, As, As if*.

as . . . as, so . . . as In negative comparisons, some authorities prefer *not so . . . as* to *not as . . . as,* but both are generally considered acceptable.

as to A wordy substitute for *about* (*He questioned me about* [not *as to*] *my plans*). At the beginning of sentences, *as to* is standard for emphasizing (*As to writing, the more he worked, the less successful he was*).

at Wordy in constructions such as "Where are you eating *at*?" and "Where is he *at* now?"

athletics Plural in form, but often treated as singular in number. See 8a(10).

awful, awfully In formal English *awful* means "inspiring awe" or "causing fear." Colloquially it is used to mean "very bad" or "unpleasant" (*an awful joke, an awful examination*). *Awfully* is colloquial as an intensifier (*awfully hard, awfully pretty*).

bad Sometimes confused with the adverb *badly*. (*He hurt his leg badly* [not *bad*]. *He felt bad* [not *badly*] *all week.*)

being that, being as (how) Nonstandard substitutions for the appropriate subordinating conjunctions *as, because, since.*

below See *above, below.*

beside, besides *Beside* is a preposition meaning "by the side of." *Besides* is an adverb or a preposition meaning "moreover" or "in addition to." (*He sat beside her. Besides, he had to wait for John.*)

better See *had better.*

between, among See *among, between.*

blame for, blame on Both are standard idioms, although some writers prefer the first. (*She blamed him for it. She blamed it on him.*)

bursted, bust, busted The principal parts of the verb are *burst, burst, burst. Bursted* is an old form of the past and past participle which is no longer considered good usage. *Bust* and *busted* are nonstandard.

but, hardly, scarcely All are negative and should not be used with other negatives. (*He had only* [not *didn't have but*] *one hour. He had scarcely* [not *hadn't scarcely*] *finished. He could hardly* [not *couldn't hardly*] *see.*)

but that, but what Wordy equivalents of *that* as a conjunction or relative pronoun (*I don't doubt that* [not *but that* or *but what*] *you are right*).

calculate, figure, reckon Colloquial when used to mean "to think" or "to expect."

can, may Informally *can* is used to indicate both ability (*I can drive a car*) and permission (*Dad, can I use the car?*). In formal English, *may* is reserved by some for permission (*Dad, may I use the car?*). *May* is also used to indicate possibility (*I can go to the movies, but I may not*).

case, in the case of Wordy and usually unnecessary. See **41a(1).**

censor, censure To *censor* means "to examine in order to delete or suppress objectionable material." *Censure* means "to reprimand or condemn."

center around, center about Common expressions, but objected to by many as illogical. Prefer *center on* (*The debate <u>centered on</u>* [not <u>*centered around*</u> or <u>*centered about*</u>] *the rights of students*).

character Wordy. *He had an illness of a serious <u>character</u>* means *He had a serious illness.*

complected A colloquial or dialect equivalent of *complexioned* as in *light-complected.* Prefer *light-* or *dark-complexioned* in writing.

complete See *unique.*

consensus of opinion Redundant; omit *of opinion. Consensus* means "a general harmony of opinion."

considerable Standard as an adjective (<u>*considerable*</u> *success, a <u>considerable</u> crowd*). Colloquial as a noun (*They lost <u>considerable</u> in the flood*). Nonstandard as an adverb (*They were <u>considerable</u> hurt in the accident*).

contact Overused as a vague verb meaning "to meet, to talk with, write," etc. Prefer a more specific word such as *interview, consult, write to, telephone.*

continual, continuous *Continual* means "frequently repeated" (*He was distracted by <u>continual</u> telephone calls*). *Continuous* means "without interruption" (*We heard the <u>continuous</u> sound of the waves*).

continue on Redundant; omit *on.*

convince, persuade Widely used interchangeably, but many careful writers *convince* people that something is so, but *persuade* them to do something. The distinction seems worth preserving.

could of Nonstandard for *could have.*

couple Colloquial when used to mean "a few" or "several." When used before a plural noun, it is nonstandard unless followed by *of* (*We had a couple of* [not <u>*couple*</u>] *minutes*).

credible, creditable, credulous Sometimes confused. *Credible* means "believable" (*His story seemed <u>credible</u> to the jury*). *Creditable* means "praiseworthy" (*He gave a <u>creditable</u> violin recital*). *Credulous* means "inclined to believe on slight evidence" (*The <u>credulous</u> child really believed the moon was made of cheese*).

criteria See *data.*

cute, great, lovely, wonderful Overworked as vague words of approval. Find a more specific word (*It was an <u>attractive</u>, <u>spacious</u>, <u>compact</u>, <u>convenient</u>,* or <u>*comfortable*</u> *house*).

43

data, criteria, phenomena Historically *data* is a plural form, but the singular *datum* is now rare. *Data* is often treated as singular, but careful writing still often treats it as plural (*These data* [not *this*] *are* [not *is*] *the most recent*). *Criteria* and *phenomena* are plurals of the same kind for the singular forms *criterion* and *phenomenon*.

deal Colloquial in the sense of *bargain* or *transaction* (*the best deal in town*); of *secret arrangement* (*He made a deal with the gangsters*); and of *treatment* (*He had a rough deal from the Dean*). Currently overworked as a slang term referring to any kind of arrangement or situation.

definite, definitely Colloquial as vague intensifiers (*That suit is a definite bargain; it is definitely handsome*). Prefer a more specific word.

different from, different than *From* is idiomatic when a preposition is required; *than* introduces a clause. See **40(f).**

disinterested, uninterested Now frequently used interchangeably to mean "having no interest." The distinction between the two, however, is real and valuable. *Uninterested* means "without interest"; *disinterested* means "impartial" (*Good judges are disinterested but not uninterested*).

don't A contraction for *do not,* but not for *does not* (*She doesn't* [not *don't*] *want a new dress*).

doubt but what See *but that.*

due to Some writers object to *due to* as a preposition meaning "because" or "owing to" (*The festival was postponed because of or owing to* [not *due to*] *rain*). Acceptable when used as an adjective (*His failure was due to laziness*).

each and every Unnecessarily wordy.

effect See *affect, effect.*

enthuse Colloquial for *show enthusiasm* or *make enthusiastic.*

equally as good The *as* is unnecessary. *Equally good* is more precise.

etc. See *and etc.* and **17a(4).**

everyone, every one See *anyone.*

every which way Colloquial for *in every direction, in great disorder.*

except See *accept, except.*

expect Colloquial when used to mean "suppose" or "believe" (*I suppose* [not *expect*] *I should do the dishes now*).

fact, the fact that Usually wordy for *that* (*He was unaware that* [not *of the fact that*] *she had left*).

factor Wordy and overworked. See **41a(1).**

farther, further Some writers prefer to use *farther* to refer to distance and restrict *further* to mean "in addition" (*It was two miles farther to go the way he wished, but she wanted no further trouble*). Dictionaries recognize the forms as interchangeable.

fewer, less *Fewer* refers to numbers, *less* to amounts, degree, or value (*We sold fewer tickets than last year, but our expenses were less*).

field Wordy and overworked. Say *in atomic energy* not *in the field of atomic energy*. See **41a(1).**

figure See *calculate.*

fine As an adjective to express approval (*a fine person*) *fine* is vague and overused. As an adverb meaning "well" (*works fine*) *fine* is colloquial.

flunk Colloquial for *fail.*

folks Colloquial when used to mean *relatives,* and in the phrase *just folks,* meaning "unassuming," "not snobbish." Standard in the sense of people in general, or of a specific group (*folks differ, young folks*).

former, latter *Former* refers to the first-named of two; *latter* refers to the last-named of two. *First* and *last* are used to refer to one of a group of more than two.

function As a noun meaning "event" or "occasion," *function* is appropriate only when the event is formal (*a presidential function*). As a verb meaning "work," "operate," *function* is currently overused and jargonish (*I work* [not *function*] *best with coffee*).

further See *farther, further.*

get A standard verb, but used colloquially in many idioms inappropriate in most writing. (*Get wise to yourself. His whistling gets me. You can't get away with it.*)

good, well *Good* is colloquial as an adverb (*The motor runs well* [not *good*]). *You look good* means "You look attractive, well-dressed," or the like. *You look well* means "You look healthy."

good and Colloquial as a synonym for *very* (*good and hot, good and angry*).

great See *cute.*

43

had better, had best, better Standard idioms for *ought* and *should,* which are more formal (*You had better* [or *had best*] *plan carefully.* More formally: *You ought to* [or *should*] *plan carefully*). *Better* alone (*You better plan carefully*) is colloquial.

had ought, hadn't ought Nonstandard for *ought* and *ought not.*

hang, hung The principal parts of the verb are *hang, hung, hung,* but when referring to death by hanging formal English uses *hang, hanged, hanged.* (*We hung the pictures. The prisoner hanged himself.*)

hardly See *but.*

he or she See **8b(1).**

himself See *myself.*

hisself Nonstandard for *himself.*

hopefully *Hopefully* means "in a hopeful manner" (*He waited hopefully for money*). It is now widely used in the sense of "it is hoped" (*Hopefully, you can send me money*). Some readers object strongly to this use.

hung See *hang, hung.*

idea Often used vaguely for *intention, plan, purpose,* and other more exact words. Prefer a more exact choice. (*My intention* [not *idea*] *is to become an engineer. The theme* [not *idea*] *of the movie is that justice is color-blind.*)

ignorant, stupid The distinction is important. An *ignorant* child is one who has been taught very little; a *stupid* child is one who is unable to learn.

illusion See *allusion, illusion.*

imply, infer To *imply* means to suggest without stating; to *infer* means to draw a conclusion. Speakers *imply;* listeners *infer* (*He implied that I was ungrateful; I inferred that he didn't like me*).

in, into *In* indicates "inside, enclosed, within." *Into* is more exact when the meaning is "toward, from the outside in," although *in* is common in both meanings. (*I left the book in the room, and went back into the room to get it.*)

in back of, in behind, in between Wordy for *back of, behind, between.*

individual, party, person *Individual* refers to one particular person. *Person* refers to any human being as a distinct personality. *Party* refers to a group of people, except in legal language. (*Jefferson de-*

fended the rights of the <u>*individual*</u>. *She is a* <u>*person*</u> [not an <u>*individual*</u>] *of strong character. You are the* <u>*person*</u> [not <u>*party*</u>] *I am looking for.*)

infer See *imply, infer.*

ingenious, ingenuous *Ingenious* means "clever"; *ingenuous* means "naive" (*Inventors are usually* <u>*ingenious*</u>, *but some are too* <u>*ingenuous*</u> *to know when they have been cheated*).

in regards to Nonstandard for *as regards* or *in regard to.*

inside of, outside of The *of* is unnecessary (*He stayed* <u>*inside*</u> [not <u>*inside of*</u>] *the house*).

in the case of, in the line of See *case.*

into See *in, into.*

irregardless Nonstandard for *regardless.*

is when, is where, is because Faulty predications in such sentences as: *A first down* <u>*is when*</u> *the football is advanced ten yards in four plays or fewer. A garage* <u>*is where*</u>. . . . *The reason* <u>*is because*</u>. . . . See **14a.**

its, it's The possessive pronoun has no apostrophe. *It's* is a contraction of *it is.*

kind, sort These are frequently treated as plural in such constructions of <u>*these kind*</u> *of books* and <u>*those sort*</u> *of dogs.* Preferred usage in both speech and writing requires singular or plural throughout the construction, as in <u>*this kind*</u> *of book* or <u>*these kinds*</u> *of books.*

kind of, sort of Colloquial when used to mean *somewhat, rather* (*She was* <u>*rather*</u> [not <u>*kind of*</u>] *pleased*).

kind of a, sort of a Omit the *a.*

latter See *former, latter.*

lay, lie To *lay* means to *place, put down* (<u>*Lay*</u> *the book on the table*). To *lie* means to *recline* (*The dog* <u>*lies*</u> *on the floor*). See **3d.**

learn, teach To *learn* means to gain knowledge; to *teach* means to give knowledge. (*We* <u>*learn*</u> *from experience. Experience* <u>*teaches*</u> *us much.*)

leave, let To *leave* is to depart; to *let* means to permit or allow. (*I must* <u>*leave*</u> *now. Will you* <u>*let*</u> *me go?*)

less See *fewer, less.*

let See *leave, let.*

43

level Overworked and unnecessary in such phrases as *at the retail level, at the particular level.* Use only when the idea of rank or degree is clearly meant (*We speak of our education as divided into three levels: elementary, secondary and college*).

liable, apt, likely Often used interchangeably. But careful writing reserves *liable* for legally responsible, or subject to, *likely* for probably, and *apt* for having an aptitude for (*He is likely to drive carefully, for he is not an apt driver, and he knows he is liable for any damages*).

lie, lay See *lay, lie,* and see **3d.**

like, as, as if *Like* is a preposition; *as* and *as if* are conjunctions. Though *like* is often used as a conjunction in speech, writing preserves the distinction (*He looks as if* [not *like*] *he were tired*). Note that *as if* is followed by the subjunctive *were.*

likely See *liable.*

loose, lose Loose means "to free." *Lose* means "to be deprived of." (*He will lose the dog if he looses him from his leash.*)

lots, lots of, a lot of Colloquial for *much, many,* or *a great deal* (*He had a great deal of money* [not *lots of*] *and bought many* [not *lots of* or *a lot of*] *cars*).

lovely See *cute.*

mad Dictionaries recognize *mad* as a synonym for *angry,* or *very enthusiastic,* but some readers object to its use in these meanings.

manner Often unnecessary in phrases like *in a precise manner* where a single adverb (*precisely*) or a "with" phrase (*with precision*) would do.

may See *can, may.*

maybe, may be *Maybe* means "perhaps"; *may be* is a verb form. Be careful to distinguish between the two.

might of Nonstandard for *might have.*

mighty Colloquial as an intensifier meaning "very" or "extremely" (*mighty tasty, mighty expensive*).

most Colloquial as a substitute for *almost* or *nearly.*

must of Nonstandard for *must have.*

myself, yourself, himself *Myself* is often used in speech as a substitute for *I* or *me* but is not standard in written English. Reserve *myself* for emphatic (*I myself will do the work*) or reflexive use (*I hurt myself*). The same applies to the forms *yourself, himself, herself,* etc.

nice, nice and *Nice* is overused as a vague word of approval meaning "attractive," "agreeable," "friendly," "pleasant," and the like. Use a more exact word. *Nice and* as an intensifier (*The beer was nice and cold*) is colloquial.

nothing like, nowhere near Colloquial for *not nearly* (*He was not nearly* [not *nowhere near*] *as sick as she*).

nowheres Nonstandard for *nowhere*.

number See *amount, number*.

off of, off from Wordy and colloquial (*The paper slid off* [not *off of*] *the table*).

OK, O.K., okay All are standard forms. But formal writing prefers a more exact word.

outside of Colloquial for *except* (*Nobody was there except* [not *outside of*] *Henry*). See also *inside of*.

overall An overused synonym for *general, complete,* as in *overall prices, overall policy*. Often meaningless, as in *Our overall decision was to buy the car*.

over with Colloquial for *ended, finished, completed*.

party See *individual*.

per Appropriate in business and technical writing (*per diem, per capita, feet per second, pounds per square inch*). In ordinary writing prefer *a* or *an* (*ninety cents a dozen, twice a day*).

percent, percentage Both mean *rate per hundred*. *Percent* (sometimes written *per cent*) is used with numbers (*fifty percent, 23 percent*). *Percentage* is used without numbers (*a small percentage*). Avoid using either as a synonym for *part* (*A small part* [not *percentage*] *of the money was lost*).

perfect See *unique*.

person See *individual*.

persuade See *convince, persuade*.

phenomena See *data*.

phone Colloquial for *telephone*. In formal writing use the full word.

photo Colloquial for *photograph*. In formal writing use the full word.

plan on Colloquial in such phrases as *plan on going, plan on seeing,* for *plan to go, plan to see*.

plenty Colloquial as an adverb meaning *very, amply* (*He was very* [not *plenty*] *angry*). Note that as a noun meaning "enough, a large number," *plenty* must be followed by *of* (*I've had plenty of money*).

poorly Colloquial or dialectical for *ill, in poor health.*

practical, practicable *Practical* means "useful, not theoretical." *Practicable* means "capable of being put into practice" (*Franklin was a practical statesman; his schemes were practicable*).

pretty Colloquial and overused as an adverb meaning "somewhat, moderately" (*pretty difficult, pretty sick*). Use a more specific word.

principal, principle As an adjective *principal* means "chief, main"; as a noun it means "leader, chief officer," or, in finance, "a capital sum, as distinguished from interest or profit." The noun *principle* means "fundamental truth" or "basic law or doctrine." (*What is his principal reason for being here? He is the principal of the local elementary school. That bank pays 5 percent interest on your principal. He explained the underlying principle .*)

provided, providing Both are acceptable as subordinating conjunctions meaning "on the condition" (*He will move to Washington, providing* [or *provided*] *the salary is adequate*).

raise, rise *Raise, raised, raised* is a transitive verb (*He raised potatoes*). *Rise, rose, risen* is intransitive (*He rose at daybreak*).

real Colloquial for *really* or *very* (*real cloudy, real economical*).

reason is because See *is when,* and *14a.*

reason why Usually redundant (*The reason* [not *reason why*] *he failed is clear*).

reckon See *calculate.*

refer See *allude, refer.*

regarding, in regard to, with regard to Overused and wordy for *on, about,* or *concerning* (*We have not decided on* [not *with regard to*] *your admission*).

right Colloquial or dialectical when used to mean "very" (*right fresh, right happy*). *Right along* and *right away* are colloquial for *continuously, immediately.*

rise, raise See *raise, rise.*

round See *unique.*

said *Said* in such phrases as *the said paragraph, the said person* occurs frequently in legal writing. Avoid the use in ordinary writing.

scarcely See *but, hardly, scarcely.*

set, sit Often confused. See **3d.**

shall, will, should, would *Will* is now commonly used for all persons (*I, you, he, she, it*) except in the first person for questions (*Shall I go?*) and in formal contexts (*We shall consider each of your reasons*). *Should* is used for all persons when condition or obligation is being expressed. (*If he should come. . . . We should go.*) *Would* is used for all persons to express a wish or customary action. (*Would that he had listened! I would ride the same bus every day.*)

shape up Colloquial for *proceed satisfactorily* (*Our plans are shaping up*).

should See *shall.*

should of Nonstandard for *should have.*

show up Colloquial when used to mean "appear" (*He did not show up*) or to mean "expose" (*She showed him up for the liar he was*).

sit, set See *set, sit.*

situation Wordy and unnecessary in expressions like *We have an examination situation.*

so *So* is a loose and often imprecise conjunction. Avoid using it excessively to join independent clauses. For clauses of purpose, *so that* is preferable (*He left so that* [not *so*] *I could study*). *Because* is preferable when cause is clearly intended (*Because it began to rain, we left* [not *It began to rain, so we left*]).

some Colloquial and vague when used to mean "unusual, remarkable, exciting." (*That was some party. This is some car.*) In writing use a more specific word.

someone, some one See *anyone.*

sometime, some time One word in the sense of a time not specified; two words in the sense of a period of time (*Sometime we shall spend some time together*).

somewheres Nonstandard for *somewhere.*

sort See *kind, sort.*

sort of See *kind of, sort of.*

sort of a   See *kind of a.*

straight   See *unique.*

stupid   See *ignorant, stupid.*

such   Colloquial and overused as a vague intensifier (*It was a very* [not *such a*] *hot day*).

sure   Colloquial for *surely, certainly* (He was *surely* [not *sure*] sick).

sure and, try and   Colloquial for *sure to, try to.*

suspicion   Dialectal when used in place of the verb *suspect.*

take and   Nonstandard in most uses (*He slammed* [not *took and slammed*] *the book down*).

teach, learn   See *learn, teach.*

than, then   Don't confuse these. *Than* is a conjunction (*younger than John*). *Then* is an adverb indicating time (*then, not now*).

that   Colloquial when used as an adverb. (*She's that poor she can't buy food. I didn't like the book that much.*)

that, which   *That* always introduces restrictive clauses; *which* may introduce either restrictive or nonrestrictive clauses. See **22a.** Some writers and editors prefer to limit *which* entirely to nonrestrictive clauses. (*This is the car that I bought yesterday. This car, which I bought yesterday, is very economical.*)

theirselves   Nonstandard for *themselves.*

then, than   See *than, then.*

there, their, they're   Don't confuse these. *There* is an adverb or an expletive. (*He works there. There are six.*) *Their* is a pronoun (*their rooms*). *They're* is a contraction for *they are.*

these kind, these sort   See *kind, sort.*

this here, that there, these here, them there   Nonstandard for *this, that, these, those.*

thusly   Nonstandard for *thus.*

try and   See *sure and.*

type   Colloquial for *type of* (*This type of* [not *type*] *research is expensive*). Often used, but usually in hyphenated compounds (*colonial-type* *architecture, tile-type floors, scholarly-type man*). Omit *type* for such expressions wherever possible.

unique Several adjectives such as *unique, perfect, round, straight,* and *complete* name qualities that do not vary in degree. Logically, therefore, they cannot be compared. Formal use requires *more nearly round, more nearly perfect* and the like. The comparative and superlative forms, however, are widely used colloquially in such phrases as *the most unique house, most complete examination, most perfect day.* Their occurrence even in formal English is exemplified by the phrase *more perfect union* in the Constitution. See **4e.**

uninterested See *disinterested, uninterested.*

used to In writing be careful to preserve the *d* (*We used to* [not *use to*] *get up at six every morning*).

wait on Colloquial when used to mean "wait for"; *wait on* means "to serve, attend" (*We waited for* [not *waited on*] *the clerk to wait on us*).

ways Colloquial when used for *way* meaning "distance" (*It is a long way* [not *ways*] *to Brownsville*).

well See *good, well.*

where Colloquial when used as a substitute for *that* (*I read in the mayor's report that* [not *where*] *many local crimes are unsolved*).

which For *and which,* see *and which;* for the distinction between *that* and *which,* see *that, which.*

will See *shall.*

wise *-wise* is a long established adverb suffix meaning "in a specific direction" (*lengthwise, sidewise*) or "in the manner of" (*crabwise, clockwise*). More recently *-wise* has been widely overworked as a suffix meaning "with regard to, in connection with" (*dollarwise, educationwise*). Many object to the use as jargon and unnecessary, and it is best avoided.

wonderful See *cute.*

would See *shall.*

would of Nonstandard for *would have.*

you all Informal Southern dialect form used as a plural of *you.*

yourself See *myself.*

44

Spelling is no longer commonly regarded as a proper field for individuality or experimentation.

STUART ROBERTSON

44 Spelling SP

Language existed first as speech, and the alphabet is basically a device to represent speech on paper. When letters of the alphabet have definite values and are used consistently, as in Polish or Spanish, the spelling of a word is an accurate index to its pronunciation, and vice versa. Not so with English. The alphabet does not represent English sounds consistently. The letter *a* may stand for the sound of the vowel in *may, can, care,* or *car; c* for the initial consonant of *carry* or *city; th* for the diphthong in *both* or in *bother.* Different combinations of letters are often sounded alike, as in *rec(ei)ve, l(ea)ve,* or *p(ee)ve.* In many words, moreover, some letters appear to perform no function at all, as in *i(s)land, de(b)t, of(t)en, recei(p)t.* Finally, the relationship between the spelling and the pronunciation of some words seems downright capricious, as in *through, enough, colonel, right.*

Much of the inconsistency of English spelling may be explained historically. English spelling has been a poor index to pronunciation ever since the Norman conquest, when French scribes gave written English a French spelling. Subsequent tampering with English spelling has made it even more complex. Early classical scholars with a flair for etymology added the unvoiced *b* to early English *det* and *dout* because they mistakenly traced these words directly from the Latin *debitum* and *dubitum* when actually both the English and the Latin had derived independently from a common Indo-European origin. Dutch printers working in England were responsible for changing early English *gost* to *ghost.* More complications arose when the pronunciation of many words changed more rapidly than their spelling. The *gh* in *right* and *through,* and in similar words, was once pronounced much like the German *ch* in *nicht. Colonel* was once pronounced *col-o-nel.* The final *e* in words like *wife* and *time* was long ago dropped from actual speech, but it still remains as a proper spelling form.

The English tendency to borrow words freely from Latin and French has given us groups like the native English *sight,* the French *site,* and the Latin *cite.* Our word *regal,* with its hard *g,* comes from the Norman French. Our word *regent,* with the *g* sounded as a *j,* comes from Parisian French. Words like *machine, burlesque,* and *suite* come directly from the French, with little change in spelling or pronunciation. *Envelope,* on the other hand, maintains its French spelling but is given an English pronunciation. From Spanish comes the proper noun *Don Quixote;* its Spanish pronunciation (dŏn kē·hō′tā) is still frequently heard, but the English adjective *quixotic* is pronounced kwĭks·ot′ĭk.

44a

The complex history of the English language may help to explain why our spelling is illogical, but it does not justify misspelling. Society tends to equate bad spelling with incompetent writing. In fact, we tend to see only the misspellings and not the quality of the writing, and correct spellings may sometimes blind us to faulty constructions. That particularly American institution—the spelling bee—has for generations put a higher premium on the correct spelling of *phthisis* than on a clearly constructed sentence. To illustrate, we might experiment with our own attitude. Which of the two selections below seems better?

Parants should teech children the importence of puntuallity.

The condition of unpunctuality which exists in the character of a great many members of the younger generation should be eliminated by every means that lies at the disposal of parents who are responsible for them.

On first reading, the first sentence seems inferior to the second. Actually the former is the better sentence—more direct and succinct. But the misspellings make it difficult for us to take it seriously. Readers have been conditioned to treat misspellings as one of the greatest sins a writer can commit.

44a   Avoid secondary and British spellings.

Many words have a secondary spelling, generally British. Though the secondary spelling is not incorrect, as an American writer you should avoid it. Here is a brief list of preferred and secondary spelling forms; consult a good dictionary for others.

1. American e	*British ae, oe*
anemia	anaemia
anesthetic	anaesthetic
encyclopedia	encyclopaedia
fetus	foetus
2. American im-, in-	*British em-, en-*
impanel	empanel
incase	encase
inquiry	enquiry

44b

3. *American -ize*	*British -ise*
apologize	apologise

4. *American -or*	*British -our*
armor	armour
clamor	clamour
color	colour
flavor	flavour
humor	humour
labor	labour
odor	odour
vigor	vigour

5. *American -er*	*British -re*
center	centre
fiber	fibre
somber	sombre
theater	theatre

6. *American -o*	*British -ou*
mold	mould
plow	plough
smolder	smoulder

7. *American -ction*	*British -xion*
connection	connexion
inflection	inflexion

8. *American -l*	*British -ll*
leveled	levelled
quarreled	quarrelled
traveled	travelled

9. *American -e omitted*	*British -e*
acknowledgment	acknowledgement
judgment	judgement

44b Proofread your manuscripts carefully to eliminate misspelling.

In writing a first draft, you are forming words into sentences faster than you can write them down. You are concentrating, not on the words you are actually writing, but on the words to come. A few mistakes in spelling may easily creep into a first draft. Always take five or ten minutes to proofread your final draft to make sure that you do not let them stand uncorrected.

The failure to proofread accounts for the fact that the words most often misspelled are not, for example, *baccalaureate* and *connoisseur,* but *too, its, lose, receive,* and *occurred.* Not trusting ourselves to spell hard words correctly, we consult a dictionary and take pains to get the correct spelling on paper. But most of us <u>think</u> we can spell a familiar word. Either we never bother to check the spelling, or we assume that a word pictured correctly in our minds must automatically spell itself correctly on the paper in front of us. This thinking accounts for such errors as omitting the final *o* in *too,* confusing the possessive *its* with the contraction *it's,* and spelling *loose* when *lose* is meant. You will never forget how to spell *receive* and *occurred* if you will devote just a few moments to memorizing their correct spelling.

On pages 352–55 is a list of 350 words often misspelled. Almost every one of them is a common word; to misspell any of them in a finished paper denotes carelessness.

44c

44c Cultivate careful pronunciation as an aid to correct spelling.

Some words are commonly misspelled because they are mispronounced. The following list of frequently mispronounced words will help you overcome this source of spelling error.

accident<u>all</u>y		note the *al*
acc<u>ur</u>ate		note the *u*
can<u>d</u>idate		note the first *d*
incident<u>all</u>y		note the *al*
math<u>e</u>matics		note the *e*
prob<u>ably</u>		note the *ab*
quan<u>t</u>ity		note the first *t*
represen<u>ta</u>tive		note the *ta*
soph<u>o</u>more		note the second *o*
su<u>r</u>prise		note the first *r*
ath<u>l</u>etics	NOT	ath<u>el</u>etics
disas<u>tr</u>ous	NOT	disast<u>er</u>ous
heigh<u>t</u>	NOT	heigh<u>th</u>
gri<u>e</u>-vous	NOT	gre-<u>vi</u>-ous
ir-r<u>el</u>-e-<u>v</u>ant	NOT	ir-r<u>ev</u>-e-<u>l</u>ant
mis-ch<u>ie</u>-vous	NOT	mis-ch<u>e</u>-<u>vi</u>-ous

However, pronunciation is not an infallible guide to correct spelling. Although, for example, you pronounce the last syllables of *adviser, beggar,* and *doctor* all as the same unstressed *ur,* you spell them differently. You must, therefore, proceed cautiously in using pronunciation as a spelling aid.

44d   Distinguish carefully between the spellings of words that are similar in sound.

English abounds in words whose sound is similar to that of other words but whose spelling is different: for example, *rain, rein, reign.* The most troublesome of such words are listed below.

44d

all ready: everyone is ready
already: by this time

all together: as a group
altogether: entirely, completely

altar: a structure used in worship
alter: to change

ascent: climbing, a way sloping up
assent: agreement, to agree

breath: air taken into the lungs
breathe: to exhale and inhale

capital: chief; leading or governing city; wealth, resources
capitol: a building that houses the state or national lawmakers

cite: to use as an example, to quote
site: location

clothes: wearing apparel
cloths: two or more pieces of cloth

complement: that which completes; to supply a lack
compliment: praise, flattering remark; to praise

corps: a military group or unit
corpse: a dead body

council: an assembly of lawmakers
counsel: advice; one who advises; to give advice

dairy: a factory or farm engaged in milk production
diary: a daily record of experiences or observations

descent: a way sloping down
dissent: disagreement; to disagree

dining: eating
dinning: making a continuing noise

dying: ceasing to live
dyeing: process of coloring fabrics

forth: forward in place or space, onward in time
fourth: the ordinal equivalent of the number 4

loose: free from bonds
lose: to suffer a loss

personal: pertaining to a particular person; individual
personnel: body of persons employed in same work or service

principal: chief, most important; a school official; a capital sum (as distinguished from interest or profit)
principle: a belief, rule of conduct or thought

respectfully: with respect
respectively: in order, in turn

stationery: writing paper
stationary: not moving

their: possessive form of *they*
they're: contraction of *they are*
there: adverb of place

whose: possessive form of *who*
who's: contraction of *who is*

your: possessive form of *you*
you're: contraction of *you are*

44e Familiarize yourself with spelling rules as an aid to correct spelling.

1. Carefully distinguish between *ie* and *ei*. Remember
this jingle:

44e

Write *i* before *e*
Except after *c*
Or when sounded like *a*
As in *eighty* and *sleigh*.

i before *e*	*ei* after *c*	*ei* when sounded like *a*
thief	receive	weigh
believe	deceive	freight
wield	ceiling	vein

Some Exceptions
leisure
financier
weird

**2. Drop the final *e* before a suffix beginning with a
vowel but not before a suffix beginning with a consonant.
A. Suffix beginning with a vowel, final *e* dropped:**

please + ure = *pleasure*
ride + ing   = *riding*
locate + ion = *location*
guide + ance = *guidance*

Exceptions:
In some words the final *e* is retained to prevent confusion
with other words.

dyeing (to distinguish it from *dying*)

Final *e* is retained to keep *c* or *g* soft before *a* or o.

	notice + able	= *noticeable*
	change + able	= *changeable*
But	practice + able	= *practicable* (*c* has sound of *k*)

B. Suffix beginning with a consonant, final *e* retained:

sure + ly = *surely*
arrange + ment = *arrangement*
like + ness = *likeness*
entire + ly = *entirely*
entire + ty = *entirety*
hate + ful = *hateful*

Exceptions:
Some words taking the suffix *-ful* or *-ly* drop final *e:*

awe + ful = *awful*
due + ly = *duly*
true + ly = *truly*

Some words taking the suffix *-ment* drop final *e:*

judge + ment = *judgment*
acknowledge + ment = acknowledgment

The ordinal numbers of *five, nine,* and *twelve,* formed with *-th,* drop the final *e. Five* and *twelve* change *v* to *f.*

fifth ninth twelfth

3. Final *y* is usually changed to *i* before a suffix, unless the suffix begins with *i.*

	defy + ance	= *defiance*
	forty + eth	= *fortieth*
	ninety + eth	= *ninetieth*
	rectify + er	= *rectifier*
But	cry + ing	= *crying* (suffix begins with *i*)

4. A final single consonant is doubled before a suffix beginning with a vowel when (a) a single vowel precedes the consonant, and (b) the consonant ends an accented syllable or a one-syllable word. Unless both these conditions exist, the final consonant is not doubled.

stop + ing = *stopping* (*o* is a single vowel before consonant *p* which ends word of one syllable.)

44e

admit + ed   = *admitted* (*i* is single vowel before consonant *t*
which ends an accented syllable.)
stoop + ing = *stooping* (*p* ends a word of one syllable but is
preceded by double vowel *oo*.)
benefit + ed = *benefited* (*t* is preceded by a single vowel *i* but does
not end the accented syllable.)

EXERCISE 44e(1) Spell each of the following words correctly and explain
what spelling rule applies. Note any exceptions to the rules.

argue + ment	= ?	change + able	= ?
beg + ar	= ?	change + ing	= ?
bury + ed	= ?	awe + ful	= ?
conceive + able	= ?	precede + ence	= ?
eighty + eth	= ?	shine + ing	= ?
associate + ion	= ?	busy + ness	= ?
hop + ing	= ?	defer + ed	= ?
droop + ing	= ?	peace + able	= ?

44e

**5. Nouns ending in a sound that can be smoothly united
with -s usually form their plurals by adding -s. Verbs
ending in a sound that can be smoothly united with -s
form their third person singular by adding -s.**

Singular	Plural	Some Exceptions		Verbs	
picture	pictures	buffalo	buffaloes	blacken	blackens
radio	radios	Negro	Negroes	criticize	criticizes
flower	flowers	zero	zeroes	radiate	radiates
chair	chairs				
ache	aches				
fan	fans				

**6. Nouns ending in a sound that cannot be smoothly
united with -s form their plurals by adding -es. Verbs
ending in a sound that cannot be smoothly united with -s
form their third person singular by adding -es.**

Singular	Plural
porch	porches
bush	bushes
pass	passes
tax	taxes

**7. Nouns ending in y preceded by a consonant form
their plurals by changing y to i and adding -es. Verbs
ending in y preceded by a consonant form their third person singular in the same way.**

Singular	Plural
pity	pities
nursery	nurseries

carry	carries
mercy	mercies
body	bodies

Exceptions:
The plural of proper nouns ending in *y* is formed by adding -*s* (*There are three Marys in my history class*).

8. Nouns ending in *y* preceded by *a, e, o,* or *u* form their plurals by adding -*s* only. Verbs ending in *y* preceded by *a, e, o,* or *u* form their third person singular in the same way.

Singular	Plural
day	days
key	keys
buy	buys
guy	guys
enjoy	enjoys

44e

9. The spelling of plural nouns borrowed from French, Greek, and Latin frequently retains the plural of the original language.

Singular	Plural
alumna (feminine)	alumnae
alumnus (masculine)	alumni
analysis	analyses
basis	bases
crisis	crises
datum	data
hypothesis	hypotheses
phenomenon	phenomena

The tendency now, however, is to give many such words an anglicized plural. The result is that many words have two plural forms, one foreign, the other anglicized. Either is correct.

Singular	Plural (foreign)	Plural (anglicized)
appendix	appendices	appendixes
beau	beaux	beaus
focus	foci	focuses
index	indices	indexes
memorandum	memoranda	memorandums
radius	radii	radiuses
stadium	stadia	stadiums

EXERCISE 44e(2) Spell the plural of each of the following words correctly and explain what spelling rule applies. Note any exceptions to the rules.

1 frame	3 branch	5 echo	7 Charles
2 rose	4 bass	6 stratum	8 no

9 dash	**12** cameo	**15** church	**18** potato
10 maze	**13** fly	**16** lady	**19** play
11 table	**14** box	**17** mass	**20** pain

44f ~~Spell~~ compound words in accordance with current usage.

Compound words usually progress by stages from being written as two words, to being hyphenated, to being written as one word. Since these stages often overlap, the correct spelling of a compound word may vary. For the spelling of a compound at any particular moment, take the advice of a good dictionary. (For the general use of the hyphen in compounds, see "Hyphen," Section 30.)

44g Use drills to help cultivate the habit of correct spelling.

Spelling is primarily a habit. Once you learn to spell a word correctly, you no longer need to think about it; its correct spelling becomes an automatic skill. But if you are a chronic misspeller you have the task not only of learning correct spellings but of unlearning the incorrect spellings you now employ. You must train your fingers to write the word correctly until they do so almost without your thinking about it. Here is a suggested drill that will aid you in learning correct spellings.

44f

44g

1. Look carefully at a word whose spelling bothers you and say it to yourself. If it has more than one syllable, examine each syllable.

2. Look at the individual letters, dividing the word into syllables as you say the letters.

3. Try to visualize the correct spelling before you write the word. If you have trouble, begin again with the *first* step.

4. Write the word without looking at your book or list.

5. Look at your book or list and see whether you wrote the word correctly. If you did, cover the word and write it again. If you write the word correctly the third time, you have probably learned it and will not have to think about it again.

6. If you spell the word incorrectly any one of the three times, look very carefully at the letters you missed. Then start over again and keep on until you have spelled it correctly three times.

Spelling lists

The following lists contain most of the words whose spelling is troublesome. The words are arranged in alphabetized groups for easy reference and for drill.

44g

Group 1	*Group 2*	*Group 3*
1. accidentally	1. arctic	1. apparent
2. accommodate	2. auxiliary	2. appearance
3. accompanied	3. business	3. attendance
4. achieved	4. candidate	4. beggar
5. address	5. characteristic	5. brilliant
6. aggravate	6. chauffeur	6. calendar
7. anxiety	7. colonel	7. carriage
8. barren	8. column	8. conqueror
9. believe	9. cylinder	9. contemptible
10. ceiling	10. environment	10. coolly
11. confident	11. especially	11. descent
12. course	12. exhaust	12. desirable
13. disappear	13. exhilaration	13. dictionary
14. disappoint	14. February	14. disastrous
15. dissipate	15. foremost	15. eligible
16. efficiency	16. ghost	16. equivalent
17. emphasize	17. government	17. existence
18. exaggerate	18. grievous	18. familiar
19. exceed	19. hygiene	19. grammar
20. fiery	20. intercede	20. guidance
21. finally	21. leisure	21. hindrance
22. financial	22. library	22. hoping
23. forehead	23. lightning	23. imaginary
24. foreign	24. literature	24. incredible
25. forfeit	25. mathematics	25. indigestible
26. grief	26. medicine	26. indispensable
27. handkerchief	27. mortgage	27. inevitable
28. hurriedly	28. muscle	28. influential
29. hypocrisy	29. notoriety	29. irresistible
30. imminent	30. optimistic	30. liable
31. incidentally	31. pamphlet	31. marriage
32. innocence	32. parliament	32. momentous
33. intentionally	33. physically	33. naturally
34. interest	34. physician	34. nickel
35. legitimate	35. prairie	35. noticeable
36. likely	36. prejudice	36. nucleus
37. manual	37. pronunciation	37. obedience
38. mattress	38. recede	38. outrageous

39. misspell	39. recognize	39. pageant
40. niece	40. reign	40. permissible
41. occasion	41. rhetoric	41. perseverance
42. organization	42. rhythm	42. persistent
43. parallel	43. schedule	43. pleasant
44. piece	44. sentinel	44. possible
45. psychiatrist	45. soliloquy	45. prevalent
46. psychology	46. sophomore	46. resistance
47. receive	47. studying	47. secede
48. religious	48. surprise	48. strenuous
49. severely	49. twelfth	49. vengeance
50. villain	50. Wednesday	50. vigilance

Group 4	*Group 5*	*Group 6*
1. allot	1. hesitancy	1. obstacle
2. allotted	2. hesitate	2. operate
3. barbarian	3. instance	3. opinion
4. barbarous	4. instant	4. pastime
5. beneficial	5. intellectual	5. persuade
6. benefited	6. intelligence	6. piece
7. changeable	7. intelligent	7. politician
8. changing	8. intelligible	8. practically
9. commit	9. maintain	9. presence
10. committed	10. maintenance	10. professor
11. committee	11. miniature	11. propeller
12. comparative	12. minute	12. quantity
13. comparatively	13. ninetieth	13. recommend
14. comparison	14. ninety	14. region
15. compel	15. ninth	15. relieve
16. compelled	16. obligation	16. representative
17. competent	17. oblige	17. reservoir
18. competition	18. obliged	18. restaurant
19. compulsion	19. occur	19. ridiculous
20. conceivable	20. occurred	20. sacrifice
21. conceive	21. occurrence	21. sacrilegious
22. conception	22. omission	22. safety
23. conscience	23. omit	23. salary
24. conscientious	24. omitted	24. scarcely
25. conscious	25. picnic	25. science
26. courteous	26. picnicking	26. secretary
27. courtesy	27. possess	27. seize
28. deceit	28. possession	28. separate
29. deceive	29. precede	29. shriek
30. deception	30. precedence	30. siege
31. decide	31. preceding	31. similar
32. decision	32. prefer	32. suffrage

44g

33. defer
34. deference
35. deferred
36. describe
37. description
38. device
39. devise
40. discuss
41. discussion
42. dissatisfied
43. dissatisfy
44. equip
45. equipment
46. equipped
47. excel
48. excellent
49. explain
50. explanation

33. preference
34. preferred
35. procedure
36. proceed
37. realize
38. really
39. refer
40. reference
41. referred
42. repeat
43. repetition
44. transfer
45. transferred
46. tried
47. tries
48. try
49. writing
50. written

33. supersede
34. suppress
35. syllable
36. symmetry
37. temperament
38. temperature
39. tendency
40. tournament
41. tragedy
42. truly
43. tyranny
44. unanimous
45. unusual
46. usage
47. valuable
48. wholly
49. yoke
50. yolk

44g

Group 7
1. accept
2. across
3. aisle
4. all right
5. amateur
6. annual
7. appropriate
8. argument
9. arrangement
10. association
11. awkward
12. bachelor
13. biscuit
14. cafeteria
15. career
16. cemetery

17. completely
18. convenient
19. cruelty
20. curiosity
21. definite
22. desperate
23. diphtheria
24. discipline
25. disease
26. distribute
27. dormitories
28. drudgery
29. ecstasy
30. eighth
31. eliminate
32. eminent
33. enemy

34. except
35. exercise
36. extraordinary
37. fascinate
38. fraternity
39. furniture
40. grandeur
41. height
42. hypocrite
43. imitation
44. interest
45. livelihood
46. loneliness
47. magazine
48. material
49. messenger
50. mischievous

EXERCISE 44a–g Following is a list of words chosen at random to illustrate some of the caprices of English spelling and pronunciation. You might like to try your skill at spelling them. Will any of the spelling rules apply here? How many of these words can you pronounce? How many can you define? Would a knowledge of pronunciations, definitions, or word origins be of help in spelling these words correctly?

1 aardvark	31 doughty	61 phthisis
2 abhorrence	32 dungeon	62 pituitary
3 alyssum	33 ecclesiastical	63 platypus
4 apocalypse	34 eerie	64 plebiscite
5 archipelago	35 eucalyptus	65 porpoise
6 arpeggio	36 flautist	66 psyche
7 baccalaureate	37 fortuitous	67 pyrrhic
8 bacchanalian	38 fugue	68 quay
9 balalaika	39 gargoyle	69 queue
10 baroque	40 gneiss	70 quixotic
11 bologna	41 gourmet	71 rheumy
12 bouillon	42 heterogeneous	72 rhinoceros
13 boutonniere	43 hieroglyphic	73 saccharin
14 catarrh	44 homogenous	74 salmon
15 catechism	45 hyperbole	75 scepter
16 charivari	46 icicle	76 schism
17 chlorophyll	47 idiosyncrasy	77 scythe
18 chrysalis	48 incarcerate	78 suave
19 cinnamon	49 jeopardy	79 svelte
20 clique	50 jodhpurs	80 tarpaulin
21 connoisseur	51 khaki	81 thyme
22 crescendo	52 knell	82 trauma
23 cryptic	53 larynx	83 tympany
24 cyanide	54 lymph	84 umlaut
25 cyclic	55 misogyny	85 vaccination
26 delicatessen	56 moccasin	86 vacuum
27 demagogue	57 myrrh	87 vitiate
28 diaphragm	58 niche	88 whey
29 discomfiture	59 nil	89 yacht
30 disparate	60 periphery	90 zephyr

44g

THE LIBRARY AND THE RESEARCH PAPER

Knowledge is of two kinds: We know a subject ourselves, or we know where we can find information upon it.

A man will turn over half a library to make one book.

SAMUEL JOHNSON

The processes of RESEARCH range all the way from simple fact-digging to the most abstruse speculations; consequently, there is no one generally accepted definition of the word. *Webster's Dictionary* emphasizes the meaning of the first syllable, *re-:* "critical and exhaustive investigation . . . having for its aim the revision of accepted conclusions, in the light of newly discovered facts." The *New World Dictionary* stresses the meaning of the second syllable, *-search:* "systematic, patient study and investigation in some field of knowledge, undertaken to establish facts or principles." The second definition more closely describes what is expected of you in your first years in college. You will not often revise accepted conclusions or establish new principles. But you can learn to collect, sift, evaluate, and organize information or evidence, and to come to sound conclusions about its meaning. In doing so you will learn some of the basic methods of modern research, and the ethics and etiquette that govern the use the researcher makes of other people's facts and ideas.

When your instructor asks you to prepare a research paper, he is concerned less with the intrinsic value of your findings than with the value you derive from the experience. Writing a research paper demands a sense of responsibility, because you must account for all your facts and assertions. If your results are to be accepted—and that, after all, is a large part of your purpose—you must be prepared to show how you got those results.

It is the citing of sources that distinguishes the research paper from the expository essay in popular magazines. A good journalist undertakes research to assemble his materials, but his readers are primarily concerned with the results of his research. He expects to be accepted on faith. The researcher, however, writes for his peers—for readers who are able to evaluate his findings; for this reason he uses footnotes to help them check his evidence if they wish to do so.

In preparing a research paper, then, remember that your audience expects you to indicate your sources. It expects you to be thorough—to find and sift the relevant evidence; to be critical of your evidence—to test the reliability of your authorities; to be accurate—to present your facts and cite your sources with precision; to be objective—to distinguish clearly between facts and the opinions or generalizations to which the facts lead you.

45   The Library

The library is one of the most valuable resources on the college campus, and every successful student draws constantly on its facilities. To use the library efficiently, you must understand something of the different kinds of resources it has and the kinds of help available to enable you to find the information you need. Many libraries provide guided tours as well as printed information about their resources and the location of different kinds of books. There is always a reference librarian whose special assignment is to help you. Never hesitate to ask for help if you are confused.

Once you have learned to use the library, you will be able to use your time on productive study and research rather than in aimless wandering about in the hope of finding random bits of information. This section is designed to help you become familiar with what is in your library and with the ways of finding what you want.

Knowing the library resources

Libraries have three principal kinds of holdings: a general collection of books; a collection of reference works; and a collection of periodicals, bulletins, and pamphlets.

General collection of books.   The general collection includes most of the books in the library—all those that are available for general circulation. Small libraries usually place these books on open shelves and make them available to all who have library privileges. Most large university libraries, however, keep these books in stacks, which are closed to everyone except librarians, graduate students, faculty members, and persons holding special permits. If you want to borrow a book from such a library, you must first present a call slip bearing the call number of the book you want, the name of its author, and its title. This information you obtain from the CARD CATALOG, which will be discussed later.

Reference books.   Reference books include encyclopedias, dictionaries, indexes, directories, handbooks, yearbooks, atlases, and guides. Most libraries place these books on open shelves in the main reading room and do not allow their removal from the room.

Periodicals, bulletins, pamphlets.   A PERIODICAL is a publication that appears at regular (periodic) intervals. BULLETINS

45

and PAMPHLETS may or may not be periodicals, depending on whether they are issued as parts of a series of publications or as separate, single publications. They are usually kept in the stacks with the main collection of books. Recent issues of magazines and newspapers are usually kept in the open shelves of the reading room. Older issues are bound in volumes and shelved in the stacks.

Finding your way among the library resources

Even a small library may have fifty or sixty thousand books— far too many for you ever to hope to search through for what you need. A large university library will have several hundred thousand books, and perhaps even a million or more. Just as you need to have a good map and know how to use it to get to a particular address in a strange city, you need to understand and know how to use the directories and guides that libraries provide to help you find the particular books and articles you want. In libraries, the equivalent of maps are (1) the card catalog, (2) the collection of reference books, and (3) the various indexes to periodicals. With a knowledge of how to use these, and a bit of occasional help from the reference librarian, you can find your way to the books and articles on any subject.

Using the card catalog. The heart of the library is its CARD CATALOG. This is an alphabetical list of all the books and periodicals the library contains. Most libraries have a separate catalog that describes all periodical holdings in complete detail.

The CLASSIFICATION SYSTEM on which a card catalog is based serves as a kind of map of library holdings. In libraries where you have direct access to the shelves, familiarity with the classification system enables you to find classes of books in which you are interested without using the catalog. But the chief purpose of a classification system is to supply a CALL NUMBER for every item in the library. When you fill out a slip for a book, be sure to copy the call number precisely as it appears on the card.

American libraries generally follow either the Dewey decimal system or the Library of Congress system in classifying books. The system in use determines the call number of any book.

The Dewey system, used by most libraries, divides books into ten numbered classes:

000–099	General works	500–599	Pure science
100–199	Philosophy	600–699	Useful arts
200–299	Religion	700–799	Fine arts
300–399	Social sciences	800–899	Literature
400–499	Philology	900–999	History

Each of these divisions is further divided into ten parts, as:

800	General literature	850	Italian literature
810	American literature	860	Spanish literature
820	English literature	870	Latin literature
830	German literature	880	Greek literature
840	French literature	890	Minor literatures

Each of these divisions is further divided, as:

821	English poetry	826	English letters
822	English drama	827	English satire
823	English fiction	828	English miscellany
824	English essays	829	Anglo-Saxon
825	English oratory		

Further subdivisions are indicated by decimals. *The Romantic Rebels,* a book about Keats, Byron, and Shelley, is numbered 821.09, indicating a subdivision of the 821 English poetry heading.

The Library of Congress classification system, used by large libraries, divides books into lettered classes:

A	General works
B	Philosophy—Religion
C	History—Auxiliary sciences
D	Foreign history and topography
E-F	American history
G	Geography—Anthropology
H	Social sciences
J	Political science
K	Law
L	Education
M	Music
N	Fine arts
P	Language and literature
Q	Science
R	Medicine
S	Agriculture
T	Technology
U	Military science
V	Naval science
Z	Bibliography—Library science

Each of these sections is further divided by letters and numbers which show the specific call number of a book. *English Composition in Theory and Practice* by Henry Seidel Canby and others is classified in this system as PE 1408.E5. (In the Dewey decimal system this same volume is numbered 808 C214.)

For most books (not periodicals) you will find at least three cards in the library catalog: an AUTHOR CARD; a TITLE CARD (no

45

title card is used when the title begins with words as common as "A History of . . ."); and at least one SUBJECT CARD. Here is a specimen AUTHOR CARD in the Dewey system; it is filed according to the surname of the author:

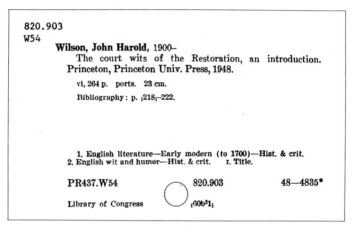

820.903
W54

    Wilson, John Harold, 1900–
       The court wits of the Restoration, an introduction.
    Princeton, Princeton Univ. Press, 1948.

       vi, 264 p. ports. 23 cm.

       Bibliography : p. [218]–222.

       1. English literature—Early modern (to 1700)—Hist. & crit.
   2. English wit and humor—Hist. & crit.   I. Title.

    PR437.W54   820.903   48—4835*

    Library of Congress   [60b²1]

1. $\dfrac{820.903}{\text{W54}}$ gives you the CALL NUMBER of the book.

2. "Wilson, John Harold, 1900—" gives you the name of the author and the date of his birth, and tells you that he was still living at the time this card was printed.

3. "The court wits . . . 1948" gives you the full title of the book, the place of publication, the name of the publisher, and the date of publication. (Note that library practice in capitalizing differs from general practice.)

4. "vi, 264 p. ports. 23 cm." tells you that the book contains 6 introductory pages numbered in Roman numerals and 264 pages numbered in Arabic numerals; that portraits appear in the book; and that the book is 23 centimeters high. (An inch is 2.54 centimeters.)

5. "Bibliography: p. [218]–222" tells you that the book contains a bibliography that begins on page 218 and ends on page 222. The brackets around 218 tell you that the page is not actually numbered but appears between numbered pages 217 and 219.

6. "1. English literature . . . Title" tells you that the book is also listed in the card catalog under two subject headings— English Literature, and English Wit and Humor—and under one title heading, "Court wits of the Restoration. . . ." Notice that the subject heading "English literature" has the subdivision "Early modern (to 1700)" and that this latter heading has the subdivision "Hist. & crit.," the heading under which you will

find the first subject card. You will find the second subject card under a division of "English wit and humor" called "Hist. & crit." The Arabic numerals indicate subject headings; the Roman numeral ("I. Title") indicates a title heading.

7. "PR437.W54" is the Library of Congress call number.

8. "820.903" is the class number under the Dewey system.

9. "48-4835*" is the order number used by librarians when they wish to order a copy of the card itself.

10. "Library of Congress" tells you that a copy of the book is housed in, and has been cataloged by, the Library of Congress.

11. "[60b^{2}1]" is a printer's key to the card.

A TITLE CARD is simply a copy of the author card, with the title typed just above the author's name. The title card is filed in the catalog according to the first word of the title that is not an article.

A SUBJECT CARD is also a copy of the author card, with the subject typed just above the author's name; it is filed in the catalog alphabetically according to the subject heading. (See item 6 above.) The subject cards, which are gathered together in one place in the catalog, help you find all or most books on a particular subject. (To find articles on a subject, use the reference tools described on pages 369–372.)

Title and subject cards for our sample catalog entry are illustrated below.

820.903
W54   The court wits of the Restoration

      Wilson, John Harold, 1900–
        The court wits of the Restoration, an introduction.
      Princeton, Princeton Univ. Press, 1948.

        vi, 264 p. ports. 23 cm.

820.903   ENGLISH WIT AND HUMOR
W54

      Wilson, John Harold, 1900–
        The court wits of the Restoration, an introduction.
      Princeton, Princeton Univ. Press, 1948.

        vi, 264 p. ports. 23 cm.

        Bibliography: p. [218]–222.

      1. English literature—Early modern (to 1700)—Hist. & crit.
      2. English wit and humor—Hist. & crit.   I. Title.

PR437.W54   820.903   48 4835*

Library of Congress   [60b^{2}1]

45

Except for the difference in the call number, catalog cards using the Library of Congress system are identical with those using the Dewey system. Note that the Library of Congress call number as well as the Dewey system number appears in the lower line of the card illustrated, although only that of the system your library uses is typed in the upper left corner.

Finding the right reference book. Explore the reference section of your library. Become familiar with the kinds of reference works available, and with the most important works of each kind. If you cannot find the book you want, or if you do not know what book will help you most, consult the reference librarian.

Following is a representative list of reference books available in most libraries.

Guides to Reference Books

Galin, Saul, and Peter Spielberg. *Reference Books: How to Select and Use Them.* 1969.

Gates, Jean Key. *Guide to the Use of Books and Libraries.* 3rd ed. 1973.

Shove, Raymond H., *et al. The Use of Books and Libraries.* 10th ed. 1967.

Winchell, Constance M. *Guide to Reference Books.* 9th ed. 1976.

Catalogs

Books in Print. Author and title indexes for *Publishers' Trade List Annual. Subject Guide to Books in Print.* 2 vols.

Cumulative Book Index. Monthly listing of published books in English. Cumulated annually.

Monthly Catalog of U.S. Government Publications, 1895 to date.

National Union Catalog. Subject and author listings of Library of Congress holdings as well as titles from other libraries, motion pictures, recordings, and film strips.

Union List of Serials in Libraries of the United States and Canada. Lists of periodicals and newspapers. Supplemented monthly by *New Serial Titles.*

Vertical File Index, 1935–. Supplements to date. (Formerly called *Vertical File Service Catalog,* 1935-54.) Monthly with annual cumulations. Subject and title index to selected pamphlet material.

General Encyclopedias

Chambers Encyclopedia. 4th ed. 15 vols. 1968.

Collier's Encyclopedia. 24 vols. 1974.

Encyclopedia Americana. 30 vols. Revised annually.

Encyclopaedia Britannica. 15th ed. 30 vols. 1974.

New Columbia Encyclopedia. 1 vol. 1975.

Dictionaries, Word Books

Dictionary of American English on Historical Principles. 4 vols. 1936–44.

45

Evans, Bergen and Cornelia. *A Dictionary of Contemporary American Usage.* 1957.

Fowler, Henry W. *Dictionary of Modern English Usage.* 2nd ed. Rev. by Sir Ernest Gowers. 1965.

Funk & Wagnalls New Standard Dictionary. Unabridged. 1964.

Oxford English Dictionary. 12 vols. and supplement. 1888–1933. Also known as *New English Dictionary.*

Partridge, Eric. *A Dictionary of Slang and Unconventional English.* 7th ed. 1970.

Random House Dictionary of the English Language. Unabridged. 1966.

Roget's International Thesaurus. Several editions available.

Webster's Dictionary of Proper Names. 1970.

Webster's New Dictionary of Synonyms. 1973.

Webster's Third New International Dictionary. Unabridged. 1971.

Wentworth, Harold, and Stuart B. Flexner. *Dictionary of American Slang.* 2nd ed. 1975.

Yearbooks

Americana Annual. 1924–.

Britannica Book of the Year. 1938–.

CBS News Almanac. 1976–.

Congressional Record. 1873–. Issued daily while Congress is in session; revised and issued in bound form at end of the session.

Facts on File. A weekly digest of world events. 1940–.

Information Please Almanac. 1947–.

Negro Almanac. 1967–.

New International Year Book. 1907–.

Reader's Digest Almanac and Yearbook. 1966–.

Statesman's Year Book. 1864.

Statistical Abstract of the United States. 1878–.

United Nations Statistical Yearbook. 1945–1968. Monthly supplements.

World Almanac and Book of Facts. 1868–.

Year Book of World Affairs. 1947–.

Atlases and Gazetteers

Columbia-Lippincott Gazetteer of the World. 1962.

Commercial and Library Atlas of the World. Frequently revised.

Encyclopaedia Britannica World Atlas. Frequently revised.

National Geographic Atlas of the World. 4th ed. 1975.

New Cosmopolitan World Atlas. Issued annually.
The Times Atlas of the World. 1975.
Webster's New Geographical Dictionary. 1972.

General Biography

American Men and Women of Science. 13th ed. 1976.

Biography Index. 1946–. Quarterly. Cumulated annually, with permanent volumes every three years.

Current Biography: Who's News and Why. 1940–. Published monthly with semi-annual and annual cumulations.

Dictionary of American Biography. 24 vols. 1922–76.

Dictionary of American Scholars. 6th ed. 1974.

Dictionary of National Biography. (British) 22 vols. 1938. Reprinted 1966 with corrections and additions 1923–63.

Dictionary of Scientific Biography. 1970–.

International Who's Who. 1936–.

Webster's Biographical Dictionary. 1972.

Who's Who. (British) 1849–.

Who's Who in America. 1899–.

Who's Who of American Women. 1958–.

Who Was Who. 1897–1960.

Who Was Who in America. 1897–1968.

Who Was Who in America, Historical Volume. 1607–1896.

World Who's Who in Science. 1968.

Books of Quotations

Bartlett, John. *Familiar Quotations.* 14th ed. 1968.

Evans, Bergen. *Dictionary of Quotations.* 1968.

The Macmillan Book of Proverbs, Maxims, and Famous Phrases. 1965.

Mencken, H. O. *A New Dictionary of Quotations on Historical Principles from Ancient and Modern Sources.* 1942.

Stevenson, Burton. *The Home Book of Bible Quotations.* 1949.

_____. *The Home Book of Quotations.* 10th rev. ed. 1967.

Mythology and Folklore

Frazer, Sir James G. *The Golden Bough.* 3rd ed. 13 vols. 1955.

Funk & Wagnalls Standard Dictionary of Folklore, Mythology, and Legend. 2 vols. 1949.

Gray, Louis H., ed. *The Mythology of All Races.* 1916–32. Reprinted 1964.

Hammond, N. G., and H. H. Scullord. *The Oxford Classical Dictionary.* 2nd ed. 1970.

Larousse World Mythology. 1968.

Literature

Cassell's *Encyclopedia of World Literature.* Rev. ed. 1973.

Columbia Dictionary of Modern European Literature. 1947.

Dictionary of World Literary Terms. 3rd ed. 1970.

Etheridge, J. M., and Barbara Kopala. *Contemporary Authors.* 1967.

Hart, J. D. *Oxford Companion to American Literature.* 4th ed. 1965.

Harvey, Sir Paul. *Oxford Companion to Classical Literature.* 2nd ed. 1937.

————. *Oxford Companion to English Literature.* 4th ed. 1967.

Hornstein, Lillian H., ed. *The Reader's Companion to World Literature.* Rev. ed. 1973.

Kunitz, S. J., and Vineta Colby. *European Authors, 1000–1900.* 1967.

Kunitz, S. J., and Howard Haycraft. *American Authors, 1600–1900.* 1938.

————. *British Authors Before 1800.* 1952.

————. *British Authors of the Nineteenth Century.* 1936.

————. *Twentieth Century Authors.* 1942. Supplement, 1955.

Literary History of England. 2nd ed. 4 vols. 1967.

Literary History of the United States. 4th ed. 2 vols. 1974.

Millett, Fred B. *Contemporary American Authors.* 1970.

Manly, John M., and Edith Rickert. *Contemporary British Literature.* 1974.

New Cambridge Bibliography of English Literature. 4 vols. 1969–74.

Whitlow, Roger. *Black American Literature.* 1973.

Woodress, James, ed. *American Fiction 1900–1950: A Guide to Information Sources.* 1974.

History, Political Science

Cambridge Ancient History. Rev. ed. 5 vols. Plates. 1970–.

Cambridge Medieval History. Rev. ed. 1967–.

Cyclopedia of American Government. 3 vols, 1949.

Dictionary of American History. 3rd ed. 8 vols. 1976.

Encyclopedia of American History. 5th ed. 1976.

Harvard Guide to American History. Rev. ed. 2 vols. 1974.

Johnson, Thomas H. *Oxford Companion to American History.* 1966.

Langer, William L. *An Encyclopedia of World History.* 5th ed. 1972.

New Cambridge Modern History. 14 vols. 1975.

Political Handbook and Atlas of the World. Published annually.

Political Science: A Bibliographical Guide to the Literature. 1965.

Schlesinger, Arthur M., and D. R. Fox, eds. *A History of American Life.* 13 vols. 1927–48.

Smith, Edward C., and Arnold J. Zurcher, eds. *Dictionary of American Politics.* 2nd ed. 1968.

Webster's Guide to American History. 1971.

The Arts

Apel, Willi. *Harvard Dictionary of Music.* 2nd ed. 1969.

Bryan, Michael. *Bryan's Dictionary of Painters and Engravers.* 5 vols. 1971.

Canaday, John C. *The Lives of the Painters.* 4 vols. 1969.

Chujoy, Anatole, and P. W. Manchester. *The Dance Encyclopedia.* Rev. ed. 1967.

Dictionary of Contemporary Music. 1974.

Dictionary of Contemporary Photography. 1974.

Encyclopedia of Painting. 3rd ed. 1970.

Encyclopedia of World Art. 15 vols. 1959–1968.

Feather, Leonard. *Jazz in the Sixties.* 1967.

Feather, Leonard. *Encyclopedia of Jazz.* Rev. ed. 1960.

Fletcher, Sir Banister F. *A History of Architecture [on the Comparative Method.]* Rev. ed. 1975.

Focal Encyclopedia of Photography. Rev. ed. 2 vols. 1969.

Grove's Dictionary of Music and Musicians. 5th ed. 9 vols. and supplement. 1954.

Hartnoll, Phyllis. *Oxford Companion to the Theatre.* 3rd ed. 1967.

Myers, Bernard S. *McGraw-Hill Dictionary of Art.* 5 vols. 1969.

Osborne, Harold. *Oxford Companion to Art.* 1970.

Popular Music: An Annotated List of American Popular Songs. 6 vols. 1973.

Scholes, Percy A. *Oxford Companion to Music.* 10th ed. 1970.

Thompson, Oscar, and N. Slonimsky. *International Cyclopedia of Music and Musicians.* 10th ed. 1975.

Philosophy, Religion

The Concise Encyclopedia of Western Philosophy and Philosophers. 1960.

Encyclopedia Judaica. 16 vols. 1972.

Encyclopedia of Philosophy. 4 vols. 1973.

Encyclopedia of Religion and Ethics. 1908–27. 12 vols. and index. Reissued, 1951.

Ferm, Vergilius. *Encyclopedia of Religion.* 1976.

Grant, Frederick C., and H. H. Rowley. *Dictionary of the Bible.* Rev. ed. 1963.

New Catholic Encyclopedia. 15 vols. 1967.

New Schaff-Herzog Encyclopedia of Religious Knowledge. 1949-50. 12 vols. and index.

45

Twentieth-Century Encyclopedia of Religious Knowledge. 2 vols. 1955.

Universal Jewish Encyclopedia. 10 vols. 1948.

Science, Technology

Besserer, C. W. and Hazel. *Guide to the Space Age.* 1960.

Chamber's Technical Dictionary. 3rd ed. Revised with supplement. 1974.

Dictionary of Physics. 1975.

Encyclopedia of Chemistry. 3rd ed. 1973.

Encyclopedia of Physics. 1974.

Handbook of Chemistry and Physics. 1914-.

Harper Encyclopedia of Science. Rev. ed. 1967.

Henderson, Isabella F. and W. D. *A Dictionary of Biological Terms.* 8th ed. 1963.

McGraw-Hill Encyclopedia of Science and Technology. 15 vols. 1971.

Speck, G., and B. Jaffe. *A Dictionary of Science Terms.* 1965.

Universal Encyclopedia of Mathematics. 1964.

Van Nostrand's Scientific Encyclopedia. 3rd ed. 1958.

Social Sciences

Encyclopedia of Educational Research. 4th ed. 1969.

Encyclopedia of Human Behavior: Psychology, Psychiatry, and Mental Health. 1975.

Encyclopedia of Social Work. 1965. (Formerly *Social Work Yearbook,* 1929-1960.)

Encyclopedia of the Social Sciences. 15 vols. 1930-35.

Good, Carter V. *Dictionary of Education.* 3rd ed. 1973.

Handbook of Business Administration. 1967.

Handbook of Forms and Model Letters. 1971.

International Encyclopedia of the Social Sciences. 17 vols. 1968.

Mitchell, Geoffrey D. *A Dictionary of Sociology.* 1968.

Munn, G. G. *Encyclopedia of Banking and Finance.* 7th ed. 1973.

A Dictionary of Psychology. Rev. ed. 1964.

White, Carl M., et al. *Sources of Information in the Social Sciences.* 2nd ed. 1973.

Using general and special periodical indexes. A library's catalog merely shows what periodicals are available. To locate the articles you may need in those periodicals you must be acquainted with and know how to use the periodical indexes, which are usually shelved in the reference section of the library. Such

45

indexes are usually classed as general or special indexes. GENERAL INDEXES list articles on many different kinds of subjects. SPECIAL INDEXES limit themselves to articles in specific areas. Representative lists of both kinds of indexes follow.

General Indexes

Readers' Guide to Periodical Literature, 1900 to date. Published semimonthly; cumulated every three months and annually. The *Readers' Guide* gives entries under author, title, and subject.

This is the most widely known and used of the general indexes. Because a great many periodical indexes use systems very similar to that of the *Readers' Guide,* it is worth examining some sample entries below.

The headings for 1 through 5 are SUBJECT ENTRIES; 6 and 7 are AUTHOR ENTRIES. Entry 8, a subject entry, indicates that an article indexed under the subject heading *Graffiti* was published in the June 1969 issue of *Science Digest,* Volume 65, pages 31 through 33. Titled "Walls Remember," it was illustrated and unsigned. (If we did not recognize the abbreviations, we could find them by looking at the first pages of the issue of the *Readers' Guide,* where all abbreviations and symbols used are explained.)

The second listing under entry 1 refers the user to a series of articles by D. Wolfle published in *Science* on the subject "Are Grades Necessary?" The first article appeared in the issue of November 15, 1968 (Volume 162, pages 745–746); the second and third appeared, respectively, in the issues for April 18 and June 6, 1969. Entry 2, under the subject heading *Graduate students,* indexes a review by D. Zinberg and P. Doty in the May 1969

1 **GRADING and marking (students)**
   Answer to Sally; multiple-choice tests. **W. R.**
   Link. Ed Digest 34:24-7 My '69
   Are grades necessary? **D.** Wolfle: discussion. Science 162:745-6; 164:245. 1117-18 **N**
   15 '68. Ap 18. Je 6 '69
   ROTC: under fire but doing fine. il U S News
   66:38 My 19 '69
2 **GRADUATE students**
   New Brahmins; scientific life in America,
   by S. Klaw. Review
   Sci Am 220:139-40+ My '69. D. **Zinberg**
   and P. Doty
3 **GRADUATION.** See Commencements
4 **GRADUATION addresses.** See Baccalaureate
   addresses
5 **GRAEBNER, Clark**
   Profiles. J. McPhee. por New Yorker 45:45-
   8+ Je 7: 44-8+ Je 14 '69
6 **GRAEF, Hilda**
   Why I remain a Catholic. Cath World 209:
   77-80 My '69
7 **GRAF, Rudolf F.** See Whalen. G. J. jt. auth.
8 **GRAFFITI**
   Walls remember. il Sci Digest 65:31-3 Je '69

issue of *Scientific American* of a book, *New Brahmins: Scientific Life in America,* by S. Klaw. The + that follows the page reference is an indication that the review is continued on a page or pages past 140. Entries 3, 4, and 7 are cross-references to the places in the *Guide* at which the user can find the subject or author listed.

There are two other general indexes that are valuable supplements to the *Readers' Guide.*

International Index. 1907–65. Became *Social Sciences and Humanities Index.* 1965–73. Divided into *Social Sciences Index.* 1974–, and *Humanities Index.* 1974–.

Poole's Index to Periodical Literature, 1802–81. supplements through January 1, 1907. This is a subject index to American and English periodicals.

Special Indexes

These indexes list articles published in periodicals devoted to special concerns or fields.

The Bibliographic Index. 1938–. Indexes current bibliographies by subject; includes both bibliographies published *as* books and pamphlets and those that appear *in* books, periodical articles, and pamphlets.

Book Review Digest. 1905–. Monthly, cumulated annually. Lists books by author and quotes from several reviews for each.

Essay and General Literature Index. 1934–. Indexes collections of essays, articles, and speeches.

New York Times Index. 1913–. Semimonthly, with annual cumulation. Since this index provides dates on which important events, speeches, and the like occurred, it serves indirectly as an index to records of the same events in other newspapers.

Ulrich's International Periodicals Directory. 13th ed. 2 vols. 1969–70. Lists periodicals under the subjects they contain, with detailed cross-references and index, thus indicating what periodicals are in the field we are interested in. Also indicates in what other guide or index each periodical is indexed, thus serving indirectly as a master index.

The titles of most of the following special indexes are self-explanatory.

Agricultural Index, 1916 to date. A subject index, appearing nine times a year and cumulated annually.

Applied Science and Technology Index, 1958 to date. (Formerly *Industrial Arts Index.*)

The Art Index, 1929 to date. An author and subject index.

Articles on American Literature. 1900–1950. 1950–1967.

45

Biological and Agricultural Index. 1964–. (Formerly *Agricultural Index.* 1907–64.)

Boyd, Anne M. *United States Government Publications.* 3rd ed. 1949.

Business Periodicals Index, 1958 to date. Monthly. (Formerly *Industrial Arts Index.*)

Catholic Periodical Index. 1930–1933. 1939–. An author and subject index.

Dramatic Index. 1909–1949. Continued in *Bulletin of Bibliography,* 1950 to date. Annual index to drama and theater.

The Education Index. 1929 to date. An author and subject index.

Engineering Index. 1884 to date. An author and subject index.

Granger's Index to Poetry. 6th ed. 1973.

Index to Legal Periodicals. 1908 to date. A quarterly author and subject index.

Industrial Arts Index. 1913–1957. An author and subject index, monthly, with annual cumulations. (In 1958 this index was split into *Applied Science and Technology Index and Business Periodicals Index.*)

Monthly Catalog of United States Government Publications. 1905–.

Play Index, 1968.

Public Affairs Information Service Bulletin. 1915 to date. Weekly, with bimonthly and annual cumulations. An index to materials on economics, politics, and sociology.

Quarterly Cumulative Index Medicus. 1927 to date. A continuation of the *Index Medicus,* 1899–1926. Indexes books as well as periodicals.

Short Story Index. 1953–. Supplements.

Song Index. 1926. Supplement.

EXERCISE 45(1) Draw a diagram of the reference room of your library, indicating the position of the following reference books and indexes.

1 *Encyclopaedia Britannica*
2 *Encyclopedia Americana*
3 *Encyclopedia of the Social Sciences*
4 *Encyclopedia of Religion and Ethics*
5 *Jewish Encyclopedia*
6 *Dictionary of American History* (DAH)
7 *Dictionary of National Biography* (DNB)
8 *Dictionary of American Biography* (DAB)
9 *Current Biography*
10 *Twentieth Century Authors*
11 *British Authors of the Nineteenth Century*
12 *American Authors, 1600–1900*
13 *Who's Who*
14 *Facts on File*
15 *World Almanac*

16 *New English Dictionary* (NED), sometimes referred to as *Oxford English Dictionary* (OED)

45

17 *General Card Catalog*
18 *Readers' Guide to Periodical Literature*
19 *International Index*
20 *The New York Times Index*
21 *Agricultural Index*
22 *Education Index*
23 *Industrial Arts Index*
24 *The Art Index*
25 *Dramatic Index*

EXERCISE 45(2) Answer each of the following questions by consulting one of the standard reference guides lised in Exercise 45(1).

1 Where can you find information on the significance of the Menorah in Jewish history?

2 Among which tribe of American Indians is the highest development of shamanism found?

3 What was the minimum equipment of a typical "forty-niner"?

4 What did the word *gossip* mean in twelfth-century England?

5 How many articles on moving pictures in science education are listed in the *Education Index* for June, 1957–May, 1958?

6 Where can you find listed a scholarly article on the training of nuclear engineers, written in 1958?

7 Where can you find listed a 1945 article on the possibility of blending aralac (a synthetic fabric) with cotton?

8 Where can you find listed articles on French stained glass, printed in 1957 and 1958?

9 What was the first invention of Peter Cooper, American inventor, manufacturer, and philanthropist (d. 1883)?

10 Where would you find information about Jacob Rayman, English violin-maker?

11 What is the price and who is the publisher for *Quest for Fire: A Novel of Prehistoric Times?*

12 How many merchant vessels were launched in the United States, 1950–1970?

EXERCISE 45(3) Write a brief paper on one of the following subjects. Be sure to answer all the questions raised. Read the prefaces or introductions to the reference works you are asked to describe, check to see how each work is organized, and make a special point of finding out how to use the works efficiently and effectively. If you have difficulty deciding what particular advantage each work has for research, consult Constance M. Winchell, *A Guide to Reference Books.*

1 Compare the *Dictionary of National Biography* and *Who's Who in America.* On what basis does each work include biographical data about an individual? Nationality? Contemporaneity? Prominence? What kinds of prominence? What kinds of information can you get about an individual in each work? Which work is more detailed? What particular research value does each have?

46

2 Compare the *World Almanac* and *Facts on File*. Both works are known as "yearbooks." How do they differ in methods of compilation of material? How does this difference affect the way in which they are organized? How does it determine the types of information included in each? How do you look up an item in each one? Under what circumstances would you consult the *World Almanac* rather than *Facts on File*? *Facts on File* rather than the *World Almanac*?

3 Compare the *Oxford English Dictionary* (OED) with the *Heritage Dictionary* or *Webster's New World Dictionary*. For illustrative purposes look up the word *kind* in each. What does each work tell you about the derivation of the word? About its history in the English language? How up-to-date is each dictionary? When would you use each one and for what purpose? What does each work tell you about the meaning of *devil* in the phrase *between the devil and the deep blue sea*? What does each work tell you about the sense in which Shakespeare meant the word *prevent*? What does each work tell you about *turbojet*? About *chemist*? About *fancy*?

46   The Research Paper

Choosing and limiting a subject

Although your own interest in, or curiosity about, a topic is a good motivation in choosing a subject for your research paper, common sense requires that you choose a subject which is appropriate for research, and which you can limit in such a way that you can cope with it satisfactorily in the space and time at your disposal. It is clear that subjects developed largely from personal experience will not make satisfactory research topics since they do not require the acquaintance with library resources and the practice of note-taking which are part of the purpose of a research paper. It is clear also that topics such as "The History of Medicine," "The American Indian," or "Modern Warfare" are far too broad and general for, say, a 1,500-word paper. If they are to be made at all workable, they will have to be narrowed to such topics as "The Discovery of Anesthesia," "The Relation of the Mohicans to the Five Nations," "The Rival Claims of Types of Army Rifles in World War II," or similar relatively specific subjects.

Certain other kinds of topics will prove unsatisfactory for less obvious reasons. Some topics offer little practice because all necessary information can easily be found in a single authoritative source. Descriptions of technical or industrial processes ("The Production of Coffee"), narratives of a man's life ("Napoleon's Military Career"), or relatively simple narrative histories

("The History of Baseball") usually fall in this group. Some topics are so controversial and complex that the time and space allowed for a student research paper are not sufficient to permit a careful weighing of evidence for both sides leading to a reasonably objective conclusion. Topics such as "Is the Supreme Court Too Powerful?" and "The Relative Merits of Federal and Local Support of Education" are of this kind.

The most satisfactory topics, then, are those which encourage you to explore the resources of the library and to develop habits of meaningful note-taking, and which give you practice in organizing and unifying information drawn from several sources. In your preliminary consideration of possible topics, you will do well to avoid those which are too personal, too broad, too simple, or too complex to accomplish these aims.

Finally, it is wise to realize that choosing and limiting a topic require more preliminary work than merely choosing a general topic you are interested in and arbitrarily narrowing it down to something you think you can manage. Unless you have already read widely about the topic you choose, you will need to begin your search for material, discover what material is in fact available in your library, and skim several articles or chapters of books before the direction you will wish to take becomes very clear to you. Even after you have made a preliminary outline and started taking notes, you will still be engaged in more and more clearly limiting and defining your topic as you read. In fact, until you have made your preliminary survey of what is available about your topic, you may have only a very general sense of how you can limit it wisely.

EXERCISE 46(1) If you do not have a topic which you are already interested in or curious about, and have not been assigned a specific topic, one good way to get started is to select a question and then search out the most accurate possible answer to it. If you lack a topic, select one of the following questions and begin working on a research paper in which you will answer it—or another question to which it leads you. Use your ingenuity to discover exactly what the question means. Check the rest of this section for guidance in finding material and getting it in order.

1 Why did Benedict Arnold turn traitor?
2 What were the provisions of the Vietnam peace agreement?
3 Was Billy the Kid a desperado?
4 Why did Israel win the Six-Day War so easily?
5 Why was Joan of Arc burned at the stake?
6 What progress have women made in securing improved wages and salaries in the past decade?
7 What caused the Reichstag fire?
8 Why was Massachusetts the only state to vote for Senator McGovern in the 1972 election?
9 How extensively did the early Algonquins engage in agriculture?

10 What is the "New Journalism"?
11 Where did the American Indians come from?
12 Why did President Nixon visit China?
13 How was Lincoln's "Gettysburg Address" received by his contemporaries?
14 What are some of the important changes that have taken place in the Roman Catholic Church in recent years?
15 Can a pitcher really curve a baseball?
16 How are Spanish-speaking children taught English?
17 What happened in the Scopes trial?
18 What are some of the important women's organizations?
19 What are the present theories on the migratory instincts of birds?
20 Have employment opportunities improved for black Americans?
21 What happened to the settlers on Roanoke Island?
22 Have many women been elected to public office since 1970?
23 What was the Teapot Dome scandal?
24 How many Protestant denominations have merged in the past two decades?
25 Is the climate growing warmer?
26 What was learned about the moon in the Apollo program?
27 What are the plausible explanations for the statues on Easter Island?
28 What federal laws have been passed to reduce air pollution caused by automobiles?
29 Does the legend that Pocahontas saved John Smith's life square with the probable facts in the case?
30 Who "won" the 1972 Munich Olympics?
31 Did Fulton invent the steamboat?
32 Has football supplanted baseball as the national game?
33 Did the Norsemen make voyages to America before Columbus?
34 What is the present ideological makeup of the Supreme Court?
35 Were Sacco and Vanzetti convicted on the basis of circumstantial evidence?
36 How did college dormitory regulations change during the 1960s and early 1970s?
37 Did Edgar Allan Poe die insane?
38 What has been done to integrate the public schools in the state?
39 What are the reasons for the disappearance of the dinosaur?
40 Have there been any significant changes in our prison system since Attica?

Finding and ordering material

1. Bibliographical aids. After your initial tentative choice of subject, research begins with your preliminary search for material and the preparation of a preliminary bibliography—that is, a list of articles, books, newspaper reports, or the like which you think are relevant to your subject. The sources for your preliminary bibliography are such reference works as the following:

Subject cards in the main card catalog.

Bibliographies at the end of pertinent articles in various en-cyclopedias.

46

Readers' Guide to Periodical Literature.

Appropriate special periodical indexes (*Engineering Index, Education Index,* etc.).

The New York Times Index.

Guides to reference books, such as those listed on pages 364–369.

Katy Benson, the writer of the specimen paper which appears later in this chapter, began to gather material with the <u>most current</u> issues of *Readers' Guide to Periodical Literature.* Katy wanted to discover what futurists are saying now—and so she had to limit her research to books and articles published in recent years. Had she been writing, say, about the Great De-pression, she probably would have looked through the bound volumes of *Readers' Guide* starting with 1929. Katy noted not only articles listed under *Future,* but also those under likely headings to which there were cross-references, such as *Twenty-first century* and *Forecasting.* She then skimmed through five or six articles with promising titles to get a sense of her topic. In two or three hours she came to the decision that at least part of her paper would be concerned with the possibility of some kind of worldwide disaster. She also realized that there were many aspects of the topic she simply couldn't handle and some she didn't care to pursue. She had by now learned enough about her topic to <u>limit</u> it intelligently; what had been a vague idea and a hazy interest was now beginning to take preliminary shape as the subject of a structured paper.

In her next visit to the library, after skimming through a few more articles with promising titles, Katy sat back, thought about her topic, and jotted down a very rough outline on one of her note cards:

I. Possible disasters (Bundy)
    A. War—compare Bradbury story
    B. Famine—controversy re supply of food
    C. Overpopulation—get more data
II. Optimistic futurists—Buckminster Fuller?—get book
III. Pessimistic futurists—???

The reminders to "get more data" and "get book," as well as the question marks, are indications that Katy is aware how in re-search one thing leads to another and that it is a mistake to depend on one's memory. As we will see, Katy later decided not to categorize the futurists as "optimistic" and "pessimistic," although she did use those adjectives once or twice. But this very rough outline did lead her to Buckminster Fuller, and in turn to some important new ideas.

The next session at the library she devoted primarily to books. Reference to the Subject Catalog led to several promising titles. Katy jotted down the call numbers, gave them to the desk, and waited, note cards in hand. She did not make the mistake of so many beginning researchers, of starting to read immediately. Instead, she looked first at all the tables of contents and the indexes, and she skimmed through the prefaces, introductions, and one or two chapters. She was then able to reject several books as being of little value or interest, in spite of their original promise. She did not, as do some students, waste a lot of time reading books or articles which later are found to be useless. The good researcher knows not only what to hold on to but also what to send back.

2. Bibliography cards. The writer of our specimen paper was careful throughout her preliminary search to make bibliography cards for each article, book, or pamphlet she thought she might use. Be careful to follow this procedure, even though it may seem unnecessary at the time. Failure to get all the necessary bibliographic information at the time you are consulting a book or article can cause frustrating delay and inconvenience later. Return trips to the library, time-consuming in themselves, sometimes result only in finding that a periodical is at the bindery or that a book is not available. At best, omission of a particularly useful piece of information may make it necessary to look through several books or periodicals to relocate an exact source.

The best method of keeping an accurate and useful record of your sources is to make out bibliography cards. The common sizes of cards are 3″ × 5″, 4″ × 6″, and 5″ × 8″. Most students prefer the 3″ × 5″ card for bibliographic entries and one of the larger sizes for note-taking.

Enter each bibliographic item on its own card and gradually build up a bibliographic card file on your subject. There are several different forms for such entries, and your instructor will give you complete directions if he wishes you to follow a form other than the one suggested here. The following is a common system:*

BIBLIOGRAPHICAL ENTRIES

| For a book with one author | Fox, Robin Lane. <u>Alexander the Great</u>. New York: Dial, 1974. |

*Bibliographic forms suggested here, like footnote forms on pp. 383–389, are based on *The MLA Style Sheet,* 2nd ed., 1970.

46

For a book with two or more authors

> Graves, Harold F., and Lyne S. S. Hoffman. Report Writing. 3rd ed. Englewood Cliffs, N.J.: Prentice-Hall, 1966.

For an edited book

> Timko, Michael, ed. Twenty-Nine Short Stories. New York: Knopf, 1975.

For a translation

> Kazantzakis, Nikos. Zorba the Greek. Trans. Carl Wildman. New York: Simon and Schuster, 1952.

For a book with an author and an editor

> Melville, Herman. Billy Budd, Sailor. Ed. Harrison Hayford and Merton M. Sealts, Jr. Chicago: University of Chicago Press, 1962.

For a book of two or more volumes

> Morison, S. E., and H. S. Commager. The Growth of the American Republic. 3rd ed. 2 vols. New York: Oxford University Press, 1942.

For an essay in an edited collection

> Wescott, Glenway. "The Moral of Scott Fitzgerald." In The Great Gatsby: A Study. Ed. Frederick J. Hoffman. New York: Scribner's, 1962.

For an unsigned article in an encyclopedia

> "Universities." Encyclopaedia Britannica: Macropaedia. 1974 ed.

For a signed article in an encyclopedia

> J[ones], J. K[nox], and D[avid] M. A[rmstrong]. "Mammalia." Encyclopaedia Britannica: Macropaedia. 1974 ed.

> Goodwin, George G. "Mammals." Collier's Encyclopedia. 1976 ed.

For a weekly magazine article

> Asimov, Isaac. "Clippings from Tomorrow's Newspapers: News Stories of 2024." Saturday Review/World, 24 August 1974, pp. 78-81.

For a monthly magazine article

> DeMott, Benjamin. "Looking Back on the Seventies: Notes Toward a Cultural History." The Atlantic, March 1971, pp. 59-64.

For a newspaper article

> Hartnett, Ken. "The Alternative Society, Part Five: It's Hip to Be Holy, Addicts Find Religion." The Boston Evening Globe, 30 April 1971, p. 2, cols. 2-5.

For an article in a journal with continuous pagination throughout the volume

> Ardery, Philip P., Jr. "Upon a Time in Woodstock." National Review, 21 (1969), 908.

46

For an article in a journal which pages each issue separately	Slater, Philip E. "America's Changing Culture." <u>Current</u>, 119 (June 1970), 15–21.
For articles with no author given	Follow form appropriate for type of magazine, journal, or newspaper cited, but begin with title of article. For example: "The Message of History's Biggest Happening." <u>Time</u>, 29 August 1969, pp. 32–33.
For a public document	U.S. Department of Health, Education, and Welfare. National Center for Educational Statistics. <u>Digest of Educational Statistics</u>. Washington, D.C.: Government Printing Office, 1968.
For an unpublished thesis or dissertation	Stein, Robert A. "Paradise Regained in the Light of Classical and Christian Traditions of Criticism and Rhetoric." Diss. Brandeis University 1968.

EXERCISE 46(2) Select one or more of the following subjects and list all the likely sources in which you would look for (1) preliminary information and (2) periodical articles on the subject.

1 Bilingual Education for Spanish-Speaking Americans
2 The India-Pakistan Wars
3 Experimental Programs in Elementary Schools
4 Women's Magazines
5 "Black Capitalism"
6 The "Jewish Novel"
7 Acupuncture
8 American Prisoners of War in Vietnam
9 The Poetry of Robert Frost
10 Bussing
11 Jazz in the 1920's
12 The Early Plays of G. B. Shaw
13 Religious Rites of the Navajo Indians
14 The Use of Hypnosis in Medicine
15 Hallucinogenic Drugs
16 Migratory Habits of Birds
17 Developments of Plastic Surgery
18 The Early History of the Teamster's Union
19 Viking Exploration of America
20 Migratory Workers in the Southwest

EXERCISE 46(3) Prepare a short bibliography (on cards) for one of the following topics.

1 Negro Colleges
2 Color Television

3 The Assassination of Robert Kennedy
4 The Theatre of the Absurd
5 Organic Foods
6 Medicare
7 Rock Festivals
8 Pop Art
9 The Assassination of Lincoln
10 Rockets and Interplanetary Travel

EXERCISE 46(4) Prepare a short working bibliography for one of the following persons and hand in a brief biographical sketch with it.

Martin Luther King	Bill Russell
Margaret Fuller	Charles Steinmetz
Henry Kissinger	Gamal Abdul Nasser
Marilyn Monroe	Tennessee Williams
Margaret Chase Smith	Charles Chaplin
Harry Truman	Luther Burbank
Pope John XXIII	Louis Armstrong
Winston Churchill	Frank Lloyd Wright
Ralph Nader	Eudora Welty

3. Preliminary organization. The processes of choosing and limiting a subject, making a preliminary search of materials available, and gathering bibliographic entries all help you bring your subject gradually into focus. As you begin to read sources, even at the preliminary stage of your research, your plan should slowly become more and more definite and clear. Try to crystallize it into some sort of outline for yourself.

Your early outlines may be quite general and will surely require considerable reworking. But they are useful as guides to let you review your own thinking about your topic, to suggest kinds of information you have and do not have, and to help you see possible patterns of final organization that you can work toward. The writer of our specimen paper was able to expand and refine her preliminary outline after several days of reading, note-taking, and thinking:

I. Summary of Ray Bradbury's "August 2026 . . ."
   A. Technological advances
   B. Nuclear disaster
II. View of Futurists
   A. Technological advances
      1. Automation in home (plenty in Kahn and Wiener)
      2. Transportation—get more
      3. Energy sources—(too complex?)
      4. Daily life—maybe something on family structure
   B. Possibility of disaster
      1. Nuclear war—need for international control

    2. Overpopulation
       a. Optimistic view
       b. Pessimistic view—get Ehrlich book?
    3. Famine—control over food production
III. Cooperation among nations
    A. Energy—????? (too complex?)
    B. Agriculture
    C. Armaments
    D. Population
IV. Conclusion—Buckminster Fuller

As you can see, the second outline still differs greatly from the outline on pp. 394–395. But at this point, Katy Benson was satisfied that she knew where she was going. There were still question marks and reminders, and there would be additions, deletions, and revisions, but the paper was almost ready to get itself written.

4. Note-taking. Once you have finished your preliminary search to assure yourself that you have a workable subject, have established some sense of the directions you may take, and have jotted down some initial list of possible headings, you will begin to take notes on everything you read that seems at all pertinent to your topic. Do not be afraid of taking too many notes. It is much easier to lay aside notes that turn out to be superfluous than it is to return to the library to search out again sources you have already gone to the trouble of finding once.

Develop the habit of entering your reading notes on standard-size cards. They are easier to carry than a notebook, easier to refer to than full sheets of paper, and easy to rearrange as you experiment with different possible outlines. In taking notes, observe the same principles that you observed in writing out your bibliography cards: Make sure that all your notes are accurate and complete. Be particularly careful that you know the exact source from which you took each piece of information. Be _very_ careful to distinguish between information which you are summarizing or paraphrasing and information which you are quoting. Place quotation marks around <u>all</u> material which you take word for word from any source. In general, force yourself to summarize, paraphrase, and record relevant facts rather than quote. Reserve exact quotation for particularly telling phrases, or for information that must be rendered precisely as you found it.

Be certain to use a separate card for each note. Do not include notes on two different subtopics in your outline on a single card. The usefulness of cards depends greatly on the convenience with which they can be shuffled and rearranged. Cards with separate notes can easily be combined when you are experimenting with arranging notes for your first draft. Cards that combine two or more notes on somewhat different items will prevent you from doing this.

The note cards on this page were prepared for the specimen paper included in this section. The first is an exact quotation. The second is a brief summary of several pages. The third records a short quotation and then summarizes the article's conclusion. Study these cards as well as those given with the text of the research paper. They do not represent the only way to take notes, but they are good notes, and more than anything else are responsible for the success of the paper itself.

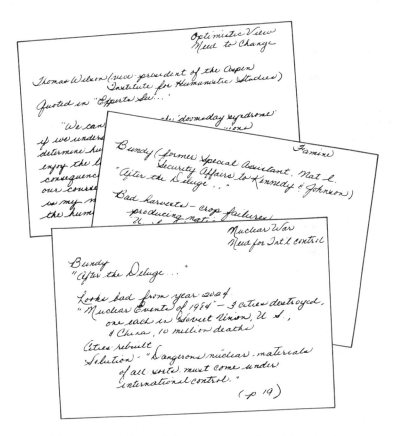

5. Footnotes. One of the purposes of making out accurate bibliography and note cards is to provide you with the information you will need for footnoting your research paper. Footnotes have three main uses:

A. To give the source of your information and quotations.

B. To add information or commentary which, though related to the subject being discussed, would interrupt the flow of the text. Because students sometimes misapply or overuse this kind of footnote, some instructors discourage its use. Employed intelligently and judiciously, however, the additional-information footnote can strengthen a research paper.

C. To give additional evidence or illustration in support of an assertion. For example, if you are arguing that Theodore Roosevelt was essentially a conservative, your footnote might cite one or more other writers who also think so. This device, known as the *See also* footnote, is sometimes the vehicle for pedantry, and is therefore disapproved of by some instructors. Still, it can be an effective technique when used intelligently and unpretentiously.

The first use is by far the most important and most common. Though today, even in formal scholarship, there is a tendency away from the extremely heavy footnoting of earlier scholarship, accurate and honest documentation is one of the basic conventions of all research writing. Only careful and thorough footnoting can ensure that you will not appear to represent someone else's work as your own, and that the interested reader can easily check the accuracy of your investigation and carry it further if he wishes.

Student research writers sometimes have difficulty determining what kinds of information require footnoting and what kinds do not. It is clear that direct quotations, charts, diagrams, tables, discussions that summarize ideas and opinions of others in your own words, and the like all require acknowledgment in footnotes. Difficulties arise principally in acknowledging opinion which the writer has paraphrased from others rather than reached independently, and in determining what is "common knowledge" and therefore does not require acknowledgment. With respect to the first, the student writer should be very careful to distinguish clearly between those opinions which he has actually arrived at independently in the course of his reading on the subject, and which therefore need no acknowledgment, and those which in fact he has paraphrased more or less wholly from a particular source and which therefore must be acknowledged. The writer should be careful to remember that ideas, interpretations, opinions, and conclusions reached by another writer are in many ways more important contributions on his part than bald facts, and therefore even more deserving of acknowledgment.

What constitutes "common knowledge" is really less difficult to determine than some students seem to feel. Any writer who reads in his subject to some depth will quickly come to see that certain kinds of facts are taken for granted by nearly all writers discussing the subject, while others are matters of dispute, or the result of special investigation. A student writing for the first time on Wordsworth may not have known when he started reading that the *Preface to the Lyrical Ballads* was first published in 1798, but he will quickly discover that everyone writing on the subject takes this as an established fact. On the other hand, the exact date at which a particular poem was written may be a matter of dispute, or at best may have been established only by someone's diligent research. Clearly, the first fact does not need a footnote, the second does. In addition, common sense will tell us that specialized facts—such as the number of Polaroid cameras sold in 1973, the estimated population of Thailand in 1960, the highest recorded tide in San Francisco Bay, or the number of earthquakes in Peru in the nineteenth century—are unlikely to be "common knowledge." In contrast, the precise date of Lincoln's assassination, the birth and death dates of John F. Kennedy, or the longitude and latitude of New York are in the usual sense of the phrase "common knowledge," even though they may be far removed from the tip of your tongue at the moment. When common sense, fortified by the knowledge you have gained from your reading in a subject, still leaves you in doubt, footnote the information.

6. Footnote form. Footnote form, as used in professional scholarship and research, is complex and varied. Most of the forms have been evolved to meet the demands of formal scholarship designed to add to the fund of knowledge. Further, the conventions followed in reports of scientific research differ from those in the humanities and some of the social sciences. If, in your future study, you have occasion to publish research in your particular field, the vitally important thing to remember is that whatever the field, it will have its own established conventions which you will be expected to follow. You will have to consult the style of the publications in your field, study the conventions, and adhere to them exactly.

As a less experienced student, even though you are chiefly concerned with adding to your own knowledge, you are expected to adopt the habits of the professional scholar and follow an established set of conventions. The conventions described here are based on those established by the Modern Language Association, and set forth in *The MLA Style Sheet* (2nd ed., 1970), which has become the guide for some eighty professional journals in languages, humanities, and some areas of social science.

Unless your instructor directs otherwise, place footnotes at the bottom of the page on which the reference occurs and number them consecutively throughout the paper. In type-written manuscript, single-space all footnotes and leave a double space between footnotes (see the specimen paper at the end of the section). Indicate the appearance of a footnote by placing a raised figure at the end of the statement to be documented. Then repeat the figure at the beginning of the footnote itself:

Text   of these about 100 were independent, over 106 more were churchrelated, and more than 500 were public institutions.[1]

Footnote   [1]Paul Woodring, The Higher Learning in America: A Reassessment (New York: McGraw T. McGraw, 1968), p. 32.

Placing footnotes at the bottom of the page is only one of several ways of handling them. You can place all of them together on a separate page or pages at the end of your paper, or you can insert each in the text directly after the reference to it:

Text   "College teachers," writes Professor Seymour E. Harris, "do not primarily seek high economic rewards, or they would not have chosen teaching in the first place."[2]

Footnote   [2]Higher Education: Resources and Finance (New York: McGraw-Hill, 1962), p. 637.

Text   It becomes increasingly apparent, however, that many who might otherwise have

Your instructor will tell you which of these methods he wants you to use.

The following list is based on footnote forms recommended by the Modern Language Association. (Note that footnote and bibliography form differ.)

FOOTNOTE REFERENCES

For a book with one author, first edition

   [1] Theodore Roszak, The Making of a Counter Culture (Garden City, N.Y.: Anchor Books, 1969), pp. 47–48.

For a book with one author, later edition

   [2] Mary Anne Ferguson, Images of Women in Literature, 2nd ed. (Boston: Houghton Mifflin, 1973), p. 268.

For a book with two or more authors

   [3] Margaret B. Bryan and Boyd H. Davis, Writing About Literature and Film (New York: Harcourt Brace Jovanovich, 1975), pp. 37–38.

For an edited book

4 Michael Timko, ed., Twenty-Nine Short Stories (New York: Knopf, 1975), p. ix.

For a book with an author and an editor

5 Herman Melville, Billy Budd, Sailor, ed. Harrison Hayford and Merton M. Sealts, Jr. (Chicago: University of Chicago Press, 1962), pp. 27-29.

For a modern reprint of an older edition

6 John Livingston Lowes, The Road to Zanadu: A Study in the Ways of the Imagination, 2nd ed. (1930; rpt. New York: Vintage-Knopf, 1959), p. 231.

For a book consisting of two or more volumes

7 S. E. Morison and H. S. Commager, The Growth of the American Republic, 3rd ed. (New York: Oxford University Press, 1942), II, 75.

For a signed article in a book by several contributors

8 Gary Wills, "The Making of the Yippie Culture," in Perspectives for the 70's, ed. Robert G. Noreen and Walter Graffin (New York: Dodd, Mead, 1971), p. 57.

For an unsigned article in an encyclopedia

9 "Universities," Encyclopaedia Britannica: Macropaedia, 1974 ed.

For a signed article in an encyclopedia

10 J. K[nox] J[ones], Jr., and D[avid] M. A[rmstrong], "Mammalia," Encyclopedia Britannica: Macropaedia, 1974 ed.

11 George G. Goodwin, "Mammals," Collier's Encyclopedia, 1976 ed.

For an article from a weekly magazine

12 Barry Farrell, "Second Reading: Bad Vibrations from Woodstock," Life, 5 September 1969, p. 4.

For an article from a monthly magazine

13 Benjamin DeMott, "Looking Back on the Seventies: Notes Toward a Cultural History," The Atlantic, March 1971, p. 60.

For an article from a journal with continuous pagination throughout the volume

14 Philip Tracy, "Birth of a Culture," Commonweal, 90 (1969), 532.

For an article from a journal which pages each issue separately

15 Andrew Kopkind, "A New Culture of Opposition," Current, 111 (October 1969), 56.

For a newspaper article

16 Ken Hartnett, "The Alternative Society, Part Two: Disaffected Depend on Society They Shun," Boston Evening Globe, 27 April 1971, p. 2, col. 2.

46

Note: Footnotes for articles with no author given follow the same format as above, with the author's name omitted. For example:

[17] "Rallying for Jesus," _Life_, 30 June 1972, p. 40.

For a public document

[18] U.S. Department of Health, Education, and Welfare, National Center for Educational Statistics, Digest of Educational Statistics (Washington, D.C.: Government Printing Office, 1968), p. 69.

For an unpublished thesis or dissertation

[19] Robert A. Stein, "Paradise Regained in the Light of Classical and Christian Traditions of Criticism and Rhetoric," Diss. Brandeis University 1968, p. 73.

The following abbreviations are customarily used in footnotes:

anon.	anonymous
art., arts.	article(s)
c., ca.	_circa_ (about); used with approximate dates
cf.	_confer_ (compare)
ch., chs. (_or_ chap., chaps.)	chapter(s)
col., cols.	column(s)
diss.	dissertation
ed., edn.	edition
ed., eds.	editor(s)
e.g.	_exempli gratia_ (for example)
et al.	_et alii_ (and others)
f., ff.	and the following page(s)
ibid.	_ibidem_ (in the same place)
i.e.	_id est_ (that is)
introd.	introduction
l., ll.	line(s)
loc. cit.	_loco citato_ (in the place cited)
MS, MSS	manuscript(s)
N.B.	_nota bene_ (take notice, mark well)
n.d.	no date (of publication) given
n.p.	no place (of publication) given
numb.	numbered
op. cit.	_opere citato_ (in the work cited)

p., pp.	page(s)
passim	throughout the work, here and there
rev.	revised
trans., tr.,	translator, translated, translation
v.	*vide* (see)
vol., vols.	volume(s)

A first footnote must be detailed because certain information is necessary to distinguish one source for all others. Later footnotes can—and should—be brief and simple.

Current practice, as encouraged by *The MLA Style Sheet* and other similar guides is as follows:

1. If only one work by a given author is used, cite only the author's last name and the appropriate page reference.

[1] Theodore Roszak, The Making of a Counter Culture (Garden City, N.Y.: Anchor Books, 1969), p. 61.

[4] Roszak, p. 110.

2. If two or more works by the same author are used, cite the author's last name and a shortened title, as follows:

[1] Benjamin DeMott, "Looking Back on the Seventies: Notes Toward a Cultural History," The Atlantic, March 1971, p. 60.

[3] Benjamin DeMott, "The Sixties: A Cultural Revolution," New York Times Magazine, 14 December 1969, p. 4.

[5] DeMott, "Looking Back," p. 62.

Although the forms described above for footnote references after the first are now widely used, some editors and instructors prefer to continue the use of the Latin abbreviation *ibid.*, meaning "the same title as the one cited in the previous note."

[1] Mary Anne Ferguson, Images of Women in Literature, 2nd ed. (Boston: Houghton Mifflin, 1973), p. 268.

[2] Ibid., p. 249.

If the second note refers to exactly the same page as the first, only *ibid.* is used; otherwise the appropriate page number is given.

The Latin abbreviations *loc. cit.*, and *op. cit.* meaning "in the same passage referred to in a recent note," and "in the same work cited in a recent note," are no longer commonly used although they appear in most older research articles.

46

7. Quoted material.

A. The ethics of quotation. Footnoting is in part a matter of manners and ethics. A failure to acknowledge one's debt to others for words, facts, and ideas is at best a breach of manners; at worst, it is a form of theft known as plagiarism, an offense subject to legal action in the courts and to disciplinary action by a university. In the academic world acknowledgment of indebtedness is especially necessary because most researchers are rewarded for what they write, not in money, but in reputation.

Questions of what kinds of material must be footnoted have been discussed above. There remain some problems worth noting about the use of quoted material itself. The controlling principle guiding the use of all quoted material is that the original writer shall be represented as honestly and accurately as possible. Here are a few basic rules which will help you hold to this principle in handling quoted material.

1. When you quote material that is clearly not public property, acknowledge the source whether you quote it verbatim or in paraphrase.

2. Always acknowledge a direct quotation unless it can be classified as a "familiar quotation."

3. Transcribe direct quotations precisely and accurately. To omit even a comma may violate the meaning of a statement. <u>Check and recheck every quotation</u>.

4. Whenever you want to omit material from a quoted passage, indicate the omission (ellipsis) by using three spaced periods (. . .). If the omission is from the end of a quoted sentence, use four periods (. . . .), the first indicating the period at the end of the sentence (see **19c**). When you omit material from a quoted passage, be sure that what you retain is grammatically coherent.

5. When you wish to substitute in a quotation words of your own for the original, enclose your own words in square brackets (see **26f**).

Even though you observe these rules, you may still be guilty of misrepresentation and deception in quoting if you are not careful to preserve the key words that indicate the <u>tone</u> of the original. Observe the following passage:

Woodrow Wilson "was more than just an idealist," Herbert Hoover has written. "He was the personification of the heritage of idealism of the American people." He was also the twenty-eighth President of the United States, one of perhaps five or six in the nearly two hundred years of our country's history who can be, by anyone's reckoning, classified as truly great. Perceptive educator, courageous reformer, international leader, Wilson in his time was the spokesman of the future.*

46

The tone of the paragraph is one of praise which comes close to adulation. In quoting from the passage, you can alter the tone as well as the intent of the writer by making small changes in the original. For example, omission of the adjectives *perceptive, courageous,* and *international* in the last sentence would distort the writer's opinion of Wilson.

B. The technique of quotation.

1. Do not quote long, unbroken stretches of material. Such a practice puts the burden of discovering the purpose of your quotation upon the reader, or forces him to reread the quotation in the light of your subsequent commentary. The use you make of a quotation, not the quotation itself, is your research contribution.

Make frequent use of paraphrase, or indirect quotation, whenever you do not need the precise words of the original, or when you can restate its point more briefly in your own words. Interpolate your own commentary and explanations whenever you feel they are needed.

2. When you work quoted material into a sentence of your own, be sure your words, grammar, and syntax are in logical relation to the quotation. Below are some examples of common errors in quoting material, followed by corrected versions.

Incorrect	Woodrow Wilson was one of the five or six American Presidents who are "the personification of the history of idealism of the American people." (This confuses the statements of Hoover and the newspaper editor.)
Correct	Herbert Hoover describes Woodrow Wilson as "the personification of the heritage of idealism of the American people."
or	The editor describes Woodrow Wilson as one of five or six American Presidents "in the nearly two hundred years of our country's history who can be, by anyone's reckoning, classified as truly great."
Incorrect	The newspaper declared that Woodrow Wilson was one of the five or six American Presidents that they could classify "as truly great."
Correct	The newspaper declared that Woodrow Wilson was one of the five or six American Presidents "who can be, by anyone's reckoning, classified as truly great."

* This and the examples given below are from *The New York Times,* December 13, 1959, Sec. 4., p. 10.

46 Specimen research paper

The research paper presented in this section is a successful student paper. The assignment required that the student choose a topic interesting to himself, gather authoritative information about it from a number of sources, and organize the information clearly in a paper of about 1,500 words that would both report the information and make some evaluation of it. The student was also required to prepare a statement of purpose, a sentence outline, and a bibliography in proper form, and to document all evidence in appropriate footnote form. The paper reproduced here, although of course not an original contribution to knowledge, is a very able paper, clearly worth an honor grade in every respect. It will repay careful study. The accompanying commentary directs attention to some of the problems of writing and documentation which were faced and solved.

The format

The title is centered near the top of the page, in capitals. The text is double-spaced, well-balanced. Two spaces (or, if your instructor prefers it, a ruled or typewritten line) separate the last line of the text from the first footnote. The footnotes are single-spaced, with a blank space between them to allow for the raised footnote numbers. Small Roman numerals or Arabic numerals may be used to number the thesis and outline pages. Pages of the paper itself are numbered with Arabic numerals consecutively throughout the entire paper, including the bibliography.

The title page, statement of thesis or purpose, and sentence outline

The first three pages give a quick summary of this research paper. Notice that this prefatory material falls into three divisions; (1) *the title,* which is a very general statement; (2) *the statement of purpose,* which explains briefly what the paper attempts to do; and (3) *the outline,* which is a rather full statement.

THE FASCINATING AND FRIGHTENING WORLD

OF THE FUTURISTS

By

Katy Benson

English 101, Section Q

Mr. G. Lapin

April 4, 1977

Research Paper Outline

Statement of Purpose:

The purpose of this paper is to report on what futurists are saying
about the threat of a worldwide disaster and the kind of technological
advances we can expect.

Outline

I. Introduction: In Ray Bradbury's science-fiction story, "August
   2026: There Will Come Soft Rains," we are given a frightening
   and fascinating glimpse into the future.

II. Many futurists are concerned with the two questions raised by
    the story: How real is the threat of worldwide disaster? What
    kind of advances can we expect?

A. Most futurists believe we can escape the "doomsday" of
   nuclear war, famine, and overpopulation.

   1. Nuclear war: Such a war would have nightmarish consequences,
      but international control of nuclear weapons can prevent it.

   2. Famine: Crop failures could result in the death of many
      millions, but futurists believe that advanced technology
      can provide enough food for everyone.

   3. Overpopulation: Uncontrolled population growth could bring
      mankind to "the brink of extinction," but most futurists
      believe we still have time to institute population control,
      and hopefully without restricting individual freedom.

Research Paper Outline   Page 2

    B. Cooperation among nations will be an absolute necessity if
we are to solve our problems.

      1. We can expect more global interdependence in the future.

      2. Americans may have to cut back on their standard of
living, but life will be far from unpleasant.

    C. Futurists predict major advances.

      1. In their daily lives Americans will make use of many
technical innovations, for which we will find the
necessary resources and energy sources.

      2. We can expect other changes in family size and housing.

      3. Americans will be healthier and live longer as medical
science makes major breakthroughs.

III. Conclusion: There is still time for mankind to avert Oblivion
and instead fulfill the dream of a peaceful, prosperous world,
and even dare to work toward a future Utopia.

COMMENTARY

Paragraph 1

Text. Although many introductions to student papers are not necessary or, for that matter, desirable, this introductory paragraph can easily be justified. The summary of the science-fiction story not only is interesting—research papers do <u>not</u> have to be boring—but it also serves as a framework to the paper as a whole. It leads to the two key questions asked in paragraph 2 and it serves as a continuing motif in paragraphs 8, 9, and 11. Katy summarizes the story effectively in a few sentences and selects a good quote to dramatize the situation.

Note that the fairly long quotation is indented and single-spaced and does not require quotation marks. Note also the use of ellipsis—three spaced periods after the sentence period.

Documentation. Footnote 1 follows MLA form for a first reference to a short story in an edited collection. The author's name is not given since it is mentioned in the text. Mention of the edition makes it possible for the reader to find the documented material; editions often differ considerably.

Paragraph 2

Text. Using the story as a link, Katy introduces the two questions she will answer in this paper. Paragraphs 3, 4, 5, and 6 will deal with the possibility of disaster, and paragraphs 8, 9, and 10 will deal with possible technological advances. Katy has divided her paper into two parts—"the fascinating" and "the frightening," or "the hopes" and "the fears." The reader is given a good direct statement about the intention and limits of the paper. The reader knows exactly what to expect.

THE FASCINATING AND FRIGHTENING WORLD

OF THE FUTURISTS

1   In 1950 Ray Bradbury, the famous science-fiction writer, published
a story entitled "August 2026: There Will Come Soft Rains." The main
character is a fully automated, almost human house full of mechanical
devices. Meals are prepared automatically according to an established
schedule; listening devices are programmed to recognize and respond to
people's voices; and the house's own "voice" entertains by reading
poetry aloud. Bridge tables miraculously appear in time for card games,
and tiny automated cleaning animals resembling robot mice continually keep
the house spotless. The house seems to function without the aid of any
human beings. And early in the story we are told that that is indeed the
case:

> The house stood alone in a city of rubble and ashes. . . .
> At night the ruined city gave off a radioactive glow which
> could be seen for miles. . . . The entire west face of the
> house was black, save for five places. Here the silhouette
> in paint of a man mowing a lawn. Here, as in a photograph,
> a woman bent to pick flowers. Still farther over, their
> images burned on wood in one titanic instant, a small boy,
> hands flung into the air; higher up, the image of a thrown
> ball, and opposite him, a girl, hands raised to catch a ball
> which never came down.[1]

2   Bradbury's imaginative glimpse into the future is both fascinating and
frightening. The future, the story seems to say, holds out the possibility
of tremendous technological advances, but also the threat of total destruction.
Today both the hopes and the fears concern not only the science-fiction

---

[1] An Introduction to Literature, ed. Sylvan Barnet, Morton Berman,
and William Burto, 6th ed. (Boston: Little, Brown, 1977), pp. 270-71.

46

Paragraph 3

Text. This paragraph is a general answer to the first question and will be developed in greater detail in the following three paragraphs. If one wished to be picky, one could question Katy's statement about "most futurists." How can she arrive at such a conclusion on the basis of necessarily limited reading? Her defense would be that she felt she had looked at a reasonably large body of material, had noted that a few authorities had also written that "most" futurists felt that way, and that her judgment was based on objective reading of what she believed were representative viewpoints. And of course that is what the reader expects from student researchers.

It is worth noting that Katy tells us something about the authorities she cites—Wilson is "associated with the Aspen Institute"; in paragraph 4 Bundy is "a former White House aide"; in paragraph 5 Abelson is "editor of *Science Magazine*." Such identification is important because it provides evidence that the authorities cited are really authorities.

Documentation. Footnote 2 follows MLA form for an unsigned article in a weekly magazine. "Quoted in" makes clear that Thomas Wilson is not the author of the article.

Paragraph 4

Text. In a good opening sentence, Katy introduces the three elements of the first part of her paper—the answer to the first question. She then begins discussion of the first element, "nuclear war." In her research, Katy had gathered a good deal of material about the horrors of nuclear war, and in the first draft of the paper she had devoted a complete paragraph to that subject. But then she decided that she was belaboring the point and was in danger of losing sight of her thesis statement.

Her decision to remove the paragraph from the final draft was wise. Writers must learn to resist the temptation to include all their researched material; and they must learn to be cruel in their rewrite.

Documentation. Footnote 3, like footnote 2, follows the form for a weekly magazine. Since the author is identified in the text, his name is omitted in the footnote.

writers but also the scientists and scholars--"futurists"--whose studies
cover a very wide range of interests. My own interest in this subject
I have limited to the two questions raised by Bradbury's story: How real
is the threat of worldwide disaster? And if we do have a future, what
kind of technological and other advances can the average American really
expect?

As for the first question, most futurists believe we can avoid the
kind of catastrophe described in the story. Thomas Wilson, of the Aspen
Institute for Humanistic Studies, seems to sum up this view: "We can ward
off the 'doomsday syndrome' if we understand that human decisions determine
human conditions. . . . We have the ability to change our course--our
social values--and this is my main cause for optimism about the human
predicament."[2]

The three most frequently mentioned causes of a future "doomsday"
are nuclear war, famine, and overpopulation. Former White House aide
McGeorge Bundy, taking an imaginative look backward from the year 2024,
speaks of the "Nuclear Events of 1984" in which three great cities were
destroyed, one each in the Soviet Union, China, and the United States, with
the loss of ten million lives. But he sees this nightmarish prophecy as
leading not to the end of the world but as a terrible lesson that teaches
the leaders of the nations to do something about international control of
nuclear weapons.[3] Certainly such a scenario can by no means be described

---

[2] Quoted in "Experts See World Perils Ahead--But 'Humanity Will
Survive,'" U.S. News & World Report, 23 June 1975, p. 64.

[3] "After the Deluge, the Covenant," Saturday Review/World, 24 August
1974, p. 19.

Paragraph 5

Text. Katy moves neatly to the second element, and again cites Bundy to point out the possible consequences. This time, however, Katy presents the views of two additional authorities. She felt she had to do so because she herself was surprised to read that experts were so optimistic about food production. Again, she exercised good judgment. There is no need to belabor a point, to indulge in what we can call "footnote overkill"; but when it is necessary to prove a point, we should not hesitate to use more than one source. In addition, she realized that she had relied entirely on Bundy in her discussion of nuclear disaster. Though he had proved a good authority, she recognized the need to support her point with additional authorities.

By comparing the note cards below with the text, we can see how effectively Katy paraphrases the Piel quotation and how she works the Abelson statement into the structure of her sentence.

Food
overpopulation

Philip H. Abelson (Editor, Science Magazine)
in Glenn

Believes "technically feasible" to feed and house in the United States a population 10 to 100 times as great as our present one."
But problem also population. As population increases, so also "contamina-tion" of environment.

Food

Gerald Piel (Former Science editor - Life
Keynote Speaker, 1976 American
Institute of Biological Sciences)
Reported in "The Next 200 Years Could Be Best"
Re: future food supplies - "confident"

"He quoted various agricultural specialists to support his optimism that advanced technology will be able to provide all the world's food needs. One bright outlook came from Roger Revelle, who estimated that the Indus, Ganges, and Brahmaputra valleys in India alone could feed the entire world."
(p. 431)

3

as "optimistic"--although other possibilities in thermonuclear, gas,
and biological warfare are more horrifying. What futurists are saying
is that if we realize how utterly destructive future wars can be, perhaps
we will learn in time to prevent such wars.

The second "doomsday" nightmare is famine in large parts of the
world. In Bundy's scenario, famines resulting from crop failures in the
grain-producing countries cause a death toll of sixty-five million.[4]
Bundy then imagines the creation of an international "World Food
Commission" with the power to prevent future famines.[5] But other
futurists are even more confident that famine can be averted. Gerard Piel,
keynote speaker at the 1976 annual meeting of the American Institute of
Biological Sciences, was optimistic about the ability of advanced
technology to provide enough food for everyone, and he cited one agricultural expert who estimated that India alone could feed the world.[6]
Philip H. Abelson, editor of Science Magazine, believes that the United
States is technically capable of feeding a "population ten to one hundred
times as great as our present one." But as do others, Abelson recognizes
that the basic problem is not insufficient food but overpopulation.[7]

And here the futurists come to the third possible "doomsday"--
overpopulation. But again the views of most futurists are more optimistic

---

[4] Bundy, pp. 18-19.

[5] Bundy, p. 20.

[6] Quoted in "The Next 200 Could Be Best," BioScience, 26 (1976), 431.

[7] "The Continuing Scientific Revolution," in Man and the Future,
ed. James E. Gunn (Lawrence, Kansas: The University Press of Kansas, 1968),
p. 57.

Documentation. Footnotes 4 and 5 require only the name of the author and the page references since all other information has already been given in footnote 3. (Katy might have used *Ibid.* for footnote 5, but we have noted on p. 389 that such Latin abbreviations are now less used than formerly.)

Footnote 6 is MLA form for an article in a journal with continuous pagination throughout the volume.

Footnote 7 is MLA form for a signed article in a book by several contributors and an editor.

Paragraph 6

Text. Katy introduces the third element, but this time she gives the first words to the more pessimistic view of Ehrlich. Ideally, she should have gone to Ehrlich's book, since Hilsman in *his* footnote tells us where *he* got the quote. The reason the original source is better is that the reader, if he desires to, can go to the source and make a judgment about whether or not the quoted writer has been treated fairly. Does the quote truly represent his view? Is it taken out of context? Have important ideas or modifications been left out?

Katy's defense was, as she put it, "What am I supposed to do—spend my whole life in the library?" It's hard to argue with the writer of a good paper, but still . . .

Note how in the last sentence Katy recapitulates the three "doomsday" possibilities by mentioning once again the Bundy scenario.

Note also the *three* spaced periods indicating ellipsis within a sentence in the quoted paragraph, and the use of brackets to indicate a change made by Katy in the Hilsman quotation.

Documentation. In footnote 10 Katy has used the full name of the publisher Alfred A. Knopf. The *MLA Style Sheet* now recommends that an appropriately shortened form of the publisher be used. Thus Katy could have used simply the name Knopf. Similarly, in footnote 28 later, Bantam would have been sufficient. And so too in the list of works cited at the end of the paper.

Paragraph 7

Text. This paragraph serves both as a commentary on the "doomsday" section and as a transition to the second part of the paper—the answer to the second question. Here again, Katy had much more material than she used. She put in the Waldheim quotation because of his authoritative position as Secretary

4

than one might expect. Roger Hilsman, for example, does not see the
future as bleakly as Paul R. Ehrlich, who wrote in 1970:

> The explosive growth of the human population is the most
> significant terrestrial event of the past million millennia.
> Three and one half billion people now inhabit the Earth, and
> every year this number increases by 70 million. . . . Mankind
> itself may stand on the brink of extinction; in its death throes
> it could take with it most of the other passengers of Spaceship
> Earth. No geological event in a billion years . . . has posed a
> threat to terrestrial life comparable to that of human over-
> population.[8]

Hilsman believes that mankind can solve this problem, and that even with
a population of seven billion in the year 2000, there is still hope to
slow down the rate of growth and to find the food, resources, and energy
to support that population. Hilsman admits he is "alarmed" by the present
threat of overpopulation, but he believes that "mankind will eventually
solve [the] problem"[9] And Dennis Gabor believes this can be done
"without any dictatorial interference with the family and with the insti-
tutionalized religions."[10] It is interesting to note than in Bundy's
futuristic scenario, population control is tied to the program to end
hunger, and thus, together with international control of nuclear weapons,
the world finds solutions to the three major problems it faces.[11]

If there is one thing that futurists agree upon it is that cooperation
among nations will be an absolute necessity. Kurt Waldheim, Secretary
General of the United Nations, states, "It is this fact of global

---

[8] Quoted in Roger Hilsman, The Crouching Future (Garden City, N.Y.:
Doubleday, 1975), pp. 503-04.

[9] Hilsman, p. 504.

[10] Inventing the Future (New York: Alfred A. Knopf, 1964), p. 210.

[11] Bundy, p. 20.

General of the United Nations, and she summarized Barber's ideas because he said so succinctly what other futurists were saying. Here are some of the cards she worked with:

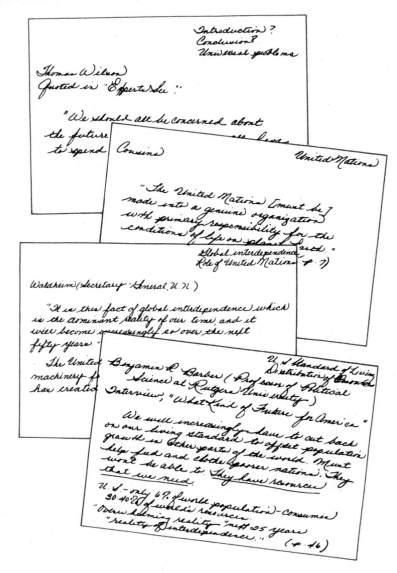

5

interdependence which is the dominant reality of our times, and it will become increasingly so over the next fifty years."[12] Such interdependence may very well result, as one authority pointed out in an interview, in the need for Americans to cut back on their standard of living. A nation which has six percent of the world's population cannot continue to use forty percent of the world's resources.[13] But, although life may change in a number of ways, the American of the future--if there is a future-- will find life not at all unpleasant.

According to at least one prediction, the automation described in Bradbury's science-fiction story will probably be part of the daily life of Americans by the year 2000. In a list of one hundred "very likely" technical innovations, the authors include such items as "Automated or more mechanized housekeeping and home maintenance . . . automated grocery and department stores . . . extensive use of robots and machines 'slaved' to humans."[14] Such large-scale mechanization would of course require unprecedented demands for energy and resources, but futurists seem to be optimistic about man's ability to discover new resources and energy sources. René Dubos stated in an interview that "resources don't exist

[12] "Toward Global Interdependence," Saturday Review/World, 24 August 1974, p. 63.

[13] Benjamin R. Barber, in "What Kind of Future for America?" U. S. News and World Report, 7 July 1975, p. 46.

[14] Herman Kahn and Anthony J. Wiener, The Year 2000: A Framework for Speculation on the Next Thirty-Three Years (New York: Macmillan, 1967), pp. 52, 53, 54. Actually some of these predictions already seem to have come true. Robot mail carts and an electronic library are already in use. A. R. Roalman, "A Practical Approach to Predicting the Future," Science Digest, November 1976, p. 75.

46 **Paragraph 8**

Text. Katy begins discussion of the second part of the report. Here the three elements are not so clearly marked as in the first part, but material does not always lend itself to clear-cut divisions or categories. Katy does well in organizing and condensing what she does have. Wisely, she anticipates a question from the reader: Where will the energy for all this automation come from? And wisely she resists the temptation to get deeply involved in the controversy over energy resources, not because she cannot find any answers but because there are just too many for her to make use of in this paper.

Documentation. Footnote 14 follows MLA form for a book written by two authors. It also contains a brief comment, documented, that Katy did not wish to incorporate into the text. Editors and teachers disagree about this use of footnotes. Some find it a useful way of calling attention to closely related material which would be digressive in the text. Others feel that it is too easily abused, and that material not significant enough to be in the text should be excluded entirely. Check with your instructor before using such footnotes. And never use them merely to display leftover scraps of your research.

Note that footnote 16 indicates a summary of six pages. Katy had four separate note cards with information about various sources of energy, but then decided that all she could spare was a one-sentence statement.

Paragraph 9

Text. Katy continues with her discussion by presenting material from several sources. This is a catch-all paragraph which could have been strengthened by the introduction of more sociological data, more predictions about "the home" rather than the house of the future. But the paragraph is well organized and begins and ends with effective transitional devices.

The bit about the contoured bathtub Katy did not find in the library. She just ran across it while reading the newspaper. This is not unusual, since good researchers give themselves plenty of time and often happen upon useful material in unexpected places.

Documentation. Footnote 19 gives a shortened form of the title first documented in footnote 17.

Footnote 20 provides information about the columns the newspaper article can be found in as well as the page.

6

until we invent them. . . . A resource is something that each generation
learns to extract and use." For example, he suggests that new technologies
will make it possible for us to make use of much that we now consider
industrial and domestic waste.[15] In addition, we will make considerable
use of new sources of energy such as solar electrical power and geothermic
energy.[16]

9   But of course a house--even a science-fiction house--is not a home.
And here, too, futurists see changes in the years to come. Families will
be smaller; there will be more single people and childless couples.[17]
Actually, the citizen of the future is unlikely to live in a single-family
dwelling, as in the Bradbury story, since such housing will not only be
too expensive for the average person but will also become a symbol of
wastefulness and thus "socially unacceptable."[18] Instead, the condominium
will replace the single-family home.[19] Heating of buildings will be made
more efficient, and even bathtubs may be contoured to the body to avoid
wasting of hot water.[20]

[15] "Looking Into the Future," Current, 171 (March 1975), 40.

[16] Gabor, pp. 95-100.

[17] "How Life Will Change for Americans in Years Ahead," U.S. News
& World Report, 12 January 1976, p. 54.

[18] René Dubos, "Recycling Social Man," Saturday Review/World,
24 August 1974, p. 10.

[19] "How Life Will Change . . .," p. 54.

[20] "Contoured Bathtub--Energy Saver of the Future," The Boston
Globe, 14 February 1977, p. 6, cols. 3-7.

46 Paragraph 10

Text. This is a well written paragraph. It begins with a good topic sentence, provides links between sentences, and contains a good mix of paraphrase, summary, and direct quotation. The information is derived from five different sources, but the paragraph flows smoothly from beginning to end. Such writing is

7

10   Conservation of energy will also probably result in a healthier
America. Since we will be less likely to use automobiles--we will see
more bicycles, mo-peds, and trolleys[21]--people will do more walking. A
reduction of meat in our diet will also be healthier for us, and the
meat we do eat will be reinforced with vegetable proteins.[22] The fact
that we will be eating less and less meat is suggested by a headline
"Remember Chickens?" in "Clippings from Tomorrow's Newspaper: News
Stories of 2024" by scientist and science-fictionist Isaac Asimov.[23]
More important, Kahn and Wiener list as "very likely" such advancements as
"general substantial increase in life expectancy, postponement of aging,
and limited rejuvenation" and as an "important possibility" a life span of
between 100 and 150 years.[24] Dr. Charles A. Berry, "the astronaut's
doctor," stated in an interview that he believes we will see a life span
of 100 years for many future Americans as well as major medical breakthroughs, including the conquest of both cancer and heart disease.[25]

11   Number 87 in Kahn and Wiener's list of one hundred very likely
innovations is "stimulated and planned and perhaps programmed dreams."[26]
This sounds like science-fiction material (what Andrew A. Spekke calls

---

[21] "How Life Will Change . . .," p. 55.

[22] "What Life Will Be Like 20 Years in the Future," **U.S. News
& World Report**, 14 January 1974, p. 74.

[23] Saturday Review/World, 24 August 1974, p. 78.

[24] Kahn and Wiener, pp. 53, 56.

[25] "What Kind of Future for America?" pp. 47-48.

[26] Kahn and Wiener, p. 55.

possible only when the writer has done the necessary research and organization. If the note cards are prepared intelligently, the paragraph practically writes itself. In writing a research paper, as in all writing, what appears to be the long way is often the short way.

Paragraph 11

Text. Katy spent a great deal of time on her final paragraph. It is a good one. It summarizes the paper; it reminds us of the science-fiction story and contrasts the story's conclusion with the vision of Buckminster Fuller. Katy came across his name many times while doing her research, and she knew very early that she would end her paper with a quotation from his works.

It is worthwhile comparing Katy's final draft of the last four sentences with her first two drafts. The time she spent on the rewriting was clearly worth it.

First Draft

R. Buckminster Fuller, who is regarded by many as the "prophet" among futurists, is more optimistic than Ray Bradbury. Bradbury seems to say that even if we attain a technical Utopia we will end in oblivion. But Fuller writes: "This moment of realization that it soon must be Utopia or Oblivion coincides exactly with the discovery by man that for the first time in history Utopia is, at least, physically possible of human attainment." Not only futurists but all people hope that he is right.

Second Draft

R. Buckminster Fuller, the "prophet," is optimistic about making the dream come true. He believes that Utopia is possible, but it will not come unless we choose it. Bradbury offers Utopia and then Oblivion, but Fuller speaks for the many futurists who feel there is still time for mankind to come to its senses. He believes that "for the first time in history Utopia is, at least, physically possible of human attainment."

Documentation. In footnote 28 Katy makes reference to a work she does not actually use in her paper. Although she took notes from this collection, she found no direct use for the material. She did feel, however, that the book was interesting enough to mention to the reader. Such footnoting is common among scholars, but student researchers ordinarily should avoid it.

8

"Buck Rogers stuff"),[27] but in a way it summarizes what most futurists
are saying. If we hope to achieve the dream of a peaceful, prosperous
world, we will have to stimulate our imaginations and plan and program
our course of action. R. Buckminster Fuller, perhaps the most respected
"prophet" among the futurists, believes that the chances of fulfilling
that dream are good. He is not afraid to speak of a future Utopia.
Whereas Bradbury seems to offer both Utopia and oblivion, Fuller speaks
for those who feel there is still time for us to come to our senses and
choose our future. He writes: "This moment of realization that it soon
must be Utopia or Oblivion coincides exactly with the discovery by man
that for the first time in history Utopia is, at least, physically
possible of human attainment."[28]

[27] "America: The Next 200 Years," _Intellect,_ 105 (1976), 50.

[28] _Utopia or Oblivion: The Prospects for Humanity_ (New York:
Bantam Books, 1969), p. 292. For some informative discussion about
Buckminster Fuller's ideas as well as selections from his writings
see Patricia Wallace Garlan, Maryjane Dunstan, and Dyan Howell Pike,
Star Sight: Visions of the Future (Englewood Cliffs, N.J.: Prentice-
Hall, 1977), pp. 107-45.

9

WORKS CITED

Asimov, Isaac. "Clippings from Tomorrow's Newspapers: News Stories of 2024." Saturday Review/World, 24 August 1974, pp. 78, 80.

Bradbury, Ray. "August 2026: There Will Come Soft Rains." An Introduction to Literature. Ed. Sylvan Barnet, Morton Berman, and William Burto. 6th ed. Boston: Little, Brown, 1977.

Bundy, McGeorge. "After the Deluge, the Covenant." Saturday Review/World, 24 August 1974, pp. 18-20, 112-14.

"Contoured Bathtub--Energy Saver of the Future." The Boston Globe, 14 February 1977, p. 6, cols. 3-7.

Dubos, René. "Recycling Social Man." Saturday Review/World, 24 August 1974, pp. 8-10, 102-06.

"Experts See World Perils Ahead--But 'Humanity Will Survive.'" U.S. News & World Report, 23 June 1975, pp. 64-65.

Fuller, R. Buckminster. Utopia or Oblivion: The Prospects for Humanity. New York: Bantam Books, 1969.

Gabor, Dennis. Inventing the Future. New York: Alfred A. Knopf, 1964.

Garlan, Patricia Wallace, Maryjane Dunstan, and Dyan Howell Pike. Star Sight: Visions of the Future. Englewood Cliffs, N.J.: Prentice-Hall, 1977.

Gunn, James E., ed. Man and the Future. Lawrence, Kansas: The University Press of Kansas, 1968.

Hilsman, Roger. The Crouching Future. Garden City, N.Y.: Doubleday, 1975.

"How Life Will Change for Americans in Years Ahead." U.S. News & World Report, 12 January 1976, pp. 54-56.

Kahn, Herman, and Anthony J. Wiener. The Year 2000: A Framework for Speculation on the Next Thirty-Three Years. New York: Macmillan, 1967.

"Looking Into the Future." Current, 171 (March 1975), 24-46.

"The Next 200 Could Be Best." BioScience, 26 (1976), 431.

Roalman, A. R. "A Practical Approach to Predicting the Future." Science Digest, November 1976, pp. 74-79.

Spekke, Andrew A. "America: The Next 200 Years." Intellect, 105 (1976), 49-50.

Waldheim, Kurt. "Toward Global Interdependence." Saturday Review/World, 24 August 1974, pp. 63-64, 122.

"What Kind of Future for America?" U.S. News & World Report, 7 July 1975, pp. 44-50.

"What Life Will Be Like 20 Years in the Future." U.S. News & World Report, 14 January 1974, pp. 72-75.

WRITING SUMMARIES AND EXAMINATIONS

47 Summaries

The ability to summarize effectively—to strip a paragraph or a chapter down to its central meaning while at the same time not distorting the author's original thought and approach—is an extremely useful ability. Writing such summaries is itself an excellent way to study closely. Having such summaries available to yourself for review is invaluable for later reference and review.

Practice in preparing summaries will also help you to read with greater accuracy and to write with greater conciseness and directness. You cannot summarize effectively if you have not read carefully, discriminating between principal and subordinate ideas. Such discrimination, in turn, will help you to sharpen your own style and to avoid the prolixity that creeps into careless writing.

Before you try to summarize a passage, read it carefully to discover the author's purpose and point of view. As you read, pick out the central ideas and notice how they are arranged. Be on the lookout for the author's own compact summaries, either at the beginning or end of a passage or at points of transition.

After studying the passage, you are ready to organize your summary. Ordinarily you will be able to reduce a paragraph—or sometimes a whole group of paragraphs—to a single sentence. Very complex paragraphs, however, may require more than one sentence.

Use a simple or complex sentence rather than a compound sentence to summarize a paragraph—unless the original paragraph itself is poorly organized. A compound sentence implies that there are two or more equally dominant ideas in the paragraph. If you find that you have written a compound summarizing sentence, recheck the paragraph to make sure that the author did not imply some subordinating relationship that you have missed. In determining the author's intent, be alert to such writing techniques as parallel clauses and phrases, which indicate ideas of equal weight, and transitional words and phrases, which show relationships among ideas.

Summarize the author's ideas in the order in which they have been presented, but avoid following the exact wording too closely. If you are overly scrupulous in trying to preserve the "flavor" of the original, you will find that your summary will be far too long. Do not hesitate, however, to pick up the author's key terms and phrases, for they are useful in binding the précis together. Discard any figures of speech, digressions, or discussions that are not essential to the "trunk and main branches." When you are all through, you should find that you have reduced the material to not over one-third of its original length. Study the following example.

> We very rarely consider, however, the process by which we gained our convictions. If we did so, we could hardly fail to see that there was usually little ground for our confidence in them. Here and there, in this department of knowledge or that, some one of us might make a fair claim to have taken some trouble to get correct ideas of, let us say, the situation in Russia, the sources of our food supply, the origin of the Constitution, the revision of the tariff, the policy of the Holy Roman Apostolic Church, modern business organization, trade unions, birth control, socialism, the League of Nations, the excess-profits tax, preparedness, advertising in its social bearings; but only a very exceptional person would be entitled to opinions on all of even these few matters. And yet most of us have opinions on all these, and on many other questions of equal importance, of which we may know even less. We feel compelled, as self-respecting persons, to take sides when they come up for discussion. We even surprise ourselves by our omniscience. Without taking thought we see in a flash that it is most righteous and expedient to discourage birth control by legislative enactment, or that one who decries intervention in Mexico is clearly wrong, or that big advertising is essential to big business and that big business is the pride of the land. As godlike beings why should we not rejoice in our omniscience?
>
> JAMES HARVEY ROBINSON, *The Mind in the Making*

Notice that this paragraph hinges on the sentence beginning *And yet most of us have opinions on all these. . . .* This sentence suggests the pattern that your summarizing sentence should probably take. The central idea of the paragraph is that we do not ordinarily take pains in forming our convictions on important matters, but we nevertheless express our opinions as a matter of right and even take delight in our apparent omniscience. The main clause of your summarizing sentence will express the second part of the central idea, retaining the author's ironic approach.

> We are godlike beings who delight in our ability to form and express convictions on birth control, on intervention in Mexico, or on the role of big business, without a moment's thought.

To preserve the author's qualification in the first part of the paragraph, however, you must precede the main clause with a subordinate clause.

47

Although the few pains we take to understand such things as the situation in Russia, the sources of our food supply, the origin of the Constitution, the revision of the tariff, the policy of the Holy Roman Apostolic Church, modern business organization, trade unions, birth control, socialism, the League of Nations, the excess-profits tax, preparedness, and advertising in its social bearings give us little reason to have confidence in our opinions on these matters, we are godlike beings who delight in our ability to form and express convictions on birth control, on intervention in Mexico or on the role of big business, without a moment's thought.

But this "summary" is almost half as long as the original. To reduce it further, replace the specific examples with general terms.

Although the few pains we take to understand such things as social, political, economic, religious, and medical issues give us little reason to have confidence in our convictions on these matters, we are godlike beings who delight in our ability to form and express such convictions without a moment's thought.

This summary, less than one-third the length of the original, would be acceptable for most purposes, but occasionally even a shorter summary is desirable.

Although we have little reason to trust our convictions on the important issues of life, we delight in forming and expressing such opinions without a moment's thought.

Clearly this last sentence does not express everything in Robinson's paragraph, where the concreteness and the vigor of the short sentences are perhaps even more striking than its central thought. But a summary is concerned only with the central thought, not necessarily with retaining the author's style, and the central thought is preserved even in the shortest statement above.

EXERCISE 47(1) Write a two-sentence summary of the paragraph by Jacques Barzun, on page 229, beginning "The whole aim of good teaching."

EXERCISE 47(2) Write a one-sentence summary of the same paragraph.

EXERCISE 47(3) Try to write a one-sentence summary of the following paragraph. Does the effort tell you anything about the weakness of the paragraph itself?

Among the many interesting aspects of dietary training is the living together of the students. This allows each to get acquainted with people from all over the States and to exchange ideas and viewpoints from different sections of the country. By living in such a home, many girls grow into more mature individuals. It proves a good chance for girls who have always lived at home to become more independent. It also helps to establish feelings of self-sufficiency in those who have never before been on their own.

EXERCISE 47(4) Write the briefest summary you can of the paragraph below.

Great care and attention is given in the organization of pageants and other popular feasts, and of these a Russian crowd is particularly appreciative, throwing itself wholeheartedly into the enjoyment of every detail. The "crowd sense," which is just another expression of the corporate instinct, is peculiarly strong in Russia, and it is often curiously reminiscent of an English crowd, particularly in its broad and jolly sense of humor. But Russians of any class have a much stronger artistic sense than we have. This was so before the revolution, and it comes out in the organization of these festivals. They are all out to enjoy themselves, and anything particularly clever or pretty gets them at once. In Kiev, still as always a beautiful city on its lovely site, in the late summer of 1936, I saw a march past of all the wards in turn. They swung past with splendid vigor, squads of men or of women—one squad of women had in the middle of it a fine old man with a long beard who looked very pleased with his company. There were flowers and dancing everywhere; each ward was preceded by a dancing band of girl skirmishers in the picturesque Ukrainian costume, sometimes singing the charming Ukrainian folk songs. At one point various forms of recreation and amusement were represented: the fishermen carrying long fishing rods with colored paper fish hooped to them, the chess players carrying enormous cardboard knights, bishops, and castles. Interspersed between the detachments came curious and fanciful constructions, sometimes very ingenious; an effigy of Trotsky with long nose and black eyes and curls made an excellent Mephistopheles. It was a family feast of old and young, and we all exchanged our comments as each new surprise went past. With the usual courtesy to guests there was a chair set for me, and when I wanted to let a lady have it, I was genially told "that I had to submit to the will of the majority." At one time a torrent of rain came down, but the marchers swung past with all the more vigor and enjoyment. And so it was with the on-lookers. After several hours of it, I asked a neighboring policeman whether I couldn't go away: "No," he said very nicely, "you must stay and enjoy it." And enjoy it they certainly did, for in spite of more downpours of rain, from my room in the hotel I could hear them singing and dancing on the square outside till two in the morning. The one thing that fell below the level of all the rest was the exhausting reiteration of the portraits of Stalin and the other "big noises" of Communism. There must have been about forty of Stalin alone: one ten foot high, of the face alone. I noticed a sympathetic cheer when there came past a single portrait of Lenin.

BERNARD PARES, *Russia: Its Past and Present*

48 Examinations

Much that we have said in this handbook about effective writing applies to the special problem of writing examination essays. Your instructor will expect you to write standard English, to organize your material intelligently, and to provide evidence and detail to support your generalizations. When you are given several days or more to write a theme (or a take-home examination), you spend a good portion of your time on prewriting—choosing and limiting your subject, thinking about it, gathering material, and outlining. You also have the time, if you have not procrastinated, to make important changes after your first draft—revising your paragraphs and sentences, substituting more precise words, and proofreading. Clearly, you cannot expect to do all this in the half-hour, hour, or even two hours you are allowed for an in-class examination. You are writing under pressure; you have so much time and no more. Nevertheless, the basic guidelines on "How to Write" that were discussed in Chapter 31 can be helpful to you if you keep in mind that time is always looking over your shoulder.

Preparation

Most of your prewriting must be done before you come to the examination. You will not have to choose a subject; it will be chosen for you—or, at best, you will be allowed to choose from among two or three that have been given. It is probably fair to say, however, that you know the general subject of the examination. It is the subject matter of the course, or of that segment of the course on which you are being examined. Your task, then, is to come to the examination with a rough outline in your mind of the course segments. This process of outlining should begin with the very first lecture or reading assignment and should continue uninterrupted to the day of the examination. If you take intelligent notes during lectures, if you underline key passages and make marginal notations in your textbooks, if you summarize your reading, look over your gathered material from time to time, evaluate it, and structure it, you will be ready for the pre-examination study and review. At that time you will be wise to prepare a more formal outline based on an overview of the course material and any guidelines suggested by your instructor. Writing such an outline and studying it from time to time will help fix the general subject in your mind and will be helpful when you are confronted with the problem of answering specific questions in a specified time.

Prewriting

At that moment your subject is limited for you. Your general subject was "History of Europe, 1815–1848"—the segment of the course on which you are being examined. Now you are given 50 minutes to answer four questions, the first of which is: *What were the four major political and social developments in Europe during the period 1815–1848?* Or, your general subject was *"Three stories by Nathaniel Hawthorne and two by Herman Melville"*—the stories you discussed in class or that were assigned as outside reading. Now you are given 50 minutes to answer two questions, the first of which is: *Hawthorne has been called a "moralist-psychologist." Define the term and evaluate Hawthorne's effectiveness as moralist-psychologist by making specific reference to two of his tales.*

It should go without saying that you will not be able to address yourself to the topic <u>unless you read the examination question carefully</u>. Too often students settle for a hurried glance at the question and start writing without thinking about what they are being asked to do. Are you being asked to summarize or to analyze? Are you expected to present information or to interpret? Are you being asked to comment on a given statement, possibly disagree with it, or to prove it by providing supporting evidence?

In the first question, you are directed to furnish information (What <u>are</u> the four major developments?). You have little more than ten minutes to answer the question. You are not being asked to go into great detail or to interpret the data—you simply don't have the time to do this. Your task is to answer the question as given, and you will be unwise to fill up half a blue book with everything you know about the subject. In the second question, you are asked to define and evaluate; you must make a critical judgment on the basis of specific evidence in Hawthorne's stories. You are given approximately 25 minutes, and you are expected to use that time for a thorough and well-reasoned presentation. Too often, haste and carelessness result in poorly written exams even when the student has mastered the subject matter. Make it a rule to take a minute or two to think about the question, and the rest will be easier.

Having done this, your task now is to gather material and to prepare a rough outline of your now limited topic. If you are

48 prepared for the examination, you will be able to do this in a few minutes. One student who answered the first question jotted down the following on the back of his examination booklet:

> 1815—Congress of Vienna
> 1848—Revolutions
> Nationalism—C. of V. denied rights to Poles, Belgians, Greeks, etc.
> Conservative—Liberal Conflict—Cons. anti-reform. Lib. underground
> Industrial Expansion—Intro. of machines. Transportation—railroads, steam transport, etc.
> Class conflict—Lower class vs. middle class

One student who addressed himself to the second question jotted down the following:

> How human beings behave (psych.) and how they ought/ought not to (moral)
> "Ambitious Guest"—psychological study of human ambitions—moralistic application
> "Wakefield"—integration of psych. and moral—people tied to systems

Then, after briefly studying their notes, the students numbered them in the order they wished to present them—and they had their outlines.

As in all outlining, you must not feel rigidly bound to the material and its structure. As you write, other ideas may come to you and a better structure may suggest itself. The student who answered the Hawthorne question, for example, decided to write on "Egotism" rather than "The Ambitious Guest." Since time, however, is looking over your shoulder, you probably cannot afford the luxury of changing your mind more than once.

Cover Statement

On the basis of your notes you should now be able to begin your examination essay by writing a sentence or two that will serve as a thesis statement. The students who answered the above questions began as follows:

> Although there were no major conflicts among the European powers between the Congress of Vienna (1814–1815) and the Revolutions of 1848, important developments were taking place that would affect the future history of Europe. Four of these developments were the rise of nationalism, the conflict between the conservatives

and the liberals, the conflict between the lower and middle classes, and the expansion of industry.

Hawthorne is a moralist-psychologist who is concerned not only with *how* people behave but also with how they *ought to or ought not to* behave. He is most successful when he integrates the two approaches, as in "Wakefield," and least successful when his moralizing gets away from him, as in "Egotism; or, The Bosom Serpent."

Often, of course, the pressure of the examination will not allow you to formulate as thorough a cover statement. You will need more thinking time before you can arrive at a judgment. If so, you will have to limit your opening to what is specifically required by the question (e.g., Define "moralist-psychologist"), then develop your ideas, and then conclude, after looking over what you have written, with the summary or evaluation (e.g., "Hawthorne, then, is most successful when. . . ."). Indeed, in some examinations you will not be in the position to summarize or evaluate until you have addressed yourself to a number of particulars. In any case, whether you begin your answer with a cover statement or not, you must resist the temptation, so powerful during the first few minutes of the examination, to start throwing in haphazardly everything you know. Do not start writing until you have a clear sense of direction.

Development

Provide supporting evidence, reasoning, detail, or example. Nothing weakens a paper so much as vagueness, unsupported generalizations, and wordiness. Do not place your grader in the position of having to thrash through acres of weeds to find a mustard seed of fact. Don't talk about "how beautiful Hawthorne's images are and what a pleasure it was to read such great stories, etc., etc." Go back to your jotted notes; if necessary, add supporting material. If you have written a cover statement, take a hard look at it and then jot down some hard evidence in the space at the top of the page.

You have been asked, for example, to "Discuss the proper use of the I.Q. score by a teacher." Your notes read: *Intelligence— capacity for learning. Must interpret carefully. Also child's personality. Score not permanent. Measures verbal ability.* You have formulated a cover statement which reads: *"Intelligence" is a vague term used to describe an individual's capacity for learning. The teacher must remember that I.Q. scores tell only part of the story, and that they are subject to change.* Now you must provide the material for development. Think about specific

I.Q. tests, specific studies that will support your generalizations. Jot down notes such as the following:

> 10% of children significant change after 6 to 8 years
> High motivation often more important than high I.Q.
> Stamford—Binet—aptitude rather than intelligence
> Verbal ability—children from non-English speaking families—culturally deprived—low verbal score
> N.Y. study—remedial courses, etc.—40% improvement in scores

You now have some raw material to work with, material you can organize and clearly relate to your cover statement.

You still have some hard thinking to do, but at least you have something to think about. Even if you do not fully succeed in integrating your data into a perfectly coherent and unified essay, you will at least have demonstrated that you read the material and have some understanding of it. Padding, verbosity, and irrelevancies prove only that you can fill up pages. There may be, here and there, a grader who weighs his blue books, but don't depend on yours being one of them. If anything, your grader is more likely to show mercy to a short, underdeveloped answer than to a lengthy padded one.

This is by no means to say that you must never toss in a few interesting tidbits not specifically called for by the question. There is nothing wrong with beginning a discussion of the significance of the Jefferson-Adams correspondence with: "In their 'sunset' correspondence of more than 150 letters, Jefferson and Adams exchanged their ideas on world issues, religion, and the nature and future of American democratic society, almost until the day they both died—July 4, 1826." While only the middle third of this sentence is a direct response to the question, the other data, although not crucial to the answer, is clearly relevant. What is important to remember, however, is that such information must not <u>substitute</u> for your answer.

To illustrate a successful examination essay, here are the first two paragraphs of an answer to the Hawthorne question:

> Hawthorne is a moralist-psychologist who is concerned not only with *how* people behave but also with how they *ought to or ought not to* behave. He is most successful when he integrates the two approaches, as in "Wakefield," and least successful when his moralizing gets away from him as in "Egotism; or, The Bosom Serpent."
>
> "What sort of a man was Wakefield?" the narrator asks, and it is immediately made clear that Wakefield himself cannot know. He is not stupid; his views are not immoral. He is simply a creature

enslaved by whim. Hawthorne studies this man both as psychologist and moralist. He must not only evaluate Wakefield but also teach his reader something worthwhile about the life of those who would follow Emerson and write *Whim* "on the lintels on the door-post." Hawthorne speaks of Wakefield's selfishness and vanity, and shows us what happens when such a person attempts to play the game of Self-Reliance. It is not enough to explain why Wakefield suddenly left his wife. It is necessary also to pinpoint the kind of moral failure that can lead to such action. And so Hawthorne follows Wakefield's every step in order to discover the moralistic source of his psychologically incredible act of rebellion. Only after Wakefield suddenly and inexplicably returns after twenty years of aimless withdrawal does Hawthorne state the moral significance of the tale: human beings are tied to systems and cannot withdraw from them without risking the possibility of their becoming "Outcasts of the Universe."

Last Look

Most instructors, when preparing an exam, allow for an extra few minutes. If possible, finish your writing a few minutes before the deadline. Check to see if you have left out words and phrases. See if you can add an additional bit of detail or evidence, possibly in the margin of the examination booklet. Correct misspellings and awkward sentences. See if your cover statement can be improved. If you have done your prewriting and have structured your material intelligently, such revisions will not take long. You are not expected to write a perfectly polished essay in an examination. Most instructors, however, do respond favorably to a well-written paper, and it is worth your while to make your essay as readable as you can.

EXERCISE 48(1) Evaluate an examination you have taken. Place +'s and
—'s in the margins, and make a list of strengths and weaknesses. Look over
your lecture notes, textbooks, and other material, and then revise your examination until you are satisfied it merits a higher grade.

BUSINESS
LETTERS

49

49   Business Letters

Form and style

In form and style business letters follow standards which emphasize efficiency, clarity, neatness, and competence, reflecting the qualities which business and industry value. Whenever possible, letters are typewritten on 8-½″ by 11″ white unlined paper, or on letterhead stationery, which of course may vary in size and color. The mechanical form of the letter—the arrangement of its parts—follows a conventional pattern. For mailing, letters are folded twice across to fit a standard long envelope of 4″ by 9-½″ or 10″, or folded once across and twice in the other direction to fit a smaller 3-½″ by 6-½″ envelope.

In style, the modern business letter, like all good writing, varies in its degree of formality according to the situation and purpose and the extent to which the writer knows his or her correspondent personally. Always, however, a good business letter style is marked by a pattern of organization which makes its central points immediately clear, an intelligible and direct style, and a language appropriate to the reader. And such letters are particularly attentive to conventions of punctuation, grammar, and spelling. The modern business letter avoids any special jargon and such now old-fashioned set phrases as "wish to advise that," or "am in receipt of"; equally it avoids an excessively breezy informality.

Parts of the business letter

The business letter has six parts: (1) the heading, (2) the inside address, (3) the salutation, (4) the body, (5) the complimentary close, and (6) the signature. The sample letter on p. 429 illustrates a widely used format for these parts, and provides a model which you can follow. The content of that letter describes the arrangement of the parts, and special conventions of the punctuation. Note the following comments on appropriate selection of the salutation, complimentary close, and other details.

   The salutation. If it is known, the last name of the addressee is used as in *Dear Mr. Howe, Dear Miss* (or *Mrs.*) *Kanski, Dear Dean Reavill. Dear Ms. Kanski* is now widely used not only when the marital status of a woman is not known, but also because many women prefer it. If a woman to whom you are writing identifies herself as Miss or Mrs., however, always address her in the same way.

In writing to organizations or to persons you do not know, use *Dear Sir or Madam, Dear Sir, or Gentlemen.* For appropriate forms of salutation and inside addresses for letters to government officials, military personnel and the like, check your desk dictionary for guidance. Of course, if you are replying to a letter, you should use the same forms as those in the letter to which you are replying.

The complimentary close. The majority of business letters use one of the following courteous closes: *Yours truly, Yours very truly* or *Very truly yours, Sincerely yours,* or simply *Sincerely.* Business letters addressed to people with whom there is frequent and friendly correspondence often use *Cordially,* or *Cordially yours.* Closings such as *Respectfully yours* and *Yours respectfully* are reserved for formal circumstances where they seem appropriate as, for example, in addressing a letter to the president of your university, or to a high government official.

Note that the first word of a complimentary close is always capitalized, but only the first.

Signature. Both the handwritten and the typewritten signature are important. If appropriate, the typewritten signature may be followed by the writer's official capacity, but neither professional titles nor degrees should be used with the signature.

Sincerely yours,

William H. Oliver

William H. Oliver
Editor

A woman may if she wishes place *Ms., Miss,* or *Mrs.* inside parentheses before her typed name. A married woman may choose to add below her typed name *Mrs.* followed by her husband's name, inside parentheses.

Sincerely,

Katherine Carlone

(Ms.) Katherine Carlone

Yours truly,

Elizabeth Phillips

Elizabeth Phillips
(Mrs. Charles Phillips)

Reference initials. Business letters that have been typed by a secretary frequently identify the author and the secretary by their initials. At the same point, the information about other material enclosed with the letter, or the fact that copies of the

49

letter have been sent to others may be identified. Such information is typed flush with the left margin as follows:

RLW/cwm	initials of author and secretary
Enc. Sample letter	enclosure indicated
cc: Patrick Q. Jay, Manager	copies sent to

Kinds of business letters*

Request letters. Perhaps the most common kind of business letter most of us write is that asking someone to do something: give us information, send us something we have seen advertised, or correct a mistake. Such letters should be direct, businesslike, and courteous, even when you are registering a complaint. Above all they must be clear. They must give the exact information the reader needs to meet your request.

Letters 1 and 2 on pp. 431 and 432 illustrate simple, clear letters of this kind.

Letters of application. Though letters requesting information, registering complaints, and the like are probably those you will write most often, letters in which you are applying for a position you want are almost certainly among the most important you will write. In writing such letters, keep the following advice in mind:

(1) Be as specific as possible about the position you are applying for. If the position was advertised, identify the advertisement. If a specific person suggested you write, mention that fact.

(2) Describe any part of your education or previous work experience which you believe may prepare you for the position you wish. Be brief, direct, and factual, but at the same time present such information to your advantage.

(3) Provide references if possible, but remember that useful and relevant references have to come from people who actually know your work at first hand. People for whom you have previously worked successfully and instructors with whom you have taken relevant courses are often among your best references. Remember that a potential employer consulting one of your references will want to know specific things about the quality of your work, your overall ability—and your reliability. In listing references, be sure to get permission from those whose names you use.

(4) For many part-time or temporary positions for which you apply, it is sufficient to describe your experience and other qual-

*Some of the sample letters on pp. 431–435 are adapted from P. D. Hemphill, *Business Communications* (Englewood Cliffs, New Jersey: Prentice-Hall, 1976).

Heading
> 521 Lake Street
> Tucson, Arizona 85702
> April 29, 1979

Mr. Peter B. McHenry
Business Manager
University of Texas
Austin, Texas 78752

Inside Address

Dear Mr. McHenry: Salutation

This letter uses a format called modified block style. All parts of the letter except the heading, the complimentary close and the signature are placed flush with the left margin. Paragraphs are not indented. The heading is placed approximately flush with the right margin; note that it includes the date. The complimentary close and typewritten signature are aligned with the heading. If you are using a letterhead stationery, the date may be typed three or four spaces below the letterhead and either centered or placed flush with either margin. In what is called the full block style, all parts of the letter are placed flush with the left margin.

The punctuation in the heading and inside address of this letter is open. That is, no punctuation is placed at the end of lines, although internal punctuation between city and state, and between day and year is retained. The salutation and complimentary close, however, are followed by a colon and a comma respectively. In fully open punctuation, no punctuation would be used after the salutation and close.

Note that spacing in the letter is an important part of its appearance. Two or three spaces should be left between the date and the inside address. Double spacing should be used between all other main parts of the letter, and always between paragraphs. It is wise to allow three spaces between the complimentary close and your typed signature. The appearance is well served also by the picture frame placement used in this letter, which maintains uniform and generous margins.

Complimentary close   Sincerely,

Signature   *Caren A. Mattice*

Signature identification   Caren A. Mattice

Body

49

ifications in the body of your letter, as the writer of Letter 3 on p. 433 does. But for full-time positions, and particularly if the listing of your background, qualifications, and references is fairly full, it is wiser to tabulate information in a clear, convenient form on a personal data sheet, or resume, as does the writer of Letter 4 on p. 434. This enables you to use your letter to highlight in summary form particularly important information, and makes the necessary factual information conveniently available to a prospective employer.

Study sample Letters 3 and 4, and the format and information in the personal data sheet included with Letter 4 (p. 435).

Letter 1

1058 University Road
Champaign, Illinois 61820
March 23, 1980

American Youth Hostels, Inc.
Travel Department CT
Deleplane, Virginia 22025

Gentlemen:

A recent local newspaper article about varieties of student
summer travel described some of the trips sponsored by
American Youth Hostels. It also reported that you have
available a free pamphlet entitled Highroad to Adventure,
which provides information about such trips.

Please send me one copy of Highroad to Adventure together
with any other descriptive material you may have, and any
special information I may need to apply for membership in
American Youth Hostels.

Sincerely,

Juan Benvenito

Juan Benvenito

Letter 2

444 West Wilson Street
Madison, Wisconsin 53715
July 9, 1979

Cambridge Camera Exchange, Inc.
7th Avenue and 13th Street
New York, N. Y. 10011

Gentlemen:

The Minolta SRT 201 camera outfit which I ordered from you
on June 21 arrived today and appears to be in good working
order. However, your advertisement in The New York Times
for Sunday, June 16 listed six items as being supplied
with this outfit, including a film holder and a sun shade.
Neither of these items was included in the package which I
have just received nor do I find any notice that they will
be sent at a later date.

I am sure that this omission is unintentional, and that you
will correct it. Will you please let me know when I may
expect to receive the film holder and sun shade, as advertised. If there is a dealer in the immediate area, I would
be happy to get them from him if you will authorize me to
do so at your expense.

Sincerely,

Marilyn S. Conway

Marilyn S. Conway

Letter 3

3481 Mountain Road
Bellevue, Washington 98004
April 14, 1979

Dr. Winthrop D. Pierce
Professor of Marketing
University of Washington
Seattle, Washington 98105

Dear Professor Pierce:

Through your bulletin posted at the University of Washington placement
service I learned that you are looking for students to work part time
for you next year in various marketing research projects. I believe my
educational background and my experience working with people could be
put to good advantage in such work.

In early June I expect to receive my A.A. degree with a marketing
specialty from Bellevue Community College. Courses I have taken include
Marketing, Advertising, Business Writing, Business Law, Accounting, and
Computer Programming. I plan to continue my study at the University of
Washington next year.

I have been holding two part-time jobs, one as an assistant to Professor
John Leonard in the Business Department at Bellevue Community College,
and one as a night dispatch clerk in the Bellevue Trucking Company. I
believe I work well with people. In my position with Professor Leonard
I supervise three other part-time students, and my work at the Bellevue
Trucking Company requires me to deal constantly with other workers.

Both Professor John Leonard and Mr. Oscar Malenko, manager of the
Bellevue Trucking Company, have assured me they could recommend me to
you. I believe you know Professor Leonard. Mr. Malenko can be reached
by telephone at (206) 912-5437.

I can arrange to come to Seattle at your convenience. You can reach
me or leave a message for me at my home phone (206) 123-7654.

Sincerely,

Ralston Phillips

Ralston Phillips

Letter 4

643 Lane Avenue
Durham, New Hampshire 03824
March 22, 1980

Personnel Office
Arthur D. Little Company
25 Acorn Park
Cambridge, Massachusetts 01517

Dear Sir:

Mr. James Hartman, who has been a research engineer with Arthur D. Little for many years, suggested I apply to you for a secretarial position. Having lived in Cambridge for much of my life, I have often read and heard about the work of the Arthur D. Little Company. Now I believe it would be an interesting and pleasant place to work.

In late May I will graduate from the University of New Hampshire with an Administrative Secretary major. My shorthand speed is 120 words per minute, and my typing about 70 words per minute.

During the past two years I have worked part time in the Business Division office at the University of New Hampshire. During the past ten months I have been assigned the composing and typing of routine correspondence and have been commended for the clarity and accuracy of my letters. I believe my training would qualify me for administrative assistant duties as well as secretarial work. My personal data sheet is enclosed.

I can easily come to Cambridge at your convenience, and would appreciate the opportunity for an interview. Should you wish to call rather than write me, I can be reached at (603) 732-6154 before 10 AM and after 4 PM.

Sincerely yours,

Ms. Maria Gonzalez

Enc.

PERSONAL DATA SHEET

MARIA GONZALEZ

POSITION SOUGHT: SECRETARY

643 Lane Avenue
Durham, New Hampshire 03824
(603) 732-6154

Education	1976-80: University of New Hampshire, Durham, New Hampshire B.S. degree; Administrative Secretary major

Courses taken that would be useful in secretarial work:

Advanced Shorthand	Administrative Secretary
Advanced Typewriting	Machine Calculation
Business English (grammar)	Office Services
Business Communications (writing)	Basic Accounting
Machine Transcription	Human Relations in Business

1972-76: Cambridge High School, Cambridge, Massachusetts

Experience	1978-present: Student assistant in office of Business Division, University of New Hampshire. General office duties: take shorthand; answer telephone; act as receptionist; file.

1974-76: Acme Travel Agency, 428 Main Street, Watertown, Massachusetts. Receptionist, typist. Part time and summers.

Special Qualifications	Bilingual: Competency in writing and speaking both English and Spanish.

Personal Data	

Age	22	Hobbies: Skiing, tennis; styling and making own clothes.
Height	5' 7"	
Weight	115	Memberships: Phi Beta Lambda,
Hair	Black	college business fraternity. FBLA,
Eyes	Brown	high school business club.

References	Mrs. Margaret W. Baird, secretarial instructor, Business Division, University of New Hampshire, Durham, New Hampshire 03824. Telephone: (603) 860-2451.

Mr. Jason L. Masters, Manager, Acme Travel Agency, 428 Main Street, Watertown, Massachusetts 02172. Telephone: (617) 321-8967.

Mr. James Hartman, 12 Longfellow Road, Lexington, Massachusetts 02173.

A GLOSSARY
OF GRAMMATICAL
TERMS

50

This glossary provides brief definitions of the grammatical terms used in this text. Cross references refer the reader to pertinent sections of the text. For further text references to terms defined, as well as for references to terms not included in the glossary, the reader should consult the index.

absolute phrase Absolute constructions modify the entire remainder of the sentence in which they stand. They differ from other modifying word groups in that (1) they lack any connective joining them to the rest of the sentence, and (2) they do not modify any individual word or word group in the sentence. Compare *Seeing the bears, we stopped the car,* in which the participle phrase modifies *we,* with *The rain having stopped, we saw the bears,* in which the construction *the rain having stopped* is an absolute modifying the rest of the sentence. The basic pattern of the absolute phrase is a noun or pronoun and a participle. (*She having arrived, we all went to the movies. We left about ten o'clock, the movie being over.*) Such phrases are sometimes called NOMINATIVE ABSOLUTES, since pronouns in them require the nominative case.

Absolute phrases may also be prepositional phrases (*In fact, we had expected rain*) or verbal phrases (*It often rains in April, to tell the truth. Generally speaking, July is hot*). For the punctuation of absolute phrases see **21b.**

abstract noun See *noun.*

active voice See *voice.*

adjectival Any word or word group used to modify a noun. Some modern grammars limit the meaning of ADJECTIVE strictly to those words which can be compared by adding *-er* and *-est* (*new, newer, newest; high, higher, highest*). Such grammars apply the term ADJECTIVAL to other words which ordinarily modify nouns, and to any other word or word group when it is used as an adjective. In such grammars the italicized words below may be called ADJECTIVALS.

Limiting adjectives	*my* suit, *a* picture, *one* day
Nouns modifying nouns	*school* building, *home* plate, *government* policy
Phrases modifying nouns	man *of the hour*
Clauses modifying nouns	girl *whom I know*

adjective A word used to describe or limit the meaning of a noun or its equivalent. According to their position, adjectives may be (1) ATTRIB-

UTIVE, i.e., placed next to their nouns (*vivid example; a boy, strong and vigorous*), or (2) PREDICATIVE, i.e., placed in the predicate after a linking verb (*She was vigorous*).

According to their meaning, adjectives may be (1) DESCRIPTIVE, naming some quality (*white house, small child, leaking faucet*); (2) PROPER, derived from proper nouns (*Roman fountain, French custom*); or (3) LIMITING. Limiting adjectives may indicate possession (*my, his*), may point out (*this, former*), may number (*three, second*), or may be articles (*a, the*). (See **1b(4)** and Section 4.)

adjective clause A subordinate, or dependent, clause used as an adjective.

The man *who lives here* is a biologist. (The adjective clause modifies the noun *man*).

Dogs *that chase cars* seldom grow old. (The adjective clause modifies the noun *dogs*.)

(See also **1d.**)

adverb A word used to describe or limit the meaning of a verb, an adjective, another adverb, or a whole sentence.

According to function, adverbs may (1) modify single words (*went quickly, quite shy, nearly all men*); (2) modify whole sentences (*Maybe he will go*); (3) ask questions (*When did he go? Where is the book?*); or (4) connect clauses and modify their meaning (see *conjunctive adverb*).

According to meaning, adverbs may indicate (1) manner (*secretly envious*); (2) time (*never healthy*); (3) place (*outside the house*); or (4) degree (*quite easily angered*). (See **1b(4)** and Section 4.)

adverb clause A subordinate, or dependent, clause used as an adverb.

When you leave, please close the door. (The adverb clause, indicating time, modifies the verb *close.*)

The sheep grazed *where the grass was greenest.* (The adverb clause, indicating place, modifies the verb *grazed.*)

Adverb clauses also indicate manner, purpose, cause, result, condition, concession, and comparison.) See **1d.**

adverbial A term used to describe any word or word group used as an adverb. Common adverbials are nouns in certain constructions (*She went home*), phrases (*She went in a great hurry*), or clauses (*She went when she wanted to go*). Compare *adjectival.*

adverbial objective Sometimes applied to nouns used as adverbials. (*They slept mornings. He ran a mile.*)

agreement A correspondence, or matching, in the form of one word and that of another. Verbs agree with their subjects in number and person (in *She runs,* both *she* and *runs* are singular and third person). Pronouns agree with their antecedents in person, number, and gender (in *He wanted his way, he* and *his* are both third person, singular, and masculine). Demonstrative adjectives match the nouns they modify in number (*this kind, these kinds*). (See Section 8.)

antecedent A word or group of words to which a pronoun refers.

> She is a *woman who* seldom complains. (*Woman* is the antecedent of the pronoun *who.*)
> *Uncle Henry* came for a brief visit, but *he* stayed all winter. (*Uncle Henry* is the antecedent of the pronoun *he.*)

appositive A word or phrase set beside a noun, a pronoun, or a group of words used as a noun, which identifies or explains it by renaming it.

> John, my *brother*   Albany, the state *capital*
> His hobby, *playing handball*   modifiers, *that is, words which describe or limit*

The appositives illustrated above are NONRESTRICTIVE: they explain the nouns they follow, but are not necessary to identify them. When appositives restrict the meaning of the nouns they follow to a specific individual or object, they are RESTRICTIVE: *my sister Ilene* (that is, *Ilene,* not *Dorothy* or *Helen*); *Huxley the novelist* (not *Huxley the scientist*). (See **22b** and Section 24.)

article The words *a, an,* and *the* are articles. *A* and *an* are INDEFINITE articles; *the* is a DEFINITE article. Articles are traditionally classed as limiting adjectives, but since they always signal that a noun will follow, some modern grammars call them DETERMINERS.

auxiliary A verb form used with a main verb to form a verb phrase. Auxiliaries are commonly divided into two groups. The first group is used to indicate tense and voice. This group includes *shall, will,* and the forms of *be, have,* and *do* (*shall give, will give, has given, had given, does give, is giving, was given*).

The second group, called MODAL AUXILIARIES, includes *can, could, may, might, must, ought, should,* and *would.* These are used to indicate ability, obligation, permission, possibility, etc., and they do not take inflectional endings such as *-s, -ed,* and *-ing.*

(See Section 3.)

cardinal numbers Numbers such as *one, three, twenty,* used in counting. Compare *ordinal numbers.*

case The inflectional form of pronouns or the possessive form of nouns to indicate their function in a group of words. Pronouns have

three cases: (1) NOMINATIVE or SUBJECTIVE (*we, she, they*), used for the subject of a verb, or a subjective complement; (2) the POSSESSIVE, used as an adjective (*their dog, anybody's guess*); and (3) the OBJECTIVE (*us, her, them*), used for objects of verbs, verbals, and prepositions. Possessive pronouns may also stand alone (*The car is his*). Nouns have only two cases: (1) a COMMON case (*woman, leopard*) and (2) a POSSESSIVE case (*woman's, leopard's*).
   (See Section 2.)

clause A group of words containing a subject and a predicate. Clauses are of two kinds: main or independent, and subordinate or dependent. MAIN CLAUSES make independent assertions and can stand alone as sentences. SUBORDINATE CLAUSES depend on some other element within a sentence; they function as nouns, adjectives, or adverbs, and cannot stand alone.

Main	*The moon shone,* and *the dog barked.* (Two main clauses, either of which could be a sentence)
Subordinate	*When the moon shone,* the dog barked. (Adverb clause)
	That he would survive is doubtful. (Noun clause)

   (See **1d.**)

collective noun A noun naming a collection or aggregate of individuals by a singular form (*assembly, army, jury*). Collective nouns are followed by a singular verb when the group is thought of as a unit, and a plural verb when the component individuals are in mind (*the majority decides; the majority were slaves*).
   (See **8a(6)** and **8b.**)

common noun See *noun.*

comparison Change in the form of adjectives and adverbs to show degree. English has three degrees: (1) the POSITIVE, which is the form listed in dictionaries (*loud, bad, slowly*); (2) the COMPARATIVE (*louder, worse, more slowly*); and the SUPERLATIVE (*loudest, worst, most slowly*).
   (See **4e.**)

complement In its broadest sense, complement is a term for any word, excluding modifiers, which completes the meaning of a verb (direct and indirect objects), a subject (subject complements), or an object (object complements).

verb complements	Give *me* the *money.* (*Money* and *me* are direct and indirect objects respectively.)
subject complements	Helen is a *singer.* She is *excellent.* (The noun *singer* and the adjective *excellent* refer to the subject.)

441

50

object complements   We elected Jane *secretary*. That made Bill *angry*. (*Secretary* and *angry* refer to the direct objects *Jane* and *Bill*.)

complex sentence   See *sentence*.

compound   Made up of more than one word but used as a unit, as in compound noun (*redhead, football*), compound adjective (*downcast, matter-of-fact*), or compound subject (*Both <u>patience</u> and <u>practice</u> are necessary*).
    See also *sentence*.

compound-complex   See *sentence*.

concrete noun   See *noun*.

conjugation   A term used to describe the changes in the inflectional forms of a verb to show tense, voice, mood, person, and number.
    (See Section 3.)

conjunction   A part of speech used to join and relate words, phrases, and clauses. Conjunctions may be either coordinating or subordinating.
    Coordinating conjunctions connect words, phrases, and clauses of equal grammatical rank: *and, but, or, nor, for*.
    Subordinating conjunctions join dependent clauses to main clauses: *after, although, as if, because, since, when*.
    See **1b(5)**.

conjunctive adverb   An adverb used to relate and connect main clauses in a sentence. Common conjunctive adverbs are *also, consequently, furthermore, hence, however, indeed, instead, likewise, moreover, nevertheless, otherwise, still, then, therefore, thus*. CONJUNCTIVE ADVERBS, unlike COORDINATING and SUBORDINATING CONJUNCTIONS are moveable and can thus occupy different positions within the main clause in which they stand.
    (See **20c**.)

connective   A general term for any word or phrase that links words, phrases, clauses, or sentences. CONNECTIVE thus includes conjunctions, prepositions, and conjunctive adverbs.
    (See **1(5)** and **32d(4)**.)

construction   A general term describing any related group of words such as a phrase, a clause, or a sentence.

coordinate   Having equal rank, as two main clauses in a compound sentence.
    (See Section 33.)

correlatives   Coordinating conjunctions used in pairs to join sentence elements of equal rank. Common correlatives are *either . . . or, neither*

. . . nor, not only . . . but also, whether . . . or, both . . . and.
(See **35c.**)

dangling construction A subordinate construction which cannot easily
and certainly be linked to another word or group of words it modifies.
(See Section 12.)

declension See *inflection* and *case.*

degree See *comparison.*

demonstratives *This, that, these,* and *those* are called DEMONSTRATIVES
when used as pointing words. (<u>*This*</u> *dinner is cold.* <u>*That*</u> *is the man.*)

dependent clause See *clause.*

determiner A word such as *a, an, the, his, our, your* which indicates
that one of the words following it is a noun.

direct address A noun or pronoun used parenthetically to point out
the person addressed, sometimes called NOMINATIVE OF ADDRESS or
VOCATIVE. (<u>*George*</u>*, where are you going? I suppose,* <u>*gentlemen,*</u>
that you enjoyed the lecture.)

direct and indirect quotation A direct quotation is an exact quotation of
a speaker's or writer's words (sometimes called DIRECT DISCOURSE). In
INDIRECT DISCOURSE the speaker's or writer's thought is summarized
without direct quotation.

Direct   He said, "I must leave on the eight o'clock shuttle."
Indirect   He said that he had to leave on the eight o'clock
             shuttle.

direct object See *object* and *complement.*

double negative The use of two negative words within the same construction. In certain forms, two negatives are used in the same statement in English to give a particular emphasis to a positive idea (*He
was* <u>*not*</u> *entirely* <u>*unprejudiced*</u>). In most instances, the double negative
is nonstandard. (*He* <u>*didn't*</u> *do* <u>*no*</u> *work. We* <u>*didn't*</u> *see* <u>*nobody.*</u>)
(See **42b.**)

elliptical construction An omission of words necessary to the grammatical completeness of an expression but assumed in the context. The
omitted words in elliptical expressions are understood (*He is older
than I* [<u>*am*</u>]. *Our house is small, his* [*house is*] *large*).

expletive The word *it* or *there* used to introduce a sentence in which
the subject follows the verb.

It is doubtful that he will arrive today. (The clause *that he will
arrive today* is the subject of the verb *is.*)

There are two ways of solving the problem. (The noun *ways* is the subject of *are*.)

finite verb A verb form that makes an assertion about its subject. Verbals (infinitives, participles, gerunds) are not finite forms.

function words A term used to describe those words, such as articles, auxiliaries, conjunctions, and prepositions, which are more important for their part in the structure of the sentence than for their meaning. They indicate the function of other words in a sentence and the grammatical relations between those words.

gender The classification of nouns and pronouns as masculine (*man, he*), feminine (*woman, she*), and neuter (*desk, it*). A few English nouns have special forms to indicate gender (*salesman, saleswoman; hero, heroine*).

genitive case The possessive case.
(See Section 2.)

gerund A verbal that ends in *-ing* and is used as a noun. Gerunds may take complements, objects, and modifiers.
(See **1c.**)

idiom An expression established by usage and peculiar to a particular language. Many idioms have unusual grammatical construction and make little sense if taken literally. Examples of English idioms are *by and large, catch a cold, lay hold of, look up an old friend.*
(See **40f.**)

imperative See *mood.*

indefinite pronoun A pronoun, such as *anybody, anyone, someone,* that does not refer to a specific person or thing.

independent clause See *clause.*

independent element An expression that has no grammatical relation to other parts of the sentence. See *absolute.*

indicative See *mood.*

indirect object See *object.*

infinitive A verbal usually consisting of *to* followed by the present form of the verb. With a few verbs *to* may be omitted (*heard her tell; made it work*). Infinitives can serve as nouns (*To swim is to relax*), as adjectives (*I have nothing to say*), or as adverbs (*We were ready to begin*).
(See **1b.**)

inflection Variation in the form of words to indicate case (*he, him*), gender (*he, she, it*), number (*man, men*), tense (*walk, walked*), etc. DECLENSION is the inflection of nouns and pronouns; CONJUGATION the inflection of verbs; and COMPARISON is the inflection of adjectives and adverbs.

intensifier A term applied to such modifiers as *much, so, too,* and *very,* which merely add emphasis to the words they modify. Words such as *actually, mighty, pretty,* and *really* often occur as vague intensifiers in much colloquial English.

intensive pronoun Any compound personal pronoun ending with -*self* used for emphasis (*I did it myself. The Dean himself wrote the letter*).

intransitive verb See *verb.*

inversion A reversal of normal word order. (*Dejected, he left the witness stand. The verdict he clearly foresaw.*)

irregular verb A verb that forms its past tense and past participle by a change in an internal vowel, or by some other individualized change rather than by the usual addition of -*d* or -*ed* to the basic form as in *walk, walked, walked* (*begin, began, begun; do, did, done; fall, fell, fallen*).
(See **3d.**)

kernel sentence A term used in some contemporary grammars to describe one of a limited number of basic sentence patterns from which all grammatical structures can be derived.
(See **1a.**)

linking verb A verb that shows the relation between the subject of a sentence and a complement. (*He seems timid. The cake tastes sweet. He is a thief.*) The chief linking verbs are *be, become, appear, seem,* and the verbs pertaining to the senses (*look, smell, taste, sound, feel*).

modification Describing or limiting the meaning of a word or group of words. Adjectives and adjective phrases or clauses modify nouns; adverbs and adverb phrases or clauses modify verbs, adjectives, or adverbs.
(See Section **4.**)

mood The form of a verb used to show how the action is viewed by the speaker. English has three moods: (1) the INDICATIVE, stating a fact or asking a question (*The wheat is ripe. Will he go?*); (2) the IMPERATIVE, expressing a command or a request (*Report at once. Please clear your desk*); and (3) the SUBJUNCTIVE, expressing doubt, wish, or condition contrary to fact (*The grass looks as if it were dying. I wish he were more friendly*).
(See Section **3.**)

nominal A word or word group used as a noun. (*The blue seems more suitable. Eating that pie will not be easy.*) Compare *adjectival.*

50

nominative case See *case.*

nonrestrictive modifier A modifying phrase or clause that is not essential to pointing out or identifying the person or thing modified.

> Smith, *who was watching the road,* saw the accident.
> The Wankel engine, *new to the market,* is promising.
> (See Section 22, especially **22a.**)

noun A word, like *man, horse, carrot, trip, theory,* or *capitalism,* that names a person, place, thing, quality, concept, or the like. Nouns usually form plurals by adding *-s,* and possessives by adding *'s,* and most frequently function as subjects and complements, although they also function in other ways. (See **1b.**)

Nouns are divided into various subclasses according to their meaning. The most common classes are the following:

Class	Meaning	Examples
common	general classes	*tiger, house, idea*
proper	specific names	*Chicago, Burma, John*
abstract	ideas, qualities	*liberty, love, emotion*
concrete	able to be sensed	*apple, smoke, perfume*
collective	groups	*herd, bunch, jury*
count	able to be counted	*chicken, slice, book*
mass	not ordinarily counted (not used with *a, an*)	*salt, gold, equality*

noun clause A subordinate clause used as a noun. (*What I saw was humiliating. I shall accept whatever he offers.*)
(See **1d.**)

number The form of a noun, pronoun, verb, or demonstrative adjective to indicate one (singular) or more than one (plural).

object A general term for any word or word group that is affected by or receives action of a transitive verb or verbal, or of a preposition. A DIRECT OBJECT receives the action of the verb. (*I followed him. Keep whatever you find.*) An INDIRECT OBJECT indicates to or for whom or what something is done (*Give me the money*). The OBJECT OF A PREPOSITION follows the preposition and is related to another part of the sentence by the preposition (*We rode across the beach*). See also *complement* and **1a** and **2c.**

object complement See *complement.*

objective case See *case.*

ordinal numbers Numbers such as *first, third, twentieth,* used to indicate order. Compare *cardinal numbers.*

paradigm An illustration of the systematic inflection of a word such as a pronoun or a verb, showing all its forms.

parenthetical expression An inserted expression that interrupts the thought of a sentence. (*His failure, I suppose, was his own fault. I shall arrive—this will surprise you—on Monday.*)

50

participial phrase See *participle* and *phrase.*

participle A verbal used as an adjective. As an adjective, a participle can modify a noun or pronoun. The present participle ends in *-ing* (*running, seeing, trying*). The past participle ends in *-d, -ed, -t, -n, -en,* or changes the vowel (*walked, lost, seen, rung*). Though a participle cannot make an assertion, it is derived from a verb and can take an object and be modified by an adverb (*Swimming the river, completely beaten*).

parts of speech The classes into which words may be divided on the basis of meaning, form, and function. The traditional parts of speech are: noun, pronoun, verb, adjective, adverb, preposition, conjunction, and interjection. See **1b** and separate entries in this glossary.

passive voice See *voice.*

person The form of a pronoun and verb used to indicate the speaker (first person—*I am*); the person spoken to (second person—*you are*); or the person spoken about (third person—*she is*).

personal pronoun See *pronoun.*

phrase A group of related words lacking both subject and predicate and used as a single part of speech. Phrases may be classified as follows:

Prepositional	We walked *across the street.*
Participial	The man *entering the room* is my father.
Gerund	*Washing windows* is tiresome work.
Infinitive	*To see the sunset* was a pleasure.
Verb	He *has been educated* in Europe.

(See **1c.**)

possessive See *case.*

predicate The part of a sentence or clause that makes a statement about the subject. The COMPLETE PREDICATE consists of the verb and its complements and modifiers. The SIMPLE PREDICATE consists of only the verb and its auxiliaries.
(See **1a.**)

predicate adjective An adjective serving as a subject complement (He was *silent.*) See *complement.*

predicate noun A noun serving as a subject complement. (He was a hero.) See *complement.*

50

preposition A word used to relate a noun or pronoun to some other word in the sentence. A preposition and its object form a PREPOSITIONAL PHRASE. (*The sheep are <u>in</u> the meadow. He dodged <u>through</u> the traffic.*)
(See **1b(5)**.)

prepositional phrase See *phrase* and *preposition*.

principal clause A main or independent clause. See *clause*.

principal parts The three forms of a verb from which the various tenses are derived: the PRESENT INFINITIVE (*join, go*), the PAST TENSE (*joined, went*), and the PAST PARTICIPLE (*joined, gone*).
(See Section 3.)

progressive The form of the verb used to describe an action occurring, but not completed, at the time referred to. (*I <u>am studying</u>. I <u>was studying</u>.*)
(See Section 3.)

pronoun A word used in place of a noun. The noun for which a pronoun stands is called its ANTECEDENT. (See **1b(2)** and **8b**.) Pronouns are classified as follows:

Personal	*I, you, he, she, it*, etc.
Relative	*who, which, that* I am the man *who* lives here. We saw a barn *that* was burning.
Interrogative	*who, which, what* *Who* are you? *Which* is your book?
Demonstrative	*this, that, these, those*
Indefinite	*one, any, each, anyone, somebody, all*, etc.
Reciprocal	*each other, one another*
Intensive	*myself, yourself, himself*, etc. I *myself* was afraid. You *yourself* must decide.
Reflexive	*myself, yourself, himself*, etc. I burned *myself*. You are deceiving *yourself*.

proper noun See *noun*.

reciprocal pronoun See *pronoun*.

relative clause A subordinate clause introduced by a relative pronoun. (See *pronoun*.)

relative pronoun See *pronoun*.

restrictive modifier A modifying phrase or clause that is essential to pointing out or identifying the person or thing modified. (*People <u>who</u>*

448

live in glass houses shouldn't throw stones. The horse that won the race is a bay mare.)

sentence A complete unit of thought containing a subject and a predicate. Sentences can be classified according to their form as SIMPLE, COMPOUND, COMPLEX, and COMPOUND-COMPLEX.

Simple	They rested. (One main clause)
Compound	They rested and we worked. (Two main clauses)
Complex	They rested while he worked. (One main clause, one subordinate clause)
Compound-Complex	They rested while we worked, but we could not finish. (Two main clauses, one containing a subordinate clause)

subject The person or thing about which the predicate of a sentence or clause makes an assertion or asks a question.

subject complement See *complement.*

subjunctive mood See *mood.*

subordinate clause See *clause.*

substantive A word or group of words used as a noun. Substantives include pronouns, infinitives, gerunds, and noun clauses.

substantive clause A noun clause. See *clause.*

suffix An ending which modifies the meaning of the word to which it is attached. Suffixes may be INFLECTIONAL, such as the -*s* added to nouns to form plurals (*rug, rugs*), or the -*ed* added to verbs to indicate past tense (*call, called*). Or they may be DERIVATIONAL, such as -*ful, -less,* or -*ize* (*hope, hopeful; home, homeless; union, unionize*). Derivational suffixes often, though not always, change the part of speech to which they are added. See *inflection* and **391.**

superlative See *comparison.*

transitive verb See *verb.*

verb A word, like *confide, raise, see,* which indicates action or asserts something. (See **1b(3).**) Verbs are inflected and combine with auxiliaries to form VERB PHRASES. Verbs may be TRANSITIVE, requiring an object (*He made a report*), or INTRANSITIVE, not requiring an object (*They migrated*). Many can function both transitively and intransitively. (*The wind blew. They blew the whistle.*) LINKING VERBS, such as *be, become,* and *appear,* are followed by complements which refer back to the subject.

50

verb complement See *complement*.

verb phrase See *phrase*.

verbal A word derived from a verb and able to take objects, complements, modifiers, and sometimes subjects but unable to stand as the main verb in a sentence. See *gerund, infinitive,* and *participle.*
(See **1b** and **1c**.)

voice The form of the verb which shows whether the subject acts (ACTIVE VOICE) or is acted upon (PASSIVE VOICE). Only transitive verbs can show voice. A transitive verb followed by an object is ACTIVE (They *bought* flowers). In the PASSIVE the direct object is made into the subject (The flowers *were bought*).
(See **1a,** Section 3, and **36e**.)

word order The order of words in a sentence or smaller word group. Word order is one of the principal grammatical devices in English.
See p. 73.

INDEX

A

a, an, 327
Abbreviations, 96–98
  academic titles, 96
  commercial, 97
  of countries, states, months, days, 97
  with dates and numerals, 97
  in footnotes, 388–89
  in formal writing, 97
  Latin, 97
  periods with, 103–4
  titles of persons, 96
  of *volume, chapter, page,* 97–98
above, below, 327
Absolute phrase, 438
absolved by, from, 306
Abstract noun, 446
Academic titles, abbreviation, 96
accede to, 306
accept, except, 327
accompany by, with, 306
Accusative case. *See* Objective case
acquitted of, 306
Active voice:
  defined, 450
  for emphasis, 256–58
  paradigm, 34
  preference for, 71
  verb forms, 33
actually, 327
ad, 327
adapted to, from, 306
Addition, transition words, 206
Addresses, comma in, 120
Adjectival, 438
Adjective(s):
  classes, 438–39
  comparison, 21, 42–43, 441
  demonstrative, 66, 443
  descriptive, 439
  form and use, 39–43
  function, 21
  hyphenated, 142
  limiting, 438, 439
  logically incomparable, 42
  predicate, 16, 439, 447
  proper, 138, 439
  in series, 119–20

Adjective(s) (*cont.*)
  suffixes, 295
Adjective clauses. *See also* Subordinate clauses
  defined, 439
  diagramed, 47
  function, 26
  as modifiers, 26
  position of, 75
  restrictive and nonrestrictive, punctuation of, 113–16
admit to, of, 306
Adverb(s):
  comparison, 42–43, 441
  conjunctive, 59–60, 108–9, 442
  defined, 439
  form and use, 39–43
  function, 21
  misplaced, 74
Adverb clauses. *See also* Subordinate clauses
  defined, 439
  diagramed, 48
  function, 26
Adverbial, defined, 439
Adverbial objective, defined, 439
affect, effect, 327
aggravate, 327
Agreement, 61–66. *See also* Agreement of pronoun and antecedent; Agreement of subject and verb.
  defined, 440
  of demonstrative adjective and noun, 66
  of verb tense in subordinate clause, 35
Agreement of pronoun and antecedent, 64–65
  with antecedents joined by *or* or *nor,* 65
  with collective nouns, 65
  with *each, every,* etc., 64–65
Agreement of subject and verb, 61–64
  with collective nouns, 63
  with predicate nouns, 63
  in relative clauses, 63
  subjects joined by *and,* 62
  subjects joined by *or* or *nor,* 62
  when plural subject has singular meaning, 63
  when subject is pronoun, 61–62